Praise for

C H A T T E R

"A most useful, challenging and provocative book."
—*Los Angeles Times*

"Keefe writes, crisply and entertainingly, as an interested private citizen. [*Chatter* is] filled with anecdotes, colorful quotes and arresting statistics." —*The New York Times*

"Intriguing . . . Keefe's useful research primer on today's surveillance society . . . open[s] the way for the creation of privacy beats for journalism's coming generation of search engineers."
—*The New York Times Book Review*

"Riveting . . . part detective story and part travelogue . . . [a] provocative investigation into the global eavesdropping network . . . Keefe addresses secrecy and the potential for paranoia in the digital age." —*The Providence Sunday Journal*

"*Chatter* has the intrigue of a spy novel."
—*The Columbus Dispatch*

"A bold and distinctive book . . . Provocative, sometimes funny, and alarming, *Chatter* is a journey through a shadowy world with vast implications for our security as well as our privacy. Keefe [is] an excellent writer with sleuth-like skills."
—*Cryptologia*

"Thorough . . . beguiling, crisply written . . . [*Chatter*] cuts through the fog on some controversial subjects." —*Time Out Chicago*

CHATTER

CHATTER

UNCOVERING THE ECHELON

SURVEILLANCE NETWORK

AND THE SECRET WORLD OF

GLOBAL EAVESDROPPING

PATRICK RADDEN KEEFE

WITHDRAWN

RANDOM HOUSE TRADE PAPERBACKS

NEW YORK

2006 Random House Trade Paperback Edition

Copyright © 2005, 2006 by Patrick S. Radden Keefe

Published in the United States by Random House Trade Paperbacks,
an imprint of The Random House Publishing Group,
a division of Random House, Inc., New York.

RANDOM HOUSE TRADE PAPERBACKS and colophon are
trademarks of Random House, Inc.

Originally published in hardcover and in different form in the
United States by Random House, an imprint of The Random House
Publishing Group, a division of Random House, Inc., in 2005.

Library of Congress Cataloging-in-Publication Data
Keefe, Patrick Radden.
Chatter : uncovering the echelon surveillance network and the secret world of
global eavesdropping / Patrick Radden Keefe.
p.   cm.
Includes bibliographical references.
ISBN 0-8129-6827-1
1. Intelligence service—United States.   2. Eavesdropping—United States.
3. Wiretapping—United States.   4. Civil rights—United States.   I. Title.
JK468.I6K37   2005
327.1273—dc22   2004058481

Printed in the United States of America

www.atrandom.com

2 4 6 8 9 7 5 3 1

Text design by Jo Anne Metsch

To Frank Keefe and Jennifer Radden,
who taught me how to write
and to inquire.

Secrecy is as indispensable to human beings as fire, and as greatly feared. Both enhance and protect life, yet both can stifle, lay waste, spread out of control.

—Sissela Bok

A mere string of figures will disclose the identity of the stringer as neatly as tame ciphers yielded their treasures to Poe. The crudest *curriculum vitae* crows and flaps its wings in a style peculiar to the undersigner. I doubt whether you can even give your telephone number without giving something of yourself.

—Vladimir Nabokov

It is frequently said about advertising that half the money spent is wasted but no one knows which half. Much the same can be said about intelligence. . . .

—James Rusbridger

CONTENTS

INTRODUCTION

PRESS: Are you confirming the existence of the Echelon system?
STATE DEPARTMENT SPOKESMAN RICHARD BOUCHER: No.
PRESS: So you're not?
BOUCHER: I don't think I am. I would have to check and see if
I am, but I don't think I am.
(Laughter)

—*From the official transcript of a State
Department Press Briefing, May 11, 2001*

IN FEBRUARY 2003, police in New York City launched a frantic effort
to protect the city's subways from a terrorist attack. Sixteen thousand
law-enforcement officials specially trained to combat terrorism were
deployed throughout the city. Authorities increased the number of
patrols and checkpoints along the myriad subterranean arteries that
pump commuters in and out of Manhattan every day. Undercover officers took up positions on trains and platforms, keeping watch, and
groups of heavily armed, bulletproof-vested cops, known as Hercules
Teams, descended on the stations. Police manned the entrances of each
of the thirteen underwater subway tunnels in and out of Manhattan
and walked hundreds of miles of platforms with bomb-sniffing dogs,
radiation detectors, and gas masks.

What brought about this sudden frenzy of protectiveness on the part
of the NYPD? What tipped them off? One word in an intercepted conversation between suspected terrorists: *underground.*

. . .

WHEN DID THE TERM *chatter* creep into the American lexicon? It's a curious little word, once so innocuous, so trivial in its connotations. It meant gossip or scuttlebutt, the babble of a child. Then, overnight, the word developed a new and ominous meaning. And now the chatter on any given day is a barometer of our national panic. Like the meteorological indications underlying a weather forecast, chatter tells us if calamity is expected, if we are on "alert" or on "high alert," the precise aural hue of the day's threat index.

After a couple of months of the Blitz, Londoners learned to live with the bombings, to distinguish instinctively among the telltale shrieks of incoming ordnance and block out everything that didn't threaten to tear them to pieces. In the aftermath of September 11, 2001, Americans have proved similarly adaptive to an uncertain environment. The daily threat level still appears on the news, jockeying on the screen with the latest stock reports, the time and date. But most of us don't give it much mind—more interested in glancing at the temperature to figure out if it's jacket weather—and treat it like the changing shades of a bruise that is slowly going away. But it's not going away; the threat index is there, shifting a shade here, a degree there, and seeming only ever to range between "elevated" and "severe."

By what peculiar alchemy does our government ascertain the level of terror we should feel on a given day? What sources of intelligence undergird this daily bulletin of our state of siege? Most Americans have no idea, choosing to trust the personnel and the technology brought to bear by our government. We hear that chatter indicated that Saddam Hussein's Iraq was producing weapons of mass destruction, and that chatter foretold the terrorist attacks on September 11, 2001. In the weeks before a disaster, we are told, a pattern emerges. Before September 11, before the Bali bombing in October 2002, before the suicide bombs in Riyadh in November 2003, there was a sudden spike in chatter, a crescendo of foreign voices. Then silence. Then disaster. We comprehend very little about the terrorists of Al Qaeda: their perverse fundamentalism, their deadly marriage of backward-looking philosophy with forward-looking technologies, their elusive, viruslike organizational structure. But we have come to know this telltale metabolic rhythm: chatter; silence; attack. Chatter has become a critical, if spectral, factor in American life in the early years of the twenty-first century. And yet very few of us understand what this word means. Who is chattering? Who is listening? How do they go about listening? And perhaps most important, how reliable is chatter as an augury of calamity to come?

HERE IS A CONSPIRACY theory for you. The United States is the dominant member of a secret network, along with four other Anglophone powers—the United Kingdom, Canada, Australia, and New Zealand—that intercepts the chatter of people around the planet. The pact between these countries was initiated a half century ago, in a document so secret that its existence has never been acknowledged by any of the governments involved: the UKUSA agreement. The network these countries have developed collects billions of telephone calls, e-mails, faxes, and telexes every day and distributes them, through a series of automated channels, to interested parties in the five countries. In this manner, the United States spies on its NATO allies, and the United Kingdom spies on its EU allies: the network supersedes any other ties of loyalty or affiliation. Each country has laws against spying on its own civilians but not against having its *allies* spy on its civilians—and in this manner the United States will occasionally have the United Kingdom keep an eye on individuals in this country, with the understanding that if Britain turns up any interesting tidbits, it will slide them across the table.

The technology used by these five powers to intercept communications is staggeringly sophisticated. Our small vocabulary for describing the act of listening in is rife with anachronisms. In his *Commentaries on the Laws of England* (1765–69), Sir William Blackstone defined *eavesdroppers* as those who "listen under walls or window, or the eaves of a house, to hearken after discourse, and thereupon to frame slanderous and mischievous tales." The word still brings to mind characters hiding behind screens in the plays of Shakespeare or Molière. Even *wiretap* is something of a quaint anomaly: much of the communications interception in the last century involved not tapping wires but simply plucking signals from the air.

Signals intelligence, or Sigint, in the shorthand of politicos and spies, is the little-known name for listening in that is used today by the eavesdroppers themselves. Eavesdropping has become an extraordinarily cutting-edge game, with listening stations inhaling conversations bounced via satellites and microwave towers; spy satellites miles above in space tuning in on radio frequencies on the ground; and silent and invisible Internet bugs clinging, parasitelike, to the nodes and junctures of the information superhighway.

Though many Americans are not even aware that it exists, the National Security Agency, the American institution in charge of electronic eavesdropping, is larger than the CIA and the FBI combined. In fact, these better-known intelligence agencies are puny by comparison. Whereas the CIA has roughly twenty thousand employees and a budget of approximately $3 billion, the NSA has some sixty thousand employees scattered around the planet, and its budget is estimated to be as high as $6 billion per year. The United States and the United Kingdom are so intimate when it comes to cooperating on Sigint that the NSA has a much closer relationship with the British eavesdropping agency—Government Communications Headquarters (GCHQ)—than it does with America's own CIA. The Anglophone network is said to hear absolutely everything, yet its existence remains a secret—unknown in some cases even to the legislative bodies of the countries that run it. The network is code-named Echelon.

Like any good conspiracy theory, this one contains important elements of truth. Like any good conspiracy, it is also nonfalsifiable: while it might be impossible to prove that it's all true, it's also impossible to prove that it's not, and the theory thrives on official denials and refusals to comment. It's the quintessential paranoid fable for the Internet age. It spread in the epidemic manner that stories online do, and it plays upon anxieties shared by those who channel large amounts of personal information through a network, without a solid grasp of how secure that information is in transit. At the same time, despite the supposedly "borderless" nature of the Internet, this conspiracy theory seems to have taken hold in Europe but not in the United States. To the extent that stories about Echelon have percolated into the American consciousness, they have done so not through newspapers or the nightly news but rather via the alarmist folklore of television and fiction. In the popular ABC show *Alias*, leggy spy Sydney Bristow struggles to access the Echelon system and announces, "Some people think there's a conspiracy—that the government eavesdrops on everyone. It's no conspiracy." Cayce Pollard, the heroine of cyberpunk novelist William Gibson's 2003 book *Pattern Recognition*, also manages to tap into Echelon—a system, Gibson writes, "that allows for the scanning of all net traffic."

When I first encountered tales about Echelon, they were presented not as fantasy but as fact. I was a graduate student in the United

Kingdom in the late 1990s when stories about Echelon started appearing in the newspaper. The picture painted was intriguing: a dramatic eavesdropping architecture, wrapping itself, gridlike, around the globe; an invisible infrastructure whereby a select handful of agencies could tap in to the chatter of nations and garner an Olympian omniscience, literally hearing everything, all the time. Yet for all the antiseptic geometry of this system, its contours were surprisingly smudgy. It was not clear whether the word *Echelon* stood for one particular satellite-interception program or the whole system of Anglophone cooperation on Sigint. The system was alluded to in quasi-mythological tones, but most reports admitted up front that they were not working on the basis of any corroborated information.

Marlow, Joseph Conrad's narrator in *Heart of Darkness*, was obsessed as a child with "the blank spaces on the earth"—those regions in the world that remained unexplored and unsurveyed in the nineteenth century. In the twenty-first century, we are no longer afforded such alluring cartographic mysteries, but I found, as I started probing the world of signals intelligence, that it occupies a similarly uncharted shadow land in our contemporary consciousness.

"The most profound technologies are those that disappear," wrote the computer scientist Mark Weiser in a seminal 1991 article, in which he introduced the notion of "ubiquitous computing." "They weave themselves into the fabric of everyday life until they are indistinguishable from it." In the intervening decade and a half, communications technologies have, in precisely this fashion, disappeared. We take for granted our landlines and cellphones, two-way pagers and wireless-enabled laptops. When Weiser was writing, the telephone was something connected to the wall that teenage children bickered over, and the Internet was for a small few an idea, a rumor, and for the vast majority something closer to science fiction. Today, our relationship with technology is umbilical: my generation was the first to arrive at college to find Internet connections waiting in every dorm room; we cannot live, or even imagine a life, without access to the web. It is not only that we use this technology daily but also that we transmit more information than ever before through the wires and over the airwaves: we pay our bills and our taxes online; meet, date, and converse online; search for the import of medical symptoms online; and type our most embarrassing and revealing questions and quandaries into Google, all online. We have an intuitive sense that this medium, which we have internalized to the point where it is almost an organic extension of our thoughts and words, is vulnerable to interception—that someone might be listening. But for most of us, this uneasy feeling remains an unsubstantiated hunch, one of the peculiar vagaries of life in a digital age.

This book is the story of my efforts to figure out how chatter works: who can listen in and how they go about it. It is the story of an epic struggle between two abstract concepts—security and privacy—that is playing out amid lightning-fast technological and social change. It's also a story about government secrecy. My endeavors to chart the secret world of signals intelligence were frustrated by something I have come to think of as the Sigint Postulate: there is an inverse proportion between how much a person is willing to talk about signals intelligence and how much he or she actually knows. The fringes of the Sigint world are peopled by conspiracy theorists and privacy advocates, paranoids and cranks—colorful characters of dubious credibility. And the heart of that world, the highly classified sanctum of America's intelligence establishment, is home to the lowest-profile and most secretive professional tribe on earth: the eavesdroppers themselves.

The United States has fewer than five thousand spies operating throughout the world today, but it has some thirty thousand eavesdroppers. Every three hours, the NSA's satellites pick up enough information to fill the Library of Congress. And yet most Americans possess next to no information about our global eavesdropping apparatus. As a result, we lack the vocabulary to discuss whether our intelligence agencies are keeping us safe, or invading our privacy, or both. We tend to digest concepts such as "privacy" and "national security" whole, to take them as undifferentiated and unexamined absolutes, and to refuse—because we have too little information or because it is just too difficult—to plot the various changes taking place in our society on the liberty-security matrix. We have no sense of how reliable an index of safety chatter really is or whether our eavesdropping operations are worth the billions of dollars we allot to them. We don't know whether Echelon exists and, if it does exist, how the shadowy network operates. It all remains an enigma.

I am not an investigative journalist, by training or inclination. When I set out to see what I could discover about global eavesdropping, it was as an average curious civilian. What I found as I started looking into the means through which the United States and its allies intercept communications is that this system serves as a window into, and a metaphor for, a broader series of issues and dilemmas that will be the defining struggles of our era: the negotiation between privacy and national security in a wired world; the profusion of paranoia and conspiracy theories in an Internet age, in which rumor abounds but hard information is in short supply; and the real dangers of unchecked government secrecy. I had little idea when I started that this quest for information would take me from a massive "listening base" in England's Yorkshire moors to the bosom of bureaucratic Europe in Brussels, from the back rooms of Washington to the cafés of Copenhagen, to an abandoned NSA base, hidden in the Smoky Mountains of North Carolina. Nor did I realize that I would encounter such a bizarre and memorable cast of characters: eavesdroppers, who spend their days listening in on headphones to the private conversations of people around the planet; protesters, hackers, and activists, who believe that privacy as we once knew it has ceased to exist; officials who contend that even talking about America's eavesdropping capability is tantamount to assisting terrorists; and a small band of intrepid researchers and reporters who have struggled, over the last three decades, to uncover the world of global eavesdropping one detail at a time.

CHATTER

RADOMES IN THE DESERT, RADOMES ON THE MOOR

The Invisible Architecture of Echelon

YOU CANNOT HELP but note the juxtaposition. Here, away from the world, amid rolling pastures, on a tract of land where the air is redolent of cow dung, lies the most sophisticated eavesdropping station on the planet. England's North Yorkshire moors are, after all, cow country. Leaving the elegant Victorian spa town of Harrogate, my taxi winds west through eight miles of verdant countryside. Just outside the city, the traffic thins, and what cars we pass seem to go much slower than they need to—a deliberate, agrarian pace. Fields are set off by a network of hedges beneath a panoramic, cloudless sky. Sheep congregate here and there, and dozens of cows lounge by crumbling stone walls, some gazing as we whiz by, others chewing their cuds, oblivious.

I have been warned, seen photos—I know what to expect. But as the first dome hovers into sight, I catch my breath. The bucolic road winds and rises and falls, and as we dip and rise again and crest a hill the tip of a great white sphere, shimmering in the summer heat, becomes visible in the distance. One giant dimpled dome, a great Kevlar golf ball. Then suddenly four domes, and then eight, as others float into view above the hill. A dip in the road and they're obscured again and then again in sight.

As the taxi rounds the perimeter fence, the base becomes visible in flashes through a row of trees. The white globes are called radomes, and each houses a satellite dish antenna, protecting it from the elements and masking its orientation—the dome itself is just a kind of skin. I count twenty-eight of these domes in all, ghostly white against the green of the countryside. They look otherworldly.

And in a sense, they are. The dishes are hidden inside the radomes because their supersensitive antennae are trained on a corresponding set of satellites hovering more than twenty thousand miles above. Some of those are communications satellites that transmit secure messages to other intelligence installations around the world. Some are spy satellites, which take photographs, intercept communications, and use Global Positioning Systems to pinpoint the locations of various individuals or vehicles around the planet. And some of the satellites are regular commercial communications satellites, the kind that transmit your telephone calls and Internet traffic across the oceans. The first two varieties of satellite were built specifically to correspond with the base. This third kind, however, was not. These satellites are managed by a company called Intelsat, and the signals they relay are private, civilian communications. But the base collects these signals, too, soundlessly and ceaselessly intercepting great flows of private communications every minute of every hour. The sign at the gate reads: RAF Menwith Hill.

I approach the sandbagged entrance, smile at the grave British military policemen who stand guard, and peer inside. RAF stands for Royal Air Force, but the name is a deliberate misnomer. The base was built in the 1950s on land purchased by the British Crown, but in 1966 the site was taken over by the American National Security Agency. Thus while the station is nominally an RAF base, it is actually home to more than twelve hundred Americans. These people live in housing within the perimeter of the fence, send their children to primary and secondary school within the fence, use their own grocery store, post office, sports center, pub, and bowling alley, all within the fence. The bowling alley, in a questionable piece of nomenclature for a base that is instrumental to America's nuclear program, is called the Strike Zone. There are houses and a chapel and a playground and a full-sized track and baseball diamond. The whole base covers 560 acres. Beneath a curling ribbon of razor wire, armed men with dogs patrol the fence.

While we are accustomed, in this age of American power projection, to the idea of full-time military personnel living in this type of enclave abroad, I was surprised to learn that the majority of the employees at Menwith Hill are in fact civilians: engineers, technicians, mathematicians, linguists, and analysts. The NSA has always employed large numbers of civilian contractors: professionals, generally with technical expertise, who satisfy the rigorous background tests and security clearances to work at the forefront of the most secret field in American intelligence. These people come from aerospace and technology firms that do regular contract work for the government. They move their belongings and their families to the base, drawn by the allowances made for them: free housing, free shipping of their furniture and cars, and most of all, a tax-free salary. They work in three eight-hour shifts, so that the great interception machine does not shut down. They work Christmas and New Year's Day, and through the routine protests outside the gates of the base on the Fourth of July. There are linguists trained in Arabic, Farsi, Hebrew, and the gamut of European languages. With another four hundred or so personnel from the British Ministry of Defence, this single quietly humming spy station, which the vast majority of British and American civilians have never heard of, has a staff as large as all of Britain's storied domestic-intelligence service, MI5.

At the Black Bull Inn, a local pub, the night before my visit to the base, a couple of teenagers drinking pints of bitter and eating chicken curry–flavored potato chips at the bar joked about the carloads of beautiful young American women, "the Menwith Hill girls," whom they occasionally see. The women drive American cars with the steering wheel on the left and head out to pubs in surrounding villages or into Harrogate or York on the weekends, before returning to disappear behind the fence. If the social life of these women has the quality of an apparition to the locals, their professional life is even more obscure. One of the boys at the bar, reed thin with dark hair and an eyebrow ring, said he had worked at "the Hill" for a while, in the cafeteria, but that the base was segregated into the Upper Hill and the Lower Hill, that there was a strict division between the living areas and the working areas, and that his security clearance, which in and of itself had required a battery of forms, questions, checks, and tests, was inadequate to let him get anywhere near the real activity on the base. He said that as far as he could tell, much of the work happens in the untold stretches of the Hill that are underground. "But from what *I* hear," he said, raising a conspiratorial brow and eyeing my notebook to make sure I was getting this, "it's an alien-testing zone." His mates cackled at this, and all the louder when they saw me dutifully scribbling it down.

I stand at the entrance and, craning my neck, gaze through the fence. The guards are toting machine guns and look at me with idle curiosity. A digital screen by a cluster of low buildings flashes messages to cars driving into the base. RAIKE AND MASSAGE TUESDAY NIGHT . . . GEICO INSURANCE EVERY THURSDAY . . . KARAOKE THURSDAY NIGHT . . . DRINKING AND DRIVING WRECKS LIVES.

"Pardon me, sir," one of the guards clears his throat. He nods to indicate something behind me.

A blue sedan is idling, waiting to get past. I move aside. The driver is a young woman in a sweatshirt, her hair pulled back. We make eye contact for a second. She's about my age—a Menwith Hill girl! The guards wave her through, and she's gone.

Inside the fence, in one-story, windowless buildings and in high-tech underground basements, the Menwith Hill girls join their colleagues in the clandestine interception of billions of communications per day. It has been claimed that all telecommunications traffic in and out of Europe that passes through Britain is intercepted by the base.

THIS IS THE INSCRUTABLE face of American intelligence in the twenty-first century. When the Iron Curtain fell, it ruptured the fixed geography of Europe and the world, unleashing a slow tectonic shift that continues to alter the geopolitical landscape to this day. The end of the cold war also changed the nature of intelligence activities for the United States and its allies. The decentralization of the threat that had been posed by the Soviets, combined with a reduced defense budget, a new sense of optimism, and a diminished American tolerance for military casualties, led to a pronounced reduction in the number of human spies on the ground. Gone are the trench-coated cold warriors of John le Carré novels, the CIA spies who were at the vanguard of cold war intelligence, sent to infiltrate the opposition or work out of embassies, recruit moles and double agents, and risk their lives in the process. Human intelligence, or Humint, was already in a steady decline by the end of the cold war, and it continued to dwindle as an American priority through the 1990s. In 1998, Porter Goss, the Florida congressman and former CIA case officer who was the chairman of the House of Representatives' Intelligence Committee and in September 2004 was appointed director of the CIA, declared simply, "It is fair to say that the cupboard is nearly bare in the area of human intelligence."

But while American politicians were unwilling to sacrifice the lives of spies in countries that no longer played a decisive role against the Soviets or those of soldiers in places such as Mogadishu or Sarajevo, they were more than willing to invest in new technologies to fight wars and gather intelligence, as it were, by remote control. In a succession of conflicts, the George H. W. Bush and Bill Clinton administrations made it clear that the United States, wherever possible, would prefer to use gadgets instead of humans. In the words of former CIA operative Robert Baer, "The theory was that satellites, the Internet, electronic intercepts, even academic publications would tell us all we needed to know about what went on beyond our borders."

Arguably, this trend was nothing new. Since the 1970s there had been a growing sense that as technology advanced, it might displace the agent on the ground. Stansfield Turner, President Jimmy Carter's director of central intelligence, met with Carter twice per week to give him tutorials on the various kinds of intelligence collection the United States was engaged in. Turner felt that he and the president shared a "technical bent" and observed that they both had come to regard the "traditional human spy" as basically outmoded.

But what was an inkling for these men became a conviction for subsequent administrations, as a combination of gadgetry and money appeared to provide a way around sending agents on risky assignments. In the July/August 2001 issue of the *Atlantic Monthly,* just weeks before the terrorist attacks of September 11, a former CIA officer named Reuel Marc Gerecht published an article deploring a total absence of effective on-the-ground human intelligence in the Middle East. He concluded, "Unless one of Bin Laden's foot soldiers walks through the door of a U.S. consulate or embassy, the odds that a CIA counterterrorist officer will ever see one are extremely poor."

SINCE THE FOUNDING, more than a half century ago, of the NSA, there has been a prevailing understanding that while the world of intelligence matters was very secret and not something that should be discussed with anyone not in the know, the world of signals intelligence was the most secret of all. You can detect this hierarchy of secrecy even in prevalent jokes about the agencies. The old saw about the NSA, which was created not by Congress but by President Harry Truman in a secret executive order on October 24, 1952, was that NSA stood for "No such agency" or "Never say anything." This mantra must have been enthusiastically adopted from the start, because for the first two decades of its existence the NSA was not acknowledged by the federal government and did not appear in any annual federal intelligence budgets, its allocations buried in other, inconspicuous-looking items. This despite the fact that at the time the agency employed more than ten thousand people. By contrast, the joke about the Office of Strategic Services, the predecessor of the CIA, which does human intelligence, was that OSS stood for, "Oh so social." This may explain why most Americans can tell you quite a bit about the CIA today, while a surprising number have never heard of the NSA. Few could tell you what it does or where it is located. It is rarely discussed in newspapers, and despite all the talk of chatter on the nightly news, the acronym NSA rarely impinges on the consciousness of the average American.

The NSA operates out of a massive edifice of reflective black glass, its headquarters at Fort Meade, Maryland. Even the architecture of the "Puzzle Palace," as it is sometimes known, repels efforts to figure out what is going on inside. It is literally a black box. We do know that the agency employs more mathematicians than any other organization in the world and that the campus at Fort Meade is the densest concentration of computer power on the planet. Just one of the agency's Cray supercomputers can handle sixty-four billion individual instructions per second.

The NSA's work is divided into two functions: communications security and signals intelligence. The former involves creating secure communications and cryptography for America's political leaders and military. The latter responsibility involves listening in. Part of the reason it is hard to gather information on the NSA is that the agency is not a user of its own intelligence. There are no gun-toting NSA agents who go out into the field and act on the intelligence the agency has gathered. The Puzzle Palace only provides intelligence to other agencies and to politicians and generals. In that sense, it is passive. It just sits and *listens*.

The reason for all of this secrecy is obvious: eavesdropping works only if the person you are monitoring does not know he or she is being monitored. When the press reported in 1998 that American intelligence was intercepting the satellite-telephone conversations of Osama Bin Laden, he promptly stopped using that phone. The lesson is clear: when your quarry knows you can break his code, he will devise a new one. Worse yet is the whole string of possibilities for deliberate deception. After spikes in terrorist chatter set off a series of alarms about impending terrorist strikes in various places around the world in 2003, some observers of the intelligence community speculated that Al Qaeda was deliberately throwing out red herrings on frequencies they knew were being monitored by the NSA.

. . .

THE NEW SPIES ARE not James Bonds or George Smileys. They are not marksmen or lotharios, lone operatives parachuted into foreign terrain. The new spies are the Menwith Hill girls: smart, motivated, on the nerdy side perhaps, more familiar with an ergonomic keyboard than a camera hidden in a wristwatch. All the contradictions of the new intelligence are captured in Menwith Hill. A space-age base, standing out cinematically against the sweep and sky of the Yorkshire countryside. A microcommunity of Americans, self-contained and secretive, in the heart of Great Britain. Two dozen dish antennae, hidden within their cocoonlike membranes, pointed at satellites thousands of miles above. And all on the old Roman road to York—a road built because the Romans knew that establishing and controlling the arteries of communications was the key to maintaining an empire. Whereas traditionally success in espionage hinged on an ability to get "in" or "inside"—to infiltrate—in the new world of intelligence an obscure base on the other side of the planet can be as great or greater an asset to military operations than an agent in an embassy. Thus it was not some forward station in Saudi Arabia that was awarded the NSA's Station of the Year prize for 1991, for its role in the Gulf War, but RAF Menwith Hill, thousands of miles away.

And Menwith Hill is only the largest of the listening stations, the brightest point in a constellation of bases large and small, with microwave towers and satellite dishes pointing at the sky: Bad Aibling in Germany; Misawa Air Base in Japan; Akrotiri in Cyprus; Guantánamo Bay in Cuba; and Pine Gap, dead in the center of Australia. Despite their locations in foreign lands, these bases tend, with the full consent of the various national governments, to be run by Americans. For most of the host countries, there is some persuasive rationale: a close military alliance with the United States, with the tacit or explicit promise of American military protection, should it ever be needed; some level of intelligence sharing, whereby the tenant operation passes any valuable intelligence collected to the host government; or often simply money. In order to maintain a base in a strategic part of the world, where a bounty of signals can be plucked from the air, the United States is willing to pay generous rents, and the presence of hundreds or thousands of American civilian and military personnel has never been bad for the economies in the kinds of remote areas where the NSA tends to set up shop.

Even America's closest intelligence allies—the United Kingdom,

Canada, Australia, and New Zealand—have only a limited amount of input into the goings-on at these bases. Certainly, there are representatives of the home government present inside the fence, and sometimes their role is substantial: they help run and maintain the collection equipment or analyze the results. But just as often, the role of these officials has tended to be merely custodial. In a trial in the 1970s, a British officer who worked at RAF Edzell, an American listening station in a farming area south of Aberdeen, Scotland, said, "I am the only British officer on the base. I do not know what it does. I do not know details of its operations. I play no part in them. I am completely isolated. My U.S. colleagues do not speak to me." Another said simply, "I'm only the land-lord's representative."

Under the leadership of the United States, five intelligence agencies—Britain's Government Communications Headquarters (GCHQ), Canada's Communications Security Establishment (CSE), Australia's Defence Signals Directorate (DSD), New Zealand's Government Communications Security Bureau (GCSB), and the NSA—have wrapped the earth in a spectral web of electronic surveillance. The details of this intimate partnership are known to very few. Politicians do not fully understand it: in the name of safety and security, intelligence agencies keep congressional oversight committees in the dark. The listeners themselves do not fully grasp it. Knowledge within Sigint agencies is allocated on a strictly need-to-know basis, and the professional universes of Sigint employees are limited to the parameters of their particular compartmentalized tasks. A cryptanalyst can spend his or her whole career at the NSA and never hear so much as the code name of some softly humming program that colleagues down the hall have been running all along. The public knows of this kind of intelligence only in anecdote: the half-heard speculations of paranoid ranters, the alarmist prognostications of the odd Op-Ed, the ongoing reification of rumors on the Internet. And that one recurring word, at once lyrical and blunt, invoking both the architectural nature of the system and the uncompromising hierarchy of the need to know: Echelon.

WHEN HENRY LEWIS STIMSON was appointed secretary of state by President Herbert Hoover in 1929 and learned that American code breakers had been intercepting and reading the communications of British, French, Italian, and Japanese diplomats, he was appalled and famously declared, "Gentlemen do not read each other's mail." Stimson's piety notwithstanding, the interception of communications is probably as old as communication itself.

The best way to chart the history of communications interception is to explore the history of efforts to keep messages private—that is, the history of cryptography. Even in the earliest forms of written communication, people knew well enough to convert or hide the messages they wanted to send privately. David Kahn, the world's foremost expert on the history of cryptography, argues in *The Codebreakers,* his magisterial, thousand-page tome, that cryptography is, in its way, as natural and inevitable in its evolution as language itself. "It must be that as soon as culture has reached a certain level, probably measured largely by its literacy, cryptography appears spontaneously—as its parents, language and writing, probably also did," Kahn writes. "The multiple human needs and desires that demand privacy among two or more people in the midst of social life must inevitably lead to cryptography wherever men thrive and wherever they write." Kahn rejects the idea that secret writing spread from continent to continent by some process of cultural diffusion, as so many other technical innovations demonstrably did, and argues instead that the presence of crude methods of encryption in even distant and isolated lands can signal only a spontaneous, organic emergence.

In *The History,* Herodotus tells the story of the tyrant Histaeus, who was in the Persian court of King Darius and wanted to send a message to his son-in-law, Aristagoras, to urge him to revolt against the Persians. The challenge was in sending a message of such sensitivity to Miletus, where Aristagoras was, when all the roads were watched. So Histaeus summoned his most trusted slave, shaved his head, and tattooed his message onto the slave's scalp. He waited until the slave's hair grew in again before sending him off, with a simple order to be delivered only to Aristagoras: shave my head. In ancient China, sensitive messages were written on thin sheets of silk or paper, then rolled into a ball and covered with wax. The messenger would hide the ball in his clothes, or in his rectum, or in his stomach and produce it only for the intended recipient. Actually, neither of these methods is cryptography per se. Whereas the word *cryptography* derives from the Greek *kryptos,* which means "hidden," and *graphein,* which means "to write," these subterfuges were more accurately what is known as steganography, or "covered writing," from the Greek word *steganos,* for "covered." Real code making and code breaking was developed later, among the Arabs in the ninth century. And cryptanalysis, the science of unscrambling a coded message without the key to the code, was pioneered by Arab scholars in the Middle Ages.

But it was the growth of diplomatic relations and the associated interception of diplomatic communications in the Middle Ages and the Renaissance that really spurred the development of cryptography. In the 1500s, European states began appointing ambassadors to live in one another's courts. The ambassadors sent reports home, and these documents were sometimes opened and read. By the end of the sixteenth century, this cat-and-mouse game of diplomatic interception had become so important that most European states kept full-time "cipher secretaries" occupied, enciphering outgoing messages, deciphering incoming ones, and trying to break the ciphers on intercepted messages. These first full-time puzzlers were the direct antecedents of the analysts and engineers at Menwith Hill today.

In Renaissance Venice, the court cipher secretary was a man of immense political importance and prestige. His name was Giovanni Soro, and his reputation as a code breaker was such that as early as 1510 the papal curia was forwarding him ciphers that no one in Rome could solve. Venice was under the control of the Council of Ten, the mysterious cadre of officials that maintained order with an authoritarian secret police and scores of informers, and code breaking was assuming a new importance. Soro worked with two assistants in a suite above the Sala di Segret in the Doge's Palace. The doors to their chambers were barred. When coded messages sent to foreign powers were intercepted, they were forwarded directly to Soro and his men. The cipher secretaries were reportedly not allowed to leave the office until they had cracked the code. The operation was so successful that they started a small school in code breaking and had examinations each September. This was, perhaps, the first Black Chamber, as the small, secretive interception and cryptography units of subsequent governments have been known. From the suite in the Doge's Palace to the literal black chamber, the great black Puzzle Palace at Fort Meade, these operations have shared remarkable similarities.

By the seventeenth century, code breaking was widely acknowledged as an activity vital to the preservation of official power. Antoine Rossignol, a supremely talented French code breaker who came to the attention of Cardinal Richelieu, became a minor celebrity in the court of Louis XIV. He worked in a room just off of the Sun King's study at Versailles, close to the monarchical bosom. So crucial was Rossignol to the dominance of France that he became a rich man, with a château outside of Paris, surrounded by gardens designed by Le Nôtre, the gardener of Versailles. Shortly before his death in 1682, Rossignol was visited at his home by Louis XIV, when the king arranged a detour on his way to Fontainebleau. In light of the fact that courtiers in Louis XIV's entourage jockeyed for an opportunity to remove his morning bedpan, this gesture says a great deal. It was Rossignol who established a tradition of formidable French cryptography, which would continue through the reign of Napoleon and his famously complex *grand chiffre,* the Great Paris Cipher.

THE INVENTION OF THE telegraph, in the mid-nineteenth century, marked the advent of signals-based communications. Signals sent along the telegraph line were quicker and more reliable than a letter sent by courier, and by the end of the nineteenth century the British General Post Office could tap out four hundred words per minute along the cables that linked London to its burgeoning empire. Most of these messages were sent *en clair,* without any encryption at all, because at this stage telegraph communication was still primarily a British technology. When a message left London for Bombay or Hong Kong, it could be intercepted only by tapping the great tentacular cables that crisscrossed the ocean floor. And the Royal Navy controlled the seas. Still, while it might be difficult to locate a particular courier and find the sensitive message on his person, telegraph lines are not hidden. From the telegraph onward, it has been an axiom of communications interception that new technologies that make it easier to communicate will make it easier to intercept communications as well. Thus, while the invention of wireless radio by Guglielmo Marconi at the turn of the twentieth century freed the user of dependence on telegraph wires, it freed the tapper of that constraint as well. Marconi set the signal free, sent it into the air, and in the century that followed that is where it remained. Only in the last several years, with the development of high-capacity fiber-optic cables, has it begun to appear that the signal might return to earth and in the process become more secure.

ON JANUARY 16, 1917, Arthur Zimmermann, Germany's foreign minister, sent a telegram to the German ambassador in Mexico City. Zimmermann's telegram read 130 13042 13041 8501 115 3528 416 and so on, for a page, a long string of numeric code. When he sent the telegram,

Zimmermann had no way of knowing that it would become the key Sigint story of the First World War and be decisive in bringing American troops to Europe. The telegram announced that Germany was about to begin unrestricted submarine warfare and proposed an alliance between Germany and Mexico. It also expressed Germany's encouragement for Mexico "to re-conquer the lost territory of Texas, New Mexico and Arizona."

The British intercepted the telegram, and the code breakers of Room 40, Britain's wartime Black Chamber, cracked the code. But one of the crucial wisdoms of code breaking was apparent to the British even then: never let them know you're listening. Britain had been endeavoring to draw the United States into the war for some time, and Admiral Sir William Hall knew that all he had to do was pass the decoded telegram on to the Americans in order to make it finally happen. But he hesitated, not wanting to show his hand and assuming that when the Germans started torpedoing civilian ships, the Americans, still grieving the loss of the 1,195 passengers aboard the *Lusitania* in 1915, would need little further impetus to join the hostilities. But on February 3, two days after the Kaiser initiated unrestricted naval warfare, Woodrow Wilson announced that America would nevertheless maintain its neutrality.

Even at this juncture, Hall was reluctant to pass the telegram directly along. Instead, he realized that if he could somehow get hold of the same telegram through human rather than Sigint channels, he would be able to preserve the integrity of his interception operation. So he contacted a British spy in Mexico, known only as Mr. H., who proceeded to infiltrate the Mexican Telegraph Office and steal a copy of a revised and decoded version of the message. Within days, this version was passed to the Americans and the press, President Wilson declared it "eloquent evidence" of the ignominy of the Germans, and by April America was at war.

THE CHARTER FOR ROOM 40 was drafted in 1914, on the eve of the war, by a young man named Winston Churchill. From this early experience, Churchill gained a fascination with signals intelligence, a fascination he would have occasion to indulge fully during the Second World War. While both Britain and the United States maintained code-breaking facilities during the interwar period, it was not until the Second World

War that their respective Sigint operations—and their cooperation in these matters—began to approach anything resembling what it is today. The technology and utility of Sigint mushroomed during World War II. Whereas the U.S. Army and Navy had about four hundred code breakers in World War I, in World War II they had sixteen thousand. In reference to the value of this esoteric field, Churchill wrote in *Their Finest Hour,*

> This was the secret war, whose battles were lost or won unknown to the public; and only with difficulty comprehended, even now, by those outside the small high scientific circles concerned. No such warfare had ever been waged by mortal men. The terms in which it could be recorded or talked about were unintelligible to ordinary folk. Yet if we had not mastered its profound meaning and used its mysteries even while we only saw them in the glimpse, all the efforts, all the prowess of the fighting airmen, all the bravery and sacrifices of the people, would have been in vain.

During the war, Churchill fixated on signals intelligence and insisted on personally reading raw transcripts of intercepted communications. Every morning, the staff at 10 Downing Street received a box marked with the insignia of Queen Victoria. None of the staff was allowed to open the box, and it was brought directly to Churchill, who used a special key he kept on a ring at his waist to open it. The box contained the most recent intercepts of enemy communications, which Churchill referred to as his "golden eggs." ("I must try to make my exceedingly complicated and highly sensitive hen lay a few more eggs," he wrote to his wife, Clementine, in 1944.) He looked through these with Sir Stewart Menzies, known as "C," the traditional code name for the head of British intelligence. By reading intercepted communications from the Italians and the Japanese and, after 1943, the Germans, Churchill was able to gain unparalleled insight into the war as it unfolded. He relished this secret omniscience and developed an insatiable appetite for it, keeping tabs on neutral countries such as Ireland, Turkey, Spain, Portugal, and most of the nations in the Balkans and South America. He listened in on allies as well: de Gaulle's Free French, the Dutch, the Czechs, and other governments-in-exile. Even when he traveled, Churchill had to have his golden eggs. When he went to meet Roosevelt off the coast of Newfoundland for the Atlantic Charter meeting in the summer of

1941, he specified that the intercepts should be sent to him in a specially weighted box, so that if the airplane was shot down over the ocean, the documents would immediately sink.

The breaking of the German Enigma codes by the tweedy dons and crossword puzzlers of Bletchley Park has become, in the last quarter century, one of the most extensively documented aspects of World War II. Yet until the 1970s, there was little information publicly available about interception and code breaking in the war. The culture of secrecy that by necessity characterized these operations in wartime somehow endured, a remnant reflex in the postwar period. In fact, it wasn't until 1978 that David Owen, then foreign secretary in Britain's Labour government, announced that those people who had worked on "Enigma material" during the war could finally admit that they had.

In the spring of 1941, a small team of American code breakers—two from the navy, two from the army—crossed the Atlantic. They were led by an army reserve officer and mathematical cryptographer named Abraham Sinkov. With them was a crate containing a tenderly packed reproduction of the Japanese diplomatic cipher machine known as Purple—a small but heavy piece of machinery that was used to convert plain text to code. It was a gift for the British code breakers at Bletchley Park, and in return the British gave the Americans an assortment of advanced cryptological equipment for use at their own operation, headquartered at Arlington Hall, a converted girls' school in Arlington, Virginia. This episode was significant for a number of reasons. First, the Purple machine was used to encipher diplomatic communications, and if you have at your disposal the means of turning a communication into code, you can generally work backward and figure out how to break that code. Second, in the spring of 1941 the United States had not yet entered the war. And third, this favor marks the beginning of a friendship that would change the balance of global intelligence and power in the cold war and beyond.

Britain had assembled a team of brilliant cryptographers to crack German and Japanese codes at Bletchley Park. Even the decision to locate this strategic nerve center amid the brick kilns and railway yards of a run-down Buckinghamshire village indicated the tremendous importance that Sigint had already acquired. One rationale was that Bletchley Park lay roughly between Oxford and Cambridge, which would allow for better access to mathematicians and code breakers. But there was another rationale as well: few places in England are farther from the sea.

The British did not want to run the risk that this, their most valuable and secret military asset, could be overtaken by a beach invasion.

Once the Americans had entered the war, another mission to Bletchley Park was dispatched in April 1943, this one led by William Friedman, the most brilliant American cryptanalyst of his day. Born Wolfe Frederick Friedman in Russia, he emigrated to Pittsburgh as a baby in 1893 and was drawn to cryptography as a young man primarily because of a young woman—Elizabeth Smith, who would become his wife—working in that field at Riverbank Laboratories in Illinois. Friedman had been a cryptologic officer in the First World War and became a distinguished and influential scholar and practitioner of the art. He was joined on the trip to England by Colonel Alfred McCormack, head of the new Signals Corps Special Branch, who had done a comprehensive review of American Sigint operations after Pearl Harbor, and by a thirty-five-year-old Harvard-trained lawyer who had been associated with the Special Branch and Arlington Hall for only five months, Telford Taylor. Taylor would become famous after the war as the chief prosecutor in the Nuremberg war-crimes trials; it is less well known that for most of the war he served as the primary American liaison in Great Britain for signals intelligence.

The three Americans were received warmly by their British counterparts. For men intrigued by the intellectual aspect of cryptography, it must have been refreshing to talk openly about the subject and learn what "the cousins" on the other side of the Atlantic had been working on. What Friedman's delegation discovered was that the British codebreaking operation was far more developed and professional than they had guessed. Bletchley Park had a personnel roster exceeding five thousand people, and the British far outpaced the Americans in their development of the practices and procedures of code breaking and interception.

Friedman, McCormack, and Taylor were there to do more than just observe. Upon arrival, they began negotiating what would be the first major written agreement binding Britain and the United States on communications intelligence, a precursor of the agreement that governs that relationship today. The BRUSA agreement, as it was known, was the first major pact of its kind: an alliance on Sigint between two nations. The thrust behind BRUSA was to prevent duplication of effort by carving up geographic spheres on which each power would focus and to coordinate the exchange of intelligence and information. The text of the agreement was secret for half a century but was finally declassified by the NSA in 1995. It held that "both the U.S. and British agree to exchange completely all information concerning the detection, identification and interception of signals from and the solution of codes and ciphers used by the Military and Air forces of the axis powers." The agreement held that the United States would assume responsibility for reading Japanese communications, while the British would focus on the Germans and the Italians. It was determined that "all intelligence available from decodes shall be made available to Liaison Officers, and if they deem necessary it will be exchanged between London and Washington." The declassified text still bears the admonition, *"Part I to be destroyed by Fire when Read."* After BRUSA was signed, Friedman and McCormack headed home, and Taylor stayed on to oversee personally the exchange of information and techniques.

Six months later, in November 1943, representatives of some thirty allied countries convened in Washington to discuss a more extensive collaboration on signals intelligence. The British and Americans were joined by intelligence officials from Canada and Australia, and it was at this gathering that the participants began to develop in embryo the broader international cooperation that would be formalized in the UKUSA agreement after the war.

AN EXTRAORDINARY NUMBER OF features of today's international landscape emerged during the last six months of 1945. On August 6, the crew of the *Enola Gay* loosed the first atomic bomb, on Hiroshima. Three days later, the crew of the B-29 known as *Bock's Car* dropped a second bomb, on Nagasaki. On September 2, Japanese officials signed an unconditional surrender aboard the battleship *Missouri,* in Tokyo Bay. On October 24, the United Nations was founded. And on November 20, 1945, the Nuremberg trials began, under the leadership of Telford Taylor and Attorney General Robert H. Jackson.

While these events are enshrined in history books as epoch-defining episodes, another development in these months that had a similarly momentous impact on the manner in which international society worked in the subsequent years has gone largely overlooked. When the war ended and the Allies prevailed, in no small measure because of their secret cooperation on signals intelligence, they elected to continue that alliance in peacetime. On September 12, 1945, just days after the Japanese surrender, President Harry Truman signed a top-secret one-sentence memorandum, authorizing the secretary of war and the secretary of the navy "to continue collaboration in the field of communication intelligence between the United States Army and Navy, and the British, and to extend, modify or discontinue this collaboration, as determined in the best interests of the United States."

Why extend this intimate cooperation into peacetime? Part of the explanation lies in enduring Allied fears about postwar security, particularly regarding Stalin's Russia. The Americans worried that their coverage of the signals flying around the world was incomplete: their naval-intercept stations were largely focused on the Pacific, in places like Guam, Samoa, and Okinawa, and their Atlantic coverage focused on the south, in Puerto Rico, Brazil, and the Panama Canal Zone. The British, meanwhile, had intercept stations in the North Atlantic and the North Sea area, as well as in the Mediterranean and around the Red Sea, the Indian Ocean, and the South Pacific. The British also had access to intercept stations in Canada, Australia, New Zealand, and South Africa. Due in part to their burden sharing during the war, the United States and the United Kingdom each possessed what the other lacked in 1945, and only through continued cooperation could either have the kind of global strategic omniscience that seemed prudent in an uncertain period.

And so in February 1946, William Friedman went to England for another round of negotiations. This time, discussions took the better part of two months, and Britain had been authorized by the governments in Ottawa and Canberra to negotiate on their behalf. Sir Stewart Menzies chaired the negotiations. A shrewd tactician, he would pause the talks when a particularly intractable issue arose and suggest that the participants adjourn to the Ritz for lunch. Back in his office several bottles of claret later, Menzies found his colleagues considerably more pliable.

At the meetings, it was decided that a U.S. liaison office would be set up in London and that various procedures should be instituted to avoid duplication of effort—a constant risk in a working environment that is so compartmentalized and secret. It was agreed that solved material would be exchanged between the two countries and that an exchange program would be set up, which would allow employees from one agency to spend several years working for the other.

Over the course of these negotiations, a document began to take shape. In its final form, it comprised some twenty-five pages, but it would remain an ellipsis in the historical record—a brief but consequential passage that was simply excised. Even the date of the document generates debate among historians. Before he died, the legendary NSA cryptographer Dr. Louis Tordella confirmed for the British intelligence historian Christopher Andrew that he was present at the signing and that it occurred in June 1948. Perhaps because the negotiations were so protracted and involved successive draft agreements, the date is often given as 1947. A Colonel Kirby and a Colonel Hayes from the army, a Captain Roeder from the navy, John Morrison from the air force, and Benson Buffham and Robert Packard from the State Department were also present, according to Tordella. And the document was known as the United Kingdom–USA Communications Intelligence Agreement, or simply: UKUSA.

Despite the fact that a fair amount of ink has been spilled about it, that its existence has been acknowledged by numerous former intelligence officers, and that it gave rise to one of the most durable and co-ordinated intelligence alliances in history, the document is still not public and has been neither confirmed nor denied by the member agencies. The initial phase of the agreement, which was signed in 1947, bound just the United States and the United Kingdom. The arrangement provided that GCHQ would use its listening stations in Britain and on Cyprus to monitor western Europe and the Middle East. The following year, Canada, Australia and New Zealand joined as "Second Parties."

A further group of "Third Parties," such as Japan, South Korea, and various NATO allies, joined the alliance in subsequent years. But significantly, it was a tiered agreement, by no means among equal parties. Even Britain, while it may have been on a roughly equal footing with the United States during the war, was gradually demoted as America solidified its cold-war position as a superpower. One former NSA officer put it thus: "[All] information comes to the United States, but the United States does not totally reciprocate in passing information to the other powers." Indeed, most of the American bases located on foreign soil, including RAF Menwith Hill, send intelligence directly back to Fort Meade, Maryland, after which it can be distributed to other powers on a need-to-know basis. Though Britain houses the giant ear at Menwith Hill, it hears only what America wants it to.

The terms of the agreement are even less generous when it comes to the third parties. For instance, Japan has allowed the United States to build a dozen eavesdropping installations on its territory and locate the

NSA Far East Headquarters there. Yet since 1981 the NSA has leaned on New Zealand's member agency, the GCSB, to intercept and monitor huge volumes of Japanese diplomatic traffic (JAD, in the shorthand of the trade). It is also interesting to note that at roughly the same time the UKUSA agreement was signed, the North Atlantic Treaty Organization was formed, in April 1948. The terms of UKUSA remained unaffected by NATO. The treaty merely broadened the scope for the overt construction of new listening stations.

Having circled the NSA installation at Menwith Hill and having gazed, mesmerized, at those white orbs appearing to bob, weightless, in the pastureland, I figured that if GCHQ wouldn't declassify the UKUSA agreement, it could at the very least acknowledge that it exists. After all, I'd *seen* this giant American installation in the middle of Britain; I'd walked around it. What could be the harm in effectively conceding the obvious? "The UK and U.S. have an excellent relationship, benefiting both us and NATO, working together for common defense purposes," Bob McNally, a GCHQ spokesman, e-mailed me. "There has been a long tradition of cooperation between us. . . . We do not comment on or discuss details of the relationship, nor the operations of our allies." This response was pretty typical. No one is denying that there is a friendship, even a "special relationship." But any effort to push past those blandishments is a nonstarter. Still, while officials will not acknowledge the alliance by name, they occasionally slip and convey relevant details. In October 2002, New Zealand's prime minister, Helen Clark, told the *New Zealand Herald* that her country was still part of something she called "the best intelligence club." When she was asked about this club later on TVNZ, Clark said that New Zealand was a "founder member" of the club, "along with the U.S., Britain, Australia and Canada."

ONE DAY IN 1970, a truck pulled out of the headquarters of the aerospace company TRW, in Redondo Beach, California. Aboard the truck was a geostationary satellite—a piece of spy technology that was to revolutionize the manner in which the United States gathered signals and draw the five nations of the UKUSA alliance closer than ever before. *Geostationary* means simply that the satellite orbits in synch with the rotation of the earth, so that it remains over a single spot. Four years earlier, TRW had received a contract from the CIA to produce four of these satellites, to be launched in the early 1970s. This was the first satellite of the program, code-named Rhyolite, and it became known to the people who managed it from the ground as Bird 1.

Because constructing satellites is so expensive, Bird 1 was to perform a number of functions. Its primary task would be telemetry: reading radio waves and atmospheric changes to detect the presence of missile testing. But another function was to intercept communications signals. Because the earth is curved, when you send a radio signal between microwave towers that are any distance apart, some of that signal will continue going straight ahead, past the tower, into space. This is called "microwave spillage." The quality of the signal will deteriorate the farther from earth it travels, but a message will still be discernible twenty-two thousand miles out, where Rhyolite satellites were designed to hover. As such, in the words of Robert Lindsey, the *New York Times* reporter who was one of the first people to write about the program, Rhyolite "could monitor Communist traffic over much of the European landmass, eavesdropping on a Soviet commissar in Moscow talking to his mistress in Yalta or on a general talking to his lieutenants across the great continent." James Bamford, who with two dense books on the history of the NSA is the uncontested civilian authority on the agency, refers to Rhyolite as "NSA's first true listening post in space."

Packed into a large container aboard the truck, Bird 1 was transported to Cape Canaveral, Florida, where it was launched from an Atlas-Agena D launch vehicle. Bird 1 was a squat cylinder, about five feet long and weighing three quarters of a ton, that was designed to unfold in space into the shape of a giant umbrella, with a shallow dish that was more than seventy feet across, from the center of which protruded a long antenna. The dish was backed by two long wings made of silicon cells, which could convert light into energy. And the whole device was encrusted with two dozen microwave receivers. The satellite most likely spent several months hovering over the United States, while lab-coated technicians fine-tuned and calibrated its sensitive components. Then it began its migration to a spot above the equator, near Indonesia and Australia—the most strategic point for gathering signals from the Soviet Union and China.

Rhyolite was not completely independent of listening posts of the terrestrial variety, and as Bird 1 was being readied for launch in the United States, preparations were under way on the other side of the planet. Deep in the sweltering heart of Australia's Red Center, about nineteen kilometers outside the town of Alice Springs, strange things were happening. The Red Center is a barren expanse of rust-colored sand and tufts of spinifex, the dry grass that is one of the few things that can grow in such intense desert conditions. Alice, as it is known to the locals, is the only outpost for hundreds of miles, a speck of a town, dusty and tough, hard in the center of the Australian landmass. In the 1960s, Alice was a small community of several thousand whites, mainly gritty ranchers with a taste for isolation, and several thousand Aborigines, whose people had been living in the area for millennia. So it must have seemed exceedingly odd to locals when, three years before the launching of Bird 1, a Texas-based outfit by the name of Collins Radio Company set up an office in town.

More surprising even than the fact that these Americans had stumbled into the heart of the Outback and could tolerate the summer temperatures of 115 degrees was the fact that they planned to stay—Collins was there to help construct a base just outside of town, in a shallow basin between rocky outcrops in the foothills of the Macdonnell Ranges. The base would initially contain just two radomes, hiding dishes that were thirty-three and twenty-one meters in diameter, respectively. These were erected in 1968 but were followed over the years by twelve more, bringing the number of radomes today to fourteen. The radomes are joined by a dozen other antennae and twenty or so one-story support buildings, including a massive computer room of almost six thousand square feet, said to be one of the largest in the world. Collins provided much of the basic infrastructure, IBM was the primary contractor for the computers, TRW produced the satellites controlled by the station, and another Texas company, E-Systems, was responsible for the management and operation of the computer room. Thus, while the base was officially, if cryptically, known as a "Joint Defense Space Research Facility," it was still very much an American operation. The name of this beachhead of the UKUSA interception system in Australia is Pine Gap.

It is difficult to convey just how isolated Pine Gap is. The base gives literal expression to the phrase *in the middle of nowhere*. It lies in the remotest stretch of the remotest continent on earth. A former E-Systems technician who spent several years at Pine Gap told me that after a short while the young Americans there went stir-crazy and indulged in progressively Bacchic fits of excess, drinking and coupling for lack of anything better to do. Of course, the location is remote by design. When the idea of using geostationary satellites for signals intelligence was conceived in the 1960s, the primary concern in choosing sites for ground stations was that the Soviets not be in any way able to intercept the downlinks. In order to maintain satellites in parking orbits over the Indian Ocean, the Americans needed a downlink site in the southern hemisphere, because the curvature of the earth prevents satellites there from transmitting directly to the United States. The downlink could not be on an island like Diego Garcia or Guam, because it would be vulnerable to Soviet Sigint vessels trawling for signals just off the coast. While this kind of tampering is always a hazard, on this occasion the concern was particularly acute, because in order to keep Bird 1 light-weight and easy to power, the architects had elected to send it into orbit without any onboard encryption system. The messages it transmitted back to earth were sent as "natural language"—totally unencrypted.

Given these considerations, Pine Gap was an ideal solution. The seven square miles around the facility are secured as a buffer zone to reduce electronic interference of any sort. The leaseholders on the pastures around the station keep visitors off the property. Thus, it would not be possible to install any kind of satellite-receiving antenna anywhere within a fifty-mile radius of the site. The air-traffic controllers at the Alice Springs airport report any suspicious flight movements, so there is little possibility of interception by overflight. And the site is hundreds of miles from the sea, so there is no danger of Russian ships picking up signals from Bird 1.

Because the satellite program at Pine Gap has always been a "black" program, there has been very little in the way of official comment regarding its operations or capabilities. The agreement to establish the base signed by the governments of Australia and the United States on December 9, 1966, says that it will be devoted to "joint space research." Yet the agreement identified the American agency responsible for the base as the Advanced Research Projects Agency, or ARPA, which is now known as DARPA. (An amendment to the agreement in 1977 replaced this reference with a more generic one, saying that the Department of Defense would oversee the station.) What acknowledgment there has been that the station even exists has consistently claimed that the facility engaged in space research or "arms control verification." There is little doubt that the station *was* an important means of checking on the nuclear research and testing activities of the Soviets and other powers through various forms of satellite telemetry. The Australian minister of foreign affairs Bill Hayden once remarked that "it is highly unlikely that some major arms control agreements between the superpowers would have been concluded if there had been no Pine Gap." But even at the height of the cold war in the 1980s, it was estimated by Desmond Ball, a professor at Australian National University and the foremost expert on Australian signals intelligence, that less than 40 percent of the resources and effort of the U.S. geostationary satellite program was actually devoted to arms control. Moreover, as Ball makes clear, the program which Bird 1 initiated had been in the works for some years by the time that first Rhyolite satellite was launched in 1970—indeed, it predated any serious discussions and treaties between the Americans and the Soviets on arms control. Ball claims that technicians in Pine Gap's Signals Analysis Section were able to listen in on communications from the start and that some had the haunting experience, during the final years of the Vietnam War, of listening to radioed cries for assistance from wounded American GIs.

But what does Pine Gap do today? One might expect the base to have closed down after the cold war. Another American base several hundred miles to the south, with the lyrical name Nurrungar (which, aptly enough, is derived from the Aboriginal word for "to listen"), was shut down in 2000, and many of its employees and much of its hardware were moved to Pine Gap. At the same time, Australian authorities announced in the summer of 1998 that the Pine Gap agreement had been renewed for another ten years.

Today, the base employs almost nine hundred people, roughly half of them Australian and half American. There have been labor disputes in the past, with Australian employees going on strike because they are paid less than their American counterparts, but otherwise relations are fairly amicable. Alice Springs is full of Americans now. They never discuss their jobs, of course, but they are involved in numerous activities: baseball leagues, Rotary clubs, the Keep Alice Springs Beautiful Society. And they bring a great deal of money to the local economy.

Though Bamford refers to Pine Gap as the NSA's first listening post in space, the base is actually run by the CIA, which coordinates with the NSA and the National Reconnaissance Office (NRO), the agency responsible for designing and developing American satellites. Initially, Pine Gap was just a relay station. It received unencrypted signals from the Rhyolite satellite, encrypted them, then relayed them to the United States, either to TRW or directly to Fort Meade. But Ron Huisken, an Australian who was head of the facility from 1995 to 2001, claims that Pine Gap has doubled in size since the Gulf War. This most likely reflects the extent to which the southern-hemispheric coverage provided by the base has become increasingly vital to American strategic considerations. It also reflects the closeness between the Australian and American intelligence communities born of the UKUSA agreement. Today, Pine Gap is the largest CIA base in the world. But it is just one of dozens of bases run by American military and intelligence agencies in Australia alone.

Over the years, the presence of so many American bases in Australia has been the source of sporadic controversy, and to this day protests are still organized around various bases, particularly around Pine Gap. When this happens, the roads to the base are shut down and manned by military police. The greatest controversy of this sort occurred in the fall of 1975. At the time, there was much concern within Australia about hosting bases that were instrumental in American nuclear telemetry and thus might become targets of a nuclear strike. While this seems alarmist today, it is worth remembering the general climate of the cold war, in which such events seemed entirely plausible and to many inevitable. In the fall of 1975, new information about the role of the CIA in Australia was becoming public, fanning the flames of the debate. At the forefront of criticism of American installations was Prime Minister Gough Whitlam. In late October, his Labour government revealed that the bases had not been supervised by the U.S. Department of Defense, as had been held previously, but in fact by a CIA official, whose name became public. The Labour party initiated inquiries, and it was revealed that not even those individuals in very senior positions in the Australian Foreign Ministry understood exactly what was done at bases like Pine Gap.

On November 10, the Australian Security Intelligence Organization received a message from its liaison with the CIA that said agency officials were extremely concerned about the danger of any further public revelations about the base.

CIA IS PERPLEXED AS TO WHAT ALL THIS MEANS. DOES THIS SIGNIFY SOME CHANGE IN OUR BILATERAL INTELLIGENCE SECURITY RELATED FIELD. CIA CANNOT SEE HOW THIS DIALOGUE WITH CONTINUED REFERENCE TO CIA CAN DO OTHER THAN BLOW THE LID OFF THOSE INSTALLATIONS IN AUSTRALIA WHERE THE PERSONS CONCERNED HAVE BEEN WORKING AND THAT ARE VITAL TO BOTH OUR SERVICES AND COUNTRIES, PARTICULARLY THE INSTALLATIONS AT ALICE SPRINGS.

This was a matter of utmost importance to the United States. The National Security Council regarded the bases in Australia as instrumental to American nuclear survival, and it was suggested at the end of the message that if the revelations continued the United States might stop giving Australia privileged access to the intelligence flowing from the bases.

Whitlam persevered, however. This was not a good time to be associated with the CIA. Revelations were beginning to emerge about the agency's involvement in the overthrow of Salvador Allende in Chile, and Whitlam was convinced that there was similar tampering with the domestic political affairs of Australia. He had begun to allege publicly that the CIA had channeled funds to the Liberal and National Country parties, both of which opposed Labour and supported the presence of the American bases. He was preparing to give another speech on the subject on November 11 but was unable to because Governor-General John Kerr removed him from office.

In the years since, theories have persisted in Australia about the CIA's involvement in this coup, but Whitlam's ouster was ultimately a hiccup in what has otherwise been a history of amicable cooperation. Though initially Australian employees at Pine Gap were excluded from the Signals Analysis Section of the base and shut off, as a result, from the rich intelligence product gathered there, the facility was desegregated in 1980, and today the relationship under UKUSA is closer than ever. The directors of the five allied agencies meet together every year to plan and coordinate. The meetings are routine and routinely secret. The public does not know which country is playing host in which year or when the meetings are convened. And the cooperation between UKUSA countries is hardly limited to the provenance of the secret agreement. Numerous other bilateral and multilateral agreements govern the exchange of intelligence among these countries, to say nothing of the countless informal conventions that arise out of sustained cooperation, which are often as or more important than the written agreements themselves.

In 1999, Bill Blick, Australia's inspector general for intelligence, was the first official in any of the UKUSA countries to acknowledge this close relationship and the Sigint network the countries maintain. "As you would expect there are a large amount of radio communications floating around in the atmosphere," he told the BBC, "and agencies such as DSD collect those communications in the interests of their national security." Asked whether these intercepts are passed on to Britain and America, Blick confirmed that "they might be in certain circumstances."

Menwith Hill and Pine Gap are just two of a great many bases that cover the globe. Their size and significance is a testament to the scope of the system the UKUSA agreement initiated more than fifty years ago and the degree to which the four non-American parties to that agreement are intimately involved with American intelligence today. On their own, they are merely an indication of the tremendous resources and investment that have been devoted to the network and merely a hint of the network's capabilities. Gough Whitlam underestimated how important the continued health of this arrangement was to the governments of the countries involved and how deftly an alliance between intelligence agencies could trump the needs and demands of local people or politicians. He also underestimated the lengths to which the agencies would go in order to keep the whole arrangement secret. A similar miscalculation would be made by a young GCHQ employee a quarter century later.

THE LEAK WAS ME

Listening to Diplomats

ON THE AFTERNOON of Monday, February 3, 2003, as the drumbeat for an invasion of Iraq intensified in Washington and London, a young blond woman named Katharine Gun tucked a document into her handbag before leaving work at GCHQ, on the outskirts of the Cotswold spa town of Cheltenham. At twenty-eight, Katharine had been working for the agency for two years, as a translator of Mandarin Chinese. She shuddered as she passed through security and exited the complex—by removing a classified document from the premises she was already breaching the rules. If the risk she assumed was high, so too were the stakes: Katharine Gun's plan, however idealistic or naïve, was to prevent the United States and the United Kingdom from going to war in Iraq.

The previous Friday had started like any other. Katharine had been seated at her workstation at GCHQ, where she spent her days wearing a pair of headphones, listening to intercepted Chinese conversations. Katharine was born in England, but her parents moved with her to Taiwan when she was three. She returned to Britain for high school, where she found that she had an unusual gift for languages, and continued to study Chinese. At the University of Durham, she picked up Japanese, and after graduating moved to Hiroshima prefecture, in Japan, to teach English in a provincial school. In 1999, Katharine returned to England and was looking for a job in which she could use her languages when her eye fell on an ad in the newspaper for work at GCHQ. She had never had a particular interest in intelligence and could not tell from the ad what precisely the job entailed, but the ad contained a list of languages they were interested in, and two of them were Chinese and Japanese. "It seemed fairly innocuous, in terms of how they do things, who they target, why they target those particular people," she later recalled. "Yes, you know you're going to work for intelligence services. Yes, you know it's secretive, and all the rest of it. But you don't know the extent." She did a little research but was not able to learn much about the particular nature of GCHQ's work. The recruiting officer she spoke with was not very forthcoming either. But it was a job. In keeping with standard practice, the agency proceeded to vet her, conducting a thorough investigation into her background, talking with friends and neighbors, old colleagues, and whoever else might be able to help establish a picture of her fitness to work in the most secret realm of British intelligence. Katharine took a series of temp jobs while she waited, a little bemused by the process and still not certain precisely what, if she was eventually given a job, she would be asked to do.

Vetting can be particularly protracted for those who have lived for any length of time in foreign countries, so it was a full year before GCHQ informed Katharine that she had the job. In January 2001, she reported for work and was immediately assigned to a team of ten or so people who were supervised by a "line manager." She found the atmosphere relatively laid-back and liked her colleagues. Most of them were quite young, because GCHQ has traditionally had a big problem with retaining linguists. As a result, there are few old hands, and the staff is fairly fluid. Katharine was confident about her language skills from the start, but she was intimidated by the blizzard of procedures and classifications and acronyms she needed to learn in order to perform the job. On top of that, she was expected to keep up with the news on a regular basis. A translator at GCHQ will often monitor the same people for months or years, getting to know the voices and temperaments of various officials and sometimes collecting news photographs of these individuals and posting them at the workplace to keep them straight. From her first day listening in, Katharine realized that you have to know who your target is: when you tune in on a given line or frequency, you have to know who it is you are listening to.

After two years on the job, Katharine had fully acclimated to the rituals and lingo of the Sigint profession and was beginning to find the work mundane. But on Friday morning, January 31, 2003, she opened her GCHQ e-mail to find a memo from a man named Frank Koza, Chief of Staff for Regional Targets, NSA. It was marked top secret and described an operation by the NSA to bug the telephones of United Nations diplomats in New York. It opened:

As you've likely heard by now, the Agency is mounting a surge particularly directed at the UN Security Council (UNSC) members (minus
US and GBR of course) for insights as to how to [sic] membership is
reacting to the ongoing debate RE: Iraq, plans to vote on any related
resolutions, what related policies/negotiating positions they may be
considering, alliances/dependencies, etc—the whole gamut of information that could give US policymakers an edge in obtaining results
favorable to US goals or to head off surprises.

Katharine scrolled down, in shock. The memo went on to explain that
in particular that meant a "surge" of eavesdropping activity on diplomats from the so-called middle six countries—the delegations on the
Security Council whose votes on the upcoming Iraq resolution were
undecided: Angola, Cameroon, Chile, Mexico, Guinea, and Pakistan.
Hesitant to leave it at that, Koza explained that the NSA had also
asked for coverage of "existing non-UNSC deliberations/debates/
votes" and that "this effort will probably peak (at least for this specific
focus) in the middle of next week, following the SecState's presentation
to the UNSC" on February 5.

Katharine read and reread the memo. She was opposed to a war in
Iraq—she'd marched in London to protest it—and felt strongly that an
invasion without proper Security Council authorization would be illegal. She went home over the weekend and stewed over the memo.
Slowly, it occurred to her that if the British public knew about the
memo and understood that British intelligence was being enlisted in
this plot to manipulate neutral countries into backing an invasion,
there might be an uproar. By the time she came to work Monday morning, Katharine Gun knew that she had to do something.

Katharine gave the memo to a friend with connections in the British
media. She did not know whether it would be published or by whom,
and she did not want to communicate further with the friend, so that
she could protect her identity. Say this for eavesdroppers: they're cau-
tious about their own communications. She went back to work Tuesday, trying to put the memo out of her mind, and all was business as
usual for the next month. On the morning of March 2, Katharine was
out picking up the Sunday papers when her eyes fell on the reprinted
memo on the front page of the London broadsheet *The Observer,*
under the headline, "Revealed: U.S. Dirty Tricks to Win Vote on Iraq
War."

. . .

KATHARINE WAS RIGHT TO think that the memo would ruffle feathers. The *Observer* article prompted angry editorials in newspapers in England and around the world—though not, as it happened, in the United States. American coverage was limited to brief articles in *The Washington Post* and the *Los Angeles Times,* both of which downplayed the significance of the allegations. Despite the fact that the "surge" outlined in the memo was directed at offices and residences on the east side of Manhattan, *The New York Times* ignored the story completely. When asked why the *Times* had not run a single piece on the story, Alison Smale, the paper's deputy editor, said, "Well, it's not that we haven't been interested. We could get no confirmation or comment" from U.S. officials. The message was clear: if the *Times* won't publish anything the government does not confirm, all the Bush administration needed to do was remain tight-lipped, and the paper of record would do the same. Sure enough, when questioned in press conferences about the allegations, Secretary of Defense Donald Rumsfeld and White House Press Secretary Ari Fleischer both categorically refused to comment.

What little American coverage there was of the memo seemed to suggest that it was a fake. By the evening of the day the story broke, Matt Drudge had alerted readers of the Drudge Report website to the fact that while Frank Koza, the supposed author of the piece, was presumably American, several of the words in the memo were rendered in British spelling. "Favorable" became "favourable"; "emphasize," "emphasise"; "recognize," "recognise." Moreover, the date on the document was written 31/01/2003, and not, as any red-blooded American would have written it, 1/31/2003.

In spite of a predictable refusal to comment by the NSA, however, the Koza memo began to appear legit. *The Observer* explained that it had edited the document's spelling for its British readers, giving further evidence to George Bernard Shaw's suggestion that the United States and the United Kingdom are two countries divided by a common language. The paper also confirmed that Frank Koza was an NSA employee. The president of Chile, Ricardo Lagos, whose country has felt particularly suspicious of American intelligence agencies since the CIA-supported coup against Salvador Allende in 1973, telephoned Prime Minister Tony Blair and demanded an explanation. And the British police arrested Katharine Gun on suspicion of having violated the Official Secrets Act.

The moment the story broke, GCHQ had launched an internal investigation, and when Katharine arrived at work on Monday morning, she was informed that everyone who received Koza's e-mail would be questioned by vetting officers, as those in charge of internal security are known. When Katharine met with a vetting officer on Tuesday, she denied responsibility, but that night she was nauseous with worry. The next day, she tracked down her line manager, and they went to a quiet room. The line manager was a sympathetic older woman, and Katharine liked her and felt guilty for having effectively betrayed her by leaking the memo. The manager could see Katharine was extremely agitated. As soon as they sat down, Katharine blurted, "The leak was me."

BRITAIN'S OFFICIAL SECRETS ACT has had a tortured history. First passed at a time of great national insecurity, in 1911, as the Kaiser's Germany threatened to unsettle the fragile balance of power in Europe, the act was a blanket provision preventing civil servants from revealing almost any government information. Officials reportedly used to joke that even the menu in the Civil Service canteen was secret, a joke made slightly less entertaining for being, strictly speaking, true. Even in its amended form, the Official Secrets Act of 1989 is a broad provision preventing members of the intelligence services from talking about any aspect of their work, from the most sensitive to the most banal. Yet while spies traditionally prize discretion and have an understandable motivation to penalize disclosures, prosecutions are an inevitably public process, and nowhere more so than in England, where a gift for rhetoric and a penchant for scandal often elevate a criminal trial to the level of theatrical spectacle. As such, the act has tended to be an ineffective weapon for the government to wield, and one that has backfired more often than not. Prosecutions under the act have seldom been successful, and even successful convictions have often followed trials that were so sensational they ended up revealing far more secrets than the initial offending leak.

The very existence of GCHQ was an official secret until Margaret Thatcher was forced to acknowledge that the agency existed, in the wake of a 1983 Official Secrets Act prosecution of a GCHQ employee who had sold secrets to the Soviets. That spy was ultimately convicted, but at the price of GCHQ's invisibility. In 1985, a British judge advised a jury to convict Clive Ponting, a former Ministry of Defense employee, of violating the act by leaking a classified document regarding the British sinking, in 1982, of the Argentine cruiser *General Belgrano,* which had resulted in the deaths of 323 people. The jury disregarded the judge's advice, however, and acquitted Ponting. In 1987, a former MI5 officer named Peter Wright published a memoir called *Spycatcher* in the United States and Australia. By the time the book came out, Wright was an old and sickly man living on a sheep ranch in Tasmania. Thatcher's government tried, in a high-profile case, to extradite him. They failed. In 2002, a judge sentenced the former MI5 agent David Shayler to six months in prison for leaking classified information about intelligence activities to the *Mail on Sunday.* The sentence was much shorter than the government had hoped for, however, and was accompanied by such a storm of negative publicity that the victory was decidedly pyrrhic.

It may have been this history of failures that explained the bizarre developments that followed Katharine's arrest. As soon as GCHQ's internal investigators had taken a full statement from Katharine, the police were summoned, and she was whisked off to the Cheltenham police station, where she was booked "on suspicion of having violated the Official Secrets Act" but not charged. She was informed that she would have to spend the night in what was euphemistically dubbed a "custody suite," attached to the station, but that her husband could come and visit her. Her husband was panicked—a team of police officers was searching their Cheltenham home—and he cried as they spoke through a glass divider. The next day, however, Katharine (whose name was not at that time publicly known) was released on bail. She returned home, unemployed now, having been dismissed from GCHQ, and waited. Liberty, the London-based human-rights organization that had defended David Shayler, contacted her through GCHQ and took on her case. But the government did not bring charges. Her legal team was led by Shami Chakrabarti, the director of Liberty and a former lawyer for Britain's Home Office. Chakrabarti thought that it would be madness for the government to charge Katharine—the last thing Tony Blair wanted was a public trial that would touch on the merits of a very unpopular war. But as the summer months wore on, the fact that the government hadn't announced that they *weren't* charging Gun became more profound than the fact that they hadn't announced that they were. She whiled away the days, finding it hard to remain optimistic, saved only by what she calls her "high boredom threshold." Her parents still lived in Taiwan, but they telephoned every day. And some of her friends from GCHQ remained supportive, staying in touch and confiding in Katharine that they shared her view that the operation she had exposed was outrageous. Other GCHQ friends cut off contact with her completely the moment she was dismissed.

In the early fall, I contacted Liberty to inquire about the status of the case and to ask whether charges could still be considered "pending" when the government had taken no action for seven months. The war in Iraq was raging, with American and British casualties mounting daily and no exit in sight. Pundits were invoking Vietnam. Barry Hugill, a spokesman for Liberty, told me, "I suspect, given the unpopularity of the war in the U.K., that they will not want a high-profile case and will let the matter drop. But only time will tell."

Time told. On Thursday, November 13, 2003, Katharine was officially charged by the Metropolitan Police Special Branch, and her identity was revealed. She was at home when one of her lawyers, James Welch, telephoned. "He didn't even say 'I've got bad news,' bless him," she later recalled. "He just said, 'They're going to charge you.' " Katharine was specifically charged with having violated section 1(1) of the act, which holds that "a person who is or has been a member of the security and intelligence services . . . is guilty of an offence if without lawful authority he discloses any information, document or other article relating to security or intelligence which is or has been in his possession by virtue of his position as a member of any of those services."

Looking at the wording of that provision, Katharine did not at first appear to have much of a case. If the prosecution could demonstrate that she leaked the memo, her defense could hardly argue that she had not violated section 1(1) on its face. No doubt aware of this and mindful of the fact that a jury would determine Katharine's fate, her lawyers decided to go on the offensive and exploit public hostility to the war by endeavoring to make the proceedings not a trial of whether Katharine leaked the memo but instead a trial of the legality of the war in Iraq and of the peculiar obligations of the special relationship between Britain and the United States.

One of the objections raised by David Shayler's defense and by indignant editorials in the British press had been that there are no loopholes in the Official Secrets Act whereby intelligence agents might be acquitted on the grounds of public policy—no whistleblower exception. While Shayler's various defenses failed, Lord Woolf, the chief justice in the Court of Appeal, did allow that in principle a defense of "necessity" might be read into the act. Under this exception, acquittal would be possible if the crime was committed "to avoid imminent peril of danger to life or serious injury to himself or towards individuals for whom he reasonably regarded himself as responsible."

This language formed the basis of Katharine's case. The day she was charged, Katharine released a statement, saying that her disclosures were justified because "they exposed serious illegality and wrongdoing on the part of the US government which attempted to subvert our security services; and they could have helped prevent wide-scale death and casualties amongst ordinary Iraqi people and UK forces in the course of an illegal war. No one has suggested (nor could they) that any payment was sought or given for any alleged disclosures. I have only ever followed my conscience."

One shrewd tactic invited another, however, and the prosecution answered with an ingenious legal ploy to hamstring Katharine's defense. Government prosecutors averred that because Katharine's work at GCHQ was secret, she could not tell her lawyers anything that was not already in the public domain without applying to the government first, for permission. This would effectively have obliged the defense to disclose its case to the prosecution before the trial had even begun; the team at Liberty aggressively fought the move.

Meanwhile, outside the courtroom, as the war in Iraq continued to unravel, Katharine became a popular hero in the world press. Paparazzi lingered outside her hearings, waiting for a shot of the pert young blonde in the pink scarf who had taken a stand on the war in Iraq. British reporters scrambled to find a new angle on the case. ("GCHQ Mother: My Girl Is Not a Traitor," *The Guardian* exclaimed.) In the United States, Katharine's case was taken up by a bizarre assemblage of personalities from entertainment and politics. The actors Sean Penn and Martin Sheen, the Reverend Jesse Jackson, Daniel Ellsberg, and the gnomish presidential candidate Dennis Kucinich all spoke in her defense, writing letters and producing petitions. Ellsberg called the leak "more timely and potentially more important than the Pentagon Papers," which he had leaked.

While the British press relished the drama of this story, however, the American press continued to ignore it completely. From New York, I followed the emerging case in the world press and looked in vain for any coverage by American papers. Certainly some native myopia has always hindered the media in the United States, but it did not take an investigative journalist to figure out that the fact that the British government had charged Katharine was a de facto admission that the Koza memo was real. And that was significant news. I was also struck by the degree to which, in the unfolding scandal, Katharine had become a proxy for the British people—the average objector to Blair's rush to war, who just happened, by virtue of her job as an eavesdropper, to be in a position to do something about it. The story seemed made for the movies: a fierce storm of government deception and hypocrisy swirling around an idealistic, attractive protagonist. Why weren't reporters picking it up? It would not be the last time I underestimated the tacit gentleman's agreement whereby the American press refrains from covering the great unmentionable game of government eavesdropping.

IN JANUARY, KATHARINE WAS due to appear for a pretrial hearing at Bow Street Magistrates Court in central London, and I decided to attend. I showed up early that morning to find a scrum of paparazzi already loitering outside the courthouse, smoking cigarettes, stamping their feet in the cold, and examining press photos of their prey so they'd know whom to shoot. At a few minutes to ten, a taxi pulled up carrying two women, one of whom was blond and wearing a pink scarf. One grizzled lout, half a dozen cameras dangling from his fireplug neck, shouted, "Oy—that's her!" and dashed toward the cab, the rest of the pack swarming at his heels. But then the door opened to reveal a teenage girl, a pink scarf wrapped around her neck, and her mother. They blinked nervously at the confused photographers on the sidewalk and disappeared down an alley in the direction of Covent Garden.

A few minutes later, another taxi pulled up, this one bearing the real Katharine Gun. Wearing a black coat and a thin smile and flanked by lawyers and supporters, she pushed her way through a succession of photographers who seemed to emerge one by one, like assailants in a kung-fu movie, to plant themselves, shutters whirring, in her path. Katharine's face was a mask of composure, but as she walked past me and into the courthouse, I registered an agitated, searching look in her small blue eyes: fear.

An old drunk with a thin cigar that had lost its spark between his lips sat on the steps of the courthouse, nursing a tall can of Carling. It did not look to be his first of the morning. With a good-natured curiosity he watched the parade of lawyers and gawkers and hacks file past him into the building. I was one of the last to enter, and as I headed in we had a comically Shakespearean exchange. "Have you got a light, gov?" he asked.

I said no.

"That young miss, who was that then?" he asked.

"It's a woman who worked for the intelligence services," I answered vaguely, preoccupied with getting inside.

"And what's she done, then?" he asked.

"Uh, there was a secret document. About the war in Iraq," I mustered. "And she gave it to the press. Which was against the rules."

The old inebriate took this in, nodded thoughtfully for a moment, then growled, "Well, good on her!" and flashed me a toothless grin.

After a brief and uneventful hearing on procedural issues, in which Katharine's lawyers pointed out that unless the judge lifted the gag on Katharine, they would not be able to develop a defense, everyone filed out of the courtroom. I walked to the offices of Liberty, in a dilapidated old building on Tabard Street, on the South Bank of the Thames. Barry Hugill had said that if I showed up, Katharine might be willing to speak with me. In a warren of offices that looked out over rooftops and soot-stained chimneys jutting with ancient, centipedal television antennae, I joined Katharine, her father—Paul Harwood, a professor of European literature at Tunghai University in Taiwan—James Welch, and Barry Hugill. I explained my project, and Katharine seemed eager to talk with me, but Welch, a thin, bald man with a young face and a lawyer's punctilious intensity, cut in to inform me that there was very little we could discuss. "You see," he said, "if the government is feeling at all litigious, and we have every indication that they are, anything Katharine tells you now could become the basis for further charges of violating the Official Secrets Act."

I said that I had read the text of the act and that Katharine could conceivably tell me all sorts of things about her background and her life outside of GCHQ that would not get her prosecuted again. Katharine's father, a rumpled looking Brit with a gentle, lived-in face, listened quietly, then interrupted. "I'm sorry," he said, "but having listened to all of this, the advice I would give Katharine is to not talk to you or anyone until after the trial."

I suggested that we could talk now, and I would promise not to publish until after the trial. Katharine shook her head. "It's quite possible that I am already under some form of surveillance," she said flatly, cradling a mug of tea. "It just doesn't make sense to take the risk." I left with the promise that when the trial was over I could come back and talk with her—and with those words about the possibility of surveillance still in my head. From anyone else, the idea would have struck me as decidedly paranoid; from a former GCHQ employee, it carried a certain undeniable authority.

Katharine's team had one good arrow still in its quiver. Since the invasion of Iraq, rumors had swirled in London that Lord Peter Goldsmith, the fifty-three-year-old millionaire barrister who was Britain's attorney general, had not been persuaded that a war without a UN resolution authorizing aggression would be legal under international law. So while the issue of Katharine's ability to talk was still pending, the Liberty team announced that they would request to see the confidential opinion on the legality of the war that Goldsmith had furnished Tony Blair. Suddenly, the burden of proof seemed to have shifted, and in claiming their defense of necessity Katharine's lawyers had dispensed with the matter of whether she had leaked the memo, focusing instead on whether the prosecution could prove that the war in Iraq had been technically legal. On Tuesday, February 24, 2004, Katharine's team formally requested Lord Goldsmith's advice. But within hours of having done so, they received word that the government was planning on dropping the case altogether. It appeared that even greater than the profound embarrassment Whitehall would suffer for dropping the case was the potential embarrassment in its own attorney general's opinion on the invasion. Katharine's husband told her not to celebrate until they were certain the charges were being dropped. He had counseled her all along to prepare for the worst, and so far he'd been right every time. Stifling her excitement, Katharine bought a new suit and started planning her remarks. She was due for a hearing at the Old Bailey the next day. On Wednesday, February 25, Katharine Gun emerged, beaming, from the courthouse to a throng of well-wishers and newspaper photographers. "I'm absolutely overwhelmed and I'm obviously delighted, and just gob-smacked," she said. "I have no regrets. I would do it again."

THE MOMENT THE CASE was dropped, the story seemed to explode and to register, at last, with the American public. *The New York Times* and *The Washington Post* suddenly covered it—for the first time, in the case of the *Times,* save a solitary column by Bob Herbert. The London papers splashed Gun's photograph across the front pages. And late Wednesday, BBC Radio's John Humphrys interviewed Clare Short, Tony Blair's former minister for international development, who had resigned in May 2003 over the war in Iraq, and asked her about the case. Quite unprompted, Short said, "The UK in this time was also . . . spying on Kofi Annan's office." Humphrys was clearly taken by surprise and asked if Short believed Britain had been involved in this operation. "Well I *know*," Short replied. "I've seen transcripts of Kofi Annan's conversations. In fact I've had conversations with Kofi in the run up to war thinking 'Oh dear, there will be a transcript of this, and people will see what he and I are saying.' "

Short's revelations were a bombshell. On Thursday, February 26, a visibly irate Tony Blair addressed reporters and called Short's disclosures "deeply irresponsible." When asked to confirm or deny the story, however, he refused, saying he would not comment one way or the other on the operations of the intelligence services. "That should not be taken, as I say, as an indication about the truth of any particular allegations," he said. "Whether intentionally or not, those who do attack the work our security services are doing undermine the essential security of this country."

A fierce animosity between Short and Blair predated this particular episode, and Short immediately shot back in a television interview, "What's he going to say? Either he has to say 'Yes it's true,' or he has to say 'No it's not true,' and then he'd be telling a lie. So he's got to say something else, so he can have a go at me." Asked by the BBC's Jeremy Paxman about Blair's suggestion that she was irresponsible, Short replied that there was no way her disclosures threatened the lives of any active spies or even jeopardized the national interest. Paxman pointed out that in making these disclosures, Short had *herself* violated the Official Secrets Act, to which Short replied contemptuously, "Well I think if you say how many orders of toilet paper [MI6] makes, you'd probably break the Official Secrets Act."

On Friday, February 27, the Australian Broadcasting Company (ABC) reported that the UN's chief weapons inspector, Hans Blix, had been monitored as well. The ABC's Andrew Fowler claimed that intelligence sources told him that each time Blix entered Iraq, his phone was targeted and recorded, and transcripts were made available to the five UKUSA partners. The same day, Richard Butler, who was chief weapons inspector from 1997 until 1999 and is now the governor of Tasmania, told ABC radio that he was "well aware" that his calls were monitored while he was weapons inspector. "I was utterly confident that . . . I was being listened to by the Americans, the British, the French and the Russians," he said. It suddenly began to appear that everyone was listening to everyone else.

DURING THE GREAT DEPRESSION, a Harvard Business School professor named George Elton Mayo conducted a series of experiments on human behavior and workplace productivity at Western Electric's Hawthorne Plant in the Chicago suburb of Cicero, Illinois. From a massive factory floor full of workers hunched over telephone-relay devices, Elton Mayo chose half a dozen women and monitored their behavior and productivity for several weeks, without them knowing he was watching. Having ascertained a base productivity level, Elton Mayo then segregated his six women in a special room, under the eye of a supervisor, and adjusted the hours in their workday, the days in their workweek, the hour of their lunch break, the frequency of breaks, and so forth. Looking for the effects of monotony and fatigue on the job, he tinkered with the conditions and monitored the women's productivity. But as he conducted his experiment, Elton Mayo noticed a baffling trend. Almost anything he did to alter the working conditions of his segregated six, even changes that should have resulted in more stress and exhaustion, seemed to increase the women's productivity relative to that on the factory floor.

What Elton Mayo had stumbled on was a much broader observation of human behavior than how many telephone parts a person can produce without a lunch break. The theory that emerged from his experiments became known as the Hawthorne Effect and holds that what made the difference in the smaller room was not the hours or the breaks or any other change Elton Mayo could have imposed. It was the fact that somebody was watching.

The principle underlying the Hawthorne Effect seems obvious: we act differently when we know we are being monitored. It has been adduced to explain why insomniacs who are brought in for sleep studies often sleep better in the laboratory and why juvenile offenders who take part in special rehabilitation programs often straighten up. And it more or less gave birth to human-resources departments in business organizations: people will be happier and more productive if they feel the company is taking an active interest in them and the work they are doing.

One area where the Hawthorne Effect has not been rigorously applied, however, is signals intelligence. On the most basic level, a crude form of the Hawthorne Effect explains why intelligence agencies like GCHQ strive so hard to prevent disclosures like Katharine Gun's. If people know you are listening, they will alter their behavior in one way or another. They may not talk on an open line. They may encrypt their communications or, if they know you can break their codes, change their encryption. They may let you listen and speak only in an indecipherable language of coded allusions, the way mobsters in films and television do. Or worst of all, if they know you are listening but you don't know that they know, they may actively mislead you or feed you false information. All of these possibilities come into play when it comes to the oldest game in the Sigint book: listening to diplomats.

WHEN ASKED WHETHER IT was legal to listen in on Kofi Annan, Clare Short replied, "I don't know. I presume so. It's odd, but I don't know about the legalities." Tony Blair assured the public that Britain's intelligence agencies "always act in accordance with domestic and international law." But there is little question that the operation described in Koza's memo was illegal on a number of grounds.

The 1946 General Convention on the Privileges and Immunities of the United Nations, a multilateral treaty signed by the United States and the United Kingdom, states that "the premises of the United Nations shall be inviolable. The property and assets of the United Nations, wherever located and by whomsoever held, shall be immune from search, requisition, confiscation, expropriation and any other form of interference." Likewise, the UN Headquarters Agreement provides that "the headquarters district shall be inviolable."

There may be some room for textual interpretation in these provisions, however. While they ensure the physical inviolability of the headquarters, state of the art communications intelligence requires no such physical intrusion to intercept a telephone call. Still, when questioned about Short's allegations, Fred Eckhard, Kofi Annan's spokesman, cited the General Convention, saying, "That's a generally worded prohibition that I think was intended to anticipate any subsequent technological innovations. So our interpretation is even satellite interception of messages constitutes interference and is prohibited by the 1946 Convention."

But whether or not you accept Eckhard's reading of the General Convention, there is a much more explicit legal prohibition against this kind of activity. The Vienna Convention on Diplomatic Relations, rat- ified by both the United States and the United Kingdom, holds that "the official correspondence of the mission shall be inviolable." Arti- cle 30, section 1, holds that "the private residence of a diplomatic agent shall enjoy the same inviolability and protection as the premises of the mission." And section 2 states that a diplomat's papers and correspon- dence shall also be inviolable. These provisions are not merely sym- bolic and could present grounds for hauling the United States or the United Kingdom into the International Court of Justice (ICJ), if it was possible to prove that illicit listening had taken place. Part of the rea- son that these cases do not fill the docket at the ICJ is an evidentiary problem: in most circumstances, listening is a remote and passive act; it leaves no fingerprints.

Another reason, however, is that while it is clearly illegal, eavesdrop- ping on diplomats is so common and accepted a practice that many UN delegates regard making noise about its illegality as equivalent to mak- ing a citizen's arrest for jaywalking. The history of the UN has, since its very inception, involved the unmentionable practice of intercepting diplomatic communications. Throughout the planning of the UN, at an organizational conference in San Francisco in the spring of 1945, Ed- ward Stettinius, Harry Truman's secretary of state, was receiving inter- cepts from the U.S. Army's Signal Security Agency, the predecessor to the NSA, of the diplomatic cable traffic on forty-three of the forty-five nations in attendance. (It is not clear whether U.S. intelligence was able to intercept Russian communications, and, then as now, Great Britain was exempt.)

This history has led to a jaundiced view among diplomats that eavesdropping is an unpleasant inevitability. When *The Washington Post* reached a UN delegate to ask whether he believed his calls were being monitored, he replied, "Let's ask the guy who's listening to us." In fact, the paper ran two stories—one immediately following the orig- inal publication of the Koza memo and one following the dropping of Katharine's case—remarking on how, the hysterical reaction of the world press notwithstanding, this was *not* a newsworthy turn of events. Former secretary general Boutros Boutros-Ghali told the BBC, "It is a tradition that member states that have the technical capacity to bug will do so without hesitation." *The Observer* reported that GCHQ has a special unit specifically to monitor communications at the UN. Diplomats told members of the press that when they wanted to have a private conversation, they routinely left the offices and took a walk in

Central Park, conjuring a cartoonlike image of a park overrun by pensive ambassadors taking morning constitutionals, all trying to conduct a little business in peace. Queried about eavesdropping, Stefan Tafrov, Bulgaria's representative to the UN, told CBS News that there is actually a "prestige factor" in being listened to, as one's maneuverings must be of some consequence to attract such attention. He added, "It's almost an insult if they *don't* listen."

CHELTENHAM IS A FEW hours from London by train, a prosperous and precious Georgian city, and when I arrived on April 1 the town green was a riot of colorful spring flowers. I made my way to the Kandinsky Hotel and had coffee in the eclectically furnished lobby. Reading material was strewn across a table, and I thumbed through the regional paper, the *Gloucestershire Echo*. Amid local-interest pieces and ads for houses promising "Short Walk from GCHQ," I stumbled on an article claiming that GCHQ planned to open its new $600 million headquarters, an imposing ring of glass and steel known affectionately as the Doughnut, to the public. The article said the agency would begin welcoming tourists and was planning a "Spy World" theme park. Incredulous, I reread the opening lines, shook my head, then realized—I'd opened the April Fool's issue.

A minute later, Katharine walked in, dressed in a gray turtleneck sweater, her hair pulled back from her face, and looking, to my surprise, a great deal less composed than the last time I'd seen her. We walked to a little tea shop Katharine knew, where we ascended to the empty second floor and began to talk.

Katharine said she was immensely relieved at the dropping of the case though curious about the government's rationale for doing so. "Why did they go ahead and charge you?" I asked.

"I have no idea," she said. "If they hadn't brought charges in November, and they'd just said, Okay, you're a very bad girl, you know, you shouldn't have done this, but we're not going to charge you, we *are* however going to gag you so you're not going to talk to anyone about this, then none of this would have come out. It would have died. . . ." Her voice trailed off.

The case has clearly taken a toll on her. She was unable to get another job during the year that the charges were pending. She was also still scared of talking too freely, for fear of inviting another prosecution under the Official Secrets Act. I asked what set her off when she first read Koza's memo, and she said that the little caveat "minus US and GBR of course" really "got my goat. . . . It just struck me as being arrogant, in the sense that you know, there's this kind of chumminess between those of us who speak the Queen's language or whatever." But, I objected, that's standard protocol for UKUSA intelligence agencies. I was perplexed about her strong reaction to what must have been a run-of-the-mill provision, but I was also trying to draw her out and get her to confirm or allude to the UKUSA agreement. She wasn't biting. "It was just the tone," she said vaguely.

"The tone struck me as oddly informal," I said. "Was it unusual for you to receive an e-mail like this from someone working at another agency in another country?"

Katharine toyed with a coral bracelet around her wrist. "We all know that there is the existence of cooperation between the five," she said carefully. "So in order for certain things to work smoothly, there needs to be direct communications between them." She paused and looked at me apologetically, unable to say more, then, shrugging, added, "If there weren't, they'd be accused of incompetence."

A young woman brought a pot of Earl Grey for Katharine and an espresso for me. Katherine eyed her with the nervousness of a horse when a stranger approaches, a wary twitch signaling that the conversation was effectively over until this woman departed. We both stopped talking and smiled wanly at the woman.

After she disappeared downstairs, I mentioned an article in *The Guardian* that appeared when the Koza memo first came to light and claimed that the memo was "sent out via Echelon." The BBC, meanwhile, said that Koza was requesting to "tap into the network called Echelon." I said I had always understood Echelon to be a system for collecting communications and not, as *The Guardian* seemed to imply, some sort of distributed mailing list. I asked which characterization of the system seemed more accurate.

Katharine took the coral bracelet off and worried it, watching the pieces slide along the string. "I don't know how the system works," she said. "I'm not a technician, so I can't comment."

"But it's a name you've heard before," I pushed.

"Yes," Katharine said slowly, looking me in the eyes. "But I can't comment on that either."

I had a particular question about some of the fallout after Katharine's story broke. Everything I had read and heard indicated that by the time policymakers saw communications intercepts they had been incorporated into finished reports. But Clare Short said that she had actually read transcripts herself. "I really don't have *any* idea what she would have been seeing," Katharine said. "Generally, everything is turned into a report, at least from my experience. If it's true that there was actually interception of Kofi Annan . . . it just goes to show how little faith we have, that the British and the Americans want to be kind of omniscient in a way, have got to see everything and hear everything."

But how could Katharine be so shocked by this? If diplomats are all so quick to acknowledge that they are being listened to, how could an employee at precisely the kind of eavesdropping agency that conducts these operations be incredulous or indignant to learn that the United States and the United Kingdom were listening in on the middle six? The whistleblower is rarely free of a certain discomforting stridency or self-mythologizing narcissism, and through all the press coverage of Katharine's ordeal this was a telling lacuna. If Katharine was a Mandarin translator who presumably spent the prior two years translating Chinese diplomatic communications, how could she be so shocked by Koza's memo?

"It wasn't just the fact that they were listening, it was what they were going to do with the information," Katharine said. "It was because it was about the issue of war, the issue of human lives, the issue of the workings of the UN and manipulating it in such a way as to secure the result of war." She said that it is unrealistic to think that eavesdroppers would stow their political predispositions before they put on the headphones. As such, leaking the memo was less an idealistic or sanctimonious expression of shock than it was a hope that she might just have the power to avert the war. "My conviction was that if anything was going to shed light on what the Bush-Blair coalition was trying to do, that could be it."

She told me that the recruitment posters GCHQ uses are colorful mock newspapers that claim that GCHQ employees are the people who create the "headlines behind the headlines." But, she explained, there is an internal contradiction in luring people with the enticement that they will have an effect on policy and then wanting them to be completely politically neutral. "They want people to be compliant," she said, "pretty much unthinking." Still, she told me, in the run-up to the war, GCHQ supervisors were careful to assure everyone working at the agency that the country would not go to war without an additional authorizing resolution from the UN. Katharine wasn't around by the time this promise was broken.

Katharine felt that the reservations of the international community about a war in Iraq were not merely the fey equivocations of lesser powers or the appeasement of a violent dictator. They were utterly sensible and ultimately prescient doubts about an impending calamity—precisely the kind of down-home common sense that the Bush administration claimed to espouse. As she watched Washington and Whitehall endeavor to elbow the middle six into a yes vote for war, Katharine Gun realized that these two great powers were short-circuiting the only institution that might still be able to rein them in. "I believed that the memo had the potential to create a situation where people would stop and think before they acted," she told me. "And the more I thought about it, the more I believed I couldn't let that go."

FOOTPRINTS OF FREEDOM

A Constellation of Bases

WE LIVE IN a world awash in signals. In the wonderful opening scene of Krzysztof Kieslowski's film *Rouge* a French man picks up a telephone in his apartment in London and dials the number of his lover in Geneva. As the man dials, Kieslowski takes his camera along the phone cord, seemingly into the line itself, through a dense weave of tiny red wires, into a communications cable running underwater, then back up out of the water, under cities and through forests, through more wires and cables and switches, and eventually up to the woman's phone in Geneva. We follow the signal in the instant it takes between the last number he dials and the ring of the phone on the other end, and we gain an insight into the hurtle and flux of the communications system we so take for granted.

Signals course through wires and are beamed by satellite ground stations; signals surge from your cellphone to a microwave tower and from that tower to another to another to another to a satellite to another string of microwave towers and to the phone of a friend in another country, all in an instant. Your Internet activity is broken down into data packets that travel by fiber-optic cable, pulses of light coursing down a strand of glass the thickness of a follicle of hair. When you make a long-distance phone call to England over a satellite network, the signal travels through copper cables or between microwave towers until it reaches an uplink station and is bounced off a satellite, hovering in geostationary orbit twenty-two thousand miles above the earth, and down again to another earth station at Bude, on the cliffs of Cornwall. The air around us and the sky above us are a riot of signals. To intercept those signals is as easy as putting a cup out in the rain.

In order to get a sense of the world of signals as a material, physical thing, I arranged a meeting with a man named Alistair Harley. Alistair is a good-natured former MI5 surveillance man in his forties, with a boyish grin and very short blond hair. In the early part of his career, when he wasn't working on "Technical Surveillance Countermeasures"—securing important government phone calls and meetings from hostile interception—he was sitting on hilltops between microwave relay towers with sophisticated listening equipment, intercepting calls and messages and acting on the intelligence they produced. Now that he is out of that world, he works as a freelance computer- and communications-security expert. From what I could glean, this seems to involve hacking into the computer systems of various companies and organizations, then telephoning them shortly after they have identified the breach and offering his services in preventing that sort of thing from happening again. I met him in the cathedral town of Ely, just outside of Cambridge, England. We walked through the train-station parking lot until we reached his car: a small blue sedan bristling with antennae. A dozen wires of various sorts jutted out all over it. "Yep, that's mine," Alistair said as we approached. "The porcupine."

Over the next several hours, Alistair and I drove around the area near his house, listening. The dashboard of his car was a jumble of receivers and switches, black wires and knobs. He fiddled to get the right frequencies as we zipped along, listening to the messages flying around us. As we drove down empty roads, without a person in sight, the inside of the car sounded like a cocktail party in full swing: cellphone conversations, the bark of walkie-talkies and CB radios, the gibberish of encrypted calls.

This was in the summer of 2002, and on the other side of the planet the war on terror was under way. We stopped at Lakenheath, the largest American air-force base in England. Bombers and supply planes bound for Afghanistan maneuvered on an endless runway. Alistair fiddled, and soon we were listening to exchanges between ground crews and the control tower as the planes were readied for takeoff. "It works out well," Alistair told me, as he took a pair of binoculars out of the glove compartment. "I can sit at the end of the runway and look like an aircraft spotter." For the first few minutes, I didn't even register that the voices crackling through the receivers and into the car were not British but American.

It was a peculiar kind of voyeurism: the knowledge that the flight plans of American F-15s would qualify as extremely valuable intelligence for a broad assortment of enemies of the United States and that the signals were right there in the air, asking to be listened to. "If you listen to the ground crews at night, you can hear their mission briefing for the next morning," Alistair told me with an excited grin. He explained that as a general rule "if it uses radio waves then there is nothing that cannot be intercepted, monitored, stored. There's certainly not a lot around here voice- and data-wise that *I* can't intercept. And with GCHQ's equipment, it must be tenfold."

ALISTAIR'S OBSERVATION THAT a signal is easy to intercept once it leaves the wires is critical, because so many of the signals we send are converted to radio waves and sent through the air. The key to much of modern communications and to the interception of these communications lies in the prosaic field of geometry. In the October 1945 issue of *Wireless World,* the science-fiction writer and inventor Arthur C. Clarke published an article called "Extra-terrestrial Relays." Clarke argued that three satellites positioned over each ocean region (Atlantic, Pacific, Indian) in geosynchronous orbit could provide communication for the whole planet. *Geosynchronous* is just another term for *geostationary:* the satellite travels in the same direction and at the same speed as the earth's rotation on its axis, taking twenty-four hours to complete a full cycle. As long as the satellite is positioned over the equator in its assigned orbital location, it will appear to be stationary with respect to locations on the surface of the earth.

A single geostationary satellite can "view" approximately one third of the earth's surface. Thus, three satellites placed at the proper longitudes could cover almost all of the earth's surface. Satellite ground stations could then be used to bounce communications off the satellites and thus jump the oceans and connect the globe. While Clarke's vision also included such period visionary artifacts as humans living in and maintaining these satellites and being provided with supplies by regular space-shuttle visits, the simple geometric calculation he laid out underlies the manner in which we communicate, trade, and make war today.

On August 20, 1964, Intelsat was formed. *Intelsat* stands for the International Telecommunications Satellite Consortium, and it was devoted to seeing Clarke's speculation become a reality. Initially, Intelsat was an intergovernmental organization; it became a private company only in 2001. On April 6, 1965, just five years before the advent of the

Rhyolite program, Intelsat I was launched—the world's first commercial communications satellite. A few months later, on June 28, officials in the United States and Europe exchanged greetings in a transatlantic ceremony.

It was a formidable step, more than one hundred years after the first transatlantic telegraph cable was sent from Queen Victoria to President James Buchanan on August 16, 1858. New Yorkers had greeted the news of that message with a hundred-gun salute and fireworks on the roof of City Hall. What was not reported at the time was that the Queen's ninety-nine-word message had taken sixteen and a half hours to transmit. The first Intelsat message, by comparison, took seconds, and satellite communications proceeded to broaden, quicken, and democratize the great changes ushered in by the transatlantic cable.

The launch of a second satellite, Intelsat II, established service between the United States and Japan in 1967, and two years later the system was complete, with the launch of Intelsat III, which covered the Indian Ocean region. On July 20, 1969, Intelsat transmitted images of Neil Armstrong's first steps on the moon, live via satellite, to five hundred million people around the world. While fiber optics will eventually supplant satellites as the primary conveyor of international signals, today much of the phone, fax, telex, and e-mail communications relayed around the globe are still bounced off of these satellites. Communications data passes through a satellite using a signal path known as a transponder. The speed with which digital information travels is measured in bits per second, where each bit represents a zero or a one. One transponder on an Intelsat satellite can handle up to 155 million bits of information per second. That's fifteen thousand pages of text—say, fifty copies of this book—per *second*. And satellites typically have between twenty-four and seventy-two transponders, so the capacity to carry information is almost beyond comprehension.

Nevertheless, the democratization of the medium means that while Clarke's formula still holds, three satellites could not possibly accommodate the volume of traffic, the sheer billions of signals that bounce in and out of space every day. Thus, the earth is encircled by a fleet of satellites, a man-made ring of Saturn. By the time Intelsat 907 was launched in early 2003, Intelsat operated twenty-six satellites. The organization had also become a publicly traded company—a quarter of the stock of which, it seems worth mentioning, is owned by Lockheed Martin, one of the principal contractors to the NSA. For the Lockheed employees at Menwith Hill who are assigned to intercept civilian communications transmitted via Intelsat satellites, it must be rather convenient that Intelsat itself is partially controlled by the parent company.

The Intelsat satellites are accompanied by weather satellites, various regional communication satellites, a network of twenty-four Navstar Global Positioning System satellites, and the unacknowledged military and spy satellites of the United States and dozens of other countries. The espionage-satellite phenomenon that was ushered in by Rhyolite in 1970 has blossomed in the intervening years. Three advanced American KH-11 "Keyhole" satellites circle the earth in highly elliptical orbits, from two hundred miles at the perigee to 22,300 at the apogee, circling the planet in twelve hours and photographing targets on the ground. They can identify objects on the earth's surface as small as six inches across. All told, the United States alone has roughly one hundred spy satellites. During the cold war, space became a very crowded place.

The geographic area over which a satellite can transmit or receive is called its footprint. Imagine a cone, the tip of which starts at the satellite itself, and the base of which expands until it reaches the earth, covering miles and miles of ground. For commercial communications companies, the collection of the transmissions simply involves putting a ground station somewhere in the footprint. Similarly, intelligence agencies who want to collect all of the signals beamed down from a given satellite need only build their own base, with a couple of dishes oriented in the right direction, somewhere inside that footprint.

ONE WAY TO GET A sense of the raw capability of the Echelon network to suck up communications is simply to develop a tally of the number of these listening stations that are strewn around the globe. If, as Clarke suggested, it takes only a certain number of satellites to cover the planet, then it should take only a certain number of spy stations to intercept all of the satellite communications bounced around the world. While much of the Sigint apparatus of the UKUSA countries is swathed in secrecy, these bases, even those in the most secluded locations, are hiding in plain sight.

Initially, the UKUSA partners needed only three bases: Morwenstow, on the cliffs of Cornwall, England; Sugar Grove, in the mountains of West Virginia; and the Yakima Training Center, in Washington State. These sites are far-flung but have remarkable similarities with one another and, indeed, with other bases established by the UKUSA powers over the past thirty years. They are all in locations that are extremely remote. This allows for a "quiet" radio environment, which won't interfere with the sophisticated listening equipment; a diminished risk of interception by foreign intelligence agencies; and minimal intrusion by a nosy press or public. But remoteness alone is not the sole criterion for choosing these locations: each of the three original bases is located inside the footprint of a large commercial communications-satellite downlink.

The base at Morwenstow clings to the edge of high cliffs at Sharpnose Point, near the town of Bude. Morwenstow was the first of the bases in the system known today as Echelon. The base was established in 1971 by GCHQ but has been run in close collaboration with the NSA. Originally, there were two satellite dishes: one aimed at the Intelsat satellite over the Atlantic Ocean and another aimed at the Intelsat satellite over the Indian Ocean. In the 1980s, these dishes were augmented with a series of new ones, and by the early nineties the base had nine dishes: two inclined toward the two main Indian Ocean Intelsats, three toward the Atlantic Intelsats, three toward positions above Europe or the Middle East, and one dish covered by a radome. This is one reason to have radomes: without them, it is fairly easy for an observer to discern which satellite is being targeted. With them, it is anyone's guess.

Morwenstow is located, not accidentally, just sixty miles up the coast from British Telecom's Goonhilly Earth Station, on Lizard Peninsula. Goonhilly is the largest commercial satellite earth station in the world, with more than sixty dishes transmitting millions of phone calls, e-mails, and TV broadcasts at any given moment. It opened in 1962, and GCHQ was quick to recognize that all it had to do in order to collect the signals intended for Goonhilly was set up a few dishes nearby. In the 1970s, the Goonhilly dishes were inclined identically to the two at Morwenstow. Several high-capacity transatlantic cables terminate at Goonhilly, which means that while it may be difficult to tap into the fiber-optic cables themselves, any messages that get converted to microwave once they have made their trip across the Atlantic will be picked up with ease. As Alistair assured me, "If it has to leave the ground, with an antenna of some form, you're going to intercept it. No doubt about it."

The base at Morwenstow performs three broad categories of satellite interception. The first category involves simply tapping individual telephone numbers and monitoring all of the traffic. The second, a "wildcard" system, allows the listeners to intercept all calls with a particular dialing code, so it is possible to seal off a city or a switchboard and take every satellite channel linked to it. Finally, "baseband surveys" trawl through the satellite basebands of various nations to discover who is using which channels and what they are saying. In the 1980s, staff at Morwenstow raised issues about the legality of the baseband surveys, and suggested that picking up the telephone calls of British citizens, whether inadvertently or not, was illegal. By 1985, the agitation over this technique had grown so intense among the rank and file that GCHQ temporarily stopped the surveys. Some staff also worried about conducting wildcard monitoring without a warrant and suspected that the reason the monitoring of individual British phone lines was so secret was because it was illegal.

Of course, none of this is officially acknowledged. The Morwenstow base has traditionally been extremely secret and has managed to attract less attention than its bigger sibling, Menwith Hill. But during a recruitment drive in the spring of 2003, GCHQ tipped its hand when it began advertising in order to fill the position of Communication Technologist and other openings at the Cornwall base. A notice titled "Morwenstow—Technical Vacancies" appeared on job-recruitment websites, announcing, "We use some of the world's most sophisticated technology to intercept telecommunications and electronic signals from around the world." This was a much more candid description of GCHQ activities than the job announcement Katharine Gun had clipped. "We're interested in anything and everything that might impact adversely on British citizens and British interests," the announcement went on, "and provide information to support the government decision making in the field of national security, military operations and law enforcement."

The second of the three original bases in the satellite collection network, Yakima, was opened in the 1970s in a barren stretch of the army's 260,000-acre Yakima Firing Center. The aim was to get coverage of the Intelsat satellite hovering above the Pacific Ocean. The base is located one hundred miles south of the satellite earth station in Brewster, halfway between Seattle and Spokane, in north-central Washington. The cover name for the base was Yakima Research Station.

Though the base had only one large dish in the seventies and early eighties, by 1995 that one had been joined by four more. Three of the five faced west, and two faced east. It has been speculated that the two east-facing dishes may be targeted on the Atlantic Intelsats, intercepting communications relayed toward North and South America, but it is also possible that one or both of these dishes is meant not for interception but as a secure relay between Yakima and NSA headquarters at Fort Meade.

In a league of mysterious bases, Yakima is the most mysterious. Not only is it isolated like the others, but it is insulated by the massive, multi-purpose Yakima Training Center. The center is an army maneuver zone where soldiers work with heavy artillery in simulated operations and use old tanks and armored personnel carriers for target practice. As such, it serves as a formidable physical buffer for the listening base: a sort of no-man's-land. The center has a website, but it makes no mention of the NSA base. There are no photos of the base on the Internet or in any books or articles. While the area allows for some visitors to come onto the reserve to hike and hunt, these visits require applications. And it would take an intrepid explorer to wander through what is effectively a rifle range in order to get to the Sigint base. The frontier-style isolation of the base is probably what inspired the code name within the UKUSA agencies for intelligence produced at Yakima: cowboy.

The third base in the original triptych of Echelon stations was Sugar Grove, hidden in the forest of the South Fork Valley in the Appalachian mountains of West Virginia. The use of this site goes back to the 1950s and early sixties, when it was home to an ill-fated effort to create a radio telescope so powerful that it could listen to Soviet radio communications and radar signals reflected off the surface of the moon. This expensive disaster involved the construction of a satellite dish that was an astonishing six hundred feet in diameter. The project was eventually abandoned, but in the 1970s the existing two-story underground operations building was augmented by a series of new satellite dishes, and the windowless Raymond Eugene Linn Operations Center was built. (The building is named after a naval technician who lost his life in the Israeli attack on the USS *Liberty,* an NSA Sigint ship, on June 8, 1967.) The station began its new operations as a listening post around 1980. The area has unmatched radio quiet, because in 1956 the West Virginia state legislature passed an unusual zoning act establishing around it a hundred-square-mile National Radio Quiet Zone, which zoned out any electromagnetic interference.

Sugar Grove is located a mere sixty miles from Etam, West Virginia, where there are dishes that receive and relay commercial Intelsat traffic. In the 1980s, there were three large dishes at Etam, and these relayed more than half of the commercial international satellite traffic entering and leaving the United States. Today, Etam is AT&T's main downlink for transatlantic satellite telecommunications and remains one of the busiest ground stations in the world. By the late nineties, Sugar Grove had six dish antennae of varying sizes, all trained on European and Atlantic regional communications satellites. The site also had two massive Wullenweber antennae, which are known as Elephant Cages, because each is a series of antennae arranged in a giant ring large enough to fence in an elephant.

Sugar Grove is run by the Naval Security Group, which is a command devoted primarily to interception and code breaking and has traditionally worked extremely closely with Fort Meade. In 1999, a former NSA employee brought a lawsuit against several officials at Sugar Grove, arguing that in the course of his job he had been mistreated and had his privacy violated. The case went as far as the Fourth Circuit Court of Appeals, where the NSA prevailed, but not before the court had acknowledged in its published opinion that Sugar Grove is essentially an NSA operation and that at the base NSA employees have "access to information about sophisticated systems for collecting intelligence data as well as information actually collected." In 2000, the intelligence scholar Jeffrey Richelson of the National Security Archive at George Washington University obtained a copy of the Sugar Grove Naval Security Group detachment's Official History for 1990, which stated that an "Echelon training department" had been established that year. Richelson also located a document titled "Missions, Functions and Tasks of Naval Security Group Activity," dated September 3, 1991, which held that the training was complete and that the task of the Sugar Grove station in 1991 was "to maintain and operate an Echelon station."

WHILE MORWENSTOW, YAKIMA, AND Sugar Grove were adequate for much of the 1970s, by the end of the decade there was already an effort under way to supplement the original posts with new locations. Another new base was created by GCHQ in Hong Kong in 1977. Before it was handed back to China in 1997, Hong Kong was a center of espionage, a hive of spies: by some estimates, there were as many as five thousand intelligence agents from different countries in the territory. The new spy station was built by GCHQ and the RAF at Chung Hom Kok, perched above the sea on the south side of Hong Kong Island. Stanley Fort satellite base, as it became known, was code-named Project Kittiwake. It was used to monitor communications from Chinese satellites and also nuclear-weapons tests. Hong Kong was such a dense urban space that anonymity was in some respects just as easy as it was at more isolated bases: the satellite dishes at the Hong Kong base blended in with the scores of public and private dishes that dot the island. Before the base was dismantled in 1994, in anticipation of the changeover, it had one dish directed east at the Pacific Intelsats, another aimed at the Indian Ocean Intelsats, and a third responsible not for interception but for the base's own secure communications with the rest of the UKUSA powers.

Before the Stanley base closed, China argued that it was an integral part of the British defense system in Hong Kong and as such should be handed over to the People's Liberation Army. Under the terms of the Sino-British declaration on the handover, the PLA had sole responsibility for Hong Kong's external defense. The Chinese insisted during the negotiations that they should send a delegation to inspect the center. Britain balked at that, and the Foreign Office and GCHQ decided to shut down the site early. Various replacement options were considered: the Philippines, Singapore, Brunei. Ultimately, the operations were shifted to Australia, and three dish antennae were packed up and shipped to a new DSD station at Geraldton, Western Australia, which had become operational in 1993. The British then proceeded to raze the eleven-hectare site: they demolished the buildings, wiping the grounds clear of any trace of espionage technology. When a reporter from the *South China Morning Post* visited the site in the fall of 1997, he found only a vestigial guard post, manned by a vagrant sheltering from the rain.

WHILE THESE ARE THE major bases in the UKUSA network, there are dozens of other minor ones. When one base closes, another is developed, or an existing base is augmented. While it was not one of the three initial Echelon bases, Menwith Hill would come, in the 1980s and 1990s, to anchor the system. The critical point is position. Thus, during the cold war, Bad Aibling, the NSA base at the foot of Germany's Bavarian Alps, was of tremendous importance for the interception of communications from the Soviet bloc. But after the fall of the Berlin Wall and growing political pressure from the German government, Bad

Aibling was scheduled to be shut down in 2002. The base had fifteen hundred American employees, about 140 Germans, and a dozen radomes. The plan was that materials and staff would be relocated to Menwith Hill. After September 11, 2001, that plan was postponed, however, and a new date was eventually established for the United States to turn the base over to German intelligence: September 30, 2004. While this shift might be cosmetically reassuring to Germans opposed to the base, the Munich daily *Süddeutsche Zeitung* quietly reported that once the base has been formally abandoned, twenty or so American personnel will stay behind, for "technical upkeep of the station."

You could intuit a great deal about the rise and fall of different geopolitical players and the balance of power in the world just by looking at where the UKUSA agencies erect their antennae in any given epoch. As Bad Aibling's target region of central and eastern Europe diminished in strategic importance, the Middle East became more critical. The GCHQ listening station at the Dhekelia Sovereign Base Area in Nicosia, Cyprus, with its valuable feed on communications from the Middle East and the Caucasus, shows no signs of shutting down.

The principle that strategic position is all-important is nothing new. The Romans built a complex of roads that expanded the boundaries of their territory while simultaneously providing for rapid military deployments. The British became the greatest naval power in the world in the eighteenth and nineteenth centuries on the hunch that even a tiny island, if it has a good strategic position, can be a greater asset than a giant mass of land. They recognized that if they colonized geographically and economically significant little islands—even a series of atolls and a deep harbor—they would control communication, trade, commerce, the planet itself. The locating of listening stations has followed this same intuition, and they have been so important over the years that they have led the UKUSA countries into a strange and secret form of Sigint colonialism—zealously expanding the empire by taking over obscure but desirable patches of real estate.

ON JULY 17, 1996, an Australian aviator named Jon Johanson was in the midst of his second solo flight around the world when he endeavored to refuel at a tiny island in the South Atlantic. The year before, Johanson had become the first person ever to circumnavigate the globe in a homemade aircraft. It was day twenty-four of his second trip, and he was making his way across an endless expanse of ocean when the oil pressure in his RV-4 plane began to fluctuate, the oil temperature began to rise, and he was forced to make an emergency landing. Fortunately for Johanson, that stretch of ocean is not as empty as it at first appears. In his path lay Ascension Island, a speck of volcanic rock, thirty-four miles square, just south of the equator, midway between Angola and Brazil. The island is so small that it was initially classified by the British Navy not as an island at all but, for a century or so, as a ship, a "stone frigate," in the words of the Lords of the Admiralty: HMS *Ascension*. Even today, it does not appear on many world maps.

Johanson tried to radio the authorities at Ascension to request permission to land. There was no reply. He tried again and then again. Nothing. This made Johanson nervous, but he kept on track in the direction of the island—for after all, he had no alternative. Finally, an American voice crackled through the radio, wanting to know who he was, asking him to maintain a holding pattern, and directing him not to land on the island. Johanson panicked and declared an emergency. Finally, he was allowed to land.

Johanson managed a smooth landing, but when he touched down he was approached by angry British and American officials who confiscated his passport, told him civilian aircraft were not allowed to land on the island, and briefly discussed whether or not they should lock him up. To his relief, they elected not to do so, but before departing the next day he was scolded by the acting administrator of the island, told he should not have landed. "The long and the short of it was simply that no civilians are allowed to land on Ascension," Johanson wrote in his diary of the flight. "None have done so for a very long time, if at all, and I was to tell everyone that should they ever be in the same situation as I was that they would not be treated as well."

Position was crucial to the British Navy when it settled Ascension almost two hundred years ago, recognizing that it was a perfect pit stop on the west-east and north-south naval routes. In 1815, the British established a garrison of eleven marines to guard against any attempt by the French to free Napoleon, who was imprisoned on the "nearby" island of Saint Helena—seven hundred miles away. Napoleon died in 1821, but the British garrison was not abandoned until 1922, when the Crown took over and made the island a dependency of Saint Helena.

The message in a bottle washed up on the shores of a deserted island is a cliché that reinforces the idea that places like this are beyond the reach of the civilized world—beyond communication. And yet, as

Simon Winchester points out in *The Sun Never Sets,* his study of the last outposts of the British empire, Ascension had always had associations with communication. Dating back to its discovery, on Ascension Day, 1501, "sailors traveling past in one direction started a custom of leaving letters there, for collection and onward transmission by ships sailing in the other. There is still a letter-box where passing vessels may drop notes; when someone looked in it recently there was a note dating from 1913." Today, the orientation of the little island is still advantageous when it comes to communications. From the top of Green Mountain to the ash-covered slopes of the dormant volcano to the beaches, Ascension is littered with aerials.

In 1922, Ascension was actually taken over by British Cable and Wireless, which ran it for the next forty-two years. It became a relay station for the submarine cables that snake their way from Cape Town to Saint Helena, the Cape Verde Islands, and on to England. More cables ran along the ocean bed from Ascension to Sierra Leone, to Saint Vincent, to Rio, and to Buenos Aires. Unassuming little Ascension became a great node. During the cold war, the U.S. military established a tracking station on the island for their Eastern Test Range, a missile range that extends from Florida into the South Atlantic. Dinner guests at the administrator's residence, high on Green Mountain, would occasionally see rockets splinter and fall over an inky horizon, fireworks detonating in the tropical night. The BBC established a relay station on the island. And an outfit called the Composite Signals Organization, otherwise known as the overseas arm of GCHQ, set up an interception station for radio signals.

As if to illustrate the oddly unnatural level of development on it, Ascension has suffered a disastrous string of ecological imbalances over the years. In 1815, the British garrison introduced cats to the island, in order to control a burgeoning population of rats, which had arrived with the first British ships. The cats proceeded to eat the rats but, not content at that, went after the many seabirds native to the region, whole colonies of which disappeared. Boobies and other distinctive native birds were effectively banished from the island, forced to avoid the hungry cats by perching on rocky outcrops off the shore. In 2001, following decades of campaigning, the British announced that they would invest £500,000 to restore harmony to the island ecosystem. This entailed killing more than five hundred feral cats by shooting, trapping, and poisoning. Day-old chicks were flown in from South Africa as bait, to lure the whiskered predators to their death. Domestic cats were equipped with reflective collars so as to avoid death at the hands of sharpshooters.

Like Gibraltar or the Panama Canal Zone, Ascension is one of those places whose value to others reveals itself only when you look at it on a map, and, like those places, it has suffered in some respects for the strength of its position. Ascension was a vital staging post for the United Kingdom in the Falklands War and became, for one day, the world's busiest airport. As the cold war waned, the island's strategic importance diminished, and in 1997 the Composite Signals Organization started sending people home. Nevertheless, in 2002 this well-positioned desert island was still home to nearly nine hundred people.

ASCENSION WAS A DESERT island when the British first arrived in that it was literally deserted: it had no native population. This has not always been the case in those distinctive areas where American and British forces have erected their listening stations. In pursuing new stations, British and American powers have been willing to run roughshod over various obstacles and have certainly not let anything like a human population stand in their way.

During the 1960s, just as Great Britain was relinquishing many of its former colonies, it was also discreetly in the process of acquiring a new one. Fifteen hundred kilometers southwest of Sri Lanka, a sprinkling of tiny islands floats on the Indian Ocean. This scattering of atolls and lagoons is known as the Chagos Archipelago. Much of the archipelago is uninhabited and would seem of limited use to Great Britain, particularly as the country had shed its more impressive colonial acquisitions. But at the southern tip of this cluster lies one island in particular that holds special strategic promise. The island was first discovered four centuries ago by the Portuguese fisherman who gave it its name: Diego Garcia.

The larger islands relatively nearby, Mauritius and the Seychelles, had been British colonies for a century and a half when in 1965 the people of Mauritius began to make tentative noises about independence. The Labour government in London proved oddly accommodating. At the earliest signs of unrest, Colonial Secretary Anthony Greenwood promptly flew to Mauritius with news that the islanders could indeed have their independence, and in fact Britain would give them £3 million as a parting gift. In exchange for this generosity, Greenwood asked only that Mauritius satisfy one condition: give up its claim to the Chagos

Archipelago and in particular to Diego Garcia, some twelve hundred miles away. Greenwood gave no reason for this odd request, but it did not take the authorities in Mauritius long to accept the deal; it was soon announced that the archipelago would form part of a new British colony: the British Indian Ocean Territory (BIOT). As the rest of the world jettisoned colonies and the trappings of colonial rule, Britain determined that BIOT would be administered by a commissioner, who would be based in Victoria, in the Seychelles. The colony would use the currencies of the Seychelles and Mauritius and would be run according to British colonial law.

The following winter, Britain and the United States signed an Exchange of Notes "concerning the availability for Defense Purposes" of the islands in the Chagos Archipelago. The notes were a complicated affair but essentially held that the United States would lease the islands for fifty years, with an optional further twenty, for free and build a defense facility there. Without any debate in British Parliament or any kind of publicity at all, the effective ownership of this faraway site was transferred. And in 1972, an agreement was signed that would allow the United States to build a "limited communications facility" at Diego Garcia. Two years after that, another deal was struck to expand the facility.

The problem was, Diego Garcia was not uninhabited. A native population had flourished on Diego Garcia and half a dozen other islands in the archipelago for two centuries. There were towns, churches, schools, prisons, farms, factories, warehouses, and a light railway. Two thousand islanders were living in the Chagos chain in the late sixties and early seventies—more than there were in the Falkland Islands at the same time. The people of Diego Garcia worked for a French-run coconut-oil company, Chagos Agalega. They were subjects of the British Crown.

But the British government physically removed every last one, "resettling" them to Mauritius and the Seychelles. Most ended up in a slum close to the Port Louis docks in Mauritius. They called themselves the Ilois. In a memo dated November 15, 1965, a British official acknowledged that "there is a civilian population, even though it is small. In practice, however, I would advise a policy of 'quiet disregard.' In other words, let's forget about this one until the United Nations challenges us on it." This was probably the most expedient policy, in light of the fact that the Pentagon had been told by the British government that only a "small migratory population" existed on the islands and that to all intents and purposes the archipelago was deserted. The U.S. Navy had declared that the area should be made "sterile"—meaning that there should be no civilian inhabitants of any sort—and that even the little islands one hundred miles north of Diego Garcia should be "swept clean."

Late in 1965, a group of islanders from Diego Garcia arrived in Mauritius on a routine trip they made several times a year for supplies. On arrival, however, they were told that they could not return home. No ship would take them, and they would have to stay in Port Louis and fend for themselves. It took eight years from that first gesture to systematically remove all the islanders. To hasten the process, the British government bought out Chagos Agalega for £1 million, then proceeded to shut it down. So now there were no jobs and no more ships coming with supplies. The man whom the British government assigned to oversee this gradual bleeding dry of the native population, a Franco-Mauritian named Paul Moulinie, later said, "We just said—sorry fellows, but on such-and-such a day we are closing up. They didn't object. But they were very unhappy about it. And I can understand this: I'm talking about five generations of islanders who were born on Chagos and lived there. It was their home." In 1966, in an almost comically sinister quip, a British undersecretary assured his superiors that when the process was complete, "There will be no indigenous population except sea gulls."

Today, those recalcitrant seagulls share Diego Garcia with more than four thousand American sailors and contractors, who refer to the island as "DG" or "The Rock." More appropriate, perhaps, is a name that derives from the island's peculiar shape, a curving filament fringed by a string of rocky dots: "The Footprint of Freedom." It's an evocative image: the little foot-shaped bastion in a great expanse of sea, the footprint in the sand that informs Robinson Crusoe that even here, on a tiny island unmoored from the rest of the world, he is not alone. But Diego Garcia's actual significance may have a lot to do with another kind of footprint: a satellite footprint. The first monitoring station was erected on the island in 1972. It was a ground-control base for the U.S.-Australian-British Classic Wizard Ocean Surveillance Satellite System. Also set up in 1974 was a GCHQ/NSA Sigint station. The island is ideally positioned to monitor naval traffic in the Indian Ocean. Diego Garcia developed a new range of responsibilities when turmoil in the Horn of Africa forced the NSA to close its listening facility at Kagnew station in Asmara, Eritrea, in the late 1970s.

All the while, the people of Diego Garcia and the rest of the Chagos Archipelago languished in the slums of Mauritius. Over the last thirty years, there have been consistent efforts by Mauritius to retake the island—and for a brief time, the prospects looked promising. In a path-breaking legal triumph in a London high court in November 2000, the islanders won the right to return to Diego Garcia. Fifty-five hundred of them, many living as second-class citizens in Mauritius, planned to do so. The trip was scheduled for November 30, 2001. It would be a re-connaissance visit primarily and an opportunity to pay respects for the first time in three decades at the graves of their relatives, which are inscribed in English and Creole and fill a cemetery on the island. Days after September 11, 2001, however, the websites of the navy and air-force units stationed on Diego Garcia, which had offered information about the base, were suddenly shut down. The reason emerged over the course of September: Diego Garcia would be instrumental in the war in Afghanistan, both in a Sigint capacity and as an important staging post for the air force. By October, the British Foreign Office had canceled the return trip indefinitely.

WHAT IS INSIDE THESE bases? To find out, I had to go to Transylvania County, in the mountains of North Carolina. About an hour outside of Asheville, I was negotiating perilous turns on a mountain road in the Pisgah National Forest, a milky mist dissolving around me. I passed a hand-painted sign that said "Jesus Loves You" and, another mile or two into the woods, one that said "Macedonia Church Road." I turned at this sign and after another mile or so turned again, through an old security gate for what used to be the NSA's Rosman Base. The gate was open and looked to have been that way for a while; a surveillance camera nodded, inoperative, overhead. I drove on through dense forest until I reached another gate, this one lined in barbed wire, and a guard shack. Feeling slightly felonious, I slowed down and glanced into the empty little room, its twin barrier wings—one to stop incoming traffic, one to stop outgoing—drawn up permissively by its sides. Then I drove right through. The first great dish was visible from the guard shack—eighty-five feet across, backed by an elaborate cross-hatching of support bars, pointed at a forty-five-degree angle into the chalk-white sky. I had looked at many satellite dishes used by Sigint bases but had never seen one this close. The parking lot was empty. I sat and gazed.

On those rare occasions when UKUSA countries abandon a base, they tend to raze it, as they did with the Stanley base in Hong Kong. They did not want the Chinese to be able to determine anything from what they left behind: what kind of collection techniques they were using, how they protected themselves against interception. The base at Rosman is that most unusual exception: a Sigint ghost town.

Until 1995, Rosman Base was a two-hundred-acre listening station. The deserted lot I parked in still has spaces for the 250 people who used to work here. Nestled in a typically unobtrusive locale for the NSA, the site hummed happily away with a dozen dishes. Plans were under way to build new dishes, and the staff had received repeated commendations for their effective completion of various missions. But suddenly it was announced that the base would be abandoned. Throughout 1995, parts and equipment from the base were disassembled and shipped to Sugar Grove, to Fort Meade, and to various storage facilities. Eventually, the NSA left, and the Forest Service took over the land. Then the story got interesting.

The Forest Service was unable to find a new occupant for the Rosman site and was considering turning the whole area back into wilderness when a group of local astronomers came calling. The astronomers, from various southern universities, had their eyes on the pair of eighty-five-foot dishes, which were some of the largest satellite dishes in the country and were too large to be moved. While the dishes had been used by the NSA to collect communications signals, they could be repositioned to capture deep-space radio signals and would allow the astronomers to study the life and death of stars. Because of a legal technicality, the Forest Service could not sell the land but could trade it. So the scientists bought a parcel of land in western North Carolina that they thought would be attractive to the Forest Service, a trade was made, and the Pisgah Astronomical Research Institute was born.

In January 2000, a team of civilian astronomers ambled onto the abandoned Sigint base, whose only tenants now were wild turkeys and the occasional deer, and set up shop. The astronomers had been expecting a fairly basic accommodation, with little apart from the major dishes left. But what they found surprised them. As they set about installing their computers they found hundreds of miles of top-of-the-line cable running under every floor. They found a self-contained water and sewer-treatment plant that could handle tens of thousands of gallons of water at a time, and a generator that could produce 235 kilowatts of energy: enough to light a small city.

There were two main buildings on the site, and the astronomers discovered a 1,200-foot tunnel system that connected the two. The floors in the buildings were covered by industrial brown carpet. The new tenants decided to replace it but found that the carpet was glued to the floor to prevent the buildings from conducting any static electricity. There were very few windows, and they were bulletproof. The security system was incredible, with an alarm that sounded in the main building if the perimeter of the site was breached, and a surveillance system that allowed the astronomers to watch on monitors as cars approached from miles away.

I had arranged for a tour of the site with Mike Castelaz, the director of astronomical studies. Mike greeted me in the main building. He is an affable scientist with a flat Wisconsin accent and a rust-colored mustache. "This used to be the main computer room," he said, leading me into a large room in which a grad student with a mullet sat at one of a dozen or so computers. "You can see the floor is raised," Mike said, stamping his foot. "Underneath it's a jumble of wires they left behind, and they left the whole place wired with fiber optics coming in and out, running through the whole site. We've got fiber optics comparable to any university." Mike seemed slightly bashful as he showed me around, like a pauper cousin house-sitting the mansion. The facility had gone from employing hundreds of people to housing PARI, which has a full-time staff of twelve, of which only four appeared to be on-site that day.

"This room and the next one and the one after that used to be one great big room," Mike said, gesturing past the computer room. We walked into the "library," which looked to be a work in progress, and into another room currently serving as a sort of storage closet. "You can see," he said as we walked, "we pass out of 2004 and into the sixties."

The site did in fact date back to the 1960s. The big dishes at what had been NASA's Rosman Satellite Tracking Station were originally used to communicate with spacecraft in the Apollo program and with the Skylab space station in the 1970s. But in 1981, the NSA took over. School groups that had regularly visited the NASA base were no longer invited to the site. Local hikers and hunters were turned away by armed guards. In 1986, Robert Windrem, a producer for NBC News, went to Rosman to do a segment on the base. He was denied access, of course, but he drove around the perimeter and did an overflight of the site in a helicopter. He counted fourteen dishes. The site was almost due north of the old Soviet headquarters in Lourdes, Cuba, southwest of Havana, and Windrem speculated that Rosman was being used in part to capture signals sent between Lourdes and the Soviet downlink at Vatutinki outside Moscow. As Windrem was preparing his segment for a series called "The Eavesdropping Wars," William Odom, then director of the NSA, called the network and threatened legal action if they aired it. NBC did air the segment, however; it was the only glimpse the public would have of Rosman Base until the astronomers of PARI moved in.

"Do you want to see the tunnel?" Mike asked. We trotted down a staircase to the basement level and walked down a series of corridors. Most of the rooms appeared to be empty. "This is kind of cool," Mike said. He showed me a door that had a double padlock and a combination lock on it. "So I assume that means you had someone who had one key, a second person who had the other, and a third person who knew the combination," he said. "Pretty secure."

"What's in there now?" I asked.

"Uh, we brought some weights down here," Mike said. "We use it as a weight room."

The tunnel was built during the NASA days and connects the two ends of the base. Along one wall, shelves hold stacks of cords and cables. The PARI astronomers found chalk etchings of animals and warriors in the tunnel—ironic cave art the eavesdroppers left behind. The tunnel ended in a small control room. "Have you seen Smiley?" Mike asked. He brought me over to a little black-and-white television monitor. The monitor showed a smaller satellite dish, about fifteen feet across, facing away from the camera, on the roof of one of the buildings. "We still have the old controls on this," he said, and as he fiddled with a dial the dish on the television screen began rotating slowly to face us. "The story is that this facility used to be imaged from space by other nations," Mike said. "And the people working here knew when the imaging satellites were going to be overhead." The dish continued to pivot toward us, and I noticed that the eggshell-white center bore some sort of pattern. "So when the NSA was here they painted it, and when they knew a satellite would be overhead, they'd point it right at the satellite and give it a smile." The dish was now facing us, revealing a big painted smiley face.

Mike chuckled. "Now it's set up for kids to use," he said.

I asked how they rotate the eighty-five-foot dishes. "Well, those ones, when we took them over, we had to slow them right down," Mike said. "They were built to rotate more than five degrees per second. So that's sixty seconds, a hundred and eighty degrees: in a minute, it could go right across the sky." I shook my head in amazement: the machine weighs 250 tons.

"We want to look at stars, which don't move anywhere near as quickly," Mike said.

"What *would* move that quickly, that you would want to be able to swing the dish around like that?" I asked.

"Satellites," said Mike.

THE MYSTERY IS WHY the NSA left so much behind. The closure seems to have taken the agency by surprise: it had recently laid the foundations for a new dish. It was as though they left in a hurry. "You had Clinton telling people the cold war was over, and for whatever reason, this place went on the cut list," Charles Osborne told me. A pudgy, mellow southerner, Osborne is the technical director for PARI. "What other bases do you think they would shift operations to?" he asked.

"Sugar Grove?" I guessed, figuring the base in West Virginia would be closest.

"That's exactly the base I was thinking of," Osborne said, nodding. "That senator, Byrd," he went on, referring to Robert Byrd, the Democrat from West Virginia, "he had sway to push choices to his state."

"But why would they leave all this behind?" I asked. "The facilities. The dishes."

"Newer technology they would have wanted to destroy," Osborne said. "Anything you can buy on the surplus market and reverse engineer could destroy the mission. Anything that was left was probably obsolete, and anything you can dig up here was already superseded by something else."

There was one feature left at Rosman that I was very curious to see: a radome. Up a hill and around a bend from one of the two big dishes, a little clearing revealed a giant radome, nestled all by itself in the woods. It was raining, and as Mike and I approached I noticed that the exterior of the radome was stained, streaked gray and black in places. "I need to get some of the students to take care of that," Mike said apologetically.

This dome was not geodesic but made up of a mosaic of different-sized triangles. There were two entrances: one little door about four feet high and another next to it of normal size. "We put the big door in," Mike said. "It was just a little strange when we had fund-raisers here and we'd bring people down in their fancy clothes, going through the little door. It's not exactly . . . dignified." The white material on the outside of the radomes was Gore-Tex, Mike told me. It was stretched tight over an aluminum skeleton, like the skin of a drum. I rapped my knuckles on it, and it vibrated, emitting a gentle hum.

Mike let me pick the door I'd enter. Feeling a little like Alice in Wonderland, I clambered through the little one. The interior was dank, but the Gore-Tex panels were translucent and admitted a wan light. A giant dish, forty feet across, dominated the space, seeming almost too big to be contained. "We aren't using it right now," Mike said. "But we'll rotate it every now and again just to keep it moving." I fingered the aluminum triangles and scratched my fingertips against the Gore-Tex. It felt like sailcloth. Equipment was strewn around the place. Rain thrummed on the roof and leaked through in places, puddling on the concrete floor. As I jotted notes, a few drops fell on my notebook.

It was an eerie experience, getting rained on in the leaky radome, at the foot of this colossal signal-collecting disc. What must have once been so sophisticated now lay dormant and beleaguered. I had come too late.

"If you start looking for information about Echelon or any of those things, whatever you find out, it's obsolete," Charles Osborne had told me. "Anything that you can Google search on the Internet is already ten years out of date."

IT'S IMPORTANT TO REMEMBER that the UKUSA bases around the world are not occupied merely with interception of communications bounced via satellites. The code name Echelon originally applied only to the satellite-interception programs, but satellite is just one element of the broader portfolio of communications the UKUSA countries collect. There are also radio listening posts, spy satellites, like those controlled by Pine Gap, and various means of tapping into land-based networks that send e-mail and other types of signals. Our communications travel through an eclectic series of lines and waves and channels, so any interception network worth its salt must embrace a similar eclecticism.

Microwave radio signals are notoriously easy to intercept. The principle is the same as with satellites: to intercept the signal, you need simply put yourself somewhere in its path. All it took for Alistair, the eavesdropper who drove me around in "the porcupine," in his MI5 days was to find the right hill, take his laptop and the appropriate receivers, and go to work. Globally, there are several dozen radio-interception stations run by the UKUSA countries. Many of these stations date back to the early years of the cold war, before satellite communications became widespread. In that period, these were the primary ground stations for intercepting Soviet communications. The most advanced high-frequency monitoring system used during the cold war was the Elephant Cage, like the two at Sugar Grove. These circular configurations of antennae are immensely effective for collection because they can simultaneously intercept and determine the bearing of signals from as many directions and on as many frequencies as necessary. In 1964, Elephant Cages were installed at UKUSA-run bases in San Vito dei Normanni, Italy; Chicksands, England; and Karamursel, Turkey.

Not all ground stations are as massive as the Elephant Cages. There is a great diversity of radio-interception stations. Some have staffs of hundreds, others are very small, and many are simply lonely aerials, automated to function without a staff, collecting signals and relaying them elsewhere for processing. The NSA has radio-collection sites of various sizes in Hawaii, Alaska, California, Japan, Guam, and the Philippines.

While all of this interception by remote antennae may seem a little sterile, microwave interception is actually one of the remaining areas in signals collection where old-fashioned cloak-and-dagger spying comes into play. It is a fortunate coincidence for Sigint agencies that most networks of microwave relay towers tend to converge in major cities. This makes sense from a demographic point of view: there will be a higher density of calls in and out of a major city than to or from other points in a country, so it is logical and manageable to designate the city as a hub from which microwave channels can radiate. For the UKUSA agencies, this arrangement is ideal, because in major cities there are embassies. And in embassies, there are spies.

Mike Frost had a twenty-year career in Canada's Communications Security Establishment, during which time he did a wide variety of work in conjunction with the NSA. In the nineties, Frost retired to Florida, cowrote a memoir of his time at the CSE, called *Spyworld*, and became a regular on the speech circuit, touting the book and warning audiences about the Orwellian dangers of Sigint agencies. The book and Frost himself are a bit too breathless to seem entirely credible. Again, the Sigint Postulate comes into play: the more Frost talks, the less you believe him. Numerous people I spoke with took issue with

Frost's stories, suggesting that he oversimplified his accounts of certain technologies in order to appeal to a broader audience. My skepticism peaked when I wrote to Frost, asking if I could interview him about his experiences, and he replied that he would be happy to talk with me, but "I am now a professional speaker and consultant so I would have to charge you accordingly."

Nevertheless, there is one claim in Frost's book that has been echoed or confirmed by other spies, and that lends an interesting dimension to our understanding of UKUSA interception of microwave communications. In 1971, Frost was assigned to a project called "embassy collection." This involved making visits to Canadian embassies in various foreign countries and, under cover of diplomatic immunity, smuggling in large amounts of radio-interception equipment. Frost makes clear that while the actual smuggling was done by Canadian agents, all the eavesdropping hardware was supplied by the NSA. The Canadian government has not denied Frost's claims. The suggestion that embassy collection is a UKUSA practice is also supported by evidence that Australia's DSD is engaged in the same activity. Leaks in the 1980s described the installation of "extraordinarily sophisticated intercept equipment, known as Reprieve" in Australia's High Commission in Port Moresby, Papua New Guinea, as well as in Australian embassies in Indonesia and Thailand.

For more daring operations, the NSA tends to rely on the Special Collection Service (SCS), a highly secret group of NSA and CIA operatives who install eavesdropping devices in hard-to-penetrate places. By dropping a tiny microphone between the keys of a computer keyboard, an SCS spy can record the sound of an adversary typing and, using the sound signatures of each individual key, reconstruct a typed message. In some cases, the SCS does not need to go to these lengths: operatives can bribe or coopt a systems administrator or code clerk.

WHAT IS MISSED BY earth stations and embassy collection can always be picked up by other means. Microwave spillage, that surfeit of radio wave that travels past a relay tower and into space, is easily intercepted by spy satellites. Dating back as far as the Rhyolite Bird 1, the United States has had satellites performing this kind of interception. While Rhyolite was devoted to missile telemetry as well as communications interception, the NSA also developed satellites exclusively for listening. Initially controlled by the base at Bad Aibling, this program was known as Canyon. Canyon was so successful that it was followed in the late seventies by a new class of satellite, controlled by Menwith Hill and code-named Chalet.

Code names in the intelligence world are a curious phenomenon. They are considered of the highest secrecy, and yet they are just words: *Echelon,* after all, is nothing more than a secret code name for a specific computer program used to sort through intercepted satellite communications. Moreover, *Echelon* should be *ECHELON.* In an custom that seems to undermine the larger goal of inconspicuousness, intelligence agencies insist on capitalizing the code names of various secret programs. Investigative journalists on the intelligence beat tend to get very excited about discovering new code names and are often a little self-congratulatory in saying, "Here, for the first time ever, I have published the code name of this top-secret program," despite the fact that the code name itself has no intrinsic significance. In fact, when the code names are revealed—and the size and nature of the military and intelligence industries are such that most code names eventually are—the intelligence agencies respond by simply changing the name. So CHALET was operated and downlinked via RUNWAY, and its intelligence was processed through SILKWORTH ground-processing systems. Except that as soon as the name CHALET appeared in the press, CHALET was changed to VORTEX, and then, in 1987, when VORTEX became public, to MERCURY. It's all a bit absurd but not without its own poetry. When the name RHYOLITE was discovered by the Soviets and published in the press, the program was renamed ARGUS—after the monster from Greek mythology, a giant with a thousand eyes.

Today, the United States has around one hundred spy satellites in space, though only ten or eleven of them are specifically devoted to Sigint. Some of these satellites are geostationary, like the Intelsat satellites; others crisscross the planet, darting from one place to another to intercept signals. In the last four decades, the United States has spent $200 billion on spy satellites, and the NRO, which works closely with the NSA and the CIA, now has an annual budget of $7 billion. The NRO has come under a great deal of criticism in recent years for cost overruns, antiquated systems, and delays in sending new models into space. In 1998, the office sought to combine the various classes of Sigint satellites into what it called an Integrated Overhead Sigint Architecture in order to "improve Sigint performance and avoid costs by consolidating systems, utilizing . . . new satellite and data processing technologies." There is a new eavesdropping satellite in the works, called Intruder, that would consolidate many of the functions tradition-ally performed by different types of Sigint satellites, but it has report-edly encountered technical problems and cost overruns. In its final report, the bipartisan 9/11 Commission suggests that part of the reason for broad cuts in personnel across the intelligence community in the 1990s was in fact the great success of satellite-imaging technology dur-ing the Gulf War. Subsequent demands for the next generation of satel-lite systems—and the enormous cost of the development of those systems—meant the downsizing of analysts and other human-intelli-gence assets.

THE REAL CHALLENGE FOR the UKUSA agencies when it comes to commu-nications interception at the outset of the twenty-first century is not satellites, but rather the reality that the signal that Marconi set free with the telegraph is migrating back to the wires, with the rapid develop-ment of high-capacity fiber-optic cables. The limited amount of band-width on satellite systems and the great cost of the satellites themselves means that increasingly communications are being routed through fi-ber optics. It has always been more difficult to tap wires and cables, particularly those that run across the ocean floor, but it was never im-possible. During the cold war, American submarines fought a valiant and unheralded battle with the Russians in the depths of the ocean, lo-cating and tapping communications cables. But fiber optics are another matter altogether. Because the signals in fiber optics are pulses of light, not electricity, the cables do not emit electromagnetic fields of the sort that allowed the United States to tap the Russian cables undetected. In order to access an optical signal, the tapper must actually breach the cable. Whether on land or at the bottom of the ocean, the dozen strands of glass that conduct optical signals are encased inside a laser-welded, hermetically sealed stainless-steel tube, which is itself wrapped in several centimeters of reinforcing steel wire and cables.

Because of this greater security and because of the greater volume of data that can be transported over fiber optics (one fiber can carry 128 times as much digital traffic as a satellite transponder), many nations have adopted the new technology over the last decade. In the early 1990s, as more and more nations began making the switch, the NSA downsized or shut down twenty of its forty-two radio-listening posts around the world. (Though in some cases, they left equipment behind to be monitored remotely.) In 1990, Saddam Hussein realized that the

United States would be able to intercept radio and wireless communications, so he hired French and Chinese companies to install a fiber-optic backbone in Baghdad. And by the end of the decade, many speculated that fiber optics might spell doom for the NSA.

But the impregnability of fiber optics has been overstated. There is no question that intercepting communications sent over optical networks is considerably more challenging than collecting satellite or microwave signals or even tapping old-fashioned copper cables. Because the signal is actually a beam of light, the only way to intercept it would be to open up the cable itself, and doing so would most likely degrade the signal to the point where the interference would be apparent. But as early as 1999, Terry Thompson, deputy director for services at the NSA, said the agency was "much further ahead now in terms of being able to access and collect fiber-optics, cellular data, all the different modalities of communications that we are targeting."

In chat rooms and newsgroups online, hackers and cryptographers have for years debated how easy it is to tap fiber optics, with some suggesting that the only way to intercept a signal is to breach its path and others claiming that it is possible to create a "vampire tap" that could sit, undetected, on a cable and gather data in transit. Some agreement seems to have emerged in the last several years that if you tease apart the fibers and bend them into a curve, a small portion of the light, known as the "conductive emission," leaks out and can be read and amplified without revealing that the network has been compromised. By April 2003, *Computerworld* magazine declared bluntly, "Fiber-optic cables . . . can easily be intercepted, interpreted and manipulated with standard off-the-shelf equipment that can be obtained legally throughout the world." John Pescatore, a former NSA analyst, said that American intelligence agencies had been tapping fiber optics "for the past seven or eight years" and added that by 2003 a resourceful college physics major with some time on his hands could figure out how to tap into these networks. In 1999, Congress authorized a $600 million set of modifications on the USS *Jimmy Carter,* a Seawolf-class attack submarine, that would allow it to tap into underwater optical cables. And while fiber optics may have provided a refuge for Saddam Hussein during the first war in Iraq, they were less tamper-proof by the second. Even before the invasion of Iraq in the spring of 2003, an American Delta Force operative had infiltrated a key Baghdad telecommunications center and placed a tap on a fiber-optic line, which provided intelligence that was reportedly decisive in pursuing Saddam.

. . .

THE FACT THAT THE UKUSA countries are developing the capability to tap fiber optics is most significant because optical networks are above all the medium of Internet traffic. It is a mixed blessing for intelligence agencies that the communications technology that has proved most revolutionary in the last decade is also the one that travels the most circuitous route. While there is a sense of the Internet as a great democratizing technology, one with which children are routinely more adept than their parents, this is an instance where the intelligence agencies had something of a head start. During the 1980s the NSA and its partners in the UKUSA agreement developed their own international intranet, based on technology very similar to that which would emerge in the Internet as we know it today. The real parent of the Internet was the Pentagon's Defense Advanced Research Projects Agency (DARPA), the obscure and Orwellian think tank that has more recently been known for developing the Total Information Awareness program and an online futures market for terrorist attacks. A new technology we all can use occasionally comes replete with a back door into it for those who effectively gave it to us. When you think about how secure communications on the Internet are, it is instructive to remember that the blueprint for the whole system was conceived by spies.

The Internet carries a massive bulk of information. In 1965, three years before cofounding the computer-processing company Intel, a little-known scientist named Gordon Moore predicted that computer power would double every eighteen months. This rule of thumb has since become known as Moore's Law, and in the intervening three decades it has held true: the quantity of information that can be processed by a given piece of silicon has roughly doubled every year since the technology was invented. Slightly lesser known is Nielsen's Law, which deals with Internet bandwidth. This law is named after usability guru Jakob Nielsen and holds that a high-end user's connection speed will grow by 50 percent per year. In combination, these two laws mean that an exponentially increasing amount of information is passing through networks on the World Wide Web. A European Parliament report on Echelon pointed out in 2000: "The highest capacity systems in general use for the Internet . . . operate at a data rate of 155Mbps" (million bits per second); a rate of 155 Mbps is equivalent to sending three million words every second, roughly the text of one thousand books per minute. That was five years ago—which in Moore's and Nielsen's terms is an awfully long time. As a result, there is simply much more in the way of information and communications that can be intercepted.

Even if the UKUSA agencies could not tap into fiber-optic networks, messages travel over the Internet in a highly circuitous way. Because of the manner in which the Internet was constructed—and the fact that the United States was so aggressively at the vanguard of that construction—many of the messages or "data packets" that pass through cyberspace, even those that do not pass from one American to another, will nevertheless be routed through intermediate sites in the United States. It is not uncommon for messages from Europe to Asia or Africa or South America to pass through various central hubs in, say, Silicon Valley, in California.

Establishing programs called "packet sniffers" at these central hubs to look at all of the information that passes through is a relatively easy process. Packet-sniffer programs can be set up to retrieve only packets containing specific data elements, and when they do this they make and store a copy of the packet without the sender or the receiver realizing it. The European Parliament report concludes that "it follows that a large proportion of international communications on the Internet will by the nature of the system pass through the United States and thus be readily accessible to the NSA." And indeed, according to a former NSA employee, by 1995 the agency had installed sniffer software to collect various kinds of traffic at nine major Internet exchange points (IXPs). Terry Thompson, the NSA deputy director, also acknowledged in 2001 that the agency has taken to hiring technicians away from the private companies that run much of the World Wide Web, such as Cisco Systems, and employing them to reverse engineer various communications technologies in order to locate vulnerabilities that the agency can exploit. This poached talent must be invaluable in sorting through the packetized and multiplexed flows of digital data.

When I asked Alistair Harley about this, he said that picking up Internet traffic is laughably easy for British intelligence agencies. "All Internet traffic from this country to the States, or from this country into Europe, goes through a link called JA Net, or Janet," he explained. "It's a backbone that runs the length of the country, from Scotland down. And that backbone runs through Cheltenham." This sounded incredible to me—that all Internet traffic running over optical cables to or from or via the UK would run through GCHQ first.

"How do you know?" I asked.

"When I worked for '5,' " Alistair said, "that's how we intercepted e-mail."

IN THE END, THE ability to intercept electronic communications seems virtually limitless. While fiber-optic technology provides a definite challenge, the full weight of the research budget of the NSA and other UKUSA agencies is being devoted to surmounting it. These agencies have traditionally dealt with the eclecticism of the signals firing around the world and the emergence of new ways to send signals by having all sensors on, picking up as many signals as possible. If a signal is not caught by the satellite ground stations, perhaps it will be caught by an interception satellite in space; if not by an Elephant Cage microwave interception site, perhaps by an embassy-collection program; if not at the central data backbone, then perhaps at an IXP.

The reaction on the part of those who really do not want to be tracked is an almost Luddite refusal to engage with the wired world. Robert Baer, who worked as a CIA case officer in the Middle East, told me, "The problem they're running up against with terrorism is that people in the Middle East don't discuss a whole lot over the telephone. They do it in person. They've always done it that way. They've always worried that the government was tapping their calls." Interestingly, in his own work Baer seems to have exercised a similar caution. "A lot of the things I've been involved in, they don't go up into the air," he told me. "It's too sensitive. It's easier to buy a plane ticket, fly somewhere."

And while Osama Bin Laden was initially every bit the twenty-first-century terrorist, in recent years he, too, seems to have come around to Baer's position. Bin Laden started out incredibly tech savvy. He used cellphones and satellite phones and often didn't bother to encrypt, not as an oversight but because he realized that encrypting the line is a way to bring attention to your signal and make it stand out from the white noise of a billion other intercepted calls. At the same time, he *did* embrace the cutting edge of cryptography and steganography. He and his associates are known to have hidden maps and photographs of targets as well as actual instructions to terrorists in sports chat rooms, on pornographic bulletin boards, and at other websites. Muslim extremists who attended his camps in Afghanistan and the Sudan were instructed not only in the use of weapons and explosives but in the techniques of cryptography as well.

However, after it was reported in 1998 that the NSA was able to intercept his satellite-phone calls, Bin Laden abruptly stopped using the phone. Wary of being detected by overhead photoreconnaissance satellites, he avoids conspicuous convoys of vehicles. When his people venture out from their caves and safe houses, they do so on foot. And he abstains from electronic communication of any kind, appreciating that remaining unplugged is the next best thing to invisibility, and chooses instead to send his messages via courier, lone men in the desert, just as Herodotus tells us Histaeus did, thousands of years ago.

BLACK PHONE/GRAY PHONE

The Hazards of Secrecy

LATE ONE APRIL afternoon in 1982, a woman named Rhona Prime walked her bicycle home from a driving lesson. Rhona lived in a châlet-style house on Pittville Crescent Lane in Cheltenham, England, with her second husband, Geoffrey Prime, and three children from her previous marriage. As she made her way up the drive, two of her sons dashed out to meet her, shouting, "The police have been at our house!"

When Rhona got inside, Geoffrey confirmed that two police officers had been by. He explained that they were investigating a string of sexual assaults in the area and that their suspect reportedly drove a car similar to his, a brown and cream Ford Mark IV Cortina. Geoffrey said the police were going to call back to speak with Rhona and that he had to go out for an hour before they did. He seemed agitated, but then Geoffrey Prime often seemed agitated. He had never been entirely at ease in the various jobs he had taken on since retiring from GCHQ, several years before. Tall and gaunt, Prime was balding in his mid-forties. He was a chain-smoker; his fingertips were stained tobacco brown.

When the police returned, they were cordial to Rhona and her husband; it appeared there were many cars in the area that fit the description, and their visit was normal procedure. They asked Prime where he had been on April 21, and he told them that he had been home all day. When the police had gone, Rhona and Geoffrey Prime left the house in order to discuss the incident in private. They drove to Cleeve Hill, overlooking the Severn Valley, and Prime pulled over by a farm gate, beyond which lay a field of grazing sheep. Husband and wife sat quietly for a moment before Prime announced, "It's me they want."

As Rhona listened in shocked silence, her husband explained that he had been the perpetrator of the sexual assaults. After a while, they drove to a local pub to pass the time until the children were in bed; Geoffrey continued to confess. They went home, poured themselves large brandies, and still Geoffrey went on. Rhona was numbed by the news, but she tried to be as supportive as possible as her husband unburdened himself. Encouraged, perhaps, by his wife's support, Geoffrey made another confession as they sat with their brandies in the gathering dark: he told her that he had been a Soviet spy for the past fourteen years.

The trial that followed was to be a severe test of the loyalties of Rhona Prime, an embarrassing debacle for the UKUSA intelligence agencies—and a telling glimpse into the role that secrecy plays in the world of signals intelligence. Secrecy is a maverick element. As a practice, it has a way of breaking its borders, metastasizing until it has touched everything—an inkblot on a piece of paper. On the institutional level, secrecy can corrupt bureaucracies and mask mismanagement and incompetence. On the individual level, it can corrupt identities, creating a profusion of secret lives and leaving nothing free of its taint.

GEOFFREY ARTHUR PRIME WAS born on February 21, 1938, in the West Midlands town of Stoke-on-Trent. Prime was a lonely and unhappy boy and was periodically molested by an older relative. At eighteen, he joined the Royal Air Force, enrolled in a Russian-language course, and was posted to RAF Gatow, a base in West Berlin. There, Prime started learning German and, later, selling secrets to Russia. Even his initial overture to the Soviets was characterized by the clumsiness that would lead the author of one later book about Prime to title it *The Imperfect Spy*. On New Year's Eve 1967, Prime wrote a message volunteering his services and wrapped it around a stone. As his car passed through a checkpoint along the corridor through East Germany linking the west to West Berlin, Prime threw the stone into a sentry post while the guard was checking his documents. Thinking the projectile was a grenade, the guard grabbed the stone and hurled it back into Prime's car; Prime then explained to him, verbally this time, his desire to betray his country.

Prime soon began meeting with a Soviet agent named Igor. It was at the urging of Igor and his handlers that Prime transferred to GCHQ in the first place. The Soviets knew very well the importance of signals intelligence and saw the utility of having a man inside Cheltenham. Prime slowly rose in the ranks of the British Sigint establishment, all the while passing information to the Russians via dead-letter drops, radio messages, and meetings in Vienna. In 1980, he spent a stretch with his handlers on a Russian barge as it transported passengers back and forth on the day trip from Vienna to the Hungarian border. Up and down the Danube for three long days, Prime passed on valuable information about British and American Sigint capabilities.

While he was rising through the ranks of GCHQ, Prime was also going through a divorce with his first wife. Prime then met Rhona. She was stuck in an unhappy marriage and a failing business when she and her first husband decided to take in a lodger for extra cash. She approached GCHQ, as Cheltenham is something of a company town, and they ended up sending her Geoffrey Prime. Rhona's first marriage ended, her marriage to Prime began, and shortly thereafter he suddenly chose to retire. After a stint as a taxi driver, Prime became a wine merchant, but his introverted and awkward way prevented him from being very effective as a salesman. The first of a catalog of odd discoveries the police made in his house was several cases of wine stacked in a corner of the garage. Prime had been forced to buy his own inventory.

After an agonizing deliberation, Rhona alerted the police that her husband had harbored not one dark secret but two, and Prime was charged with violating the Official Secrets Act. The trial was at the Old Bailey, and the details that emerged were grotesque. While Prime's actual sexual assaults occurred on only a few occasions, his preparation was alarmingly thorough. The police found a collection of index cards, each bearing the details of a young girl. "Wendy—11 years . . . M works 2 hrs w/day mornings." There were almost 2,300 of these cards, each relating to a different girl. Prime would scan local newspapers for mentions of young girls and then begin developing his cards, replete with the daily routines of the girls' families, noting in particular when the children were home alone. Despite all the ink that has been spilled over the last twenty years on the subject of Geoffrey Prime, no one has remarked on the uncanny similarity between the manner in which Prime monitored these girls, collating press clippings and cataloging the ephemera of their daily routines, and the curious occupation in which he spent his days.

Prime's trial provided one of the first public glimpses into the nature of that occupation and the existence of the UKUSA relationship. Most Britons hadn't heard of the blandly named agency where Prime worked until the trial made clear how damaging the presence of a defector within that agency had been. On May 12, 1983, Margaret Thatcher stood before the House of Commons and acknowledged that GCHQ existed and that its function was "to provide signals intelligence in accordance with requirements laid upon it by the government in support of the government's defense and foreign policies." The government was also forced to acknowledge the proximity of the relationship between GCHQ and the NSA, as there was evidence that the nature of this partnership was one of the things Prime had leaked to his handlers. In the wake of the trial, the British Security Commission released a report acknowledging a "close and fruitful cooperation between the signals intelligence organizations of the United States . . . and the United Kingdom, to the mutual advantage of both countries." The report pointed out that while the existence of the relationship was no secret, "the methods by which their operations are carried out, the targets at which they are directed, and the nature of the intelligence derived from them are among the most important [secrets] which it is in the national interest of both countries to protect." For giving up these secrets, and for keeping so many secrets of his own, Geoffrey Prime was sentenced to thirty-eight years in prison: thirty-five for espionage and three for sexual assault.

THE PRIME STORY REVEALS a great deal about the dynamics of secrecy in Sigint. For the agencies that do this work it is a salutary tale, because people will always be fallible, and Prime is hardly alone in the history of Anglo-American intelligence. From Guy Burgess, Donald Maclean, Kim Philby, and Anthony Blunt, the so-called Cambridge Spies, who became enamored with Russia between the world wars; to Bernon Mitchell and William Martin, two code breakers at the NSA who defected to the Soviet Union in 1960; to David Sheldon Boone, an NSA cryptanalyst who was sentenced to twenty-four years in prison in 1998 for selling secrets to Russia, there has been a long history of secrets leaked by intelligence insiders. An NSA handbook that was given to new arrivals to the agency in the 1990s puts the problem succinctly: "Vast amounts of information leave our facilities daily in the minds of NSA personnel, and this is where our greatest vulnerability lies."

In a cover letter to the handbook, Philip T. Pease, then director of security, describes something called "The Total NSA Security Program" and makes it clear that this program extends beyond any set of mere regulations. "It is based upon the concept that security begins as a state of mind." *Security begins as a state of mind.* For those engaged in signals intelligence, this credo, repeated with incantatory regularity, represents a sine qua non of day-to-day life and the governing constraint of a career. The handbook cautions employees that while they may inform their spouses and family that they work at the agency, they must not divulge anything about the particular nature of their work. In fact, that forty or so hours per week when they are at work is to be so vacuum-sealed and separate from the rest of their lives that NSA employees cannot even refer to it in diaries. "Classified information acquired during the course of your career or assignment to NSA may not be mentioned directly, indirectly, or by suggestion in personal diaries, records, or memoirs." In this manner, even one's memory is edited, lest it leave a paper trail. It is this principle that gives rise to a curious turn of phrase, invoked in the handbook and probably unique to such organizations: "classified waste." Even the trash at NSA is secret. The agency disposes of forty thousand pounds of classified documents each *day,* recycling them into pulp, which is then turned into tissue paper. This side venture has reportedly become quite profitable.

For the Sigint rank and file, the security state of mind can transcend not only the ties of family and friendship but the very instinct for survival. On April 1, 2000, a navy EP-3E reconnaissance plane, stuffed with sensitive listening equipment and two dozen American eavesdroppers, collided with a jet off the coast of China. The collision ripped the jet in half, sending shards pinwheeling to the sea below. The EP-3E remained intact but began to shake and abruptly dove toward the sea, plummeting twenty-two thousand feet. After several minutes, the pilot was able to regain some control and announced that they might be able to engineer a rough landing.

At this point, the crew did not do what you or I might do. They did not cry or pray or try to communicate with their loved ones. Instead, as the pilot issued maydays and endeavored to steer the plane toward land, the eavesdroppers opened an air hatch and started madly shoving out stacks of classified documents. Reams of technical manuals and frequency lists flapped out into space as the plane made its wobbly descent. Others on the crew began attacking the banks of sensitive equipment with an ax, denting and destroying it, doing anything to keep it from falling into Chinese hands. Because if the Chinese *knew* what we could listen to, there would be no point in listening at all. When the pilot managed to land the plane at the Lingshui military airfield on Hainan Island, the dazed crew did not scramble out to safety but stayed in the plane and started hand-shredding documents as fast as they could. A navy report later conceded that "the destruction of classified material was accomplished while the aircrew was probably still in shock from the aircraft collision and the subsequent rapid descent of the aircraft." But remarkably, the report lamented the fact that not enough of the classified material onboard the EP-3E was adequately disposed of before Chinese officials boarded the plane. It called for better emergency destruction procedures in the future. This unflinching devotion to maintaining secrecy is hardly unique to the NSA. Analysts at the Government Communications Security Bureau (GCSB), the signals agency in New Zealand, are instructed that in the event of a fire or earthquake, they must clear away all of the sensitive material on their desk before they think about exiting the building.

In order to maintain security, Sigint agencies augment emergency procedures, triple fences, and tempest-proof black vaults with a corresponding series of psychological motes and parapets, walls and secret rooms. The more I read about classification and security at the NSA, the more it seemed that the life of an individual working in signals intelligence is, of necessity, a fractured one, a life split into discrete parts. This schizophrenia is enacted even in the telephone system at the NSA. According to the handbook (which may be dated at this point), there are two types of phones at Fort Meade: gray phones and black phones. The gray phones are secure, and the black phones are not. Employees are encouraged to develop the instinctual habit of picking up the right phone for the right purpose and ensuring that "use of either telephone system does not jeopardize the security of classified information." Apart from suggesting, alarmingly, that even within Fort Meade the telephone line is not something that should be treated as secure, the two-phone principle seems to capture the idea of a life cleaved into parts. One of the guidelines is that you should avoid using the nonsecure phone in the vicinity of a secure phone that is in use. The suggestion seems to be that whomever you are talking with may be untrustworthy and could overhear some classified information that they might then pass on to the enemy or to a journalist—who, when it comes to Sigint, is just the enemy by proxy.

WHEN SECRECY SEEPS INTO the life of an individual, dribbling like mercury into the fault lines separating the parts of one's identity—husband, colleague, traitor, friend—it has a way of segregating those different parts, changing them from facets of the same personality to different personalities altogether. Geologists call it "frost wedging": most rocks have tiny cracks and fissures running through them, and when it rains, water seeps into these joints. As the temperature cools, the water freezes and expands and ruptures the rock from within. Similarly, secrecy can filter into a life and harden into routine, eroding a coherent identity and resulting in a profusion of different and discrete personae.

Studying the Prime story, I could not help feeling that the lives of Geoffrey Prime, the whole categories of secrets to which Rhona Prime was not privy, were perhaps an indication that at some point all of the secrecy in an organization like GCHQ might begin to affect the employees. In a life in which an individual is told from day one on the job that he must keep many things secret even from his own wife, that he must make of his life two entirely separate spheres—work and home—and keep any interaction between those spheres to an absolute minimum, there is surely some tendency to internalize that kind of division. While he was sequestered in New Mexico, helping create the atomic bomb, Robert Oppenheimer wrote in a letter, "For the last four years I have had only classified thoughts." What could that have done to his relations with others?

In October 2002, the *Gloucestershire Echo* ran a charming item about Daphne and Peter Pennell, a married couple, each of whom worked at GCHQ for three decades. During those thirty years of professional and married life, Daphne and her husband never told each other what precisely it was that they did. "It sounds strange to say," seventy-year old Daphne told the paper, some time after Peter's death, "but, with the Official Secrets Act, we didn't talk about our work. I don't know what my husband did and he didn't know what I did. This was accepted by the many married couples that worked there."

But once a fissure like this develops, what is to stop others? It may be a mere coincidence—but if it is, it's an interesting one—that many of the moles within the agencies over the years, many of the individuals who sold the secrets of their masters, also harbored secrets of their own. If you can live a life in which you keep from your wife that you break Russian codes, why not keep from your wife and your employer that you have a secret sexual life? And if you can keep your secret sexual life from them all, why not sell secrets to the enemy and keep that a secret, too? Rhona Prime actually said, despairingly, at her husband's trial, "I do not know how he lived his triple life."

Perhaps this tendency is present only in those of weak disposition or those whose patriotism was wavering to begin with. Or perhaps the people who find their ways into the most secret realms of their nations' defense communities are in fact a self-selecting crowd, already prone to secret keeping and most at home in a murky world. What is clear, though, is that in several of these cases, the self seems to split. You get a prismatic effect, where once the game is up and the individual is exposed to the unblinking light of investigation, each rotation of that individual exposes an entirely different face. Guy Burgess and Anthony Blunt were homosexuals who were compelled, the better part of the time, to closet one aspect of their identities. Mitchell and Martin may have been as well. Forced by their societies to cloister themselves to various extents, they lived their romantic lives in private.

A linkage between a sexuality deemed aberrant by society and the tendency to be a double agent may not be purely coincidental. During the cold war, Soviet spies trawled for potential moles in the bars and nightclubs of Vienna and Berlin. Gregarious handlers would strike up friendships with British and American diplomats and servicemen, ply them with drinks, and try to find a weakness—for women, men, children, anything that would provide fodder for blackmail. They called this the "Honey Trap." In 1955, an English admiralty clerk named John Vassall was stationed at the British embassy in Moscow when he was lured into an affair with an attractive Russian soldier. Vassall had little idea that this indiscretion would effectively secure his allegiance to Soviet intelligence for seven years or that he would ultimately be arrested by the British and sentenced to eighteen years in prison. In Berlin, the Russians tried to entrap Prime in a similar manner but were not clear on what precisely suited his fancy. He was a bachelor at that time, so it was useless attempting to catch him in some sort of heterosexual liaison. At one point early on, his handlers invited a young blond man to the contact apartment. The man made it clear to Prime that he was available, but Prime was repulsed by what he regarded as an easy ruse. Prime later claimed that the failure of this ploy was enough to prevent his handlers from attempting any such thing again, but it has been widely speculated that some more characteristic impropriety in Berlin became the source of subsequent blackmail.

It is tempting to regard the traitor as just another persona that flourishes in the compartmentalized and closeted life of the secrecy-crazed spy, a paradoxical by-product of the security state of mind. But it is difficult to test this hypothesis, because in the tumult surrounding the exposure of various traitors over the years, the real or perceived sexual deviance of the double agent has often become a leitmotif of ensuing denunciations. Dating back to the exposures of Guy Burgess and Anthony Blunt, public denouncements of the mole have tended to hold that communism, homosexuality, and treachery are so mutually compatible as to be almost indistinguishable. The bloodlust that follows the exposure of a spy is often animated by a fixation with that spy's outsider status and a denial of his masculinity.

You can see this very clearly in the case of the two most notorious defectors from the NSA, Mitchell and Martin. On June 24, 1960, these two close friends told their supervisors that they were going on vacation to visit the homes of their parents. They then bought one-way tickets to Mexico City, flew from there to Cuba, and boarded a Soviet trawler bound for Russia. In August, the Department of Defense announced that the two men were missing and that there was a "likelihood that the two employees have gone behind the Iron Curtain." Mitchell and Martin were both smart but disaffected. They had met at the Naval Radio Intercept Station at Kamiseya, Japan, and struck up an intense friendship. Through the late 1950s, both Mitchell and Martin became increasingly alarmed at what they regarded as unfair American intelligence practices. In particular, they objected to reconnaissance aircraft skirting the borders of the Soviet Union, listening in.

On September 6, 1960, the two men suddenly reappeared, at a massive press conference in Moscow's House of Journalists. They sat at a long table, each flanked by a Russian interpreter. In prepared statements and a brief Q&A, Mitchell and Martin proceeded to disclose a great deal of information about an agency that most Americans had never heard of. "We were employees of the highly secret National Security Agency, which gathers communications intelligence from almost all nations of the world for use by the United States Government," Martin announced. He said that the NSA collected and decoded messages from "Italy, Turkey, France, Yugoslavia, the United Arab Republic, Indonesia, and Uruguay," then added, "That's enough to give a general picture, I guess."

The Pentagon released a statement following the press conference that painted Mitchell and Martin as deviants. "Their appearance in Moscow gives final confirmation that these young men—one mentally sick and both obviously confused—have sacrificed everything that Americans and other free men hold dear." The House Un-American Activities Committee conducted a thirteen-month investigation of the incident and concluded, absurdly, that the primary reason for the defection was homosexuality.

. . .

OF ALL THE PEOPLE I read about or spoke with, a British spy-turned-writer named James Rusbridger seemed closest to getting at the dynamics of secrecy in the lives of spies and signals people. "This mania for secrecy based on the excuse of protecting national security has steadily grown," he wrote, "until today it [has] become a form of paranoia that intrudes into every aspect of British life, often to the detriment of the very people it is supposed to be protecting." Intrigued by this idea, I wanted to learn more about Rusbridger himself and looked up his other books and some of the details of his career as a writer and a spy. What I found was fascinating. Rusbridger was, by all accounts, an urbane figure who loved intrigue. As a writer on the subject of intelligence, he would entertain his various contacts with smoked-salmon sandwiches at his cottage in Bodmin, Cornwall, not far from the listening station at Morwenstow. He had a fondness for nice Chablis. He was a prolific writer of letters to newspapers, with hundreds invariably alleging conspiracies and charging the government with one thing or another.

While Rusbridger was often tagged with the amorphous epithet "former spy," I had trouble nailing down exactly what his espionage background had entailed. Rusbridger himself often said he had worked behind the Iron Curtain for MI6 as a "bagman," or courier. According to his own account, he started off in the 1950s in the London office of a Cuban sugar company but by the sixties was smuggling parcels of American dollars into eastern Europe. Stories from those who knew him at the time, and from Rusbridger himself, paint a picture of a dashing young spy, traveling under the guise of a businessman and tooling through the streets of Warsaw and Prague in a Jaguar E-Type. On the strength of this rumored affiliation with the intelligence services and led by a true conspiracy theorist's nose for the duplicitous machinations of government, Rusbridger wrote a book called *The Intelligence Game* and another called *Betrayal at Pearl Harbor*.

Nevertheless, there were those in the intelligence establishment who denied that he had ever been affiliated. I was reminded of a conversation I had during graduate school with a professor at Cambridge University. Cambridge has a long historical association with the intelligence services, and while the days when dons tapped promising students for careers in MI6 have passed, many still detect and relish the residual whiff of subterfuge in the musty halls and common rooms. I mentioned to my professor that there was another instructor in the program who seemed occasionally to drop oblique hints that he was a spy. With a sage chuckle, my professor replied, "I'll tell you a good rule of thumb for making your way around Cambridge: the only way to tell that someone *doesn't* work for British intelligence is when they imply that they *do*."

It was with a shudder that during my research on Rusbridger I learned of the fate of this particular chronicler of the hazards of secrecy and secret lives. According to a spate of obituaries, Rusbridger was found dead at sixty-five, hanged in his cottage from an elaborate system of pulleys, with a rope around his neck and ankles, naked but for an oilskin coat and a World War II gas mask, and surrounded by a lavish collection of pornography.

HAVING PEERED INTO THE labyrinth of secrecy and the individual, I wanted to learn about the manner in which secrecy affects institutions, so I went to visit Steven Aftergood, who heads the Project on Government Secrecy. On a frigid January Monday, slate gray and streaked with rain, I took the train to Washington, D.C., and was buzzed into the brightly lit suite on K Street that houses the Federation of American Scientists. FAS, as it is generally known, was founded by Manhattan Project scientists who were deeply troubled by the technology they had unleashed and worried about the dangers of scientific research that is not guided by sound and responsible policy. As a result, FAS has become a kind of lobby group for the scientific perspective on various issues related to defense policy.

Aftergood abandoned a graduate degree in electrical engineering just as the cold war was ending and started out at FAS working on nuclear-power issues associated with the Strategic Defense Initiative— or as it was more commonly known, "Star Wars." Then one day in 1991, he received a package in the mail from an anonymous source inside the government. The package contained a stack of documents concerning a classified program to develop a nuclear rocket engine. As Aftergood flipped through the documents, he realized that the name of the project and the very fact of its existence were classified. This struck him as an excessive degree of secrecy, and he contacted the inspector general of the Department of Defense to complain that the project, which was code-named Timber Wind, was overclassified. After a year-long investigation, the inspector general agreed. And the Project on Government Secrecy was born.

"The secrecy shrouding Timber Wind got me wondering, What else is there that's classified?" Aftergood said to me, settling into a fraying office chair. "What other things am I as a private citizen not permitted to know about? What is the scope of the secret portion of government, what are the rules governing its operation, how does it comport with the democratic structures that govern the rest of the system? These are questions I've been pursuing, fruitfully and without boredom, ever since." Aftergood is in his forties, with black hair, small glasses, and a hint of a cleft in his chin. He was wearing khakis and a checked shirt and spoke in careful, ruminative tones. But for long pauses and frequent *ahhhs* and *umms,* he tends to speak in perfect paragraphs.

Aftergood works full-time trying to chart the boundaries of the secret world and, when appropriate, push them back. Each day, he checks his numerous sources in the government and around the world along with the fifty or so websites that he monitors. When he has gathered an interesting array of information, he compiles it into his e-mail newsletter, "Secrecy News," which he sends out two or three times per week. The newsletter is distributed to almost nine thousand people. About 30 percent of the subscribers are in the government and military. Ten percent live outside the United States. Sometimes he will get angry responses from officials who demand to know under what authority he has posted various pieces of information. He has been known to shoot back e-mails that read, "Authorization for publication of material on our web site is contained in U.S. Constitution, Amendment 1" and include a hyperlink to an online version of the Constitution. On the day I talked with him, Aftergood had just received an e-mail from someone at the Department of Defense congratulating him on an excellent issue. Of course, the individual had noted that the congratulations were off the record, lest word get out that the Pentagon is reading "Secrecy News."

Aftergood is a strange relief from the people I've spent months talking to. While his conviction and persistence are almost evangelical, his rhetoric has none of the flinty inflexibility that is present in die-hard civil libertarians or law-and-order types. In an intellectual arena dominated by two stratified, static positions, Aftergood seems to be that rare thing, a nuanced and dynamic thinker. Moreover, he is so patient and persuasive in articulating his position that he often makes a radical idea seem positively middle-of-the-road. "I'm not dogmatic about this," he told me, and explained that he receives large amounts of information that he would not put in his newsletter. "There have been a few cases where people sent me information having to do with nuclear weapons design, where I just thought, This guy is crazy, and so no, I just ended up destroying it because I didn't want it around."

In fact, much of what Aftergood publishes is oddly prosaic. One of the major victories he has had over the years was in forcing the CIA to publish its aggregate intelligence budget for 1997. Intelligence spending has traditionally been considered extremely secret, and while he concedes that an itemized budget might be legitimately classified, Aftergood thinks that American taxpayers have a right to know the overall dollar amount our government spends on intelligence each year. He applied for access to the figure under the Freedom of Information Act (FOIA); after some protracted resistance, the CIA gave in. (The number was $26.6 billion.) While 1997 was a victory, it was only one year, and Aftergood soon filed a FOIA claim for the 2002 budget. "Their position is that it would damage national security if that were disclosed," he told me. "I say that is nonsense, transparent nonsense. I don't think if it was published it would change the tactics of Bin Laden or anyone else in the slightest. Rather, I think it is an effort to curtail debate on intelligence spending, which is not a legitimate use of classification." The vagaries of the classification system are such that while the 1997 intelligence budget is now public, when I met Aftergood he was having trouble getting the CIA to release the budget for *1947*.

BUT WHO CARES, I asked? Much of the information Aftergood is after seems of very little utility to the average citizen. Aftergood replied that there are two reasons: one principled, the other pragmatic. From a principled point of view, he began, "It is an axiom, or an article of faith, that the best way to structure society is to maximize openness and democratic procedures, to offer a robust deliberative process. The question is not why information should be open, it's why *shouldn't* it be open. Everything should be open unless there is a good articulable reason why it shouldn't be. So I resist the question why *should* this be disclosed." He pointed out that the Freedom of Information Act allows access to any kind of information that does not fall into one of nine categories of exemption. "It doesn't have to be interesting, it doesn't have to be newsworthy, it doesn't have to be useful, it doesn't have to be anything at all. If it's not exempt, and it's a government record, I have a legal right to it."

While Aftergood's norm-driven argument has a definite appeal, there is a more pragmatic and immediate reason for diminishing the amount of official secrecy surrounding the intelligence community: while the rationale for secrecy is very often linked to national security, excessive secrecy can actually make us less secure. When the bipartisan 9/11 Commission released its final report in the summer of 2004, it concluded that reflexive bureaucratic secrecy was to blame for some of the failures of congressional oversight and intelligence sharing that led to the success of the attacks of September 11. In particular, the commission recommended that "the overall amounts of money being appropriated for national intelligence and to its component agencies should no longer be kept secret. Congress should pass a separate appropriations act for intelligence, defending the broad allocation of how these tens of billions of dollars have been assigned among the varieties of intelligence work." The commission allowed that specific allocations within the intelligence budget should remain classified but stressed that "when even aggregate categorical numbers remain hidden, it is hard to judge priorities and foster accountability."

In some respects, Aftergood is carrying on the legacy of New York senator Daniel Patrick Moynihan, who died in the spring of 2003. Moynihan famously estimated that if every newspaper in the United States devoted every page to printing the classified documents produced by the government on any single day, there would be room for nothing else. Moynihan established a bipartisan commission on reducing government secrecy, which issued a 1997 report concluding that the government's security system was classifying far too much and at far too great a cost. (The infrastructure of secrecy is extremely expensive: it costs a great deal to maintain classification systems, both in tagging documents with appropriate designations and in administering the clearance system for government employees.) Ironically, the report held, the broadness of this reflexive approach to secrecy meant that certain vital national secrets were *not* adequately protected because of the resources devoted to needlessly classifying so much else. The report also concluded that secrecy had a range of intangible negative consequences and eroded public confidence in government, because much secrecy was geared less to protecting national security than to insulating the careers and reputations of bureaucrats and policymakers. Moynihan published an elegantly persuasive book on the topic, *Secrecy*, which sits prominently on Aftergood's shelf. In that book, Moynihan suggested that secrecy is an institution that is "distinctive primarily in that it is all but unexamined. There is a formidable literature on regulation of the public mode, virtually none on secrecy. Rather, there *is* a considerable literature, but it is mostly secret."

MOYNIHAN AND AFTERGOOD MIGHT be right, but the prevailing wisdom tends to be that if there is one area that *must* remain classified, it is signals intelligence. One of the challenges in writing about eavesdropping is balancing a desire to unearth and pass along information about Sigint with a very real awareness that publishing certain details could jeopardize national security. In the summer of 2002, the CIA circulated a memo to national security officials stating that captured detainees had reported that Al Qaeda members closely scrutinize the American media for information about intelligence capabilities and alter their strategies accordingly. Aftergood said he is sympathetic with all of the secrecy surrounding Sigint and pointed disapprovingly to articles by *The Washington Times* reporter Bill Gertz, who has extraordinary access to classified documents. "He will report that, oh, a missile from North Korea is believed to be en route to Pakistan, has been learned from communications intercepts. . . . What you've just done is you've told the embassies of those two countries, and every other embassy, Go revisit your communications protection. And for what, you know?"

Sure, I said, but aren't there more difficult cases? For instance, should the UKUSA agreement still be classified? "I don't find it credible that the UKUSA agreement cannot be disclosed even in part. I don't believe it," Aftergood said. "I think the people who say it are either deluded or dishonest." At fault was the same reflexive classification, Aftergood said. And sure enough, several weeks after my chat with Aftergood I had a conversation with a Pentagon official in which I asked him why the UKUSA agreement was still classified. His answer: "Why not?"

In her book *Secrets*, Sissela Bok identifies the challenge of drawing this line between openness and national security—precisely the challenge Aftergood has chosen as his vocation—as the most difficult ethical calculation of all of those that the issue of secrecy raises. "In matters so fundamental to national self-preservation, both secrecy and openness carry risks that may present a genuine impasse," she remarks.

"The public is asked to take on faith the need for secrecy on the grounds that an open debate of the reasons for such a need might endanger national security."

But in general, Aftergood told me, he does not concern himself with these hard cases. "As a practical matter, what I do is focus on the easier, outrageous instances. If you're asking me where to draw the line between what's classified and what's not, the answer is I don't know. But there are a lot of things that are so far over the line, classified when they shouldn't be, that I have my hands full tackling those." According to the government's Information Security Oversight Office, there were more than 23 million new secrets created by the United States government in 2002. "I have to do that math," Aftergood says, "but I think that's around sixty thousand times a day." (It's sixty-three thousand.)

The U.S. government now spends more than $5 billion per year maintaining the classification system and the apparatus that surrounds it. That includes the clearance system, physical security, and so forth. And the numbers are going up every year. The tide of classification is rising and gathering an apparently inexorable momentum. Meanwhile, Aftergood works alone. An imposing row of file cabinets lines one wall of his office, and there are stacks of papers everywhere: on the bookshelves, on the cluttered desk, on the floor. I notice some tape that appears to be holding his desk together. He's funded by grants mainly and by the small contributions of people who read "Secrecy News." But at the end of the day, Steven Aftergood is a man engaged in a distinctly Sisyphean task.

IN NOVEMBER 2003, AN interesting document popped up on the Web. Titled "Interviewing with an Intelligence Agency (or, A Funny Thing Happened on the Way to Fort Meade)" and attributed to "Ralph J. Perro (a pseudonym)," this comic, first-person account of applying for a job with the NSA offers a rare insight into how seriously Sigint agencies take secrecy and security.

Perro was a midcareer computer programmer who had worked as a software developer in Silicon Valley and was in a "period of professional transition" when the combined lure of high-tech code breaking and post–September 11 patriotic duty drew him to the NSA. After all, "the agency has historically measured computing resources in acres," he points out. "*Acres*! One can only imagine the top-secret high-tech synthesis of agricultural and computer science phraseology: 'Go out and data-mine the back-40. Harvest the intelligence. We had a problem with the combine on last night's batch job.' Awesome!"

Perro's enthusiasm got him through an initial "pre-screen" interview and an "operational interview" with a hiring manager. By the end of his day at Fort Meade, he was given a CJO, or conditional job offer, pending full security clearance. But it was the clearance process that bedeviled him. First, he was subjected to a battery of psychological exams, involving everything from basic questions about age and marital status to questions about his relationship with his mother and father, and true-or-false questions running the gamut from "I would like the job of a forest ranger" to "I hear voices in my head." Perro then met with a psychologist, who declared that on the basis of the tests he was a "low to medium risk." Before leaving, Perro was subjected to a polygraph test, which he counts as the most grueling ordeal of the process.

After the polygraph, Perro headed home, while the NSA did its background investigation, interviewing friends, neighbors, and former colleagues. Some time later, he was sitting at home when a woman called, identified herself as a Department of Defense investigator, and asked if she could come by for a while. She pulled up in a tan Cadillac and invited Perro to join her in the car, where they proceeded to talk:

> The interview-in-a-sedan was physically awkward. The natural inclination of a body when sitting in the front-seat of an automobile is to sit back and look through the windshield. However, if I kept my eyes to the front the investigator would be 90 degrees to my left ear and that would look *really* deceptive. But if I kept my shoulders to the seat and only turned my head to the left I would look like a freak, if not an uncomfortable freak. So I recall opting for rotating my body about 45 degrees counter-clockwise to the left, with my left elbow resting on top of my seat, but not extended [so] that my arm reached over to *her* seat, lest I look *too* friendly.

The questions were fairly routine, and many of them similar to the ones Perro had been asked during the polygraph exam. Still, there were a few surprises. At a certain point the investigator asked Perro if he had ever engaged in wife swapping. "I'm sitting in a Cadillac at the end of my driveway, talking to a DoD investigator about whether I'm a swinger. It simply cannot get any weirder than this." Ultimately, after three and a half months of the security-clearance process, Perro was rejected.

PART OF THE IRONY of these measures is that they have tended, historically, not to work. A tough "positive vetting" system was introduced to British intelligence agencies after the Cambridge Spies defected in the 1950s. The system involves a deep investigation, not unlike the one Perro endured, that is repeated periodically throughout an agent's career. But Geoffrey Prime went through five positive vettings without GCHQ ever having a glimmer of his traitorousness, to say nothing of his other predilections. "In order for secrets to be safeguarded, privacy must be invaded," wrote the sociologist Edward Shils in his 1956 classic, *The Torment of Secrecy*, published at the height of the McCarthy era. "The security of secrets has come to require not only physical security and classification; it requires very understandably the selection of personnel." But in Shils's view, "The science of personnel selection for the reliable handling of secret information is still unborn."

The polygraph in particular is a notoriously ineffective means of ensuring loyalty and secrecy on the part of intelligence officers. Polygraphs measure cardiovascular activity, depth and frequency of respiration, and perspiration, but there is no unanimous agreement on what these responses *mean*. Perro argues that the anxiety engendered by the situation could easily produce readings that would augur poorly for the job applicant. When the Los Alamos scientist Wen Ho Lee was subjected to a polygraph test by the Department of Energy in 1998, the examiner found that on the basis of the results Lee was innocent of the charges of espionage leveled against him. In fact, the test generated unusually strong readings indicating a lack of deception, and that finding was subsequently reviewed and endorsed by two other polygraphers. But when FBI polygraphers later examined the same set of data, they concluded that Lee had failed. Meanwhile, Aldrich Ames, the notorious CIA officer who, with the help of his wife, sold valuable secrets to the Soviets for nine years, passed the polygraph free of so much as a trace of suspicion. In 1998, the Supreme Court concluded that "there is simply no way to know in a particular case whether a polygraph examiner's conclusion is accurate, because certain doubts and uncertainties plague even the best polygraph exams."

As it happens, the polygraph exam is a side interest of Steven Aftergood, and in 2000 he wrote an article in *Science* magazine in which he criticized the test. Shortly thereafter, he received a handwritten letter from Aldrich Ames, care of Allenwood Federal Penitentiary in Pennsylvania, where Ames is serving a life sentence. In the letter, Ames agreed with Aftergood's criticisms, arguing that the polygraph is a form of pseudoscience that "just won't die," likening it to astrology and homeopathy. He pointed out the complicated role that secrecy plays with regard to the polygraph. The NSA and other intelligence agencies use the test to protect their secrets by endeavoring to determine whether the subject of the test has any secrets. It may or may not work, but whether it truly does is itself a secret. "The polygraph is asserted to have been a useful tool in counterintelligence investigations," Ames wrote.

> This is a nice example of retreating into secret knowledge: we know it works, but it's too secret to explain. To my own knowledge and experience over a thirty year career this statement is false. The use of the polygraph (which is inevitably to say, its misuse) has done little more than create confusion, ambiguity and mistakes. I'd love to lay out this case for you, but unfortunately I cannot—it's a secret too.

LIKE SO MUCH ELSE in the Sigint world, the polygraph issue entails a baffling profusion of symmetries and asymmetries, ironies and paradoxes. Sissela Bok points out that "there can be no presumption either for or against secrecy in general" but insists that, "whatever control over secrecy and openness we conclude is legitimate for some individuals should, in the absence of special considerations, be legitimate for all." But Sigint agencies have long inhabited the loophole world of "special considerations." They are privy to the secrets of civilians around the planet but are hell-bent on keeping their own secrets, including often the very facts of their existence. In order to do this, the agencies subject their employees to an invasive examination, not so much a violation as an eradication of privacy—a suggestion that inside such an agency, personal privacy cannot exist. The NSA subjects its employees to polygraph exams, probes their psychologies, and investigates their private lives. But the rest of us cannot even know the employees' names. On the NSA website you will find the name of the director and those of a few other top officials, but there the trail runs cold. The whole edifice, six *billion* dollars a year, sixty *thousand* employees, *acres* of computing power, is swathed in secrecy.

"Secrecy is privacy made compulsory," Edward Shils declared. "It is privacy with higher, more impassable barriers. Yet secrecy is the enemy of privacy." A similar idea is captured in that great hobbyhorse of paranoids and cultural theorists, Jeremy Bentham's Panopticon. As Michel Foucault was quick to point out in his book *Discipline and Punish*, the signature characteristic of Bentham's circular prison with a central, all-seeing tower was that the inmates in perimeter cells could not see *into* that tower. "One is totally seen, without ever seeing," Foucault observed. "In the central tower, one sees everything without being seen." Foucault's gloss on this was that the architecture assumed a coercive function: the authorities did not even need to watch anymore, so much as persuade the inmates that they *might*. This idea had been articulated earlier, of course, as Orwell's Winston Smith realized that "there was no way of knowing whether you were being watched at any given moment. How often, or on what system, the Thought Police plugged in on any individual wire was guesswork. It was even conceivable that they watched everybody all the time."

In these passages, secrecy and privacy reveal themselves as partners in a tense dialectic. But if it is an intimate and antagonistic dance the two are engaged in, the development of a system called Total Information Awareness was an opportunity for privacy to seize the lead.

IN THE LATE SUMMER of 2002, the Pentagon announced that it was developing a new program to combat terrorism, known as Total Information Awareness (TIA). TIA would be developed by DARPA, the small and secretive organization that has traditionally represented the avant-garde of Pentagon research and development. DARPA gave the world the computer mouse and the Internet, which started life as the Arpanet. But as the war on terror got up to speed, research money was going to increasingly esoteric ventures, such as technologies that could identify a human by his face, iris, gait, or, bizarrely enough, smell. When the military historian John Keegan remarked that "the secret world has always occupied a halfway house between fact and fiction, and has been peopled as much by dreamers and fantasists as by pragmatists and men of reason," he might have had DARPA in mind.

In essence, TIA seemed animated by the same intuition as systems like Echelon. The airwaves and wires overflow with information about individuals: names, addresses, credit-card numbers, passport details. If you could just find some means of organizing all of that information, of harnessing the chaotic jumble and placing it connected and cross-referenced into a searchable database, you'd have something of a crystal ball. We all leave different trails, some of them more distinct than others, and the most distinctive trails are transactional. (An early overview of the project identified something called the "transaction space.") Terrorism, too, requires transactions, the thinking goes, and these transactions "will leave signatures in this information space." It was a visionary and poetic idea, in its own way: the transaction space is a pond—all you need do is watch for the ripples.

Of course, it was the application that was new, not the idea. The practice of "data mining" had already flourished in the go-go days of the Internet boom. When it became clear that advertisers and marketers could track not only where consumers live and how they spend money but even what websites they visit, what links they open, and how long they linger on a given page, companies sprang up to create searchable databases of consumer profiles. It's a testament to the strength of the Internet bubble and the relative peace of the 1990s that spyware, as the invidious versions of this sort of software program have come to be known, was the brainchild not of the Department of Defense but of run-of-the-mill advertising companies. Long before TIA, companies such as DoubleClick were secretly sowing your hard drive with "cookies" and other innocuously named parasitic programs that cling quietly, often unbeknownst to the computer user, recording every Web peregrination, every keystroke, every move. I was vaguely aware of this development before September 11, 2001, and of some of the hysterical reaction to it among privacy advocates, but I tended not to worry too much. Of course, there are certain Orwellian dangers lurking when you create a system that links everyone and tracks their transactions. But I tended to agree with Lawrence Lessig, the Stanford law professor and author of the early bible of Web architecture and legislation, *Code,* when he said, "No one spends money collecting these data to actually learn anything about *you*. They want to learn about people *like* you." It was the consumer profile they were after, not the individual consumer.

But TIA aimed to change all that. The idea was to link various private databases, such as the ones developed by credit-card companies and companies such as DoubleClick, with existing public databases from immigration, the IRS, and law enforcement to create one colossal, searchable "metabase," in which all of the loose strands of information about individuals would be knit together into a neat, legible braid. According to the program-objective description on TIA's website, the project would increase information gathered on American civilians "by an order of magnitude." Some people might venture into the transaction space more frequently than others, but even the modern-day Luddite who refuses e-mail and writes checks would likely eventually rent a car or apply for a mortgage, and when he did that information would make its way into a database. Normally, these various little ventures into the networked world go unconnected—a series of apparently random, discrete transactions stored in different databases. TIA aimed to connect the dots. By DARPA's own accounting, the data drawn upon would include financial, education, travel, medical, customs and immigration, housing, communications, and government records. Transportation records such as parking tickets and E-ZPass data would be fed into the system. Curiously, DARPA's website suggested that veterinary records would be included as well.

The strength of this idea was that once a terrorist ventured into the observable matrix of the networked world, an alarm would sound; in the words of DARPA's program description, TIA would generate "focused warning within an hour after a triggering event occurs or an evidence threshold is passed." If credit-card databases were linked with airline-ticket transaction databases, immigration databases, and lists of suspected terrorists, the thinking goes, a whole series of alarms might have sounded on July 19, 2000, when ten thousand dollars was wired to a Florida SunTrust bank account in the name of Mohammed Atta; or on July 10, 2001, when Zacarias Moussaoui used a credit card to pay for a simulator course in commercial flight training; or in the last days of August 2001, when more than a dozen men, mainly from Saudi Arabia, some of them on terrorist watch lists and others on lapsed visas, all bought one-way tickets on flights departing at roughly the same hour on the morning of September 11.

THE PROBLEM WAS, DARPA's public-relations instincts were atrocious. To say that the leaders of the agency's new Information Awareness Office had a tin ear would be to grossly understate the case. In fairness, the system was so ambitious and seemed to have so little regard for personal privacy that it was a hard sell from its very inception. As details about TIA emerged, Marc Rotenberg, the director of the Electronic Privacy Information Center (EPIC), the watchdog group in Washington, D.C., described TIA as "the perfect storm for civil liberties in America." In an editorial, *The Washington Post* remarked, "Anyone who deliberately set out to invent a government program with the specific aim of terrifying the Orwell-reading public could hardly have improved on the Information Awareness Office." Seemingly oblivious to the danger of such a reaction, TIA's architects made one gaffe after another. Who, for instance, thought up the name *Total Information Awareness*? Did no lowly functionary at any preparatory meeting pipe up and suggest that if the Pentagon was going to unveil a system that would unsettle those concerned with individual privacy and nervous about the prospect of an all-seeing branch of the government, it would be a little counterproductive to give the program a name that screamed *1984*? Similarly, no voice of reason intervened when the agency opted to have the symbol of the Information Awareness Office be a pyramid with an eye at the top of it that looks out at the planet earth in the foreground. If you have spent any time among conspiracy theorists, you'll know that pyramids and eyes are laden with symbolic importance for your average paranoid. Take the pyramid and eye on the one-dollar bill. These are seen by many (among them Alistair Harley) as incontrovertible evidence of a Masonic conspiracy at the bosom of the Treasury Department, if not the U.S. government itself. There's another centuries-old conspiracy theory about the Illuminati, a tiny cadre of powerful politicians and businessmen who rule the world. Their symbol is an eye atop a pyramid.

In case anyone had any doubt about the program's intentions, the website bore the motto *scientia est potentia*, "knowledge is power." Eventually, in May 2003 the wily strategists at DARPA opted to change the name to something that while still radiating strength and competence would seem at least cosmetically a little more geared toward capturing bad guys. The new name? *Terrorism* Information Awareness. You can imagine the satisfaction in not having to ditch all of that monogrammed stationery. Nevertheless, this gesture was widely regarded as too little too late and reminded me of the Stasi's decision, in the waning moments of the German Democratic Republic, to change its name from the Ministry for State Security to the Office of National Security (*Amt für Nationale Sicherheit*), which might have succeeded in softening the image of the secret police, had it not resulted in the disastrous new acronym *NASI*.

And then there was the director of the TIA program, chosen with the tact and savvy DARPA had made its very own: Admiral John Poindexter. As national-security adviser to Ronald Reagan in 1985 and 1986,

Poindexter had been a key figure in the Iran-contra scandal, in which the Reagan administration secretly sold arms to Iran and diverted the profits to help rebels in Nicaragua. (It was Poindexter himself who reportedly came to the Department of Defense with the idea for TIA, shortly after September 11.) The man at whose fingertips DARPA chose to place the personal secrets and information of all American citizens had been convicted in 1990 of five felony counts of lying to Congress, destroying official documents, and obstructing Congress's inquiry into Iran-contra. Those convictions were ultimately overturned—because testimony was used against Poindexter at trial that he had given Congress under a grant of immunity—but the taint of Iran-contra clung to him nevertheless, stale as cigar smoke, and should have rendered him unemployable on any high-profile government project, let alone one so apparently prone to abuse.

It's hard to tell which was the final straw, but the combination of the program, the name, the symbol, and the director struck a nerve with the public, particularly the Web-savvy public, and before long Poindexter found that venturing into the waters of secrecy and privacy can make for a treacherous crossing. On November 27, 2002, Matt Smith, a columnist for *SF Weekly*, an alternative newspaper in San Francisco, wrote about TIA. There was nothing unusual in this. DARPA's clumsiness and the program's ambitions had raised the ire of journalists and columnists all over the country, including William Safire, the conservative columnist in *The New York Times* and a strange bedfellow indeed for the privacy advocates and "hacktivists" who had led the outcry.

But Smith's column was different. He started out by lamenting the emergence of TIA and wondering to what uses this powerful new database would be put. Then he changed course, "Optimistically, I dialed John and Linda Poindexter's number—(301) 424-6613—at their home at 10 Barrington Fare in Rockville, Md., hoping the good admiral and excused criminal might be able to offer some insight. A pleasant-sounding woman I think might have been Linda, the former Episcopal priest and now effusive Catholic, answered the phone."

Smith's point was hard to ignore: what happens when the tables turn? The information he gathered was all publicly available. He had simply been resourceful enough to see what he—one journalist, without the formidable resources of DARPA at his disposal—could gather. And he was able to gather a great deal. "Why," the column continued, "is their $269,700 Rockville, Md., house covered with artificial siding, according to Maryland tax records? Shouldn't a Reagan conspirator be able to afford repainting every seven years? Is the Donald Douglas Poindexter listed in Maryland sex-offender records any relation to the good admiral? What do Tom Maxwell, at 8 Barrington Fare, and James Galvin, at 12 Barrington Fare, think of their spooky neighbor?"

Reading the column generated a strange mix of feelings in me. On the one hand, I felt a terrific excitement, the warm glow of vindication in watching the mighty brought down. On the other hand, this information was all so readily available that it was unsettling to think how much more can be obtained through TIA and programs like it. And finally, there was a Wizard of Oz sensation. Without the mystique of secrecy, even the supposedly all-powerful doyens of the surveillance establishment were exposed as ordinary people, living in houses with artificial siding.

Smith was well aware of this and decided to turn the screws, urging his readers

> to embark on a . . . campaign of social impropriety: Call Poindexter's home number, all of you, several times a day. If you get Linda, ask about her conversion from Episcopal priesthood to Catholicism; if you get John, ask why he needs our tollbooth records. For those of you revolutionaries with private investigator friends, ask for even more sensitive information on Reagan's former national security adviser. I'd be glad to publish anything readers can convincingly claim to have obtained legally.

What followed was a full-fledged assault on the Poindexter clan. Smith may not have appreciated quite how rich was the vein he was tapping into. He told me recently that his column does not generally deal with technology or civil liberties and that he had been on deadline on a Friday night and unhappy with another column he'd been planning when a friend suggested he write about Poindexter. Within days, however, Smith's call to arms had raced around the country and the world; and it goes without saying, the telephone at 10 Barrington Fare was ringing off the hook. Almost immediately, the Poindexters disconnected the line.

At about the same time, the TIA website, which had been surprisingly forthright in explaining what the DARPA program was designed to do, began, like a photograph left out in the light, to fade. It started with the career biographies of Poindexter and several other leaders of the program, which had vanished from the site a few days before

Smith's column ran. Then the TIA logo and motto disappeared, as did a series of links. This practice became so common in the Bush administration that *The Washington Post* gave it a name: Web scrubbing. Steven Aftergood had imparted an important lesson when I spoke with him: if you see something interesting online, always print it out, because it won't necessarily be there tomorrow. Of course, DARPA should have known better than to treat the Internet as such an impermanent medium. In the end, the agency was hoisted on its own petard. Noticing that the site was withering away, some shrewd watcher resurrected the vanished files from Google's cached version of the DARPA home page and created what is known as a mirror site, which would keep track of everything DARPA erased.

In the wake of the Smith column, John Gilmore, a cofounder of the Electronic Frontier Foundation in San Francisco, wrote a widely circulated essay that urged readers to go beyond even Smith's mandate. Gilmore's suggestion was that Poindexter himself should serve as the guinea pig for this type of surveillance, that the Poindexter family could be a test case. "Photographs and videos of the target, their house, car, family, and associates, can be made and circulated to demonstrate facial recognition techniques," he suggested. "Employees at various businesses . . . could demonstrate denial of service to such targeted people." Gilmore made no effort to mask the horror of this kind of tactic and sought to emphasize and exaggerate the invasiveness inherent in depriving an individual of his anonymity. "This is how TIA is intended to work," he pointed out. "The government would get privileged access to all these databases, access that the rest of us do not normally have." Before long, a new website, the John Poindexter Awareness Office, had sprung up. "If you are a store clerk, study the photos above. Learn this face. If you are a shipping clerk, study this name," the site directed. "When and if you see Mr. Poindexter purchase something, travel somewhere or do, well, anything—send us a tip describing your observations. We will display the information received right here on this Web site."

While I was encouraged by this kind of activism, I nevertheless felt that these guerrilla tactics somehow missed the point. One undercurrent that ran though the whole exchange was a strange twinness that I had noticed in many of the activists I talked to. Those who are most strenuously opposed to a very strong government surveillance power often also seem to be the most titillated by its possibilities. Karl Kraus once said of psychoanalysis that it was a symptom of the disease of which it was meant to be the cure. The assault on Poindexter and his family seemed like a similar misprescription. Alistair Harley had demonstrated for me the porous nature of online security with a strange mix of horror and voyeuristic satisfaction. The same concoction was present in the handling of Poindexter and his family. It was difficult to determine where a pragmatic resistance that objected to these kinds of powers ended, and an emotional and voyeuristic loathing for Poindexter and everything he stood for took over.

An argument could be made that Poindexter chose this rather sinister line of work and thus deserved this treatment. But it seems to me that there is no similar justification for Gilmore's decision to one-up Smith by publishing the phone numbers of Poindexter's neighbors. And yet, the activists had the last laugh. During the summer of 2003, it was quietly announced that John Poindexter would be ending his association with DARPA. The precipitating incident was not TIA but another Poindexter proposal, this one for a futures market in terrorism— essentially an online betting parlor in which customers could put money on the odds of possible terrorist attacks. Asked about Poindexter's dismissal, a Pentagon official said, "It's difficult for any work that he might be associated with to receive a dispassionate hearing." The official described the programs developed under Poindexter's leadership as "cutting edge," then added, "and beyond that in some cases perhaps."

"AS A MATTER OF course I don't publish home addresses or private phone numbers—just because there are crackpots out there who will call every number they see," Aftergood told me. He said he was pleased that Poindexter became a lightning rod for public attention but that he regrets that Poindexter "became the issue the way that he did, because it trivialized the larger policy debate." In early 2003, an amendment to an appropriations bill sponsored by Senator Ron Wyden, Democrat of Oregon, held up funding for TIA until the Pentagon was able to explain the program in detail to Congress, and barred any use of it on U.S. citizens without prior congressional approval. Still, Aftergood is quick to point out that "TIA goes on in different forms, and we haven't developed the political tools to meaningfully discuss it and deal with it. It seems like a missed opportunity."

John Gilmore and his ilk are sort of the civil libertarian equivalent of DARPA—cutting-edge and beyond that in some cases perhaps. Like virtually everyone in the world of tech-savvy activists who congregate in the virtual communities of websites such as Politech and Cypherpunks, Gilmore has a fascinating story. He was the fifth employee at Sun Microsystems and retired a very wealthy man while still in his thirties. Since cofounding the Electronic Frontier Foundation, he has devoted himself to a distinctive brew of activism—one that is informed by a millennial paranoia and a deep understanding of computers and their implications but is also shot through with a sixties-era sense of play. He caused a small furor in the summer of 2003 when he was thrown off an airplane before takeoff for wearing a pin that said "Suspected Terrorist." He has not flown since, in protest, and currently has a lawsuit pending against the government, in which he is suing to be able to fly without presenting ID. Gilmore is on the fringes, but along this particular fringe he exerts a distinct influence.

He is joined by the likes of John Young, the editor of the website Cryptome, who is, to put it mildly, another character. A cantankerous, bespectacled New York architect in his sixties, Young took a sideline interest in military affairs and secrecy and turned it into Cryptome in 1996. As its name suggests, the site is interested in cryptography issues, but it is also a tome, a library—a life's work. Young has put up thousands of files over the years, including large amounts of classified military and intelligence material and has generally made a habit of publishing what Aftergood will not. Most controversial of Young's projects has been the "eyeballing" series, in which Young uploads aerial photos he has taken from commercial satellites. You can imagine the frustration of the Pentagon when various secret intelligence and nuclear installations, hidden on remote islands or in deep forests, are suddenly revealed to the world in high-resolution, full color aerial photos on Young's site. When the TIA affair blew up and Gilmore distributed the telephone numbers of Poindexter's next-door neighbors, Young was happy to oblige with a satellite photo of the admiral's house.

When he is not posting classified documents and satellite photos, Young works as an architect; over the years he has taught at Columbia and been involved in a number of high-profile projects, from a media center for the Council on Foreign Relations to an apartment for the actor Raul Julia to—incredibly—the new headquarters of the secretive Catholic organization and conspiracy-theorist favorite, Opus Dei.

Young has not, thus far, been served with a court order to take any documents off of Cryptome. He was visited by the FBI, however, when two agents dropped by his Upper West Side apartment in the fall of

2003. Demonstrating the same desire to *name* the authority figures, to exert some autonomy by watching the watcher, Young scrutinized the agents' ID badges and told them that he would publish their names on his website and make them famous. "Really," one of the agents smiled, "I haven't heard that before."

"I RESPECT THE WORK of John Young at Cryptome," Steven Aftergood told me. "But I would not do all the things he does. I would not publish overhead pictures of where does Ambassador Wilson live, where does George Tenet live. I wouldn't do that."

I was troubled that those speaking out about TIA and programs like it seemed to have yielded the resistance to the kooky fringe. Why was there not more agitation on the part of the broader public? And wouldn't the antics of a John Gilmore or a John Young only undermine the possibility of any mainstream support for greater transparency? I told Aftergood that while many of the people I'd been speaking with seemed extremely paranoid and distrustful of government to a fault, my sense was that these individuals formed a marginal subset of the population and that most Americans were much more ready to take for granted the entitlements of being an American citizen and not worry so much about issues of privacy and secrecy, openness and accountability. My hunch is that most people walk around every day with a great deal of trust. They may not mind if the government *can* read their e-mail, because they trust that it won't. Or they may not mind that the government *does* read their e-mail, because they trust that the government will not do anything wrong with it.

In perfect-paragraph form, Aftergood agreed.

In the past decade, more than a billion—with a *b*—pages of historically valuable documents have been declassified at the National Archives. And most of them have gone unreviewed by members of the public, including myself. Part of the sense of trust that most of us feel is predicated, consciously or unconsciously, on the notion that if something went wrong, we would find out about it. In other words, I don't personally have to go and take meat samples at the market searching for mad-cow disease, because I have confidence that somebody somewhere will be looking for it, and if it's there they will find it. Similarly, I have confidence that somebody somewhere will find out if the intelligence agencies are running amok, or if the SEC is doing or not doing something improper, and so on. That tacit trust is predicated on access to information. When information becomes inaccessible, the ability of that someone somewhere to detect what is going wrong is eliminated altogether. So if you ask me if I have read the latest bulletin on Social Security the answer is hell no, I have no intention of doing so. But I am hopeful that some public-interest group or reporter or somebody somewhere either has or will. If that information is taken out of the realm of public access, then my trust won't go away immediately because I won't know about it, but the *basis* for my trust will have vanished. And the consequences will follow somewhere down the line.

At one point Aftergood told me, "I'm not some high-powered reporter with *The Washington Post*, I'm just a guy with a little newsletter." He is anything but. He is the proxy that is watching out for the things you should be, he is the basis of the trust with which you go about your day-to-day business—in a very real sense, this unassuming guy in the ratty chair in a drab and anonymous office is an advocate for us all.

GOLIATH PROTESTS

Making Sense of Signals

ON JANUARY 24, 2000, at around seven o'clock in the evening, the central network of the NSA at Fort Meade suddenly and inexplicably shut down. For the next seventy-two hours, there was a virtual blackout on intelligence gathering while technicians struggled to get the colossus going again. The UKUSA relationship being what it is, Britain's GCHQ and the other partner agencies sprang into action to cover for the faltering system. Eventually the NSA was able to restore operations, but only after thousands of man hours and $1.5 million had been devoted to solving the problem. In keeping with the agency's policy of maintaining a tight lid on things, Americans learned of the shutdown only long after it was over.

It turned out that a software anomaly was to blame for the blackout and that the outdated communications infrastructure at Fort Meade had failed, preventing the agency from processing or forwarding any intelligence data or even from communicating internally. Oddly, observers of the American intelligence community were not altogether surprised. After all, it was not outside the realm of possibility that at some point the great listening machine would just gag on the sheer quantity it was taking in. In those seventy-two hours, it appeared that the Echelon system's eyes were bigger than its stomach.

The life of an intelligence agency tends to adhere to the well-worn rhythms of something known as "the intelligence cycle." This cycle is simply a diagrammatic means of conceptualizing the work of intelligence, but it has become a boilerplate idea in the profession and today governs the operating procedures of Sigint and Humint agencies alike. The cycle starts with planning and target selection, which then leads naturally to collection of raw intelligence. Next, the collected intelligence goes through processing, then analysis and production of finished intelligence reports, and ultimately distribution to interested parties, before starting back at the planning stage again. What the blackout at the NSA demonstrated was that at a certain point, far from being mutually compatible and reinforcing segments of the same organic cycle, intelligence collection and intelligence production are at cross-purposes. The principle is so simple it should almost go without saying: the more you collect, the more difficult it is to make any sense of what you have collected. In July 1999, Bob Kerrey, then the ranking Democrat on the Senate Intelligence Oversight Committee, said in a speech on the Senate floor that the problem was not only the difficulty of finding a needle in the haystack but that "the haystack is getting larger and larger and harder to search." Hence the bravado with which, in the late 1990s, Osama Bin Laden occasionally talked on an unencrypted telephone—he recognized that there is so much chatter out there that he might just go unnoticed. "The whole world is wired now," one Pentagon official told me. "And that has constipative effects."

This is the emerging paradox of signals intelligence. The better you are at collection, the harder it will be to do good production. The image that is usually invoked when discussing the Echelon network is that of a vacuum cleaner—a giant ear that indiscriminately sucks up everything it can. The challenge faced by the NSA, GCHQ, and the other Echelon agencies is that they have on their hands a clumsy and colossal Hoover, when what they really want is something more akin to the baleen of a whale. Baleen whales take in huge gulps of seawater but immediately push the water back out into the sea, straining it through a fine filter that catches the plankton and other microscopic crustaceans on which they feed. Intelligence agencies, unfortunately, lack such a fine-tuned apparatus.

IT IS ONE OF the peculiarities of the history of the NSA that when the agency finally began to show its face to the public—during the tenure of Director Michael V. Hayden, in the late 1990s—it did not show its brave face. On the contrary, the public image that the agency began to put forward at the turn of the new century was one of profound weakness. Hayden has an open, friendly face, and from the moment early in his tenure when he announced "A Hundred Days of Change" he aimed to tackle one of the anomalies of America's Sigint apparatus: the fact that despite the NSA's role as an agency of the future, with one eye always on emergent technologies, it is also hopelessly attached to tradition. Decades of insularity and secretive success at the NSA are widely thought to have bred a culture of institutional arrogance, an attachment to outmoded technologies and procedures, and a refusal to take any lessons from the outside world. Hayden seemed to recognize this. He took to the job with a conviction that the agency needed to change, and that if change meant opening up a little, then so be it. Hayden, after all, was an unusual man for the job. While he is a lieutenant general in the air force and has had a long and distinguished military career, he also holds a master's degree in American history. Far from exhibiting the blanket distrust of the media that so characterized his predecessors, Hayden actually seemed to court the press. An apt illustration of the changing face of the agency is the career of James Bamford, the foremost chronicler of the NSA. When Bamford was writing his first book, *The Puzzle Palace,* in the early 1980s, the agency did everything it could to thwart his efforts along the way, denying him access and even threatening legal action. When he published a follow-up book, *Body of Secrets,* in 2001, it featured an extensive interview with Hayden, and the book party was thrown, at Hayden's invitation, at Fort Meade. Wayne Madsen, a former NSA employee who now works for the Electronic Privacy Information Center, had trouble explaining to me just how different Hayden was from the old guard. "He might be a *Democrat* for all we know," Madsen sputtered. "He's from Pittsburgh. And that's a pretty Democratic city."

Hayden presided over a period of openness like none the agency had ever seen. But the leitmotif of his various appearances and statements for the record was that the agency was in grave trouble, because it lagged behind the technological curve. Less than a month after the January 2000 blackout, Hayden gave a talk at American University in which he addressed the problems of the NSA in light of the sheer proliferation of electronic communications and the extent to which the shutdown was in part a symptom of the agency's failure to keep up. "Forty years ago there were 5,000 stand-alone computers, no fax machines and not one cellular phone," Hayden pointed out.

Today, there are over 180 million computers—most of them networked. There are roughly 14 million fax machines and 40 million cell phones. And those numbers continue to grow. The telecommunications industry is making a $1 trillion investment to encircle the world in millions and millions of high bandwidth fiber optic cable.

They are aggressively investing in the future. . . . So far, the National Security Agency is lagging behind.

This was an important and increasingly undeniable point. While traditionally the NSA had been a decade or so ahead of any type of private research and development in communications technology, that gap had narrowed considerably with the digital and dot-com revolutions of the eighties and nineties. And as Hayden was all too keenly aware, this narrowing of the margin was something the NSA could ill afford. "For others, technology is an enabler. It's an investment that makes their jobs easier," he said. "For NSA, technology is the foundation upon which all of our processes rest; it is not an option."

By the late nineties, a series of news reports in Europe and the launching of the Temporary Committee on the Echelon Interception System in the European Parliament had fueled widespread public distrust of the NSA and GCHQ and ignited a host of allegations and speculations. While Americans may have been oblivious to the uproar over Echelon in Europe, Mike Hayden most certainly was not. He was aware that in Brussels and Strasbourg a public-relations debacle was brewing. The German government, suspicious of any intelligence alliance that could supersede NATO, was pressuring the United States to close the cold-war listening station at Bad Aibling, saying effectively, Not in our backyard. The European press was engaged in daily bouts of alarmism about the growing surveillance powers of the NSA and its partner agencies. *The Guardian* ran an article titled "Big Brother Echelon," while *Le Monde diplomatique* warned of the all-hearing "*Grandes Oreilles Américaines.*" While these particulars may have been little known in the United States, the theme of an omnipotent and omniscient NSA was quite familiar. Tony Scott's paranoid thriller *Enemy of the State* had recently been a big hit. In that film, the agency was portrayed as a stupendously powerful dark force that could reposition satellites to track civilians at a moment's notice, in the interests of propagating and covering up various heinous acts of treason. When Hayden started speaking out, it is fair to say, the agency had an image problem.

And what Hayden did was to thoroughly confuse that problem. In no time at all, the agency's image issue was strangely twofold. While on the one hand there was this idea of the NSA as arch-eavesdropper, able to home in on single individuals and call up their current communications, their credit-card history, their every liaison and sordid affair, there was now another thrust, which was suggesting that the agency was not so powerful after all. This view held that strong cryptography, the Internet, and the increasing shift of communications from airborne channels to fiber-optic cables were all working together to undermine the agency's success.

Hayden had some help in advancing his point of view. The investigative journalist Seymour M. Hersh has had a long career as a thorn in the side of the American military and intelligence communities. From early articles in which he broke the story of the My Lai massacre in Vietnam to a series of articles in the spring of 2004 in which he revealed the mistreatment of prisoners at Abu Ghraib prison outside of Baghdad, Hersh has consistently taken evident pleasure in muckraking and catching the authorities unaware, exposing them at their most corrupt and inept. So one wonders how those at the NSA received a 1999 article by Hersh in *The New Yorker* that took the agency's technical capabilities head-on. The article was called "The Intelligence Gap," and Hersh opened it with a characteristically declarative salvo: "The National Security Agency, whose Cold War research into code breaking and electronic eavesdropping spurred the American computer revolution, has become a victim of the high-tech world it helped to create." Hersh cited the failure to foresee India's May 1998 nuclear tests as an instance in which the agency was outdone by the profusion of fiber-optic cables and encryption.

When it comes to this kind of news coverage, a Hersh story is sui generis. Over the years he has developed a formidable stable of reliable sources, almost none of whom will agree to go on the record. It is speculated that Hersh targets midlevel bureaucrats who are frustrated by the system and relish the opportunity to take potshots at their superiors from behind the veil of anonymity. Hersh managed to interview some two dozen "signals intelligence experts" for his article, an impressive number by any measure. The conclusion he came to was that due to bureaucratic inertia and internal mismanagement, a brain drain to outside industry, and the development of strong cryptography, the agency was falling behind in its grasp of new technologies. In particular, Hersh pointed out that "the vast majority of telephone calls, E-mails, and faxes are not encrypted—almost all are sent as plain text—but the NSA has been overwhelmed by the sheer volume of the intercepted data, much of which is irrelevant." The article briefly discussed the Echelon system, confirming that the agency does routinely collect vast amounts of data and that it is capable of targeting an individual telephone line or computer terminal on the other side of the planet. But, Hersh cautioned, "active and retired NSA officials have repeatedly told me that the agency does not have the software to make sense out of more than a tiny fraction of the huge array of random communications that are collected."

The problem with a Hersh article—and more generally with coverage based on any kind of anonymous leak—is that one never knows to what extent the leak is on or off message. One cannot help but notice that in this instance Hersh was for all intents and purposes parroting the director of the NSA. To his credit, Hersh seemed aware of this, and quoted Whitfield Diffie, one of the pioneers of modern cryptography, who now works at Sun Microsystems, speculating that the whole thing might be a ruse. "What bothers me is that you are saying what the agency *wants* us to believe—they used to be great, but these days they have trouble reading the newspaper, the Internet is too complicated for them, there is so much traffic and they can't find what they want. It *may* be true, but it is what they have been 'saying' for years," Diffie said. "It's convenient for NSA to have its targets believe it is in trouble. That doesn't mean it isn't in trouble, but it is a reason to view what spooky inside informants say with skepticism."

Still, Hayden and Hersh were not the only voices in the chorus. At a lunch of retired CIA officers in October 1998, John Millis, the forty-seven-year-old staff director of the House Intelligence Oversight Committee and himself a former CIA operations officer, talked frankly about the problems facing the NSA. Millis was a last-minute replacement at the lunch. (His boss, Representative Porter Goss, the Florida congressman and former CIA officer who was chairman of the committee until being appointed head of the CIA by George W. Bush, had been scheduled to speak.) This might explain the tremendous candor with which Millis spoke. His prognosis was extremely grim, and he returned again and again to the theme that the intelligence community was in dire trouble. He complained about massive cost overruns at the National Reconnaissance Office to support satellite intelligence-collection programs. "We spent incredible amounts of money on overhead collection and it threatens to overwhelm the intelligence budget," he told the retirees.

We have already spent more than twice as much money on the NRO than on any other intelligence agency. You do both imagery and Sigint from satellites, but it doesn't make a lot of sense doing Sigint from there any more. . . . You shouldn't be spending one dollar more than we do to try and intercept communications, regular voice and data-type communications from space. But we do make that investment. This is something that we think that we have to move away from.

After reading a transcript of the lunch talk, I decided to look Millis up and see if he might elaborate on some of his views. But in the spring of 2000, less than a year after his lunch remarks, Millis was put on paid administrative leave by Goss. It has been speculated that he was also placed under investigation by the House committee, on suspicion of having leaked classified information. At a February 15, 2000, speech at the Smithsonian Institution, Millis had criticized former CIA director John Deutch, saying he was the worst director in the CIA's history and that he had inflicted "major damage" on the CIA's espionage branch. The criticism apparently prompted some officials to speculate that Millis may have improperly disclosed information about an investigation of Deutch by the CIA's inspector general. On June 4, Millis took his own life with a shotgun in a run-down motel in Fairfax, Virginia.

Even without Millis, however, there was no shortage of evidence to bolster the weak-NSA claim. In fact, the degree to which the NSA was lagging behind private industry was essentially conceded by the agency even before Hayden's arrival, when it allowed in members of the Technical Advisor Group (TAG). The TAG was set up in 1997 by senators Richard Shelby and Bob Kerrey. The group included a number of civilians from outside the agency—research-and-development experts from Microsoft, the Lawrence Livermore National Laboratory, and the Walt Disney Company. The group got full clearance at Fort Meade, which represented a considerable and perhaps slightly humbling lowering of the guard for the agency. You can imagine the disdain of agency oldtimers, still reliving the quiet success with which the NSA pulled this country through the cold war, when they had to unlock their doors and open their files to a man who works for Walt Disney. And the TAG report was unsparing. It held, among other things, that "declining budgets and obsolete equipment are impeding NSA's ability to maintain their technical edge," and "advanced research and development must receive greater emphasis and more funding." One official involved told Hersh that the TAG members informed the NSA, "unless you totally change your intelligence-collection systems you will go deaf."

WHILE THE KIND OF access to the internal workings that the TAG representatives enjoyed is highly unusual, we do, as it happens, know a good deal about the manner in which signals intelligence processing and production work. The very name *Echelon* refers to a particular type of computer that is used to sort through large amounts of data for items on a given watch list. The watch list is the fundamental conceptual tool used by the UKUSA agencies to wade through the streams of communications they intercept. The systematic use of these lists dates back to the 1960s and 1970s. But even before that, indeed, at the advent of the UKUSA alliance, there was an understanding that each partner agency would be familiar with individuals and areas that were of importance to the other partner agencies and would make any relevant intelligence available to them. By the seventies, with the early-model Intelsat birds being launched and the volume and speed of communications increasing by orders of magnitude, it became clear to the UKUSA agencies that the bulk of messages would be too formidable to process manually. According to former NSA employees, it was at this point that the first Echelon computers were used to automate the process.

As the technology developed and it became possible to automate searches, the five partner agencies established a practice that endures to this day. Each agency is in possession of a list of targets from each of the other agencies. These lists are collated into a distribution catalog. Some of the subject categories in the catalog—say, anything relating to North Korea's nuclear program—are designated for distribution to hundreds of recipients, from organizations such as NATO command down to individual intelligence officers in an American embassy.

This swift and intricate process is referred to as "churning" and is performed by the devices that give the whole network its name: the Echelon Dictionaries. For each target of interest, there will be a series of red flags: names, addresses, telephone numbers, Internet addresses, aliases, affiliates, and so forth. For a given category of target there might be anywhere from ten to fifty such red flags. Each Echelon Dictionary computer holds a vast database of these words and numbers and works like a search engine, sorting for matches. The process is more complex and discerning than a simple word-recognition program: an Echelon Dictionary can be programmed to identify particular patterns of words or to search for a word but exclude messages in which that word is used in combination with another. When a message is intercepted, it is automatically run through this bevy of criteria, and if a match of any sort is found the message is forwarded for further analysis. The lists of keywords are maintained and updated locally by employees known as dictionary managers. But the whole process is centralized and tends to take its lead from the NSA. The agency compiles, supplies, and updates a digest of intelligence targets from all over the world. The code name for this digest is Texta.

When an intercepted message has been processed for forwarding to an analyst, the computer marks it with a three- or four-digit code for the category of intelligence it represents. So, even in the individual databases of the various agencies, all intelligence on a given target can be quickly retrieved by searching by number. Thus, for example, during the 1980s the NSA intercepted and processed traffic designated FRD (French diplomatic) at its bases in England, while GCHQ deciphered ITD (Italian diplomatic) messages in Cheltenham. The process is entirely automated; the dictionary managers are there just to maintain the system. By the time the computer actually spits out a piece of raw intelligence for a human analyst or translator to toil over, a great deal of analysis has already been done.

For the actual human analysts, the work of doing the listening, watching the messages, and preparing the reports is routine and often boring, but not without moments of great excitement. Everette Jordan, an African American linguist in his late forties, was based at Fort Meade for two decades. Jordan was a full-time listener. In high school, he had no trouble learning French and Spanish, and when he was posted to Germany in the army, he tackled German and Russian. He started work for the NSA in 1982 and was a frontline translator, listening through headphones to Soviet military officers discussing their work and their lives. In 1990, Jordan took up Arabic, his linguistic energies shadowing larger geopolitical trends. Throughout the nineties, he reported to Fort Meade every day, put on headphones, and listened to tapes of other people's conversations, just as Katharine Gun was to do at GCHQ. As Jordan listened, he translated, and this was no simple task. "You have to listen for irony, for sarcasm, for tension," he explains. "You have to listen for rhetorical statements being made. You also have to listen for humor." Jordan insists that while many of the conversations he listened to were run-of-the-mill, he was persuaded to continue because over the years he had heard conversations that were of vital significance to national security. "One of the fun things about being a linguist is knowing that the work you have done has gone right downtown to the President of the United States or the United States Congress," he says. Not every analyst is so enthusiastic. Much of the listening at GCSB stations in New Zealand has traditionally been monitoring communications among long-haul Russian fishing trawlers. A former analyst from New Zealand told Nicky Hager, the author of the book *Secret Power*, "It was like being on an assembly line, you put in your bit and then it went on to someone else. There was no sense of influencing the job. You just reported what was put on your desk."

To get a better sense of the experience of listening in, I contacted Michael Erskine. Erskine worked in a variety of roles for E-Systems, as a contract employee for the NSA, and in this capacity he did spells as a linguist, a traffic analyst, and a cryptanalyst. He described a linguist's life as "periods of intense boredom interspersed with moments of sheer terror." There is "a very heavy weight of responsibility knowing that you might miss something you should have heard," Erskine told me. "An intercept operator is the point of contact with the target. His task is to give the 'first alert.' . . . If he has a difficult language (e.g. Korean, Russian, Chinese, Arabic) he lives with the knowledge that he can't understand everything he hears all the time."

A traffic analyst is a slightly different position, monitoring the traffic that comes in for various patterns. In this case, Erskine said, the experience involves "long hours of drudgery, sorting, re-sorting, identifying, and filing voluminous sets of data. Worrying that you might fail to notice something you should have reported. You know that you are the one person on the team who can give a heads up to everyone else far enough in advance that your linguists might not be caught sleeping." He explained that as a traffic analyst you have two nagging fears: "The constant concern that your 'lingies' are non-native speakers who might fail to translate something correctly and preclude your noticing that tell-tale clue," and "the worry that you might fail to notify the cryppies of something which wasn't 'practice' after all."

The "cryppies" are the cryptanalysts, who are charged with breaking the codes of anything that comes in encrypted. "This guy is the 'computer cracker' of the Comint business," Erskine told me. "He fancies himself the smartest of them all. He lives for the *Ah Ha!* moment, the instant when he becomes certain he has broken into a system. Having done it once or twice, I can say with confidence, there is nothing like the feeling you get when you know you have the enemy by the proverbials."

While each discipline is different, Erskine told me that they all share one common anxiety: "You fear discovery. What you do absolutely has to be done in secret because you have no control over your intelligence source. The target controls the ON-OFF button and he controls what you hear. If he knows you are listening, he can stop talking or worse, he can just tell you a bunch of lies." When I asked Erskine about how the machines themselves work, how it is that the agency goes about sorting the wheat from the chaff, he was reluctant to get into the details. I was relieved by his reserve—nothing bespeaks authenticity like a refusal to talk. But just to be sure, I pushed him by asking again. Erskine opted to answer with an illustration. "Go to Google and play with the advanced features of its search engine," he told me. "Then imagine what kinds of things you might do to make it even better. Then spend twenty years refining it."

One of the questions I had was about how effective the Echelon Dictionaries and other programs like them are at sorting through *voice* recording. Text-based messages are the easiest to process, because there is already a solid foundation of technologies for sorting them. But what about voice recordings? According to Mike Frost, the former CSE spy, as far back as the 1970s the NSA was using a program called Oratory that was able to sort through spoken communications. "It didn't matter if the intercept was voice, Fax, or teletype," Frost maintains. "Oratory selected only what CSE wanted to see or hear." In fact, it is this sort of claim, and one story on this particular subject, that have led many to question Frost's credibility. In February 2000, Frost was interviewed about Echelon on *60 Minutes II*. To illustrate the manner in which keywords operate, he related an episode that he claimed occurred while he was working at CSE. "A lady had been to a school play the night before, and her son was in the school play and she thought he did a lousy job," Frost explained.

> Next morning, she was talking on the telephone to her friend, and she said to her friend something like this, "Oh, Danny really bombed last night," just like that. The computer spit that conversation out. The analyst that was looking at it was not too sure about what the conversation was referring to, so erring on the side of caution, he listed that lady and her phone number in the database as a possible terrorist.

Something about the folksy simplicity of this episode rings untrue, and a number of former intelligence officers I spoke with raised a skeptical eyebrow when I recounted it. Moreover, one of the interesting features of the European Parliament reports on Echelon is that they directly refuted this sort of claim. "The processing of telephone calls is mainly limited to identifying call-related information, and traffic analysis," one report held. "Effective voice 'wordspotting' systems do not exist and are not in use, despite reports to the contrary." Moreover, when in 1993 former NSA director Bobby Ray Inman was asked about technologies that allow for word spotting in speech, he replied, "I have wasted more U.S. taxpayer dollars trying to do that than [on] anything else in my intelligence career."

Still, the systems are always evolving. At some point, the Echelon program was updated with a successor program, Echelon II. In his report to the European Parliament, Duncan Campbell stated that "documents show that when the Silkworth processing system was installed at Menwith Hill for the new satellites, it was supported by Echelon 2 and other databanks." While Echelon II would seem to be as secret, if not more so, than the original program, I was surprised to find a reference to it in the publicly available career history of one of its architects, Bruce McIndoe. McIndoe is now the head of a private organization called iJET, a consultancy that advises executives on security for business travel. On iJET's website, McIndoe's career biography explained that he had worked as a contractor for the NSA and that "Bruce was one of the lead architects for the National Security Agency's Echelon II program, identified as one of the most productive programs in the agency's history." In the spring of 2002, Kenan Seeberg and Bo "Skipper" Elkjaer, two journalists at the Danish tabloid *Ekstra Bladet,* found McIndoe's site and got in touch. Kenan and Skipper are an oddball pair of journalists who have written more than two hundred articles on Echelon and whom I got to know on a trip to Copenhagen. In their article, they quote McIndoe as saying that Echelon II was designed because "Echelon has existed for a long time, as you know, and they needed to update the system. . . . Echelon II is the successor, so to speak, of the original Echelon system."

Hoping for a followup interview, I contacted McIndoe at iJET myself. In my first e-mails to him, I mentioned that I had read the interview by the Danes and that I knew them. This was, as it turns out, a mistake. When he did reply to me, McIndoe said that he was not at all happy with the way that interview had come out and that he felt that they had taken some liberties with his comments. After kicking myself for having so oafishly dropped their names in the first place, I replied that this might be an opportunity for McIndoe to set the record straight. McIndoe stonewalled and said that he felt no need to correct anything. I wrote back again, emboldened and obnoxious, inquiring whether he had Googled himself lately, pointing out that five or six of the first ten hits that come up are links to the interview that he now wanted to disown. Again, I asked if he could at the very least tell me what was incorrect in the interview. No dice. Another dead end. It seemed enough at the time that McIndoe had not altered or removed the reference to Echelon II on his company's website: a validation of the code name, if nothing else. But when I checked back at the site a week after our last exchange, the reference to Echelon was gone.

HAVING FOUND LITTLE SUCCESS in getting people to talk to me about the inner workings of the Echelon system, I stumbled upon a vast cache of information on precisely this subject in an unlikely place—the website of the U.S. Patent and Trademark Office. The devil's bargain at the heart of patent law is that in order to obtain the right to patent a particular invention, the inventor must divulge its details to the public. For most of its history, this was no attractive option for the NSA. The agency existed at the very crest of technological discovery and was light-years ahead of consumer research and development in the fields of telecommunications and cryptography. As such, there was no need to file a patent. But gradually, that calculation changed. As private research improved in the 1980s, the NSA began to lose some of its edge. Rather than having to compete with the outdated research operations of a waning Soviet empire, the agency was being undermined by the quick and fluid telecommunications industry of its own country. In February 2001, Mike Hayden complained, "Osama Bin Laden has at his disposal the wealth of a $3 trillion a year telecommunications industry that he can rely on." And so, eventually, the agency started filing for patents. A few drops in the seventies became a trickle in the eighties and a gush in the nineties, and over the course of the last thirty years the NSA proceeded to obtain more than two hundred patents.

No official from any of the UKUSA countries has publicly confirmed or denied that they use Echelon Dictionaries to sort through the deluge of signals. But it takes very little sleuthing to browse through U.S. patent 6,169,969, for a "device and method for full-text large-dictionary string matching." The patent was received on January 2, 2001. The inventor who developed the device for the agency is Jonathan Drew Cohen, of Hanover, Maryland. The patent states that the invention is designed to assist in "locating all keyword occurrences" in a given set of documents. It then proceeds to confirm more or less precisely what we know of the dictionary system. "In advance of processing any text, words of interest are compiled in a 'dictionary,' " it says. "Each text sample is then processed by consulting the dictionary, looking for matches between dictionary words and substrings of the text." The patent specifies that "for simplicity, these arbitrary dictionary entries are termed 'keywords,' " and that the invention is able to work extremely quickly with an extremely long watch list of keywords. "Dictionaries need to accommodate tens of thousands to hundreds of thousands of keywords. The scanning is to be performed at current digital data rates— on the order of tens of megabytes per second or more."

Because the various signals-collection devices employed by the UKUSA countries tend toward broad and undiscriminating collection, it might be useful to sort out what kind of signals are being gathered. We know, for instance, that when an antenna is positioned to intercept communications coming from a new satellite, it will initially also intercept signals for television or other useless communications but will then be reoriented to weed those signals out. To this end, another interesting invention was patented by the NSA in November 1999, after being invented by Richard Allen Shaner of Seabrook, Maryland. The patent spells out the challenge quite clearly:

> The amount of data being transmitted electronically is ever increasing. Electronic data may be in any language, may have been generated using any type of word-processor, may or may not be in a format that can be executed by a computer, may be uncompressed or compressed using any type of compression scheme, and so on. To automatically process electronic data properly, a truly automated data processing system must be able to identify the type of data contained in a received electronic file.

In order to meet this challenge, Shaner's invention will "automatically identify the type of data contained in an electronic file . . . automatically identify the language used in an electronic file," and "automatically identify the type of wordprocessor used to create an electronic file."

As for speech searches, an NSA patent from 1999 explains that identifying words or topics in speech "has been an area of growing interest," but that it is a challenge "since much of the information conveyed in speech is never actually spoken and since utterances frequently are less coherent than written language." This problem, while clearly a major concern for the NSA, appears to remain largely unresolved.

One logical way of sorting through intercepts would be to attempt to isolate material that is encrypted. After all, who would encrypt if they didn't have something to hide? Might this not be one useful means of culling intercepts that might have some intelligence value? In November 2000, the NSA patented a method of distinguishing "between normal text (natural language) and non-text (files of any type not containing natural language) messages." The patent explains that the method aims to distinguish any "electronic message which is not normal text," such as "program code, images, data, encrypted messages, etc."

A perusal of the patents indicates that even steganography—the practice of implanting an encrypted message in an innocuous-looking image on, say, a website—is not going unpursued in the labs at Fort Meade. Terrorists have been known to implant a whole text message into one picture or letter on a random website, which their allies can then extract by going to the website and using the appropriate key. But on February 11, 2003, a patent was obtained for a "method of extracting text present in a color image."

NEVERTHELESS, THERE ARE BILLIONS of websites, and it is unclear whether any computer, no matter how powerful, could possibly know in *which* image a steganographic message was implanted. For that kind of intelligence you likely need spies. It may be that the problems the NSA faces are technological, but couldn't it also be that these problems are being conceptualized in the wrong way? Because technology has always been what communications-intelligence agencies have excelled at, it seems natural that when they start to fail, they point a finger at technological failures. And it is no doubt true that the UKUSA agencies have become too good at collection at the expense of production. But couldn't it also be true that the solution lies in old-fashioned humans, either of the Humint variety—people out there on the ground gathering intelligence—or at the very least in the form of human analysts?

In 2002, Maureen Baginski, the NSA's director of Sigint, declared that agency employees need to be "hunters rather than gatherers." Currently, when Dictionary selects messages that might be of interest, the messages pass into the hands of a human analyst. If the message is worth reporting on, the analyst can work on it, translating it, either in its entirety or as a gist, then write it up in the standard intelligence-report format and distribute it within the network. The discretion exercised at this juncture is critical. The problem is that there are not enough of these analysts and not enough translators.

On September 10, 2001, the NSA intercepted two messages, both in Arabic, from Afghanistan to Saudi Arabia. While the speakers were not identified, the calls were picked up on the assumption that they were affiliated with Al Qaeda. One of the messages said, "The match begins tomorrow." The other said, "Tomorrow is zero hour." While in retrospect it seems irrefutable that the two messages were referring to the terrorist attacks of September 11, neither message was translated until September 12. To be sure, it is unlikely that intercepting and translating either message on time would have provided enough actionable intelligence to prevent the attacks the following day. But it is nevertheless a cautionary illustration of what can happen when the computers are left to operate without adequate human staff.

And in fact, this should not be in the least surprising. During the 1990s, the number of cellphones around the planet increased from 16 million to 741 million. Globally, Internet users went from about 4 million to about 361 million. Half as many landlines were laid in the last six years of the 1990s as in the whole previous history of the world. And international telephone traffic went from 38 billion minutes to over 100 billion. During this period of growth and ferment, the NSA cut its staff by roughly one third.

While the NSA's computers are very good at extracting communications from various targets and even at ranking those communications in order of urgency, that ranking depends only on the relative urgency assigned to the target. And that assignation is performed by a human. This is one of the interesting features of the two calls intercepted on September 10: it was not that they were not selected for analysis or selected and then thrown out. These two calls were flagged by the computers precisely because they were in some way affiliated with Al Qaeda, but the number of intercepted communications on that day *just from Al Qaeda* was so great that no human analyst got to the messages for forty-eight hours.

The episode also makes clear that analysts need to be very, very good. In October 2002, Hayden told the House and Senate intelligence committees:

Thousands of times a day, our front-line employees have to answer tough questions like: Who are the communicants? Do they seem knowledgeable? Where in the conversation do key words or phrases come? What is the reaction to these words? What world and cultural events may have shaped these words? . . . How much of the conversation is dominated by these events and are any of the phrases tied to them? And, if you were responsible for the management (and oversight) of NSA, you would have to ask other questions like: Where was the information collected? Were any of the communications targeted? How many calls a day are there from that location? In what languages? Hazar? Urdu? Pashto? Uzbek? Dari? Arabic? Is there a machine that can sort these out by language for you, or do you have to use a human? If there is such a machine, does it work in a polyglot place where one conversation often comprises several languages? How long does it take NSA to process this kind of material? (After all, we are not the intended recipients of these communications.) Does our current technology allow us to process it in a stream? Or do we have to do it in batches? When the data is processed, how do we review it? Oldest to newest, or newest first?

Clearly, computers themselves will not be able to make these nuanced distinctions and decisions, and for such a job experienced human analysts are absolutely essential. And yet, far from investing in these analysts and translators, in the years prior to September 11, the NSA downsized repeatedly. In a March 2002 speech, the associate director of human resources services for the NSA, Harvey A. Davis, conceded that "in the mid-1990's, NSA focused heavily on technology as the solution for many of its complex challenges. Facing massive technological advances, while downsizing and trying to maximize our return on investment, the Agency focused its hiring and development initiatives on computer science, engineering and mathematics at the expense of language and analysis."

LANGUAGE IN PARTICULAR HAS always dogged intelligence agents. The famous Navajo "code talkers" employed by the American military in the Second World War were not speaking in some memorized mathematical formula—they were speaking "code" only insofar as their own language was cryptic to those who did not speak it. It seems strange that while the technology of espionage has progressed to the point where satellites thousands of miles above the earth can take a clear photograph of a license plate in enemy territory, the challenges posed by the varieties of human speech have remained largely insurmountable. In 2002, the NSA made the rare move of publicly advertising for trained linguists, specifying which languages they wanted, and in so doing acknowledging a dire institutional weakness.

As an NSA Linguist, you will be involved in activities that focus on research translation, transcription, reporting, and analysis of materials of national concern. You may be involved in projects that have global ramifications. We are particularly interested in those individuals who are proficient in Asian, Middle Eastern, or Slavic languages. Although the Agency's language requirements may change at any time, we are currently hiring people with the following language skills:

> Amharic
> Arabic
> Chinese
> Dari
> Greek
> Pashto
> Persian-Farsi
> Somali
> Swahili
> Tagalog
> Tigrinya
> Turkmen
> Urdu/Punjabi
> Uzbek

Unfortunately for the agency, interest in learning foreign languages at the high school and college level in the United States has been on the decline for years. And even if there was a growth in interest in the wake of September 11, fluency in a language is not acquired overnight. In fact, according to the Integrated Postsecondary Education Data Systems statistics, in 2002 American colleges granted only 339 degrees in Russian, 183 in Chinese, and a mere six in Arabic. And even when there are linguists in a given language, it is extremely challenging to maintain the necessary level of fluency without leaving the base. "We take as many courses as we possibly can," Everette Jordan says of his fellow linguists. "We have other avenues of trying to keep our language skills up. We have a lot of foreign films we listen to or watch at the agency." Having spent so much time listening to Russians talk among themselves, Jordan harbors a desire to go to Russia himself one day. "There will always be a soft spot in my heart," he says.

In keeping with the tendency to continually reinvest in what it has traditionally been good at, even when that is not precisely what is currently required, the intelligence community proceeded after September 11 to collect even more intercepts—far more than it was able to translate. As a result, there was a massive backlog of documents and recorded phone calls, sitting in databases, untranslated and unexamined. In the fall of 2003, Everette Jordan was charged with devising a radical solution. The project he now oversees is called the National Virtual Translation Center, and it involves forgoing the traditional security-clearance requirements for intelligence translators and farming material out to civilian linguists, to work on in their homes or offices. "We're feeling trapped in the way we've always done things," Jordan says. "Historically we brought linguists to the material, but now we'll get the material to the linguists. . . . It means we can move a lot faster." He is optimistic about the center but guarded in his enthusiasm. He cites a profound distrust between the intelligence community and academia, and wonders whether rank-and-file intelligence analysts will be willing to entrust sensitive intercepts to their academic counterparts. "To them, it's having strangers do your work," Jordan explains, "a bit like sending your kid off to kindergarten in another town."

In preparation, Jordan spent much of 2003 scouring the country for various nongovernment professionals who know languages such as Arabic, Farsi, Pashto, Bahasa Indonesian, and Korean. In March 2001, however, Jordan appeared in a CNN documentary about the NSA, and since that time the agency has not allowed him to travel. Though he appeared on the show with his superiors' blessing, they feel that now that his name and face are out, he could be a target. After all, in addition to the gaggle of languages, Jordan's head contains thirty years of secrets.

Even the best linguists will face serious challenges if they are nonnative. Milt Bearden, a good-natured bear of a man who was the CIA officer in charge of running the Mujahideen in Afghanistan during their war against the Soviets in the 1980s, told me that "speaking Arabic" can mean a variety of things. "You might have some guy using the headphones who is a level three or four with the language, but then the two guys he's listening to know each other, and they start shucking and jiving, and it's all dialect and he has no idea what's gone on," Bearden said. Bob Baer told me, "You've got to have the linguists. Look at the guys who brought down the World Trade Center. They were all Baluch. Christ, I don't know anyone who speaks Baluch. I don't think NSA had anyone that speaks Baluch." (Baluchi is an Iranian branch of the Indo-European language family, spoken by the Baluch people, of whom there are only an estimated 100,000 in the world, most of them in Pakistan.) "The fact is that [Mohammed] Atta and his cousin were both Baluch and who knows who else they had in a support network working out of Karachi," Baer continued. "And NSA barely had any Dari speakers." (Dari is the Afghan dialect of Farsi.) "I think they just had one when the war started in October. So I can't imagine they trained any Baluch speakers."

Some have suggested that training American linguists will never be an adequate response—that what is really needed is a push to train informants on the ground in target countries, people who grew up in the milieu that is being observed. "You can't get a white kid who speaks Arabic with a Harvard accent and get him into Al Qaeda," says former senator Gary Hart, a longtime expert on American intelligence and national security. "You've got to deal with some unsavory people."

The problem can also have to do as much with cultural context as with the knowledge of any particular dialect. Arab languages especially are notoriously nonliteral: even in the context of a casual conversation, they can progress through metaphor and allusion in such a way that even the best classroom-trained speaker will have little sense of what is being said. Baer enunciated this problem. "I've done listening before, and it's a lot of hitting the rewind button," he told me.

> If you're listening in Arabic or Farsi, people slur words, and they say, "Oh, your friend's uncle." What uncle? You know, what does that mean to the guy listening in on them? And they say, "Oh, you know, the friend we met last year in Sudan." "Oh yeah, him." And then the conversation's gone forever. Because they don't use people's names. Nothing is clear, especially if they have something to hide.

Even proper names themselves can be a problem. Given how Echelon Dictionaries work, banalities such as spelling can create major obstacles. Mohmmar Qadaffi or Muammar Gaddafi? Al Qaeda or al-Qa'ida?

The name *Mohammed* alone can be rendered in more than one hundred ways. In fact, there's a company called Language Analysis Systems whose whole purpose is proper name recognition and searching products for large databases of text. Seventy-five percent of its business now comes from the U.S. government.

ONE WINTER MORNING, I visited the midtown Manhattan offices of a company called Meaningful Machines. I was there because, all the new resolve about human capital notwithstanding, the NSA and the UKUSA countries are still on the lookout for silver-bullet solutions. And companies like Meaningful Machines are at the vanguard of trying to devise them.

Even in the agency's mea culpa for cutting back so much staff in the mid-nineties, Harvey Davis maintained that the rationale behind those cutbacks was fundamentally sound.

This was largely due to the belief that better technology would increase the capability of analysts to process large amounts of data more effectively and efficiently. While this has undoubtedly been the case, the loss over the last several years of experienced linguists and analysts has created difficulties for the Agency in target knowledge, less commonly taught languages, and in training the next generation of analysts.

The suggestion here is that while it may be crucial to maintain a good stable of linguists in the meantime, the end goal will still be to work toward new technological solutions.

One such solution is automated translation, and that is what Meaningful Machines does. "Eli should be here any minute," Steve Klein said, pouring me a cup of coffee. Steve is a former corporate lawyer, occasional filmmaker, and new-economy investor with a broad face and a salesman's smile that reveals a gap between his two front teeth. In 2000, he met Eli Abir. Steve told me Eli's story in rapturous tones. He grew up in Israel, never graduated from high school, and served as a paratrooper and tank commander with the Israeli Defense Force. Eli arrived in the United States speaking almost no English and did not turn on a computer until 1993, when he set out to teach his six-year-old son how to use one. He bought the game Sim City and locked himself in a room with it for three days. When he emerged, he had figured out not only how to succeed at the game but how the game itself was programmed and how the computer he had been playing it on was designed. Before long, he was developing algorithms and filing patent applications. In the late nineties, Eli had been working on some Internet driver technologies that could translate World Wide Web addresses into non-Latin alphabets, like Japanese, Chinese, and Hebrew. After September 11, 2001, he and Steve saw an article in *The New York Times* about how U.S. intelligence had a shortage of translators. "Even from an altruistic point of view," Steve said, "from the point of view of protecting our own families, we thought, we might have something interesting here." What they had was a new technology invented by Eli that they believed would revolutionize machine translation.

The appeal of automated translation is obvious: it would reduce the need to rely on so fickle a resource as a population of human linguists and would allow for sorting by the Echelon Dictionaries to become all the quicker. There is a huge amount of private research going into automated translation; it has been estimated that by 2007 the translation market—almost all of which is manual today—will reach $13 billion per year.

The technology that Meaningful Machines is developing compares huge volumes of previously translated texts, employing sophisticated mathematical models to determine the most likely translation. It also upgrades itself, "learning" from its successes and mistakes. Thus, a correct translation of a given phrase will mean that the probability score assigned to that phrase in future translations goes up. Currently, accuracy rates in even the best machine translation are between 70 and 80 percent. But Meaningful Machines is aiming to better that by creating what Steve refers to as "automated understanding."

"Gentlemen!" A door slammed in the next room.

"Here's Eli," Steve said.

A stocky little man clad entirely in black strode into the room. Black leather boots, black leather pants, black leather biker jacket, and a reflective black motorcycle helmet. "Eli Abir. Very nice to meet you." Eli took off his helmet and extended a hand. With close-cropped gray hair, a little goatee, and olive skin, he is the spitting image of Billy Joel. But in leather. "What is this book about?" Eli asked, unzipping his motorcycle jacket to reveal a black leather button-down shirt tucked into his black leather jeans. "By the way, I rode my motorcycle into work today," he said. "I do not normally dress this way."

"It's about communications intelligence," I told him.

"Aha!" Eli said. "Let me tell you something." He sat down in a chair next to me and paused for dramatic effect. "Everything is everywhere, all the time."

I jotted this down, waited for more. Eli crossed his arms and smiled.

"Everything is everywhere, all the time," he said again.

"How so?" I ventured.

"Everything is everywhere, all the time," he said once more. "So if someone is in the middle of the Sahara desert right now, saying something on a telephone, he is actually saying it here right now. And if you have the tools," Eli said, leaning forward, "you can pull it *right out of the air.*" He snatched the air between us.

Eli explained that what makes Meaningful Machines' technology stand apart is that it is focused not on language at the level of words but at the level of meaning. "The basic unit of an idea might be two or three words," he said. "There is no separation between those words. We understand the whole before we understand the parts."

"Take my daughter," Steve broke in, seeming to want to ground his philosopher guru. "She understood *cup of milk* before she understood *cup.*"

"Language gets created not by algorithms," Eli said, "but by some charismatic kid in Harlem who makes up a word. It has to do with his charisma. It has nothing to do with math. With our program, even someone speaking broken English, it can understand."

Steve and Eli will feed the program a corpus of documents in a given language. The program can scan those documents and develop a vocabulary; it will then be able to do pattern recognition not of individual words but of concepts. "This is a huge delta in the intuitive nature of thinking about these issues," Steve declared. "If the computer is embedded with understanding and can search nonlinearly and has processing power . . ."

It all sounded a little elusive to me, but Meaningful Machines has received the stamp of approval of Dr. Jaime Carbonell, a computer scientist at Carnegie Mellon who is considered one of the world's experts on machine translation and who created some of the text-mining technologies currently used by American intelligence agencies. After Carbonell met Eli and saw his blueprint, he joined the board and became chief science officer. Steve was reluctant to get into too much detail but acknowledged that he has been talking with intelligence agencies about

Meaningful Machines' products. An article in *The Washington Post* reports that one of those agencies is the NSA.

"So I have to apologize when we show you the demo," Steve said, "that the computer's only working on a corpus of nine million pages." Whereas conventional wisdom would suggest that having too much material to draw from will always be a liability for pattern recognition or word-spotting programs, the technology developed by Meaningful Machines actually thrives on vast flows of input and *learns* from them. Thus, billions of intercepts represent not an obstacle but an opportunity. "It will be much quicker in a month or so when we have a terabyte to search," Steve said. (That's about 5 percent of all the text in all the collections in the Library of Congress.) "You need enough references to a word or phrase. You need enough related material to ferret out related concepts—synonymous expressions, or things that have strong antonyms." The old formulation is turned on its head here: the bigger the haystack, the easier it will be to find the needle.

Eli and Steve ran a few tests for me. At this stage, the program seems to work like a search engine: enter a word or concept, and the machine will pull matches in order to identify it. When they entered the word *money,* the first level of sorting selected documents relating to money but also to time, because the two are so often equated. The second level of sorting, which entails some discrimination, ruled out the references to time. Expressions and idioms do not seem to trip up the machine. *No laughing matter* produced results for *important.*

"Humans don't actually translate that well," Eli said. "This system will translate *better* than humans."

ANOTHER MAJOR QUEST that is under way is for speech and voice recognition technologies. If a computer can currently sort through billions of written documents and in seconds retrieve any documents that contain a preselected series of keywords, isn't it conceivable that a computer could listen to a million telephone calls and extract the one call that matches a preselected voice? Databases full of fingerprints can already search through thousands for a complete or partial match. The NSA is developing biometric face-recognition technology so sophisticated it can distinguish between identical twins. And the human voice is, in some respects, like a fingerprint or a human face. No two human voices are the same—differences in the dimensions of the vocal cords, lips, teeth, and jaw muscles mean that each voice is distinct. In fact, forensic speaker identification—whereby experts verify that a recorded voice actually *is* that of a particular person—is now admissible as legal evidence in thirty-five states.

Shouldn't it be possible, then, to program a machine to listen for a particular voiceprint? Not necessarily. The human voice varies a great deal from day to day and is influenced by stress, sickness, energy level, and even diet. In fact, while voiceprints are admissible in many courts, there is great professional debate and an arguable margin of error even when it comes to positively identifying a recovered recording of one voice. So the validity of the taped statements attributed to Osama Bin Laden that run on the Al Jazeera satellite channel is often contested. Moreover, the presence of any background noise at all can adulterate a voiceprint to the point where it is impossible to confirm, and this problem is only magnified when endeavoring to cherry-pick a single voice out of the ether.

Another, more modest technology underlies these efforts toward automated translation and effective voice recognition: speech recognition. Systems that can "understand" speech are already in wide use, from Moviefone to the perky automated teller who answers when you dial 1-800-USA-RAIL to buy an Amtrak ticket. By the summer of 2003, 43 percent of North American companies had either purchased interactive voice-response software for their call centers or were conducting pilot research. This form of speech recognition works by breaking down the audio input into phonemes, the basic sound units of words. These are then fed into a phoneme database, which uses statistical modeling to classify them and identify words. Finally, these words are analyzed for their grammatical structure and compared with a series of words or phrases in another database in order to make sense of the response. (Importantly, this last phase occurs at the level of text: the identified words are transferred into text and compared with text words in the database.)

Most contemporary speech-recognition technologies draw on language databases that are very small, however. This is the technological equivalent of an experience you might have at a small ethnic restaurant. You might find that your waiter has a perfect command of the English necessary to tell you the specials and take your order but not to field a question about your lost umbrella. Likewise, if you were to explain to the automated teller on the Amtrak hotline that you left your umbrella on the train, you would be in for frustration, as the word *umbrella* probably does not match any of the words, like *ticket* or *express* or *Boston,* that are in the computer's database.

Even if machines can be programmed with ever larger databases of words, effective machine "understanding" will most likely remain an elusive goal. Think about the sheer complexity of language and meaning. Take a sentence such as "He saw the girl with the telescope." What would a computer make of that sentence? What about more complicated idiomatic expressions? That one September 10 phone call has been rendered in English as "Tomorrow is zero hour." But was the original expression in Arabic literally those words or some idiomatic equivalent? While it is conceivable that for some languages a machine could be programmed with the basic idioms and expressions, this would increase the necessary size of databases by orders of magnitude. And even with those infinite databases, a computer would struggle to read nuances of tone and expression. Everette Jordan, the NSA translator, says that it is tricky to understand the conversation of someone who is drunk. What they mean "depends on what kind of drunk they are," he says.

Before he died, John Millis, the staff director of the House Intelligence Oversight Committee, said, "An analyst costs less than $200,000 a year, including salary, retirement benefits and the cost of putting the PC's and such on the desk. We can afford many more analysts than we have. Instead, we spend more money on one satellite in one year than we do on all the analytic capabilities combined." Millis thought that these priorities needed to change, but it is unlikely that they will. Research for silver bullets continues, even as the NSA is inundated by young people seeking careers in Sigint. In the year after the September 11 attacks, the agency received 73,000 résumés. Everette Jordan is struggling to get his National Virtual Translation Center up to speed, and Dr. Jaime Carbonell believes that it is right that he should try—"in the short run." But Carbonell cautions that those who are pouring resources into the center "may have to revisit that decision when technology overtakes it." And it may be ultimately that Carbonell is right, because one thing that is consistently true of individual human analysts is their eventual obsolescence. After a three-decade career listening to headphones, Everette Jordan has recently been diagnosed with the beginnings of high-frequency hearing loss at high decibels. The listener himself is going deaf.

ROGUE ELEPHANT ON A RAMPAGE

Privacy on the Line

"IF I WANT to kiss my girlfriend or kiss a boy or kiss a stranger, I know right where to stand," Bill Brown said. We were in downtown Manhattan, on the corner of Houston and Mercer, staring up at an imposing surveillance camera, perched like a vulture above a swish boutique. Brown dashed toward the wall so that he could stand underneath the camera, outside of its line of sight. "Here!"

It was an overcast Saturday in June, and I met up with Brown and a few other curious people for one of the walking tours he guides through Manhattan neighborhoods. He is a wiry man in his mid-forties, dressed that day in work boots, black jeans, and a blue parka. He has big hair, salt-and-pepper stubble, and a nervous tenacity about him. We met in Soho, and proceeded to walk around the neighborhood while he drew our attention to various surveillance cameras.

There's an argument that I encountered again and again as I researched this book, which essentially goes: why should I worry about privacy if I have nothing to hide? One of the reasons I wanted to go on Brown's tour was to get a sense of how pervasive visual surveillance is in New York and determine whether, in the scheme of things, I should care. Bill Brown certainly thought I should.

"The Fourth Amendment is still on the books," he said, as he pointed out long, slender, pinpointed "first generation" cameras and round, black, corpuscular "third generation" ones. To illustrate, he stopped beneath one camera and said, "There is no judge or magistrate sitting on the other end of this camera saying that at exactly 2:29 there was probable cause to think that a crime was going to happen here." This is certainly true, but his constitutional law was a little shaky. The Fourth Amendment protects us from unwarranted searches and seizures, but the Supreme Court has held that it applies only in situations where we have "a reasonable expectation of privacy." Whether you have a reasonable expectation of privacy on a busy street is up for debate. Brown thinks you do.

After teaching American literature for several years at the Rhode Island School of Design, Brown started a group called the Surveillance Camera Players in 1996. Initially, the players were just an art-school prank, performing plays in front of cameras and engaging in a particularly antic form of protest. But Brown realized that cameras were sprouting up all over the city and began giving the tours. As we walked down West Broadway and along Prince Street, Brown pointed out various new types of cameras that might be hard to recognize as such. The third-generation ones often masquerade as old-fashioned street lamps, a drooping, black bud hiding a powerful camera within. He talked about certain cameras that are "orphans"; the city won't take responsibility for them, nor will any private organization. When he saw these, Brown slapped a sticker on them that read, "You Are Being Watched!"

Two beefy guys in tank tops and sunglasses walked by, noticing the small crowd forming around Brown. "What's this about?" one asked.

"Protecting privacy," Brown said amiably, hoping, perhaps, that they would join the tour.

"There's more important stuff going on," one of the guys said.

"Oh yeah, what?" Brown asked.

"Twenty blocks downtown," the guy said, pointing down Broadway toward where the Twin Towers used to be.

PART OF ME AGREES WITH the tank-top guy; in any contest between the demands of security and the right to privacy, security will always trump. The Bill Browns of this world, and I met plenty of them in my travels, strike me as a trifle dogmatic on the issue of privacy. Of course, they point out that there is little evidence that surveillance cameras catch real criminals. The cameras are often strung up with the promise that they will help prevent terrorism or kidnappings, but in fact they end up doing little more than deterring petty crime. Nevertheless, it may be that the feeling of greater security, however illusory, that they provide the average civilian justifies their existence. In England, this appealing illusion of safety has brought us to the point where it's estimated that the average Londoner has his image captured on three hundred different cameras per day. After the city of Palm Springs, California, chose, in the wake of September 11, to introduce new surveillance cameras, David H. Ready, the town's city manager, told a journalist, "I think we now think of it less like Big Brother and more like a little friend."

But if the cameras are merely there to make civilians and politicians feel better as they stroll the boardwalk, to demonstrate that *somebody* is doing *something* to deter acts of terrorism and violent crime, then that is not perhaps the forcefully articulated trump on privacy rights it at first appeared. The question that repeatedly arose when I met with people who were exercised about the encroachments of electronic surveillance was, If you're generally behaving yourself, what is there to fear? Many people, when they wonder whether the government can read their e-mail, reply, If I'm not doing anything wrong, why would I care if they can? I don't subscribe to this argument—it seems too easy, too quick to assume the absoluteness of the phrase *doing anything wrong*—but it has a certain rhetorical force. And lurking behind this argument is a suspicion that all of these people who rabble-rouse about privacy rights are a little off themselves, suffer from some millennial mix of narcissism and paranoia, and tremble in the camera's gaze. Guilty always thinks he's caught, the saying goes.

In Bill Brown's case, this argument is not far off the mark. More than a year after the tour, on January 8, 2004, Brown was charged with misdemeanor aggravated harassment for placing obscene phone calls from the law firm where he temped and making sexual threats to a nine-year-old girl. It emerged that in the early nineties, when Brown was teaching in Rhode Island, he was arrested six times for calling random telephone numbers until a young girl would answer the phone, then launching into rants that were menacing and obscene. In New York, he had made seven hundred phone calls from the law firm on the night of December 28, 2003. Investigators told *Newsday* that a surveillance camera caught Brown. He knew where most of the cameras in the fifteen-floor law firm were and averted his face as he passed them. But on that night, he missed one.

IN THIS CASE, a surveillance camera actually did a good thing: it caught Bill Brown. But should the rest of us be concerned? There are so many communications out there, and intelligence agencies are so overwhelmed as is, and there are laws against monitoring civilian communications—so why should we worry? This argument is exceedingly difficult to overcome without recourse to an intuitive and possibly irrational *feeling*. Think of insects, and you will start to itch; research Sigint, and you'll become a little paranoid. The discomfort is more instinctive than intellectual, and part of the problem is that our vocabulary for discussing privacy is remarkably undeveloped. "Few values so fundamental to society as privacy have been left so undefined in social theory or have been the subject of such vague and confused writing by social scientists," Alan Westin remarked in his classic *Privacy and Freedom,* in 1967, and the situation has not improved much since.

One reason privacy may be so hard to define and evaluate relative to other social values and agendas is that it is a classic example of what the philosopher Isaiah Berlin called "negative liberties." Privacy is not a positive right, like the right to free speech, but on the contrary seems always to be defined by reference to intrusions of it. In *Legislating Privacy,* the political scientist Priscilla Regan points out that "the ambiguous nature of privacy is further complicated because people assume they possess a certain level of privacy and appear unconcerned about privacy—until their privacy is threatened or invaded. When this occurs, the definition of privacy is dependent upon, or derived from, the nature of the threat to privacy." It is much easier to talk about violations of privacy, in other words, than about some notion of privacy on its own. Even Justice Louis Brandeis, when offering his famous definition of the right to privacy, called it "the right to be left alone."

While this conundrum may appear purely semantic, the peculiar nature of our nation's jurisprudence on privacy issues means that what we think about when we think about privacy may have serious legal consequences. During Prohibition, a Seattle bootlegger named Roy Olmstead was convicted on the basis of a Treasury Department wiretap. Olmstead appealed the verdict, claiming that using evidence gleaned from an illegal wiretap was a violation of the Fourth Amendment's protections against unreasonable search and seizure. But the Supreme Court held 5–4 that the Fourth Amendment did not apply to wiretapping, because there was no physical trespass involved, which would be necessary in order for it to constitute a "search," and because telephone communications are immaterial and cannot therefore be "seized." *Olmstead* demonstrated the paucity of the American vocabulary when it comes to defining privacy: the idea had to be tethered to notions of the sanctity of property and the home, and in this case, despite Justice Oliver Wendell Holmes's dissenting cry that wiretapping was a "dirty business," there was no physical trespass in a home.

Olmstead would not be overturned for almost forty years, when in 1967 *Katz v. United States* came before the Supreme Court. *Katz* involved an FBI wiretap that had been obtained without a warrant and was attached to the outside of a telephone booth that the FBI knew was being used to facilitate a gambling operation. The Court reversed *Olmstead* by holding that the Fourth Amendment applied even in the phone booth and should protect people, not places. But here Justice John Marshall Harlan introduced a notoriously slippery standard that bedeviled Fourth Amendment cases for the rest of the century. Harlan suggested that individuals should be protected by the Fourth Amendment only in places where they have "a reasonable expectation of privacy."

This test is extraordinarily malleable and can be read in both an expansive and restrictive way. Thus, while Katz could "reasonably" expect that his conversation in a public phone booth would be private, the Supreme Court has held that it is also reasonable to expect that the government can search through your trash on the sidewalk. The moment the trash leaves your house, you no longer have any reasonable expectation that it will remain private. Because we pay our phone bills and individuals at the telephone company are able to see the numbers we have dialed, the Supreme Court has held that an expectation that the police should get a warrant to find out whom you have been calling and who has been calling you is unreasonable. But isn't it risky to allow so much to hinge on our expectations of privacy when our vocabulary for discussing privacy is so patently inadequate? And doesn't the ever-changing nature of communications technology in particular make this calculation all the more difficult? For instance, do we have a reasonable expectation of privacy on the Internet? Given that you do your web browsing through America Online and AOL knows the sites you have visited, would it be reasonable for you to expect the police to get a warrant before obtaining that information from AOL? In the wake of the *Katz* decision, Telford Taylor, the BRUSA drafter and Nuremberg prosecutor, who was by this time a professor at Columbia Law School, remarked, "No doubt it is comforting to be told that one's privacy is as fully protected in a public telephone booth as it is in the home. But it is less reassuring to realize that one's privacy is no better protected at home than in a public telephone booth."

The question, in the end, is whether privacy has any currency as an abstract principle. If you assume, for a moment, that none of us has anything to hide and also that the government is a benign force that would never abuse its surveillance capabilities, then what value does privacy have? In a 1994 essay, Stewart Baker, the former general counsel of the NSA, argued that "the risk to civil liberties" from various forms of eavesdropping and surveillance "is largely theoretical." This is a provocative claim, as any negotiation between security and civil liberties will be significantly altered if it is thought that civil liberties are not, in any practical sense, at risk. It is also a claim that, in light of the history of intelligence in the twentieth century, seems slightly naïve.

IN 1978, TIMOTHY GARTON ASH had just graduated from Oxford and decided to move to Berlin. The city was still bifurcated by the Wall, and Garton Ash lived in both West Berlin and East Berlin over the next several years, oblivious to the fact that the Stasi, the secret police of the German Democratic Republic (GDR), was slowly amassing a file on him. While the Stasi watched, Garton Ash traveled around the divided city, studied, wrote, met friends, and carried on a series of romantic relationships. The dour men in cheap suits who monitored his encounters gave him the code name Romeo.

The Stasi engineered the most perfect surveillance state of all time. Their experience is a useful one to look at not only because it demonstrates what happens when privacy is eradicated in the name of greater security but because it is also the only real instance in which a simple idea—what if we just watched everyone all the time?—was put into practice. The aim of the Stasi was to be everywhere and see everything. In 1988, the Ministry of State Security had 90,000 full-time employees and 170,000 *Inoffizielle Mitarbeiter*—"unofficial collaborators." These IM, as they were known, composed a dense weave of informants. Under the Third Reich, it is estimated that there was one Gestapo agent for every 2,000 citizens. In Stalin's Russia, there was one KGB agent for every 5,830 citizens. In the GDR, however, there was one Stasi officer or informant for every 63 people. If you count part-time informers who gave the occasional tip, some estimates have the ratio as high as one informer for every 6.5 citizens. The Stasi operated on tips, photographs, and transcripts of bugged conversations. The aim was to attain a godlike omniscience—and also to instill enough terror that no one would think of acting in a way that might raise Stasi eyebrows. The logic of coercion is, among other things, highly efficient: far more important than actually watching people all the time is the ability to make people believe you might be.

The Stasi's almost taxonomical impulse to tag and follow and know, to leave nothing to chance or individual will, was so strong that it resulted in some bizarre and tragic experiments. They developed a series of radioactive tags to mark people and objects they wanted to track. Agents would tuck an irradiated pin into a person's clothing or sneak into a person's apartment and spray the floor using a hand pump, so that the person would leave a set of radioactive tracks everywhere they went. Then it was up to an agent to follow with a Geiger counter, which would tremor silently when it got a reading. A subsequent investigation found no evidence of radiation being used to deliberately kill or injure a marked target but also found that this particular technique was employed with no regard whatsoever for any collateral health consequences.

Berliners used to refer to the Stasi headquarters on Normannenstrasse as the House of One Thousand Eyes. Over the years, files like Garton Ash's swelled and multiplied, for files beget files. As the 1980s drew to a close, so, too, did the reign of the Stasi, and as protestors ringed the building, officers inside directed a furious effort to destroy the files. Of course, this being East Germany in the waning hours of the Soviet era, there were shortages to contend with, among them a paper-shredder shortage. Agents were dispatched undercover to West Berlin to buy more, and these were used and burned out. When the Stasi had been through their paper shredders—more than one hundred were later found in one building alone—they proceeded to rip up the documents by hand. In a terrific parody of German orderliness, however, the ripping was all done in a very precise fashion, and in the years since the fall of the Wall, a group of "Puzzle Women" have been sorting through sacks upon sacks of neatly torn-up files, piecing together the surreptitiously collected records of peoples' lives. Some years back, a memo was distributed to these diligent women. It read:

1 worker reconstructs on average per day 10 pages
40 workers reconstruct on average per day 400 pages
40 workers reconstruct on average in a year of 250 working days
100,000 pages
There are on average 2,500 pages in one sack
100,000 pages amounts to forty sacks per year
In all, at the Stasi File Authority there are 15,000 sacks
This means that to reconstruct everything it would take 40 workers
375 years.

Miraculously, the Stasi's record of Garton Ash's years in Berlin remained intact, and in his extraordinary book *The File* he describes going back to Berlin, sifting through the material, and piecing together those years for himself. The result is a palimpsest of memories, observations recorded by informants and agents, and the recollections in his own diaries of that time. Garton Ash remarks, "I was not a victim of these informers. . . . They did me no serious damage." And parts of the book are quite funny, displaying a curious double voyeurism, as Garton Ash looks back at the rambling notes of encounters with him that various informers submitted more than a decade before. ("In volume four I appear—drinking, as he sourly notes, rather a lot of his brandy. Perhaps he hopes for a refill from the Stasi.") But there is a line toward the end of the book that I found troubling.

> The East European dissident's principle of As If said: Try to live in a dictatorship as if you were in a free country! As if the Stasi did not exist. My new principle is the opposite: Try to live in this free country as if the Stasi were always watching you! Imagine your wife, or your best friend, reading the Stasi record of what you said about them to another friend last Saturday night, or of what you did in Amsterdam last week. Can you live so you would not be embarrassed by it? Not seriously embarrassed, I mean. A little embarrassment will be unavoidable; such is the crooked timber of humanity.

Inadvertently, perhaps, this line captures the abstract value of privacy. As distinct from really having anything "seriously" embarrassing to hide. As distinct from a fear of a malevolent government. Is it not natural that one behaves one way in a certain context and another in a different context? Doesn't it make sense that we confide in some people and not in others? The public/private distinction is precisely what the novelist Milan Kundera gets at when he describes the fact that we act different in private than in public as "the very ground of the life of the individual," the "value one must defend beyond all others." As the legal scholar Jeffrey Rosen points out in his book *The Unwanted Gaze,* "A liberal state respects the distinction between public and private speech because it recognizes that the ability to expose in some contexts parts of our identity that we conceal in other contexts is indispensable to freedom." It is also indispensable to the formulation of identity itself and to one's sense of dignity. "It is in order to guard against such encroachments that we recoil from those who would tap our telephones, read our letters, bug our rooms," Sissela Bok argues. "No matter how little we have to hide, no matter how benevolent their intentions, we take such intrusions to be demeaning."

But isn't all of this a little alarmist? you might object. After all, this was the Stasi, a veritable caricature of Orwellian malfeasance. Such a state of affairs would never come to pass in the United States. The government is not hell-bent on stifling dissent or identifying a fifth column. And in any event, there is the Fourth Amendment and various statutes protecting against overzealous surveillance and congressional oversight of agencies like the NSA.

IN 1975, a young Washington lawyer named Britt Snider got a new assignment. Snider was thirty years old, with a law degree from the University of Virginia and a tour of duty as a signals officer in Vietnam under his belt. He had been working as a lawyer on the Senate Subcommittee on Constitutional Rights when he was offered a position as counsel on the staff of a new committee headed by Senator Frank Church from Idaho.

Several months earlier, on December 22, 1974, Seymour Hersh had published a story on the front page of *The New York Times* under the headline "Huge CIA Operation Reported in U.S. Against AntiWar Forces, Other Dissidents in Nixon Years." Hersh had gotten wind of an effort by the intelligence community to spy on civilians who opposed the Vietnam War. When he telephoned then-Director of Central Intelligence William Colby for comment on the story, he promised the revelations would be "bigger than My-Lai," the exposé for which he won a Pulitzer Prize. He was right: 1975 would go down in history as the Year of Intelligence.

The story set off a furor in the press, and on January 3, 1975, President Gerald Ford met in the Oval Office with a handful of close advisers, including Colby, Secretary of State Henry Kissinger, and his young chief of staff, Donald Rumsfeld. One damage-control plan that was discussed was the formation of a blue-ribbon commission to investigate the allegations. The case for such a commission had been made several days before, in a memo sent to the president by his deputy chief of staff, an insider on the rise named Dick Cheney. Because secret intelligence had usually been the exclusive province of the executive branch, it was decided that the commission should be congressional, and in the early months of 1975 the House and Senate established two committees. The investigations of these two committees and the reports they produced would expose as never before a dark side of American secret intelligence.

The Senate committee was led by Church, who was regarded by his colleagues as somewhat aloof and moralistic and who intended to use the investigation as a launchpad for a bid for the presidency in 1976. The committee set out to ascertain what truth there was to Hersh's allegations and how extensive this program of domestic surveillance actually was. At this time, the NSA was still a very low-profile institution, which most Americans had never heard of, and most of the momentum in Church's investigation was directed at gathering information on the CIA and the FBI. Snider and another young staffer, Peter Fenn, were left with the unglamorous job of trying to crack the NSA.

Not surprisingly, this proved difficult. Snider and Fenn started by asking the Congressional Research Service for anything and everything in the public record that dealt in any way with the NSA. The CRS obliged, turning over a one-paragraph description from the Government Organization Manual and a largely inaccurate piece from *Rolling Stone* magazine. They managed to locate and interview a few retirees, but these old-timers could only cite trivial abuses, like misallocation of parking spaces among employees. They realized, in Snider's words, that "NSA's operations were so compartmented that, unless we had the right person, others were not apt to know" anything of misconduct.

It wasn't until several months later, in May 1975, that Snider and Fenn had a break, when they obtained a copy of a document the CIA referred to as its "Family Jewels." The Family Jewels earned its name because of the degree of care with which the CIA had hidden it from the outside world. It was a seven-hundred-page compendium of recollections of current and former employees about abuses and improprieties on the part of the agency. In private, Colby referred to the Jewels as the skeletons in the CIA's closet. The list ran the gamut, from wiretapping of journalists; to assassination attempts against foreign leaders Patrice Lumumba, Rafael Trujillo, and, naturally, Fidel Castro; to the effective murder of a young CIA scientist named Frank Olsen, who was without his knowledge administered LSD in order to test its results and who proceeded to take his own life. (Colby recalls, remarkably, "Perhaps I revealed my own long career in, and resulting bias in favor of, the clandestine profession, when I concluded that this list . . . really was not so bad.")

Buried in the Family Jewels were two references to the NSA. The first of these mentioned an office in New York that the CIA had provided the NSA, for the purposes of copying telegrams. The second disclosed that the CIA had asked the NSA to monitor the communications of certain U.S. citizens who were active in the antiwar movement. These two revelations would turn out to be intricately connected. Snider contacted the NSA, asking for information or confirmation on this office in New York and any documents that might pertain to it. Months later, only after an August press leak appeared in *The New York Times* alleging that the NSA had listened in on the international communications of U.S. citizens, the agency had someone meet with Snider. A clean-cut man in his early forties showed up and acknowledged to Snider that the NSA had for many years had access to most international telegrams leaving New York for foreign destinations. The program was known to only a very few people in the government, he said. It was code-named Shamrock.

The NSA man explained that every day a courier took the train from Maryland to New York and returned with large reels of magnetic tape, on which were copies of all the international telegrams sent from New York the preceding day that had passed through the facilities of three companies: RCA Global, ITT World Communications, and Western Union. He said that once the tapes arrived at Fort Meade, they were scoured for messages sent by foreign establishments in the United States, and for messages that were in code. Telegrams sent by American citizens were present in the tapes, the man said, but generally no one looked at them. "We're too busy keeping up with the real stuff," he assured Snider. In any event, he said, the program had been terminated in May by the secretary of defense. He claimed that the program was ended not because the Church committee was on to it but because it "just wasn't producing very much of value."

Snider was dissatisfied. The man could not tell him how long Shamrock had been going on, who started it, or who approved it. He suggested Snider contact Dr. Louis Tordella, the courtly mathematician who for sixteen years was the civilian deputy director of the NSA. Tordella had been present at the signing of the UKUSA agreement after the war, but at this point he was in his sixties and retired. On a Sunday afternoon in 1975, Snider went to Tordella's home in suburban Maryland. "He was a tough cookie if there ever was one," Snider told me. "Steely little eyes. Didn't laugh, didn't smile. It was all very serious."

The old code breaker and the young lawyer sat on Tordella's veranda and began to feel each other out. Tordella was cordial to his guest but suspicious of him and his intentions. By this time, the congressional committees had gained a reputation as being out to get the intelligence community. (The outright hostility between the intelligence community and the House investigative committee, led by Representative Otis Pike of New York, was such that Donald Gregg, a CIA officer who dealt with the committee, would later say that his tour in Vietnam compared favorably to the experience.) Tordella asked what Snider knew about Shamrock. Snider spelled out what he had learned. Tordella then let out a protracted sigh and began talking. The conversation continued into the early evening.

As it turned out, Shamrock predated the NSA itself. It started out as a continuation of the censorship program during the Second World War. During the war, interception had not merely involved efforts to track down German and Japanese military communications but had focused also on civilian mail going in and out of the country. Internal scares of the Japanese internment-camp variety should indicate the level of paranoia about a fifth column in America in the early 1940s, and in order to detect developments of this sort, a censorship service was developed and grew to employ more than fourteen thousand people and occupy ninety buildings throughout the country. The censors opened one million pieces of mail every day and listened to massive numbers of telephone conversations. They also scanned movies, magazines, and radio scripts. Because it was wartime, this was perceived as acceptable, or at any rate inevitable, and Americans would often receive mail that bore a sticker that read "Opened by Censor." So scared were the censors of having not only to contend with the massive bulk of mail but also with any form of message in code that they banned a whole series of apparently harmless exchanges that *might* be code. During the 1940s there was a serious crossword fad in the United States and people often mailed one another challenging puzzles. When the censors encountered a crossword puzzle in a letter, they extracted the whole thing, rather than have to solve the crossword in order to determine whether there was a code. Likewise, listing students' grades by mail and signing off to a lover *XXOO* were banned. Many Americans sent blank paper to relatives in other countries where paper was in short supply. The censorship office, fearing that these papers might bear messages in invisible ink but lacking the energy or ingenuity to see if this was so, simply removed the paper from the envelope and, courteously, replaced it with blank sheets of their own.

And it was not just mail that was controlled. The Radio Intelligence

Division of the Federal Communications Commission, which had become extremely successful in the interwar period at policing the airwaves in the United States, continued and expanded its operations, becoming so successful that German and Japanese spies in the States did not dare transmit messages by radio at all. During the war, all of the international telegraph carriers turned copies of cables over to the government, but, Tordella said, "none of 'em ever got a nickel for what they did." Shamrock was the same program that allowed the State Department to listen in on the delegates to the United Nations conference in San Francisco in the spring of 1945. The war ended, but Shamrock kept going. The program evolved from punched paper tape in the 1950s to magnetic tape in the 1960s. With this shift, the companies wanted to maintain the actual reels of magnetic tape. It was for this reason that, in 1966, Tordella had personally asked the CIA to rent office space in New York so that the NSA could make its copies there.

Tordella explained that because of the compartmentalized nature of work at the NSA, years would go by without him ever hearing reference to Shamrock. He said he believed that President Truman was aware of the continuation of the program after the war, but no subsequent president had known about Shamrock. The program just quietly progressed for almost three decades, unbeknownst to Congress or the president or even many employees at the NSA itself. The three companies in question did not ask the agency what it did with the telegrams. They did not even interact regularly with NSA officials. They simply turned the telegrams over to couriers.

Snider asked if the program was ever used to monitor the international communications of Americans. Tordella replied, "Not per se," but then admitted that there had been instances in which the names of particular American citizens had been entered as a selection criteria so that the agency could read their communications. It later emerged that the NSA did indeed have a watch list of names of U.S. citizens whose international communications were intercepted. The agency had begun using these lists in the 1960s, on a limited basis, in order to monitor travel to Cuba, threats to the president, and the like. But in 1967, the list was expanded to include the names of U.S. citizens involved in antiwar and civil-rights activities. In principle, these individuals were added in order to determine whether they were under the influence of any foreign power. At the height of this activity, in 1973, Snider says there were six hundred people on the list. The agency later admitted that analysts were pulling out roughly 150,000 individual messages per *month* for further review. When Snider asked Tordella if it was, strictly speaking, legal for the NSA to read the telegrams of American citizens, Tordella replied, rather disingenuously, "You'll have to ask the lawyers."

THE FINDINGS OF THE Church and Pike committees were an indictment of an intelligence community run amok, what Church referred to as a "rogue elephant on a rampage." Revelations about Shamrock were accompanied by news about an overlapping program, called Minaret, and a string of other scandalous abuses of intelligence capabilities. The public learned that included on the NSA's watch list of antiwar civilians were such figures as Jane Fonda and Dr. Benjamin Spock. It eventually emerged that Henry Kissinger was particularly fond of wiretaps and surveillance and that he had instructed the FBI to compile an elaborate surveillance dossier on the sexual life of Dr. Martin Luther King, Jr. When Roger Morris, then a young staffer in the Nixon administration, expressed his surprise at this activity to Lawrence Eagleburger, another aide, Eagleburger assured Morris that this sort of activity was routine and that the file had been assembled "to blunt the black antiwar movement." Kissinger's penchant for wiretaps went so far that he authorized eavesdropping on staffers from his own National Security Council. (One target of this operation, Morton Halperin, sued when he found out, and he eventually received an apology from Dr. Kissinger.)

In a bizarre permutation of the secrecy-privacy dynamic, Kissinger also initiated wiretaps on journalists—Henry Brandon of the London *Sunday Times* and Marvin Kalb of CBS News—because he wanted to figure out the identities of their sources within the administration. In fact, Kissinger was so controlling and his vise grip on the intelligence community so complete that he was able to reroute any NSA intercepts that involved mentions of his name by figures in Washington, so that they went not directly through the normal intelligence channels but first to Kissinger's desk. He objected, as it were, to negative chatter.

THE FINAL REPORT OF the Church committee was elaborate and unsparing:

Too many people have been spied upon by too many Government agencies and [too] much information has been collected. The Government has often undertaken the secret surveillance of citizens on the basis of their political beliefs, even when those beliefs posed no threat of violence or illegal acts on the behalf of a foreign power. The Government, operating primarily through secret informants, but also using other intrusive techniques such as wiretaps, microphone "bugs," surreptitious mail opening, and break-ins, has swept in vast amounts of information about the personal lives, views and associations of American citizens.

The committees' findings demonstrated that the example of the Stasi is not an altogether inappropriate or alarmist one when it comes to American intelligence. At the very least, the excesses in both cases should serve as salutary examples. And these excesses were hardly unique; there has been a history of overreaching and abuse in the United Kingdom as well. Just as Shamrock represented a silent bargain between the NSA and commercial telegraph carriers, British Telecom colluded with intelligence agencies in a similar fashion. In 1997, during a trial of two protestors who had been prosecuted for trespassing at Menwith Hill, it emerged that BT had routed high-capacity fiber-optic cables, capable of carrying more than one hundred thousand calls simultaneously, from Hunters Stones, a major microwave station, *directly through the base* at Menwith Hill. In a letter to the York Crown Court, BT admitted that the British Post Office (which subsequently became BT) had first provided two high-capacity wide-bandwidth circuits to Menwith Hill in 1975. These circuits were connected on a coaxial cable to the BT network at Hunters Stones. In 1992, the system was upgraded with the new fiber-optic cable, which dramatically increased the quantity of communications that could flow through Hunters Stones and thence directly to Menwith Hill.

There is an ever-present danger that the power of intelligence agencies will be abused. In some instances, the abuse has been for personal gain, directed by meddling and insecure bureaucrats such as Kissinger, who wish to solidify their power. But more often, excesses on the part of intelligence agencies are symptomatic of national panic. What allowed programs such as Shamrock to spread out of control was a genuine fear that the United States was being undermined from within by communists, hippies, and others opposed to American engagement in Vietnam. At the present juncture, the United States feels as insecure and threatened as it has at any time since Vietnam. While there may be no danger that our intelligence agencies would go to the extremes that the Stasi did, it seems inarguable that a similar underlying motivation is detectable in the current situation: a ravenous, panicked desire to see and hear everything all the time.

The name *Total Information Awareness* rather elegantly captures this particular instinct, but an even better contemporary analogue to the sorts of operations the Stasi initiated is the TIPS program. First announced by George W. Bush in his State of the Union address in January 2002, the Terrorism Information and Prevention System was a project of the Citizen Corps, which aimed to get civilians involved with homeland security, and was described as "a national system for reporting suspicious, and potentially terrorist-related activity." TIPS was scheduled to get under way in the summer of 2002 and was slated to recruit one million volunteer informants in ten cities: letter carriers and utility technicians, people who would be in a position to notice suspicious things. Attorney General John Ashcroft told the Senate Judiciary Committee, "I believe that there are substantial numbers of individuals in this country who endorse the Al Qaeda agenda" and suggested that TIPS would be a way of identifying them. In the face of a broad public outcry against TIPS, the Texas congressman Richard Armey ultimately killed the program by adding a provision to the November 2002 homeland-security bill that would prohibit the Justice Department from implementing it. But it is not the specifics of the plan, however eerily similar to the Stasi, that are troubling. It's the motivation behind it. When Ashcroft was attacked by congressional Democrats for his heavy-handed tactics, he replied with the now infamous remark, "To those who scare peace-loving people with phantoms of lost liberty, my message is this: your tactics only aid terrorists. They erode our national unity and diminish our resolve."

Not the least of the problems with the type of do-it-yourself intelligence espoused by proponents of TIPS is that the general public is hardly equipped to assume the responsibility of performing intelligence work. After September 11, a Yemen-born trucker who lived in Michigan, named Mohamed Alajji, was jailed for seven days on a tip before FBI agents got around to interviewing his accuser, who turned out to be a family enemy embroiled in a feud. In Texas, a student from Morocco named Esshassah Fouad was detained because his former wife accused him of being involved in a terrorist plot. She was ultimately discredited and jailed for one year for the false tip, but Fouad was then arrested on immigration charges, because he had violated the terms of his student visa by missing school during the time he was in prison on the original false charge. On June 5, 2003, Ashcroft told a congressional panel that he would continue to detain suspects until authorities could prove that they did *not* have terrorist ties.

These examples are interesting because they bring into question not only the motivations or integrity of intelligence agencies but their competence. One reason to worry about the government compiling various databases full of private information about U.S. citizens or developing the capability to scan rapidly through our private communications is that even if you trust the agencies not to abuse their powers, that trust should perhaps not extend to their ability to keep all of that information safe. You might believe that a networked clearinghouse of personal information on American civilians would not be abused by the government, but might not the presence of such a trove be an invitation to hackers, identity thieves, and others who are not so trustworthy? When in 2002 Congress's General Accounting Office issued its annual computer security "Report Card" to various government agencies, the highest grade went to the Social Security Administration—and that was a B-minus. The lowest mark was shared by the departments of Justice, State, and Defense, precisely the departments which would oversee these types of databases—and that grade was a D.

There is an old Latin expression occasionally invoked to describe the hysterical or lawless reactions of governments that feel threatened from without or within, *Inter arma silent leges:* During wartime, laws are silent. No less an authority than William H. Rehnquist, chief justice of the U.S. Supreme Court, has asserted that "at least in the purely descriptive sense," this expression holds true. Power may corrupt, but vulnerability corrupts as well. Everyone is familiar with the old saw about power corrupting and absolute power corrupting absolutely, but this little piece of hyperbole was originally attached to the end of a more compelling and nuanced observation by Lord Acton. The whole passage reads:

> I cannot accept your canon that we are to judge Pope and King unlike other men with a favorable presumption that they did no wrong. If there is any presumption it is the other way against holders of power, increasing as the power increases. Historic responsibility has to make up for the want of legal responsibility. Power tends to corrupt, and absolute power corrupts absolutely.

The question is, why *would* it be our default expectation that intelligence agencies would do no harm and would not overreach, when it is arguably a fundamental element of their makeup to do so? People tend to misbehave when left unattended. We take chances when we think there is a good probability that no one will ever find out. The understandable professional hunger for knowledge and control will always represent a temptation for intelligence agencies to bend or break the rules when they think no one is watching. So the question, to invoke another old Latin phrase, *Quis custodiet ipsos custodes,* is: who is watching the watchers?

THE SOCIOLOGIST ANTHONY GIDDENS has suggested that trust is a precondition for and the very lifeblood of modern society. When our institutions become sufficiently bureaucratic and complex and our interaction with them becomes sufficiently attenuated, it is necessary to trust those institutions to do the right things. In some respects, this principle underlies representative democracy as well: I do not have the time or the expertise to oversee everything that my government does, but I will elect someone who will try to do just that. If the system works, it is built on these sorts of proxies. It is this trust that keeps threats to civil liberties purely "theoretical."

The Church committee investigation demonstrated that a blind trust in institutions is misplaced and that some form of oversight is necessary. In the wake of the investigation, the committees recommended the establishment of permanent congressional committees to oversee the activities of intelligence agencies. "The Church committee was the first time that Congress had ever conducted an investigation of the intelligence community," Gary Hart, who as a young senator was a member of the committee, told me. "Our reforms helped save the CIA." Hart cited the Senate Intelligence Oversight Committee as an example of what saved the agency, and in doing so he echoed the remarks of numerous officials with whom I spoke, who assured me that there was adequate oversight in the committees. But there was part of me that wondered how effective this oversight could really be. Because of the high level of secrecy, there is still a great deal of information that even the committees would not have access to. "Oversight," one friend said when I mentioned that the committees seemed to overlook as much as or more than they oversaw. "That's one of those Janus words."

"There's an awful lot of people who go on the committee for the travel," Bob Kerrey told me, implying, incredibly, that the senators on the oversight committee are drawn to this all-important job primarily by the perks. "Our oversight efforts are weak." Kerrey was a senator for Nebraska for twelve years, and during those years was the ranking Democrat on the Senate Intelligence Oversight Committee. Today, he is president of the New School for Social Research, in Greenwich Village. I wanted to see Kerrey because in reading transcripts of debates on the Senate floor, I always felt he had particularly nuanced views and a willingness to be frank that is unusual when dealing with intelligence matters. I was also interested to talk to him because he was an outspoken member of the National Commission on Terrorist Attacks upon the United States, the bipartisan "9/11 Commission" that investigated the failure of intelligence to avert the events of September 11.

Kerrey is a small, graceful man, dressed, the day we met, in an impeccable blue suit and crimson tie. He has a ready, ingratiating grin, but his eyes are deep set and have a wary cast to them, betraying less mirth than the gregarious smile does. He explained that the founding resolution for the House and Senate committees has a deliberate weakness built into it and that the weakness has to do with the structure of the legislative process. When the Senate committee has finished holding hearings and debating and marking up a bill—a budget authorization, for example—it must then submit that bill to the Armed Services Committee for review. "Because the Armed Services Committee was then and is today sufficiently powerful, they weren't going to let another committee dealing with national security be created that had independent power from them," Kerrey told me. As such, the word of the oversight committee on budget issues, or anything else for that matter, is not the final one. "So in the debate today, one of the things that people say is that we shortchanged intel in the 1990s, and why did the Intelligence Committee do that?" Kerrey said. "It's unlikely that you'll hear anybody say it has something to do with the Armed Services Committee— because they take the damn bill and whack it down to size, every single time."

I understood that some of what Kerrey was telling me might just be residual internecine rivalry. The Senate is a cluster of warring fiefdoms, in some respects, and as a legislator you can do all you want to a bill while it's on your own turf, but if it's passing through someone else's on the way to the president, you may not recognize it when it's signed into law.

"The best way of seeing that the intelligence committee doesn't have much power inside the intelligence agencies," Kerrey said, is to "go to the Committee on Responsive Politics that tracks contributions. There's not a lot of contributions going to members of the intelligence committee. If they had real power, there would be. There'd be contractors queuing up forever trying to get access to them. But they don't. Oversight is weak."

Some of this may be due to the fact that the community is so bureaucratically compartmentalized that no one really has an overview, even within the intelligence community itself. William Odom, former head of the NSA, has remarked, "Rare is the senior intelligence officer who has the overall picture. Moreover, many of them do not even understand their own mineshaft very well because they have grown up in some small tunnel within it." If that is the case, how could we expect the members of an oversight committee, all of whom have other responsibilities to committees and constituents, to even approach a holistic understanding of how an agency like the NSA is meant to work?

Exacerbating this state of affairs, the intelligence community holds the committees at arm's length, doling out information on a strictly need-to-know basis. " 'We do believe this, but we can't tell you why we believe it, because if we do then the other side will know how we collect our information,' " Gary Hart says. "This cat chases its tail all the time. . . . You say, 'All right, now, well how do you know this?' And they say we'd love to tell you, we just can't because it'll jeopardize our sources." In the memorable phrase of Norman Mineta, a Democratic congressman from California who served on the House Intelligence Oversight Committee during the Reagan years: "We are like mushrooms. They keep us in the dark and feed us a lot of manure."

In its postmortem of the attacks of September 11, the 9/11 Commission argued that because the business of the intelligence community is so shielded from the public and the press, it is all the more essential that the agencies be straightforward and forthcoming with the committees. "The overall budget of the intelligence community is classified, as are most of its activities. Thus, the Intelligence committees cannot take advantage of democracy's best oversight mechanism: public disclosure," the commission's report pointed out. "This makes them significantly different from other congressional oversight committees, which are often spurred into action by the work of investigative journalists and watchdog organizations." If the committees do not initiate and maintain rigorous oversight of intelligence activities, no one will.

Some have contended that the close relationship between the committee members and the intelligence community has become a little too close. Today, the intelligence committees "seem to think their primary role is *protection* of the intelligence community," James Bamford says. "That wasn't the original reason why they were there in the first place. But if you look at their actions in the last five or eight years, they became more of a cheering chorus of the intelligence community, as opposed to oversight."

"THE BASIC STRUCTURE OF the intelligence committees works," Bob Barr told me. "But whether or not that system works in practice is another matter altogether." Barr is a curious political animal. As a right-wing congressman and former prosecutor from Georgia, he took the lead in pushing for the impeachment of President Bill Clinton. But Barr also had a strong libertarian streak, and on losing a bid for reelection in 2002 he was hired as a consultant by, of all places, the American Civil Liberties Union (ACLU). "If you have a committee like the House or Senate that essentially rubber stamps what intelligence agencies want, then we're effectively back to where we were in the 1960s," prior to the Church committee, he told me. He said that members of the oversight committees often have inadequate access to the information they need in order to assess with any sort of accuracy the efficiency and legality of the intelligence community's behavior. "Membership of intelligence committees is limited, and most members do not take time to find out what's going on. You need committee members that will be bold in asserting their committee's jurisdiction." He said that too often the committees will simply take the intelligence community at its word. "We have to protect against committees essentially getting co-opted by the intelligence community."

Barr pointed out that when in 1999 the House intelligence committee requested that the NSA turn over any legal memoranda, opinions rendered, or other documents from the agency's general counsel's office that dealt with whether and when the NSA was intercepting the communications of American civilians, the agency demurred, citing attorney-client privilege. This was a sly and pernicious tactic. By this rationale, government lawyers would not have to turn over any documents on which they were working at their agencies, and dropping any document on the desk of some junior legal adviser would be adequate to evade any request or subpoena for it from an oversight committee. The committee chairman, Porter Goss, explained that the committee was interested in such documents because,

> if the NSA General Counsel provided too narrow an interpretation of the agency's authorities, it could hamper the collection of significant national security and intelligence information. If, on the other hand, in its effort to provide timely intelligence to the nation's policy makers, the NSA General Counsel construed the Agency's authorities too permissively, then the privacy interests of the citizens of the United States could be at risk.

The matter was clearly one of line drawing—precisely the kind of line drawing between robust intelligence and civil liberties that the committees were created to oversee. The agency stonewalled, however, and Goss protested the fact that "perhaps for the first time in the committee's history, an Intelligence Community element of the United States Government asserted a claim of attorney-client privilege as a basis for withholding documents from the committee's review." The episode seems indicative of the kind of poor or nonexistent oversight that Kerrey and Barr were alluding to, and it is worth noting that the cost of this poor oversight is not merely privacy: the committees were instituted not simply to protect civil liberties but to crack down on corruption, inefficiency, and mismanagement as well.

Though Barr was not on the House Intelligence Oversight Committee, he is a former CIA analyst himself, and when he first started hearing about the Echelon system in the late 1990s, he became irate that he could not learn more. In late 1999, he published an article under the alarmist headline "Is the U.S. Spy Shop Listening to Your Call?" The article pointed to the work of "a handful of intrepid journalists," which indicated that "Project Echelon" was able to search a huge volume of transmissions—Barr put it at two million per hour—for "keywords, voice prints, or particular telephone numbers." Barr's version betrayed an inexact acquaintance with the system, but in a way it was precisely the suggestion about "voice prints" and other inaccuracies that were disturbing: how could members of Congress be unable to sort between myths and facts about the capabilities of their own intelligence community? "What concerns me is not the Intelligence Community's monitoring activities per se; but the scope of the activities, and the refusal to provide any public assurances these activities are being conducted with appropriate respect for the privacy rights of American citizens, and within the bounds of our law and Constitution," Barr wrote, adding, "When a government agency acts like it has something to hide, it's a pretty good bet it does."

In response to Barr's agitation and to a *60 Minutes II* report dealing with Echelon, Kenneth Heath, the chief of staff of the Legislative Affairs Office at Fort Meade, sent an open letter to the House of Representatives saying,

> As is the long-standing policy within the United States Intelligence Community, we must refrain from commenting on actual or alleged intelligence activities; therefore, we can neither confirm nor deny the existence of specific operations. However, we can tell you that NSA operates in strict accordance with U.S. laws and regulations in protecting the privacy rights of U.S. persons.

Again, the message from the black box was, Trust us. We can't tell you why you should trust us. But trust us.

On April 12, 2000, the House Intelligence Oversight Committee held a hearing on the Echelon system and invited both CIA Director George Tenet and NSA Director Mike Hayden to testify. The directors' line was strictly nondenial denial, and they did little to add to the bland assurances of Heath's letter. They would not confirm or deny the existence of what Tenet referred to as "the so-called Echelon program." But they wanted to reassure the committee that the NSA does not eavesdrop on American citizens. Tenet explained that the agency does not collect intelligence on "U.S. persons" unless they are agents of a foreign power. Hayden pointed out that the NSA is subject to restrictions both by statute and executive order. There is an executive order governing Sigint, with specific restrictions imposed on the NSA's collection techniques, and on the retention and dissemination of "unintentionally acquired" information on U.S. persons. But the principal piece of legislation Hayden was invoking was the Foreign Intelligence Surveillance Act (FISA).

Signed into law in 1978, the FISA is an artifact of the uneasy climate in the wake of the Church committee investigation. The chief thrust behind the law was to create a two-track system for eavesdropping and other forms of surveillance. The procedural bar for obtaining a warrant to perform domestic surveillance for the purposes of law enforcement was set very high, whereas the procedural bar for bona-fide foreign-intelligence investigations was considerably lower. What the FISA did was create a firewall between these two systems, so that law enforcement would not be tempted to use the mandate of a "foreign intelligence" operation against domestic, civilian targets. Under the FISA, agents were obliged to show probable cause that the person they wanted to tap was an agent of a foreign government or terrorist group.

There is a concept from the field of information systems that has gained a great deal of recognition among privacy advocates: the idea of function creep. One definition of function creep is "the secondary use (deliberate or inadvertent) of information that was originally divulged for one purpose only." What the FISA traditionally did was prevent information collected under the auspices of foreign-intelligence gathering from creeping into the realm of law enforcement.

This new law for spying was accompanied by the creation of a new institution to oversee that law: the FISA Court, an intensely secretive spy court created to "hear applications for and grant orders approving electronic surveillance anywhere within the United States." The court is composed of a rotating panel of eleven federal district judges selected (in secret, of course) by the chief justice of the Supreme Court. (For most of the court's history there were only seven judges, but in 2001 the Patriot Act raised the number to eleven.) In the first two decades of its existence, the court approved some ten thousand applications for surveillance. An approved application means a ninety-day leave to monitor at will by any electronic means. Since September 11, the numbers have gone up, and the court has been approving one thousand applications per year.

The court meets in a windowless, soundproof, cipherlocked room on the sixth floor of the Department of Justice building in Washington. Its writs and rulings are permanently sealed from review. The public cannot access these records and knows very little about the court, and Congress doesn't know much more, because there is next to no oversight of the FISA Court. The court is obliged to turn over the number of surveillance orders approved every year, along with a brief semi-annual report. The 1997 report weighed in at a circumspect two paragraphs.

Perhaps it was precisely this obscurity that explained the stir the court caused in May 2002 when, in a highly unorthodox step, it published an opinion. The panel's 7–0 ruling stated that the Justice Department and the FBI had supplied erroneous information to the court in more than seventy-five applications for search warrants and wiretaps.

In the wake of September 11, Attorney General John Ashcroft was seeking to break down the wall between law enforcement and intelligence. The Justice Department had gotten flak because the FBI did not seek a FISA warrant to search Zacarias Moussaoui's laptop in the weeks before September 11, because they feared they couldn't satisfy the FISA requirement of a connection to a foreign terrorist group. In any event, the USA Patriot Act altered the FISA so that the foreign-intelligence aspect need only be a significant, not the primary, purpose of the investigation in order to obtain a wiretap. Nevertheless, the panel pointed out that a reading of the text of the act demonstrated that "collection of foreign intelligence information," as opposed to law enforcement, "is the *raison d'être* for the FISA." Having enumerated the instances of mistakes and inaccuracies in FISA applications, the court emphasized the importance of preserving the firewall "to protect the privacy of Americans in these highly intrusive surveillances and searches."

With his customary evangelical zeal, Ashcroft wasted no time before launching an appeal of the court's ruling. And in the fall of 2002, it emerged that not only was there one FISA Court most Americans never knew existed, there were two. Throughout the quarter century of the FISA Court's existence, there had been a FISA Court of Review. *The Washington Post* described the Court of Review as "a kind of ghost within the American judiciary." It was established back in 1978 "to review the *denial* of any application." And in twenty-four years, no one had ever launched an appeal of a FISA Court decision on a wiretap application—because the FISA Court had never denied one. This particular three-judge panel held the peculiar distinction of being the only court in the country that had never heard a case. In November 2002, the panel reversed the limits placed on the Justice Department by the FISA Court and argued, effectively, that it was time for the wall between foreign-intelligence gathering and law enforcement to come tumbling down.

ONE PERSON WHO SUPPORTED the overturning was Stewart Baker, former general counsel for the NSA. "On September 11, 2001, that wall probably cost us 3,000 American lives," Baker says. And he has a story to prove it. In February 2000, two men, Nawaf al-Hazmi and Khalid al-

Mihdar were living in San Diego. In early 1999, the NSA had analyzed a set of communications regarding a terrorist facility in the Middle East, and two names that came up were al-Hazmi and al-Mihdhar. The names were flagged, and the connection between them was noted, but at the time the analyst reviewing the intercepts chose not to distribute them through the normal Sigint channels. At some later point, it came to the attention of the FBI and the CIA that the two men were in the United States, but the agencies could not locate them.

By August 2001, a New York FBI agent looking for al-Mihdhar and al-Hazmi needed better resources and applied to FBI headquarters to open a criminal investigation, because intelligence resources were thin. They turned him down, saying in an e-mail,

> If al-Mihdhar is located, the interview must be conducted by an intel agent. A criminal agent CAN NOT be present at the interview. This case, in its entirety, is based on intel. If at such time as information is developed indicating the existence of a substantial federal crime, that information will be passed over the wall according to the proper procedures and turned over for follow-up criminal investigation.

The New York agent wrote back, on August 29, 2001:

> Some day someone will die—and wall or not—the public will not understand why we were not more effective and throwing every resource we had at certain 'problems.' Let's hope that [the lawyers who gave the advice] will stand behind their decision then, especially since the biggest threat to us now, UBL (Bin Laden) is getting the most 'protection.'

Two weeks later, Khalid al-Mihdhar and Nawaf al-Hazmi boarded American Airlines flight 77 and helped fly it into the Pentagon.

Baker feels that our failure to find al-Mihdar and al-Hazmi that August can be blamed squarely on the wall. "We had imposed too many rules designed to protect against privacy abuses that were mainly theoretical. We missed our best chance to save the lives of 3,000 Americans because we spent more effort and imagination guarding these theoretical privacy abuses than against terrorism." He is troubled that libertarian Republicans have joined civil-liberties Democrats to drive home the lesson that "you won't lose your job for failing to protect Americans, but you will if you run afoul of the privacy lobby."

. . .

in arguing that the wall between law enforcement and foreign intelligence is partially to blame for September 11. The bipartisan 9/11 Commission concluded in its final report that the NSA's insistence, from December 1999 onward, on attaching caveats to its Bin Laden reports that specified they should not be shared with criminal investigators and prosecutors "further blocked the arteries of information sharing." In fact, there is evidence that it was precisely in order to avoid even the appearance of violating prohibitions on spying on Americans that the NSA did not pursue FISA warrants that might have provided some early warning of September 11.

But Baker dramatically overstates the power of the "privacy lobby," particularly in the post–September 11 world. Whether you agree with current policies or not, it is hard to argue with the objective assessment that security, not privacy, is the trump card. In the fall of 2002, it emerged that a new intelligence program was monitoring thousands of Iraqi citizens and Iraqi-Americans with dual citizenship who were attending American universities or working at private corporations, because of a fear that they might pose a risk in the event of a war in Iraq. The NSA was part of the operation. Since September 11, John Ashcroft has also been using a special measure called "emergency foreign intelligence warrants." These warrants can be enforced for seventy-two hours before they are subject to review and approval by the FISA Court. By the spring of 2003, he had authorized 170, which is three times the total number in the preceding twenty-three years.

It seems clear that the United States needs to engage in a serious debate about these issues, as a nation, but that we lack the language in which to do so. To his credit, Mike Hayden seems to understand this and to heed, one hopes, Benjamin Franklin's famous admonition, "They that can give up essential liberty to obtain a little temporary safety deserve neither liberty nor safety." In a 2002 statement to Congress, Hayden asked,

In the context of NSA's mission, where do we draw the line between the government's need for CT [counterterrorism] information about people in the United States and the privacy interests of people located in the United States? Practically speaking, this line-drawing affects the *focus* of NSA's activities (foreign versus domestic), the standard under which surveillances are conducted . . . the type of data NSA is permitted to collect and how, and the rules under which NSA retains and disseminates information about U.S. persons. These are serious issues that the country addressed, and resolved to its satisfaction, once before in the mid-1970's. In light of the events of September 11th, it is appropriate that we, as a country, readdress them. We need to get it right.

VOICES IN THE DARK

Muckrakers, Whistleblowers

ONE APRIL NIGHT in 1996, a man stepped out of a house in Chechnya. The house was hidden in a quiet forest outside the village of Gekhi-Chu, thirty kilometers southwest of Grozny. The location was deliberately out of the way: the man was Dzhokhar Dudayev, leader of the Chechen Army, which was locked in a protracted and bloody war with Russian troops. He was the most-wanted man in Russia.

At fifty-two, Dudayev was a striking figure, even a little flamboyant, with military bearing, a creased uniform, dark eyes under a stern brow, and a neatly trimmed mustache. As a younger man, he had been the first Chechen ever to attain the rank of major general in the Soviet military, when he commanded a division of bombers based in Estonia from 1987 to 1990. After retiring, he returned to Chechnya and became involved in the movement for autonomy from Russia. In 1993 he declared Chechen independence, becoming the first president of the Chechen Republic, and a warlord of considerable grit. In the subsequent years, he emerged as a dashing character, always one step ahead of the Russian Army, managing to survive repeated assassination attempts and still turn up to grant televised interviews to foreign correspondents. His ability to outfox the massive Russian military time and again led to speculation about how he survived. It was one of the enduring mysteries of the war.

At this point, the war over Chechen independence had been raging for more than a year, and the Russian Army was suffering. Two weeks earlier, on April 5, 1996, President Boris Yeltsin had declared a cease-fire, saying, "We have proposed negotiations instead of military actions, including talks with Dudayev through mediators." Yeltsin's gesture of goodwill notwithstanding, Dudayev had determined that it would be too dangerous to go to Moscow or Grozny to meet with Russian officials in person. He would negotiate through intermediaries, by phone.

Dudayev headed into a field and took out his Inmarsat (International Maritime Satellite) telephone. These phones, which are bulkier than normal cellphones and have longer, thicker antennae, communicate via satellites and are favored by those in the government and military for their security and reliability in any terrain. Alone in the darkness, Dudayev placed a call to Konstantin Borovoi, a liberal deputy in the Russian Parliament, who was one of his contacts in Moscow and with whom he was working to negotiate peace.

As Dudayev spoke on the phone, he heard the sound of a plane above, and then, suddenly, two air-to-surface missiles ripped through the night, hurtling toward him—or more precisely, toward his phone. One of the missiles landed farther off, but the other detonated just a short distance from where he stood. He died moments later, a piece of shrapnel in his head.

Of this much, we are certain, or almost: there are still conflicting reports about the precise hour at which Dudayev met his fate, whether there was one missile or two, whether it really *was* Borovoi with whom Dudayev was speaking, and if so, how complicit Borovoi was in the operation. In fact, no photograph of Dudayev's body was ever released, and his aides initially claimed that he had not been killed, leading to subsequent speculation that perhaps the event was staged. The layers of insinuation and doubt surrounding the incident serve to illustrate the difficulty of knowing anything objectively when it involves secret electronic intelligence—and particularly Sigint.

There is, however, a consensus among those who have researched and written about this event that the missile that killed Dzhokhar Dudayev was targeted at his satellite phone. Had the killing occurred today, it would have been no trick to pull off: even run-of-the-mill cellphones now come with a Global Positioning System chip implanted in them, which allows the wireless provider or police to trace the phone's location to within a couple of yards. In 1996, Dudayev's assailants would have first had to use satellites to identify the frequency of the phone and then Global Positioning Systems to triangulate the signal and identify the location. They would then have required a plane with eavesdropping equipment that could lock onto the signal, program missiles to home in on the radio wave emitted by the phone, and destroy their target. The catch is, it has been speculated that in the spring of 1996 Russia did not have that kind of technology. But the United States did.

The suggestion that the United States assisted in this assassination has been floated by a number of intelligence commentators, most prominently by Wayne Madsen. Madsen is a rumpled and amiable former spy with a mustache and a dry sense of humor. "From what I heard there was a deal worked out between Yeltsin and Clinton," he told me. "Clinton didn't want Yeltsin losing to the communists, because he would be accused of helping give Russia back to communism. So he was giving them all kinds of intelligence." I asked Wayne where he'd heard this, and he said, elusively, "From people in the military here at the time."

Having worked for two decades in computer security for the navy, the NSA, and then for private companies, in 1997 Madsen became a senior fellow at the Electronic Privacy Information Center. Now he speaks out regularly, and with more authority than many of his colleagues due to his own experience in the field and his continued contacts on the inside, about abuses of signals intelligence. Shortly after the killing of Dudayev, Madsen published an article in which he claimed that Russia could not possibly have carried out the operation on its own and was most likely assisted by the United States. Madsen speculates that the satellite used in the operation was the NSA's Vortex, Orion, or Trumpet.

He argues that Russia did not have the necessary satellite technology. A similar point was made by Martin Streetly, editor of *Jane's Radar and Electronic Warfare Systems,* who thought that the state of Russia's armed forces was such that they wouldn't be able to pinpoint Dudayev's location. Madsen also suggests that Dudayev knew of the capabilities of the Ilyushin-76 aircraft and its A-50 Mainstay radar, which could pinpoint a phone's signal if the user stayed on the line for longer than four or five minutes. Thus, he normally kept his satellite phone calls to a minimum. In fact, during the first three months of 1996, the Russian Army had endeavored four times to lock onto Dudayev's signal.

But why would the United States help Russia? After all, the whole apparatus of American signals intelligence and Echelon as we know them today emerged in large part as a response to the perceived threat of the Soviet Union. Madsen seems on shakier ground here. His suggestion is that this was a political favor on the part of Bill Clinton and possibly a quid pro quo for Yeltsin's assistance on behalf of an American consortium that was building a pipeline through Chechnya. This explanation seems decidedly dark and has the whiff of conspiracy theory about it.

Yet perhaps by coincidence, Bill Clinton was in Moscow for a G7 summit the week Dudayev died. The Clinton administration had shown bizarrely unstinting support for Yeltsin and had come under fire for it. Yeltsin had admitted that his bid for reelection might depend on the outcome of the war in Chechnya, and the issue would no doubt have arisen in his conversations with Clinton. In fact, in a twist that is no less poetic for being basically circumstantial, Yeltsin stood at a press conference on the very day that Dudayev was killed, with none other than Bill Clinton at his side, and announced that "military actions are *not* going on in Chechnya."

It might be countered that the United States is stingy with its Sigint, even with its closest allies—indeed, even with other parties to the UKUSA agreement. But it turns out that the Americans had helped the Russians with Sigint before. In August 1991, President George H. W. Bush defied his advisers and allowed Yeltsin access to American intercepts of Russian military communications in order to try to prevent a coup against Mikhail Gorbachev. When the coup did take place, Bush ordered, over the fierce objection of the NSA, that essential communications intelligence be provided to Yeltsin. This, in turn, helped Yeltsin emerge a hero. In this case, the transfer of intelligence was conducted secretly. The House and Senate intelligence committees were not informed, which is required by law. (It's interesting to note, actually, that this was only law as of August 14, 1991, four days before the coup began, when Bush signed a congressional amendment to the 1947 National Security Act, which held that it was illegal for the president not to inform Congress about covert actions.)

There are others who disagree with Madsen's hypothesis. When I asked Milt Bearden, the veteran spy who ran the CIA's operations against the Soviets in Afghanistan during the eighties, whether he thought the Russians had received American assistance in targeting Dudayev, he scoffed. "I would be careful about underestimating Soviet capabilities—even at that point," he told me. Moreover, on the third anniversary of Dudayev's death, a man named Vladimir Yakovlev, who claimed that he was the deputy head of the Russian military group that had been tracking Dudayev, granted an interview with the newspaper *Komsomolskaya Pravda*. He said that the Russians *did* have the technology to track the phone call. In any event, a Russian unit had identified the gully where Dudayev was killed as a place where he sometimes went and had set a bomb there. Once they confirmed that he was in the gully, the bomb was detonated, and seconds later the rocket landed.

Still, Madsen insists, he has strong evidence that his theory is correct. He told me that in May 1996 he was invited to speak at an information-warfare conference in McLean, Virginia, and mentioned his suspicions about the Dudayev case. After his remarks, "this guy from NSA came up and he was all irate and he said, 'Don't you realize we have people on the ground over there?' And I said, 'Thanks for the confirmation my friend,'" Madsen told me. "I was only repeating what was in Reuters and the *Financial Times,* but he thought I was talking about something classified. . . . I guess he figured I had a clearance and he put two and two together. He might have been briefed on something very similar to what I was talking about at the session."

The point, in the end, is that as things stand we *cannot* know. Researching signals intelligence is an imperfect science. You can look at the installations, try to read into the interstices in State Department speeches, keep track of what satellites are launched when and how espionage technology develops, to the extent that it is possible to do so, but this is all, in the end, so much material around a central void.

As a result, there are often rumors and strange allegations, and if there is a reason why one would take the Madsens of the world with a dose of skepticism it is that the kind of speculation he engages in teeters on the edge of a slippery slope, at the foot of which is the whole repository of Internet-perpetuated conspiracy theories. If, after all, there is only circumstantial evidence to support an allegation of the United States assisting an ally in a political assassination—an event which, if it happened, would most certainly be illegal but not unprecedented—then there is no more or less evidence that the United States uses its various Sigint installations as Area 51–type locations for testing UFOs and other such fantasies. Trolling through the scores of websites that devote space to speculations about the Echelon network, one invariably encounters a full range of kooky theories about mysterious aircraft around Roswell, the assassination of JFK, or prior knowledge of the September 11 attacks on the part of America or Israel. Any investigation of Sigint involves a navigation between acceptance of the party line on the one hand and something closer to rank paranoia on the other.

This is complicated by the fact that when people talk about signals intelligence in general and Echelon in particular they tend to employ a rhetoric of absolutes. Mike Frost, the former spy for Canada's CSE, says bluntly, "Echelon covers everything that's radiated worldwide at any given instant. . . . Every square inch is covered." James Rusbridger wrote in the late eighties, "Around the world GCHQ and the NSA have a series of powerful listening stations that scoop up every transmission that ventures into the ether. No matter how faint or how brief each transmission may be it can be snatched out of the air and analyzed." There seems to be a compulsion to imagine listening networks as all-powerful, all-seeing, all-hearing.

Some of this is generated by journalists, who, when it comes to Sigint capabilities, seem to have an almost genetic predisposition toward hysteria. In a media environment saturated with news stories, it has always been in the interests of journalists to overplay their hands a bit, insinuating that capabilities are more expansive than they can prove and insisting that if intelligence capabilities and abuse on the part of intelligence agencies are concerned, where there's a way, there's a will.

On the rare occasions when a former spy has chosen to speak out, there is a characteristic breathlessness and excitement to the accounts, like a child who has kept a secret to the point where he feels he might burst and perhaps feels the need to embellish it slightly when the truth comes out. As a result, researching signals intelligence involves negotiating the pass between nondenial denials by current officials and overly florid accounts by former spies.

The Sigint Postulate plays into this: the inverse proportion between how much someone is willing to talk about signals intelligence and how much they actually know. And so does the perplexing extent to which signals-intelligence networks lend themselves to conspiracy theorizing. "We have all glimpsed somewhere—in our families, schools, workplaces, communities—that hypervigilant over-the-edge look in the paranoid eye, that bottomless rage against the system, that obsessive compilation of signs that 'they' are up to no good," write the anthropologists Susan Harding and Kathleen Stewart, in an essay on conspiracy theories in millennial America. They describe the endless wild talk of paranoids as "sort of like valves blowing off steam, the effluvia of postmodern life." And a lot of steam has been blown about Echelon. It is invisible. It is nonfalsifiable. And it plays on that property that animates most contemporary conspiracy mongering: global connectivity. All of the marionette strings of planetary power converge in some secret place, a mahogany boardroom or sterile control room, where an elusive cadre of Machiavellians—the Masons, the Jews, the Illuminati, the Bilderberg group, the NSA—run the planet.

Wayne Madsen is one face in a rogue's gallery of odd individuals who have chronicled the UKUSA Sigint alliance. He embodies all of the contradictions that mark the other muckrakers and whistleblowers who have devoted their lives to working out what happens inside and spreading the word. He is fascinated by the possibilities of listening in and suspicious of government power, devoted to working out in a pragmatic manner what is technically possible, but also at times a trifle drunk on his material.

IN COPENHAGEN, NOBODY LOCKS their bikes. The city is quaint, in an antiseptic, scrubbed sort of way, and healthy citizens ride their bikes down spotless avenues and dismount obediently as they traverse the many pedestrian streets. The whole place feels clean and modern, trusting and progressive—painfully Scandinavian, in other words.

I had come to Copenhagen to meet with Kenan Seeberg and Bo "Skipper" Elkjaer, the self-styled Woodward and Bernstein of Danish journalism, who write for the Copenhagen tabloid *Ekstra Bladet*. Working back-to-back in a little office at the paper, Skipper and Kenan spent much of the late nineties furiously chronicling the Echelon network and Denmark's role in it. Their articles were translated from Danish into English and French and replicated again and again on the Web, posted on Cryptome and debated by Cypherpunks, forwarded around by e-mail. "When we first started out, our editor told us, 'These stories should come like bullets from a machine gun,'" Kenan told me. "'Fire off your rounds. Pause. See who is still moving.'" And he and Skipper complied. When I met them they were on their fourth year of researching Sigint, and had published two hundred stories on the subject.

Kenan is the more gregarious of the two, with the rakish grin and nefarious cackle of a rock star. When I walked into their office, he had the phone in one hand and a cigarette in the other and was spinning in his chair from a computer where he was typing an e-mail to a television where he was watching a bike race on mute. He's a handsome guy, with ginger hair, an angular face, and, on that day, a Hawaiian shirt; the walls around his desk had an unusual number of photos, many of which appeared to be of Kenan himself. "Welcome to Copenhagen," he whispered, beckoning me in.

Skipper, who walked in with me, is more reserved. Dressed in dark colors, he wore a small hoop earring and glasses that magnified his green, glistening eyes. Skipper had done some graduate work in computer science before deciding to become a freelance journalist. He started digging up some good material on Echelon in the late nineties, but he couldn't get anyone to run his stories. Kenan was working as a radio and television journalist at the time and was hired to do a story on Echelon for public radio. "Skipper phoned me and said, 'Hey, I have some stories.'" Kenan told me. "I said, 'I'll do it on the radio, then you can write a newspaper article about the radio program.'"

And so a partnership was born. The two journalists complement each other's skills and through a kind of symbiosis have become immensely productive. Skipper finds sources. He scours the Internet for résumés, patents, corporate slide shows, conference announcements— anything that might shed light on NATO intelligence and defense operations and the role Denmark plays in them. "Skipper is the genius in this," Kenan said. "He's vacuuming the ether finding the new, fantastic stuff." When Skipper has located someone who looks like a promising source, Kenan gets in touch and turns on the charm.

WHEN SKIPPER FIRST READ about Margaret Newsham, he felt it might be worth trying to talk with her. "Duncan Campbell talked to her briefly in '88," he told me, referring to another investigative journalist in the field. "But Duncan's working on a different level than we are, not emphasizing firsthand sources as much as we are. He's more relying on documents." Skipper figured out that she lived in Nevada and found her in the white pages. Then he turned the phone over to Kenan, who called and talked to her for hours. They e-mailed and talked more, and eventually Kenan persuaded her to agree to a visit. The result was a classic piece of Skipper and Kenan reportage. Published on December 21, 1999, the article was called "Echelon Was My Baby" and painted a vivid, if hysterical, portrait of a whistleblower.

Margaret Newsham, who goes by Peg, grew up in the 1950s. She was married and had children but then divorced and was looking for a good job. In the 1970s she found work as a computer-systems manager for Ford Aerospace and Lockheed, in Sunnyvale, California. At the time, she was briefed and told that she could never tell anyone about the work she did there—as these companies did contract work for the NSA. "After the briefing I was shocked, stunned and said, I need to think about this for a while," Peg told Kenan. But the project involved cutting-edge technology, so she agreed to stay on. From 1974 to 1984, she worked on satellites and computers, and in 1977, as a Lockheed contractor to the NSA, she was posted to Menwith Hill.

Peg had some misgivings about the work but was pleased at her own professional advancement. She was ultimately one of the architects of the Echelon system and told Kenan and Skipper, "I don't mean to brag, but I was very good at what I did, and I actually felt like Echelon was my baby." She told them that the system was immensely sophisticated even then. "In 1979 we could track a specific person and zoom in on his phone conversation while he was communicating. Since our satellites could in 1984 film a postage stamp lying on the ground, it is almost impossible to imagine how all-encompassing the system must be today." She revealed that the NSA came up with the name Echelon and that it referred to the computer network used to sort through the communications. She said the computers used software programs called Silkworth and Sire.

"On the day at Menwith Hill when I realized how utterly wrong it was," Peg told the Danes, "I was sitting with one of the many translators. He was an expert in languages like Russian, Chinese, and Japanese. Suddenly he asked me if I wanted to listen in on a conversation taking place in the U.S. at the office in the U.S. Senate Building." Peg—naturally curious—said yes and slipped on the translator's headphones. On the line, she heard a mellifluous southern accent that sounded strangely familiar. She asked the translator who it was, and he said, That's Senator Strom Thurmond. It was at this point, Peg told Skipper and Kenan, that she realized, "We're not only spying on other countries, but also on our own citizens."

Peg was eventually fired from Lockheed for complaining about corruption and sexual harassment and for making allegations about overcharging by contractors. At this point, Peg sprung into action. She brought a lawsuit over what she claimed was a pervasive problem of false charges by Lockheed on government contracts. She claimed that she had been fired because in 1984 she was asked to do something at work which she was not willing to do, because she believed it could harm the government. (She would not say publicly what this task was.) In a separate case, she sued for wrongful termination and contacted the internal-security commission, the Defense Contract Audit Agency, which arranged a series of hearings in which Peg could describe her ordeal and her observation of abuses. An article appeared in the Cleveland *Plain Dealer*, outlining her allegations about listening in on Strom Thurmond. Thurmond himself professed to be unpersuaded and unworried by the charges. But in 1988, Peg testified before a closed-door session of the House Intelligence Oversight Committee. Her testimony and subsequent discussion of it by Congress have been sealed.

Peg Newsham is hardly the only UKUSA employee to go public over the years. In 1991, the British television program *World in Action* aired a segment about abuses of power at GCHQ. A former GCHQ officer who spoke anonymously described a nondescript brick building at 8 Palmer Street, London, where GCHQ secretly intercepts every telex that passes into, out of, or through the city. He said technicians feed the intercepts into powerful computers and that the computers run on a program called Dictionary. Moreover, this anonymous whistleblower said that 8 Palmer Street was staffed not only with GCHQ employees but also with carefully vetted representatives from British Telecom. "They take everything," he told the show, "the embassies, all the business deals, even the birthday greetings. They feed it into the dictionary."

This was a classic Sigint leak, complete with numerous reasons to question the credibility of the source. He was a former employee, not current. He was a single voice; the story was not corroborated. His refusal to be identified was clearly so as not to run afoul of the Official Secrets Act, but it also prevented the viewer from assessing his seniority—where he would rank on the inverted pyramid of the need to know. Yet at the same time, the details of what he said match perfectly the many other accounts of the Echelon system.

A year later, in the summer of 1992, a group of current "highly placed intelligence operatives" with GCHQ told *The Observer*, "We feel we can no longer remain silent regarding that which we consider to be gross malpractice and negligence within the establishment in which we operate." These whistleblowers had a litany of complaints. "Telephone, telex, and facsimile messages of legitimate companies and individuals [are] freely intercepted and disseminated to individuals and companies, and 'concerns external to normal procedures' without governmental or committee consent," they began. They suggested that surveillance targets routinely included "public and media figures, academics, social, charitable and commercial concerns," and that the agency listened in under lapsed warrants or without warrants, without any effective oversight or proper grounds for surveillance. The operatives said it was "possible to key in a triggerword which enables us to home in on the telex communications every time that word appears." In particular, they claimed that GCHQ had intercepted the communications of three charity organizations, including Amnesty International and Christian Aid. Like Peg Newsham, these insiders became emboldened by the ability to air their grievances, and—rather than limit their disclosures to the inadequacy of the warrant situation, the dangers to personal privacy, or the spying on Amnesty—they went on to point out that GCHQ was spying on companies and occasionally passing information to competitors, as a quid pro quo for "services rendered"; that internal security at Cheltenham was "generally lax to the point of absurdity"; and that the agency was inefficient, for "at least 20 percent of the workforce is idle half of the day."

When *The Observer* questioned the group about details at GCHQ in order to confirm that they worked there, the whistleblowers demonstrated an intimate knowledge of the place. When asked to provide some kind of proof about listening in on Amnesty, they furnished details from a private telex supposedly sent by Amnesty. John Merritt, the reporter on the story, contacted Amnesty to verify the details, and Amnesty, no doubt a little unsettled, confirmed that yes, such a telex had been sent.

PEG NEWSHAM ALSO HAD her credibility questioned, but this did not render her beyond the pale for Kenan and Skipper. *Ekstra Bladet* is, after all, a tabloid. "It has lots of tabloid characteristics, but mixed in there are higher quality researched articles," Kenan assured me, a little defensively. The paper is colorful, with blaring headlines, a scantily clad "Page 9 Girl," and heavy doses of celebrities and sports. But it has also won numerous Cavling Awards—the Danish equivalent of the Pulitzer—Kenan said. And it has half a million readers, which in a country of about five million is an impressive circulation. Nevertheless, where another journalist might carefully omit Peg's paranoid rambling, *Ekstra Bladet* gave it center stage. She told Kenan and Skipper that "certain elements" in the CIA and NSA wanted to silence her and that she sleeps with a loaded pistol under her mattress. Her best friend is a 120-pound German shepherd, trained to be a guard and attack dog by the Nevada State Police. The dog's name is Mister Gunther.

I asked the Danes if they thought Peg was paranoid or if they really believed the agencies were trying to harass her. "I don't think it's the agencies that are harassing her," Kenan said.

"I'm glad to hear you say that—" I started to say, but Kenan wasn't finished.

"But it might be people *affiliated* with the agencies," he said. "Crazy, patriotic types. I don't think she's paranoid."

"You know she had all of the mails from us erased from her computer," Skipper added, nodding, one eyebrow arched suggestively.

"I don't think she's paranoid," Kenan said again.

KENAN AND SKIPPER WERE hardly the first at this game. That would be a man named David Kahn. As a boy, Kahn saw a book on codes and ciphers in the window of the public library in his hometown of Great Neck, New York. The book ignited a lifelong interest, and as a thirty-one-year-old reporter for *Newsday* Kahn published *The Codebreakers,* a scrupulously researched, copiously footnoted history of secret writing. The book became a classic the moment it was published, by Macmillan, in 1967: it was a monumental feat of scholarship in a field that was until then largely overrun by hacks and dilettantes.

But *The Codebreakers* was almost never published, because David Kahn had decided to include a chapter on the NSA. "The then director of the NSA went to my publisher in New York and tried to negotiate with them," he told me recently. Today, Kahn is a dapper old gent in a houndstooth jacket, his gray hair slicked back, his grin quick and conspiratorial. "But that didn't work. They considered breaking into my house, which was actually my father's house, in Great Neck to try to get the manuscript," he chuckled.

As the book neared completion, the NSA continued to badger Kahn and his publisher. They endeavored to purchase the copyright for the book, which might then allow them to quash it, but were unable to do so. When all their tricks had failed, the NSA realized that the book was going to come out but appealed to Macmillan to delete several passages that it regarded as particularly incendiary. Kahn eventually agreed and deleted the passages. One of these involved Enigma material, which was still considered highly sensitive. Another outlined the close cooperation between the NSA and GCHQ.

KAHN WAS FOLLOWED, over a decade later, by a young man from Boston named James Bamford. Straight out of law school, with no writing experience to speak of, Bamford had decided he did not want to be a lawyer and was making ends meet by working part-time as a private investigator. The gumshoe skills he picked up were to help a great deal in the project he was about to undertake.

In the wake of the Church-committee hearings, Bamford decided he would write about the NSA, and he approached Kahn. "He came to me and said he was going to do a book on it," Kahn told me. "And I said here, take my files. I wasn't going to use them anymore. And I made a lifelong friend." Bamford approached Houghton Mifflin in Boston in 1979. Hardly anyone at the publisher had even heard of the NSA, but Bamford was able, over the course of several lunches, to persuade the company to take on the book.

He started with the records of the Church committee hearings, which he found at a government-documents repository at Wellesley College. In the footnotes of the hearings he stumbled on references to dozens of specific documents, which were useful, as the Freedom of Information Act will often allow you to obtain a specifically requested document but will not furnish all of the documents on some generic subject. Bamford put together an initial three-page list of documents. The agency rejected it entirely.

Bamford was undeterred, however, and managed, through a series of brilliant maneuvers, to glean information about the NSA. For instance, the listening stations around the planet did not appear in reports of the Senate appropriations subcommittee on military construction, but Bamford discovered that when a base wanted to build a bowling alley or basketball court, the requisition for that construction was unclassified. Comparing this sort of data with unclassified phone directories and personnel rosters, he was able, through a kind of triangulation, to compile a list of listening stations around the world. He learned that the internal newsletter of the NSA bore the warning, "for NSA employees and their immediate families." Bamford argued that because families of NSA employees had not been granted security clearance, he should be entitled to look at the newsletters as well. He requested every newsletter going back twenty-five years.

At this point, agency officials realized that Bamford was serious and, their backs against the wall, became cooperative. The agency agreed to give him a tour of Fort Meade and allowed him to interview several top officials. Wondering how closely the NSA cooperated with Britain and Canada, Bamford drove through the parking lot, jotting down the license plates of all of the cars parked in choice spots for top officials, close to the buildings. He then traced the cars and found that one belonged to an Englishman and another to a Canadian. He wrote to the agency to tell them what he had learned, and several months later, with Ronald Reagan in office, the NSA attempted, unsuccessfully, to prosecute Bamford under the Espionage Act for jeopardizing national security.

The Puzzle Palace came out in 1982 and became a bestseller. This was the first full-length book about the NSA and the only significant advance on Kahn's research. Many Americans had still never heard of the agency. When Bamford was doing his book tour, he found himself sharing a car ride to the taping of a television show with the New Jersey senator Bill Bradley. Bradley asked Bamford what his book was about, and Bamford replied, "It's about NSA, the National Security Agency." Curious, Bradley asked, "What's that?"

Bamford's book exposed the agency to the first real public scrutiny of its workings, and agency officials deeply resented Bamford for it. Two decades after the book appeared, former NSA director William Odom laid the blame for many dried-up sources directly on Bamford's door, claiming that in the 1980s *The Puzzle Palace* "became the handbook for hostile intelligence services (in particular the Soviet and Chinese) seeking to penetrate, evade, or otherwise deceive the NSA." But Odom's objections notwithstanding, *The Puzzle Palace* has, in the years since its publication, undergone a peculiar transformation: it has gone from heresy to dogma. The book became a standard text at the U.S. Defense Intelligence College (now called the Joint Military Intelligence College) in Washington. Bamford, meanwhile, has gone from being the scourge of the NSA to the agency's hagiographer.

Such a gradual transformation is not unusual. Bob Woodward was a thorn in the side of the establishment in the 1970s, and rose to prominence by helping to expose the Watergate story, which the Nixon administration desperately wanted to stifle. Yet by 2003, when he published his bestseller *Bush at War,* Woodward seemed to have gone from being the ultimate gadfly outsider to the consummate insider: he made a devil's bargain and got far greater access, but perhaps at the cost of his objectivity. It is a strange by-product of the upheavals of the second half of the twentieth century that the establishment comes to embrace, if not outright co-opt, those who once were its most vociferous detractors. Thus, on the fiftieth anniversary of the founding of the NSA, David Kahn stood beaming before a group of NSA employees at Fort Meade and told them that he felt like Harry Truman after he won the election in 1948, holding up the *Chicago Daily Tribune* with the banner headline saying "Dewey Defeats Truman." "Well," Kahn said, relishing the moment, "Kahn beat NSA."

And indeed, while they were once banned by the NSA, today *The Codebreakers* and *The Puzzle Palace* probably sell more copies to employees of Sigint agencies than to any other market. They are the books that prospective employees read to get a sense of the place where they will be working. Because of the compartmentalized nature of Sigint agencies, it is only from these books, written by outsiders, that employees can glean an aerial sense of the topography and scope of the institution beyond their individual rabbit holes. When after two decades, during which time no one else had published a full-length book on the NSA, Bamford wrote a follow-up, *Body of Secrets,* he included an in-depth interview with Director Mike Hayden himself and thanked Hayden first in the acknowledgments. The book party was thrown at Fort Meade, and a line of NSA employees hoping to get their books signed stretched out the door.

ONE RAINY NIGHT IN February 1977, three men met in a basement flat in the Muswell Hill section of London and talked over a bottle of cheap Chianti. They were Crispin Aubrey, a reporter for *Time Out* magazine; John Berry, a social worker and former Sigint officer; and a young Scot named Duncan Campbell. At the time, Campbell was twenty-four years old and had been something of a scientific prodigy, having already gained his Ph.D. in physics from Oxford before deciding, like Skipper Elkjaer would later do, to become a freelance journalist. Campbell's mother had spent the Second World War breaking codes at Bletchley Park, and he was fascinated by Sigint. When he was pursuing his Ph.D., he began to notice that the British countryside was dotted with radio and satellite stations—and it was the mystery of these stations that led him into investigative journalism. As they sat and talked, the three had little idea that their conversation would soon become the basis for a major prosecution for violating the Official Secrets Act (a crime that, in Campbell's case, could mean thirty years in prison) and a case that would become known by the initials of the three men's names: the ABC trial.

Six months earlier, Campbell and Mark Hosenball, the twenty-five-year-old son of a Washington lawyer, who was working as a freelance journalist for the *Evening Standard,* had published an article in *Time Out.* The article, called "The Eavesdroppers," revealed the existence of

GCHQ, years before it would be publicly acknowledged by the British government, and detailed many of the workings of the agency. Hosenball was consequently ordered out of the country by Home Secretary Merlyn Rees, on national-security grounds. Because Campbell was Scottish and couldn't be deported, he was more difficult for the authorities to deal with. An Official Secrets Act prosecution was not pursued because it appeared that Campbell had somehow managed to compile all of his information from anodyne public sources like phone directories.

John Berry had been a corporal in a Sigint regiment in Cyprus. He wrote a letter to a committee representing Mark Hosenball, in which he identified himself as a former member of "an organization spending vast amounts of money in total absence of public control." The letter ended up in the hands of Crispin Aubrey, an environmental reporter. Because Sigint was hardly Aubrey's beat, he contacted Campbell and asked him to come along for the interview. "I want you to decide whether he's a bullshitter," he said. The three men met at Berry's flat, and the conversation itself was quite dry. Berry described the life of a signals officer, sitting for hours fiddling with wireless dials. While the account was colorful—he described listening to an Egyptian soldier cry to Allah as his tank was hit by an Israeli shell during the Six-Day War—it was not revelatory or sensitive in its disclosures. Berry confirmed that his base intercepted communications from other NATO members, but while that was secret it was not surprising; it would result in ruffled diplomatic feathers but no major security risks.

What Aubrey, Berry, and Campbell did not realize was that MI5 was tapping Campbell's telephone and knew all about the meeting. At ten o'clock, when the men had been talking for three hours and Crispin Aubrey's tape recorder ran out of tape, thirteen Special Branch officers suddenly burst into the apartment and arrested the three men for violating section 2 of the Official Secrets Act, which punished anyone who gives "official" information, whether it is secret or not. The men were held in prison for two days and were not allowed to see lawyers. While they were being held, police descended on Duncan Campbell's apartment in Brighton. They rifled through his things and transferred his library and files to Scotland Yard. The police leveled a second charge against him, because of nine hundred pages of material found in his apartment that was considered to be of "direct or indirect" use to a potential enemy, despite the fact that all of the material was from previously published sources. Eventually A, B, and C were tried before a jury and found guilty. Campbell and Aubrey were given conditional discharges, sparing them from serving any time; Berry received a six-month suspended sentence.

The government was right to worry about Campbell. He had a formidable technical mind and the scientific background that most investigative journalists lack and that would set him in good stead for understanding the complex dimensions of listening in. And he had an uncanny knack for sifting through public source material to get at a story and extract salient and revealing details. In the breathless words of Geoffrey Robertson, the human-rights lawyer who took up his defense, "What the security services wanted to put in solitary confinement was Duncan Campbell's brain."

IN 1988, DUNCAN CAMPBELL was the first journalist anywhere in the world to publish the code name Echelon. The article ran in *New Statesman and Society* magazine and opened with the hyperbolic salvo, "Somebody's Listening, and they don't give a damn about personal privacy." Campbell described a UKUSA project, code-named P415, that drastically expanded the electronic-surveillance capabilities of the five agencies. He described the Echelon computer system and identified Menwith Hill as one of the major anchors of the network. No one knew it at the time, but Campbell's main source for the article was none other than Peg Newsham.

From that article on, Campbell has left an indelible mark on the field. He is a frustrated and frustrating man—a brilliant and tireless researcher who is hindered by purple prose and an instinctive antiestablishment and anti-American bias. Throughout my research, everyone I encountered who knew Duncan Campbell warned me that "Duncan is prickly" or "Duncan is difficult," though none of them would question his bona fides. I heard him give a talk about Echelon in the late 1990s, which featured PowerPoint slides and graphic displays, but the presentation struck me as fueled by paranoia. Bald and intense, Campbell wore jeans and thick glasses and peppered his talk with asides that by turns expressed terror at and fascination with the technology he was describing. His slides revealed a net of listening stations and Sigint satellites that appeared so finely woven that nary a private communication might slip through unread.

That Campbell was followed, bugged, and burgled by the authorities in his early twenties goes some way to explaining the alarmism that has marked the rest of his career. Still, it is hazardous to write off paranoid-sounding assertions on the grounds that they are paranoid. Reading an account of the ABC trial in the memoirs of Geoffrey Robertson, I chuckled when I learned that Campbell had told his lawyer he would not put it past the authorities to vet the jury, effectively rigging his trial. His lawyer was naturally adamant that this was not something that happened, and as I read I jotted *PARANOID!!* in the margin and underlined it twice, only to keep reading and learn that in this case, Campbell was right. The government *did* try to rig the jury in the case.

Still, chances are you have never heard of Duncan Campbell and are unfamiliar with his work. Campbell is certainly the foremost chronicler of the Echelon network, something he is fond of pointing out in irascible posts to Cryptome and the like. But if his visibility is a good index of the visibility of the Echelon issue in general, it would appear that the issue still very much occupies the lunatic fringe of Internet conspiracy mavens and self-publishing ideologues. From 1978 to 1994, Campbell was at *New Statesman* as an investigative writer, associate editor, and finally chairman. In 1990, he founded a television production company called IPTV and has since focused on investigative documentaries. But without the imprimatur of a magazine or publisher, Campbell has consigned himself in the last decade to the periphery.

When I did approach Campbell, he was in fact hostile on learning that I was writing about Anglo-American signals intelligence. He implied that I was interested only in poaching his contacts and plagiarizing his research and told me that it would be a waste of his time to answer any of my questions. I tried to assure him that I wanted to write about *him* and his work in the field. He replied that he could not very well answer open-ended questions about something he had spent the better part of his life researching. It crossed my mind that this was part of the reason the Echelon story was not more widely known. This particular tale is the province of paranoids and investigative journalists, two types that share a ruthless and suspicious territoriality.

"DANISH BEER IS LIKE sitting in a canoe," Kenan said. I wondered if something was lost in translation. "Fucking close to water!" he roared, and he and Skipper laughed. We were sitting at Café Europa, a lively outdoor spot on a bustling square in the center of Copenhagen.

"See that guy?" Skipper asked, gesturing to a man in a suit, walking quickly past with a bulging briefcase. "That's the minister of the environment. It's a small country. You could just walk up to him."

"When we started, we had to tell people about what we were doing, nobody knew about it," Kenan said.

"It was so unknown we couldn't use the word in a headline," Skipper added. "But just recently, Danish *Jeopardy* had a question about it."

I asked if the contestant got it right. "Yeah," Kenan muttered, shaking his head and drawing on his cigarette, "it was one of the easy ones."

Their stories in *Ekstra Bladet* have had a profound impact in Denmark, raising public awareness about the close ties between Danish and American intelligence and leading to five parliamentary debates on different issues. They have exposed Danish listening stations—one just outside Copenhagen, at Sandagergard, and one at Aflandshage, on Amager Island in the Baltic—and have sought to demonstrate that Denmark is a third party to the Echelon network. In 1999, the Danish minister for defense admitted that Danish intelligence had been involved in a global interception system but would not confirm or deny that the NSA was involved.

In gathering their information, Skipper and Kenan have engaged in a protracted game of poker with Danish intelligence that is not unlike the game of code making and code breaking itself. At one point, Skipper wanted information about a base the code name of which, he suspected, was Station C. He made requests to the local administration on the building files. "There were three eighteen-meter dishes," Skipper told me. "And they were building another three. If you compare it to other European countries, per capita, it's the biggest station in Europe." Skipper and Kenan filed Freedom of Information requests with the Danish Ministry of Defense and received in reply an e-mail, with a Microsoft Word document attached. Skipper opened the document in the Notepad Editor program so that he could find out about the computer it was written on. What he found was the previous name of the document. The document they received was titled, "Answer to Kenan concerning Hjoerring." Hjoerring was the location of the base. The original title was "Answer to Kenan Concerning Station C."

"Don't get Skipper behind a computer," Kenan said. "He's like a fisherman pulling in the fish."

"We waited a few months, so they wouldn't figure out that's how we knew," Skipper told me, sounding like Admiral Sir William Hall sitting on the Zimmermann Telegram so as not to give away his code-breaking abilities. Then they slipped a casual aside into an article in which they confirmed that the code name of the Hjoerring site was Station C. "But they stopped sending us Word files," Kenan said. "So they must have figured it out."

THE AMERICAN FLAGS FLUTTERED upside down at Menwith Hill. I had been invited to join the annual Independence from America rally outside the gates by Lindis Percy of the Campaign for the Accountability of American Bases (CAAB). Lindis has watery blue eyes in a lined, very tanned face and a quick, toothy smile. Her hair is cropped in a sandy, wind-blown mullet. She has an uncanny resemblance to Vanessa Redgrave. Together with her partner, Anni Rainbow, a wheelchair-bound chain-smoker with a gruff way and an easy laugh, she campaigns tirelessly against the American military and intelligence presence in the English countryside. Her protests sometimes involve marches like the one planned for that day, the Fourth of July, but more often seem to involve Lindis simply jumping a fence and waltzing onto a base. In the name of "research," she routinely penetrates the defenses at various bases and wanders around, making her way into storage rooms and cafeterias before being apprehended by military police. The situation at Menwith Hill was sufficiently bad that several years ago the base received an injunction barring Lindis from the site—an injunction that Lindis proceeded to violate 114 times. The local lads at the Black Bull Inn seem slightly baffled by the generally female peace campaigners who have occasionally camped out near the base over the years. For reasons that I suspect are less than scientific, they refer to these women simply as "the lesbians." Lindis they know only as "the Head Lesbian."

As my taxi pulled up outside Menwith Hill for the first time since my initial visit to the site, a British policeman walked toward the car with a handheld video camera, pointing it at me. It was a strange feeling, but I soon found that when you're running with Lindis, you get used to such things. About a dozen people, some young, nose ringed, and dreadlocked, others women in middle age, were gathered around a blue van parked on the road facing the base. The bus was draped in an upside-down American flag, with the words "Independence from America" silk-screened on it. A handful of police in bright yellow jackets stood uncomfortably by the entrance. A guy walked around handing out copies of *Socialist Weekly*. Aging hippies exchanged pleasantries over enormous Thermoses of tea.

Inside the van, Lindis was filling balloons, with whiny gasps from a helium canister. She told me about a possible contact, a former Sigint officer she knew. "And I think he's legitimate," she said. "I've checked him out. Because . . ." She looked at me knowingly as her voice trailed off.

I nodded, knowingly, thinking she meant that some of these people can be paranoid cranks, and said, "Oh, I *know.*"

"Because, well," she continued, "infiltrators, you know."

The balloons said "Stop Star Wars," and as Lindis filled them volunteers tied them to a makeshift table holding flyers and CAAB newsletters. The morning was cool, and the balloons bobbled and snapped on their strings in the wind. The papers were held down with stones and seashells. I flipped through the newsletters ("Bylaw Fiasco Continues"; "Latest on ECHELON") and became aware that the squat military policeman who had registered me with his camcorder when I got out of the taxi was still pointing the damn thing at me. He stood on the street, holding the camera in front of him, looking at me through the viewfinder. I glared. I did not want to adopt the combative rhetoric of my hostesses—after all, this guy was just doing his job—but his persistence struck me as a fairly transparent bid at intimidation. Our staring contest continued until a station wagon slowed down next to him and a woman in a tie-dyed T-shirt said, "Excuse me, where would it be best for me to park?" Startled by this sudden demotion from Big Brother to Little Traffic Cop, my quarry lowered his camera and gave her directions.

"I find it offensive to be photographed like that," an old woman standing next to me at the table announced. "And you know, I know what the Africans mean when they say it takes away your soul. Because that's the way it feels."

With traffic flowing smoothly, my policeman raised his camera again. On a whim, I walked over and said, "Excuse me. Why are you filming me?"

"Evidence gathering," he said. "Are you American?" He seemed surprised.

"Yes," I said. "If you're gathering evidence, what was the crime?"

"We're gathering it in advance," he said. "In case a crime is committed."

I contemplated this for a moment.

"Have you been to York?" he asked, suddenly dropping the pretense of hostile authority.

"Uh, no," I said. "I haven't."

"Most of our American friends love York," he said.

"Is it mainly Americans inside then?" I asked.

"Well," he said, then paused. "We're not really allowed to say. But yeah, we've got a lot of Americans." Then he gazed out at the array of upside-down American flags and added, "We have very good relations with the Americans."

Back at the van, Lindis had taken up a megaphone and was encouraging people to join her in reciting from a document that was being passed around: the Declaration of Independence from America. She pointed out that this year the Americans inside had been forced to hold their Independence Day "jamboree" the week before, because they knew CAAB was coming. And with that, the assembled crowd began intoning the preamble. ("When, in the course of human events, a greater state imperils the safety and continuance of a lesser . . .") Feeling a bit awkward in my role as the only American outside the fence, I gazed around. There were about thirty protesters by now, and the age range was astonishing. Two girls who looked to be about fourteen, wearing baggy jeans and with chipped nail polish, held a banner that said, "We Need Trees, Not Bushes." Next to me, a thirty-something woman whispered in the ear of a paraplegic in a wheelchair.

An elderly woman with a wooden peace sign hanging around her neck held a banner with her husband, who leaned on a cane. "What annoys me is we walked from Brighton to Selby, and our son Jonathan was on my back," she said. "And now Jonathan is fifty." They had been decrying the American bases for half a century and had achieved nothing, and still they came, early on this July morning, to protest.

I wondered how effective it was as anything but a stunt. The flower-child aesthetics. The anti-Americanism undermined, somehow, by its own virulence. And that tragic flaw of the radical left, a surfeit of different agendas. As the reading of the declaration progressed I overheard a young Irish girl, wide-eyed and dreadlocked, remark to a new acquaintance, "The other thing I'm into now is refugees."

As I looked at Lindis and the van and the protesters and the gates to Menwith Hill, I noticed that the declaration was hardly reverberating over the ancient moors. On the contrary, those protesters who weren't chatting among themselves seemed to be mumbling and flubbing the words—the way you would a prayer whose gist you remembered better than its particulars, or the Declaration of Independence itself.

. . .

IT IS TEMPTING TO take these activists lightly, but as it happens one of the most ingenious and reliable chroniclers of the Echelon system is an activist of the Lindis Percy school—hell-bent on exposing America's geopolitical manipulations and not afraid to sneak into a Sigint base to do it. "If this book contained only information that the intelligence authorities were prepared to make public," Nicky Hager writes at the beginning of his extraordinary 1996 book, *Secret Power,* "it would be very short and much of its content would be misleading."

Hager is an incredibly intrepid reporter, and by focusing just on GCSB, the New Zealand signals organization, was able to reveal more about the Echelon system than any other journalist. Hager spent twelve years probing GCSB, and he started the way James Bamford did before him: looking at lists. He compared various lists of public servants and job titles and personnel directories and was able to construct a roster of all of the New Zealanders working at GCSB. "Lists of names . . . were the key for me, because I live in a small country," he says. "Our capital city, where I live, is only 150,000 people. And within that city . . . I started to be able to locate people who might be prepared to talk to me." He approached current intelligence officers working at the agency and found, to his surprise, that most of the people he approached were willing to talk with him. Word got out that he was researching the agency, and GCSB warned staff about him. This only increased the leaks, however, directing anyone with a grudge to settle or a story to tell to Hager's sympathetic ear. For years, Hager got a thrill every time he reached into the mailbox, wondering whether someone had sent him leaked information or secret documents. Because Sigint agencies are so compartmentalized, Hager had to meet with different people from different parts of the organization in order to get a broad overview of GCSB's operations. "The person working in this office quite likely doesn't have much idea at all of what the people would do in the office next door, and they probably have no idea of what happens in the floor below them in the building," he says. "And so to build up a picture of what was happening I had to locate people in all different parts of the organization who were prepared to talk to me. And there is something about the easygoing or casual character of New Zealanders that meant that I was able to find a large number of people who would speak to me, and I could win their trust." An easygoing approach to security helped Hager as well. Following Bamford, he requested personnel newsletters and received them with sensitive information blacked out. But Hager realized that by holding the newsletters up to his desk light he could make out the deleted words.

Like Lindis, Nicky Hager is something of a daredevil, and he gathered some of his information about the Waihopi Echelon station, which was built on New Zealand's South Island in 1989, just by walking in. The base is surrounded by fences and razor wire, but Hager blithely says that he "went there several times while writing the book," to have a look around. He also managed to sneak in a television crew, who used a ladder to point their camera through a window into one of the operations buildings. There was no one there but a night watchman, and he was asleep. Hager's crew filmed Echelon equipment in the main operations room and, zooming in, captured the titles of Intelsat manuals on the desks. Hager claims that this confirms the facility's role in intercepting Intelsat traffic.

Early on in his investigation of GCSB, Hager began to realize that "the technical systems they were using and the targeting lists and the regulations and manuals . . . had another agency's name on [them], and the target lists came from the NSA." In this manner he discovered "that New Zealand was actually a little window into finding out about the whole alliance." The officers he talked to had been trained in London, Washington, and Canberra, and the new equipment that they were installing had been planned in five-nation working groups, generally in Washington. Hager concedes that "it's a strange thing that international systems should be exposed from a far-flung country like New Zealand" but credits his access to insiders.

When he finished the book, he took the manuscript to David Lange, who had been prime minister of New Zealand for five years, during which time he was theoretically overseeing GCSB. Hager sat in Lange's office while Lange read. When he finished, Lange was outraged. He said he wanted to write the foreword to the book, and did so. In it, he announced that prior to reading *Secret Power* he had no idea that New Zealand was even a part of Echelon. Lange had presided over the opening of Waihopi and had been led to believe it would actually be an independent New Zealand base—a gesture of autonomy from the United States in intelligence. Hager set him straight. "An astonishing number of people here told him things that I, as Prime Minister in charge of the intelligence services, was never told," Lange wrote.

. . .

THE LOOSE CLAN OF journalists, activists, and whistleblowers who have worked, over the last four decades, to bring some details about Anglophone Sigint operations to light is very small and very strange. It is an embattled little group, as either blowing the whistle from the inside or writing stories from the outside mean flirting with serious jail time. It is a rivalrous, secretive, and very paranoid tribe, arguably as interesting in and of itself—as an anthropological curio, a particular evolutionary adaptation to our suspicious century—as any of the rumors and revelations it has produced. For decades, these individuals worked to elevate the profile of the low-profile agencies, to get people worried about personal privacy and America's neoimperialist ambitions, to raise the hue and cry. And no one seemed to listen—until the late 1990s, when a group of politicians in Europe finally did.

TOOTHLESS TALKING SHOP

The European Parliament Investigates

THE EUROPEAN PARLIAMENT complex in Brussels is an imposing hodgepodge of stone and semireflective glass, the whole place ubiquitous with cranes, reminding the visitor that this monument to a united Europe is, like the city of Berlin today, in a perpetual state of *becoming*. The parliament is the legislative body of the European Union, and, in an act of diplomacy and largesse, its seven hundred–odd elected members, from the twenty-five countries in the union, split their time between cushy seats in Brussels, Strasbourg, and Luxembourg. I had come to Brussels because in 2000 the parliament had launched a major investigation into the existence and activities of the Echelon system. I had been corresponding with Ilka Schroeder, a Green Party member of the European Parliament from Germany who was a key figure on the investigative committee of three dozen. Every time I talked to a journalist or activist or Echelon watcher, they told me that Ilka was the woman to get in touch with. Ilka had sent me some useful information and done her best, by e-mail, to educate me on the manner in which the parliament functions. Ilka's assistant, a friendly, prematurely graying guy in a dark sweater, met me in the lobby of the main building, named for the European federalist Altiero Spinelli, and ushered me through the security procedures. We took an elevator up to Ilka's floor and entered a clean, new suite of offices. Ilka walked in, beaming, a very small woman with short blond hair and elfin features, dressed in dark Levi's and a velvet jacket. Having grown accustomed, on my travels, to being the youngest person in the room, I caught my breath. Ilka Schroeder was twenty-four years old.

· · ·

EUROPEAN CONCERN OVER ECHELON began in the early days of 1998, with the presentation of a report called "An Appraisal of the Technologies of Political Control." The report had been commissioned by the Scientific and Technical Options Assessment (STOA) committee of the parliament. It was written by a Manchester-based researcher named Steve Wright, who worked for the Omega Foundation. The report addressed a broad range of new and intrusive technologies, from surveillance cameras to "crowd control weapons," "prison control systems," and the technologies and techniques of interrogation and torture. Reading Wright's report, I was reminded of a passage from Richard Hofstadter's seminal essay, "The Paranoid Style in American Politics":

> The plausibility the paranoid style has for those who find it plausible lies, in good measure, in this appearance of the most careful, conscientious, and seemingly coherent application to detail, the laborious accumulation of what can be taken as convincing evidence for the most fantastic conclusions, the careful preparation for the big leap from the undeniable to the unbelievable.

The report adopted the rhetoric and emulated the conventions of social science, but the pretense of sober empiricism failed to mask what was ultimately a little piece of alarmism. One particular leap from the undeniable to the unbelievable that caught the attention of the parliament was a short section on communications interception, which gave an account of the Echelon system, cribbed largely from Nicky Hager's *Secret Power*. "Within Europe, all email, telephone and fax communications are routinely intercepted by the United States National Security Agency," the report declared, "transferring all target information from the European mainland via the strategic hub of London then by Satellite to Fort Meade in Maryland via the crucial hub at Menwith Hill in the North York Moors of the UK."

Glyn Ford, a British MEP with a technical background and the head of STOA, was persuaded by the allegations. "Frankly, the only people who have any doubt about the existence of Echelon are in the United States," he said in late September 1998. "These spy systems were seen as a necessary part of international security during the Cold War," he added several days later. "But there is no military reason for spying on Russia now unless they want to listen to the sound of the proto-capitalist economy collapsing." This sentiment seemed to echo across initial discussions of the system in Europe. The idea borrows from the

American political philosopher Francis Fukuyama's suggestion that the end of the cold war was really the End of History, that the Hegelian dialectic of the twentieth century had reached its teleological resolution and that the west had won. While the allegations generated outrage and incredulity in the parliament and the European press, it did not seem initially as though the story would go anywhere. And indeed, Ford conceded, "there is not enough information on Echelon, beyond its existence, to debate the matter fully."

What the parliament did do was commission another report, this one from Duncan Campbell, the person who exposed the code name Echelon back in 1988. Released in the summer of 1999, Campbell's report was titled *Interception Capabilities 2000,* and from the beginning it caused a stir. "This report describes how Comint organizations have for more than 80 years made arrangements to obtain access to much of the world's international communications," Campbell began. "Comprehensive systems exist to access, intercept and process every important modern form of communications, with few exceptions." Campbell claimed that this was achieved because the "UKUSA nations are between them currently operating at least 120 satellite based collection systems."

To Campbell's credit, he went some way in resisting the temptation to exaggerate capabilities. "Contrary to reports in the press, effective 'word spotting' search systems automatically to select telephone calls of intelligence interest are not yet available, despite 30 years of research," he wrote, deflating Mike Frost's alarmist claim that if you say the word *bomb* on the telephone you might end up in an NSA database. Campbell also made a nod in the direction of the legal guidelines governing Sigint agencies. "Although European communications passing on intercity microwave routes can be collected," he wrote, "it is likely that they are normally ignored." Here, Campbell seemed eager to counsel some restraint and temper the alarmism with more evenhanded reassurances.

BUT ONE ASPECT OF Campbell's report generated a great deal of controversy. As Glyn Ford suggested, one of the End of History questions on peoples' minds when they consider a system like Echelon is: if they're not listening to the Soviets anymore, whom are they listening to? In the safe world we occupied post–cold war but pre–September 11, whom did the UKUSA countries eavesdrop on? Duncan Campbell had an answer: corporations.

Interception Capabilities 2000 suggested in no uncertain terms that the UKUSA Sigint network was being used for economic intelligence, to advance the interests of corporate industrial giants in the countries involved. "Each UKUSA country authorizes national level intelligence assessment organizations and relevant individual ministries to task and receive economic intelligence from Comint," Campbell wrote.

> Such information may be collected for myriad purposes, such as: estimation of future essential commodity prices; determining other nation's private positions in trade negotiations; monitoring international trading in arms; tracking sensitive technology; or evaluating the political stability and/or economic strength of a target country.

He pointed out that on May 5, 1977, a secret new U.S. department, the Office of Intelligence Liaison, was created by the NSA, the CIA, and the Department of Commerce. Its task was to handle "foreign intelligence" of interest to the Department of Commerce. In 1993, the existence of the office was revealed by a British television program, and the name was changed, in a bid for the most cosmetic level of secrecy, to the Office of Executive Support.

While the general suggestion that the agencies were doing this kind of monitoring was already fairly controversial, the most incendiary passages in the report detailed specific allegations of abuse. Campbell cited three particular instances. The first involved a deal between the Panavia consortium, a European defense contractor, and Saudi Arabia. He cited a 1993 television program about Menwith Hill in which a former American National Security Council official named Howard Teicher described how Panavia was specifically targeted over sales to the Middle East. "I recall that the words 'Tornado' or 'Panavia'— information related to the specific aircraft—would have been priority targets that we would have wanted information about," Teicher said.

The second case involved the French defense contractor Thomson-CSF and Brazil. According to Campbell, in 1994 the NSA intercepted phone calls between Thomson-CSF and Brazil concerning SIVAM, a proposed $1.3 billion surveillance system for the Amazon rain forest. There had been allegations that Thomson-CSF had bribed Brazilian officials in order to secure the contract. Ultimately, the contract was awarded to Raytheon, a major American technology firm and, Cambell hastened to add, a major contractor at the Echelon satellite-interception station at Sugar Grove. As circumstantial evidence, Campbell offered a statement by Raytheon after winning the contract: "The Department of Commerce worked very hard in support of U.S. industry on this project."

The most notorious case involved another defense contractor for the U.S. government. In 1994, Airbus Industrie, the French aerospace firm, lost a $6 billion contract with Saudi Arabia to the American giants Boeing and McDonnell Douglas. Shortly thereafter, an article appeared in the Baltimore *Sun*, which Campbell claims was "well informed." The article contended that

> from a commercial communications satellite, NSA lifted all the faxes and phone calls between the European consortium Airbus, the Saudi national airline and the Saudi government. The agency found that Airbus agents were offering bribes to a Saudi official. It passed the information to U.S. officials pressing the bid of Boeing Co and Mc-Donell Douglas Corp [*sic*].

CHARGES OF INDUSTRIAL ESPIONAGE by Sigint agencies are nothing new. The "highly placed signals intelligence operatives" from GCHQ who blew the whistle to *The Observer* in 1992 suggested that "commercial information" was "being gathered from firms and disseminated to rival companies in return for 'services rendered.' " In fact, Katharine Gun told me that even today eavesdropping is divided into three classifications: "national security"; "serious crimes"; and "economic well-being." She added that she believes "economic well-being was added fairly recently." A former employee at Pine Gap told the Australian defense expert Desmond Ball that the eavesdroppers there listened to satellite intercepts of early-morning stock-exchange and other business calls. "We listened to many business conversations and transactions," he said. "We could have made a fortune." If the thought crossed the minds of analysts on the ground, it must have occurred to those who determine watch lists at the UKUSA agencies. And certainly during the Clinton years it may have seemed that the agencies were simply reorienting. Warren Christopher, then secretary of state, said in testimony to the Senate Foreign Relations Committee, "In the post–Cold War world, our national security is inseparable from our economic security."

"No is the short answer," British prime minister Tony Blair said when asked whether intercepts were used for these purposes. "These things are governed by extremely strict rules, and these rules will always be applied." James Rubin, the State Department spokesman said, "U.S. intelligence agencies are not tasked to engage in industrial espionage or obtain trade secrets for the benefit of any U.S. company or companies." It may indeed be that the United States and the United Kingdom don't *task* their agencies to look out for this sort of information, the Baltimore *Sun* article notwithstanding, but given that the take tends to be broad, analysts may well notice certain pieces of intelligence that come in with everything else. (When the NSA acknowledged that it held secret files on Princess Diana in 1998, an agency official claimed that information was gathered and retained not because the princess was a target but because her communications were sucked in incidentally, along with all the other flotsam and jetsam of global interception.)

Nevertheless, Director of Central Intelligence George Tenet told the House Intelligence Oversight Committee during the summer of 2000:

> I recognize that it is standard practice for some countries to use their intelligence services to conduct economic espionage, but that is not the policy or practice of the United States. If we lose the confidence of the American people because they think we are violating their privacy rights, or if we were to violate the trust of our allies and steal their business secrets to help U.S. companies increase their profits, we would put your support for our SIGINT programs in jeopardy, and risk losing our eyes and ears—as well as U.S. influence—around the world. I cannot afford to let that happen.

Tenet pointed out that maintaining the trust of America's allies and trading partners is of greater importance than prevailing on a big-ticket contract here or there and added, "If we did this, where would we draw the line? Which companies would we help? Corporate giants? The little guy? All of them? I think we quickly would get into a mess and would raise questions of whether we are being unfair to one or more of our own businesses."

The difficulty faced by the intelligence community was the same with industrial espionage as it was with privacy. The best they could do was say, Trust us, particularly because Tenet did not explicitly deny that the United States collects economic information. "Sigint does provide economic information that is useful to the United States Government," he conceded.

It can provide insight into global economic conditions and trends and assist policymakers in dealing with economic crises. On many occasions, it has provided information about the intentions of foreign businesses, some operated by governments, to violate U.S. laws or sanctions or to deny U.S. businesses a level playing field. When such information arises, it is provided to the Treasury Department, the Commerce Department, or other government agencies responsible for enforcing U.S. laws.

IT WAS ON THE momentum of industrial-espionage charges that the European Parliament's Temporary Committee on the Echelon Interception System got up and running in the summer of 2000, when the parliament appointed thirty-six members to spend one year looking into the allegations in Duncan Campbell's report. The aim was, predictably at this point, to produce yet *another* report. Carlos Coelho, a debonair Christian Democrat from Portugal, was selected to head the committee. "Some things were published that were not true, that are not technically possible," he said of the existing literature on Echelon. "But there are others we have to look into and find out if this can happen and in what way. We have to protect our citizens and our enterprises. That's our duty."

Enterprises rather than citizens were transparently the source of the political momentum for the investigation from the beginning, however. While privacy might have been a tough sell, as it means different things to different people, the losses of lucrative jobs or contracts in the home countries and constituencies of MEPs were able to generate political outrage more easily. What followed was a year of investigation in which the parliamentarians sought to cobble together everything they could on Echelon from the public sphere and interview the whole assemblage of individuals who knew about Sigint and were willing to talk. Part of the problem was that under the broad rubric of "industrial espionage" lay a wide range of activities, some of which the American intelligence community freely admitted, such as monitoring trade conferences and enforcing embargoes, and some of which it flatly denied, like passing foreign-trade secrets to American corporations and rigging competitive bidding on contracts. Moreover, this particular mystery of Echelon—whether it was being used to spy on companies—would be the most impossible one to solve.

"I have never found any indication that NSA takes information from European countries and passes it on to U.S. commercial companies," James Bamford said. He had been invited to testify before the committee in late April 2001, and he wanted to set them straight. "First of all, NSA has a natural reluctance to share intelligence with almost anyone. I've even had directors of the CIA tell me that they can't get the NSA to give them the information they want." Bamford explained that in order to pass intercept information on to U.S. companies, even if the NSA did so through some liaison at the Commerce Department, it would be necessary to give clearances that ran higher than top secret to people at the companies. And if you started making this kind of exception for one company, you would have to do it for others. The whole system of classification would be in jeopardy.

"I spent twenty years as a journalist in Washington writing about government," Bamford told the committee members, "and I know about leaks. That's how my job works: I get the leaks, and that's how we get the news. And if NSA was passing top-secret intercept information to Boeing or to Lockheed or to any of these other companies, it would leak probably within an hour."

Asking James Bamford was going to be as close as the committee would get to asking the NSA directly. Bamford has scores of contacts, both active and retired, from the agency, and is on a first-name basis with Mike Hayden and numerous former directors. He cautioned the committee that he was not an apologist for the agency and mentioned, rather defensively, that the NSA had tried to prosecute him way back in 1982—but he said he did not think this kind of activity was happening.

This pronouncement may have been disappointing to those eager parliamentarians who, in some sense, almost seemed to *want* it to be true that the United States was engaged in this sort of deplorable activity—and in any event wanted to disclose a smoking gun. But they had only to wait, as Bamford proceeded to qualify and undermine his own position, saying, "And if they *did* decide to do that, I'm sure I wouldn't be told. And none of you would be told. . . . I could be totally wrong here, they could be doing it right now, but that's just my opinion." He added that the NSA is involved in eavesdropping on European companies in order to stop trade in embargoed materials, such as chemical weapons or engine parts for cruise missiles. He said that they also routinely monitor any type of international trade meetings, such as NAFTA conferences. "That's one of the reasons why the U.S. likes to have all these conferences on U.S. soil or close to U.S.

soil," he said, "because it makes it easier for the eavesdropper to listen in."

This seemed more in character, the parliamentarians thought, though many would not give up believing in the more muscular conception of industrial espionage that Duncan Campbell had articulated. The Europeans also held great stock in the remarks of a man who had managed to singularly complicate the debate over industrial espionage: former Director of Central Intelligence James Woolsey. Never one to mince words, Woolsey takes a certain pride in calling things as he sees them and has been known to tell journalists investigating the NSA, "I wish you nothing but bad luck."

In the spring of 2000, as Duncan Campbell's allegations were echoing through the corridors of Brussels and Strasbourg, Woolsey wrote an Op-Ed piece for *The Wall Street Journal* that was a direct response to the report and wore the unapologetic headline, "Why We Spy on Our Allies." "My European friends, get real," Woolsey wrote. "True, in a handful of areas European technology surpasses American, but, to say this as gently as I can, the number of such areas is very, very, very small. Most European technology just isn't worth our stealing." Woolsey acknowledged that America eavesdrops on its allies and sorts through intercepts by looking for keywords. And he claimed the justification for this activity was in the pages of Duncan Campbell's report. "That's right, my continental friends," he jeered, "we have spied on you because you bribe. Your companies' products are often more costly, less technically advanced or both, than your American competitors'. As a result you bribe a lot. So complicit are your governments that in several European countries bribes still are tax-deductible."

WOOLSEY'S SWAGGER MAY HAVE seemed characteristic of a typical American bravado, contemptuous of European industry, the European Parliament, and Duncan Campbell's piddling compendium of hypotheses and allegations. But as the parliamentarians sat in Brussels wringing their hands and producing one histrionic report after another, there was a sense in which they seemed more intent on adolescent posturing than on achieving any substantial change. On hearing that the Parliament had elected to create a committee to investigate Echelon, John Young, the Cryptome editor, said, "I don't believe for a moment the Parliament will do anything more than cloak this. Watch for hearings that don't go anywhere." A Green Party member who was interviewed by the German online publication *Telopolis* referred to the committee as a "toothless talking shop." Though the powers of the Parliament have grown steadily since the 1980s, they have done so for the most part to the degree that the Parliament cooperates or consults for the more powerful European Council, and as a result it *does* remain something of a toothless organization.

And a very peculiar one. While I was visiting, Ilka invited me to attend a conference run by the delightfully named Radical Italians, one of the many parties represented at the Parliament. The conference was held in a large, round room, with state-of-the-art booths manned by simultaneous translators and a windowed wall looking out at cranes against a gray Belgian sky. The subject of the conference was "Democracy, Freedom and the Internet: How Digital Technologies Empower or Undermine Civil Liberties." There were a good number of MEPs in attendance, but I noticed a lot of familiar faces as well: Marc Rotenberg, the smooth, suited president of the Washington-based Electronic Privacy Information Center; Simon Davies, the bald, chain-smoking head of the London-based Privacy International; Yaman Akdeniz, of Leeds-based Cyber Rights and Civil Liberties. It was very much the same crowd I had encountered at a conference on surveillance cameras in a bland Washington ballroom the month before. I reflected on this itinerant troupe of activists, cellphones in hand, PowerPoint presentations at the ready, and the degree to which they seemed to flit around the world, addressing groups that were like-minded, primarily because they were more often than not the same people. "They're the digital elite," Ilka said, nodding in the direction of Simon and Marc. "They meet every six weeks in a different city."

Ilka had been an elected member of the Parliament since she was twenty-one, and as chair of the morning panel discussion she seemed to know everyone and have the kind of studied, slippery political instincts one normally sees in much older dignitaries as they work the room. (Ilka's youth may just be a German thing; she is the youngest member of the European Parliament, but she's an elder stateswoman next to Anna Lührmann, who was elected as a Green Party member to the Bundestag, the German Parliament, at the seasoned age of eighteen.)

I may be too readily duped into thinking that age and formality equate to gravitas, but there was something unmistakably undergraduate about the gathering, a kind of inescapable inconsequentiality that the participants were able to keep at bay only by ratcheting up the rhetorical temperature. The Parliament Members were uniformly young and deeply tanned—not the kind of tan you get from a weekend in the south of Spain, the kind of tan you *cultivate;* at any rate, not the kind of tan that can be achieved in Brussels, Strasbourg, or Luxembourg, a gray triptych of cities if ever there was one. As Ottavio Marzocchi, a Radical Italian with thinning hair and chunky glasses, delivered his remarks, I noticed he had an eyebrow ring. The whole thing was oddly reminiscent of that great exercise in pedagogical pantomime that ambitious American high school kids take part in each summer: the model United Nations.

The talks were generally interesting. Simon Davies spoke about the degree to which the events of September 11 changed the debate about privacy and surveillance. Marc Rotenberg discussed cryptography. Maurice Wessling, president of European Digital Rights, said there are ten thousand wiretaps per year in the tiny Netherlands alone—"and that's not conversations, that's telephone lines." But I could not help but feel that the portfolio was a little too broad. Again, there was this strange notion of connectivity: surveillance cameras, export restrictions on cryptography, grocery-store rewards cards that take note of how often you buy a dozen eggs. In the minds of the participants at the conference, these things were all connected on some deep level, all part of the same inexorable shift. The whiff of conspiracy was discernible in the sterile air of the conference room. And where there is a whiff, there is generally a theory. Erich Moechel, an Austrian technology journalist with emphatic English and a gray goatee, talked about Customer Relations Management (CRM), a new corporate strategy for improving customer service by developing and analyzing profiles of individual consumers. Having sketched out some of the more malevolent uses to which such profiles could be put, Moechel said, "And some of us are disturbed by this, because, and I just say this without weighing it, most of the companies that do this are *Israeli* companies."

A classic conspiracy theorist line. When it's not the Masons or the Illuminati sitting in a room planning global domination through CRM, it's the Jews. I looked up, a little incredulous. There were about forty people in the room. No one batted an eye.

DURING THE ECHELON INVESTIGATION, Duncan Campbell and Nicky Hager seemed to detect this penchant for hysteria at the Parliament and to understand the risk that it would undermine the proceedings. When he appeared before the committee, Hager stressed that it was important to look at the limitations of the Echelon system. He told the committee that there had been many "exaggerated second-hand accounts" of what he and others had written about the UKUSA Sigint apparatus and that these accounts lent "an air of unreality" to the discussion of Echelon. "In my opinion it is in the interest of the intelligence agencies that when the public talks about intelligence it all sounds very vague and rather akin to talking about flying saucers," Hager said. "It is very much in the interest of people like us here, people with a serious interest in the subject, to be able to be as precise and factual as possible, as it is only in that way that we can get proper public scrutiny and questioning of what is going on."

Duncan Campbell seemed to agree and, having spent the prior decade raising fears about Anglophone surveillance, now proceeded to chastise those who had grown alarmed. "In the torrent of press that followed [the original reports], a great deal of nonsense was written," a crotchety Campbell announced to the committee, "the capabilities were exaggerated, the seriousness was exaggerated, many statements were made which I have, when I speak to meetings, to falsify before I can get on to talking about the truth." He emphasized that while the committee had seized on the name Echelon, that name referred to one particular component of one type of satellite-interception operation. "Not every satellite interception system in the English speaking alliance is called Echelon," Campbell said. "And that is only a small part of what that alliance does to collect information." While he confirmed that a single Echelon station could intercept two million communications in an hour, Campbell stressed that the vast bulk of those intercepts would be of no interest to the intelligence agencies and that of every two million intercepts only four actual reports would emerge.

James Bamford agreed that speculation about the "NSA being able to eavesdrop everywhere, anytime, everyone is completely not the case." He broke down the winnowing process whereby the network sorts the wheat from the chaff in more specific terms than Campbell did. If a single station gathers one million intercepts every half hour, Bamford said, all but "6,500 are filtered out through these electronic filters." Most of that 6,500 still do not meet what the agencies call "forwarding criteria," so they will be thrown out too, leaving one thousand. "Out of a million now you're down to about a thousand messages in this half hour. Those are the ones that actually get looked at a little more closely," Bamford explained. "Sometimes it's just looking at it very quickly to see if it looks interesting, you know, just quickly going through it. Out of that thousand, they normally would get ten that they find interesting, and out of that ten, there will usually be only one report that will come out."

Yet even Bamford seemed to have concerns about the personal privacy issue. In his testimony, he was able to offer the committee that rarest of things: an account of the Echelon network actually working. It is almost impossible to substantiate a case of eavesdropping without access to those on the inside, but because of his contacts Bamford was able to do it. He told the story of a French salesman whom he gave the pseudonym Dècle. Monsieur Dècle worked for a Toulouse-based company called Microturbo, which made turbojet engines. One of Microturbo's engines is used to make the C-802 missile, an antiship cruise missile that can also deliver a chemical or biological payload, which China had traditionally manufactured and sold to Iran. As relations between China and the United States improved during the Clinton years, China gave signs that it would stop selling the C-802 to Iran, and Tehran began planning to construct the missile in Iran. Despite the French government's assurances that Microturbo would cease selling the engine to both China and Iran, it appeared that the company was negotiating with Tehran. In 1997, Monsieur Dècle faxed back and forth with an official in Tehran, and the Iranian government sent Microturbo a bank letter of credit for $1.1 million. This correspondence was intercepted, Bamford said, by GCHQ's antennae at Morwenstow, and a report was prepared by an analyst at Cheltenham who specialized in the C-802. The Americans contacted the French, outraged. The French proceeded to the port at Antwerp, where the shipment from Microturbo to Iran was ready to sail. And when they opened the crate, it contained an innocent generator, unrelated to the C-802.

"The bottom line here was that in these messages that the NSA was picking up, there was not just the name of Microturbo, but . . . the names of company employees," Bamford told the committee. He pointed out that Dècle's name would be forwarded to Canadian and Australian and New Zealand intelligence as well. "So, there is an enormous showing of this information. The person's name gets distributed not just to the intelligence agencies in these countries," Bamford went on,

> but [to] the law enforcement agencies in these countries, the customs services, even the Commerce Department in Washington gets these reports. So, you have the possibility that somebody's name could

turn up in these reports. They are associated with something illegal or very terrible, you know, sending embargoed equipment to terrorist states or whatever, and maybe that information is totally wrong.

While he was not much worried by the dangers of industrial espionage and eager to downplay estimations of the NSA's capabilities, Bamford seemed genuinely alarmed by the risks that Echelon posed for personal privacy. Even after the events of September 11, Bamford was still reiterating this theme. "Disembodied snippets of conversations get snatched from the ether, perhaps out of context, and are misinterpreted by an analyst who then secretly transmits them around the world," he wrote in September 2002.

The erroneous information gets placed in NSA's near-bottomless computer storage system—a system capable of storing five trillion pages of text, a stack of paper 150 miles high. Unlike information on U.S. citizens, which cannot be kept longer than a year, information on foreign nationals can be held eternally. Like Indian ink, the mark will likely remain with the person forever. They will never be told how, when, or why they were placed on a customs blacklist, turned down on a contract—or worse.

THROUGHOUT BAMFORD'S TESTIMONY and that of Nicky Hager and Duncan Campbell and Kenan Seeberg and Skipper Elkjaer, who came as well—throughout the entire life of the Committee to Investigate Echelon, in fact, from the first meeting on July 6, 2000, to the day they produced their finished report—committee members were intrigued to note the presence in the back of the room of a single, unspeaking American. He was a representative of the U.S. State Department, there to observe the proceedings and, presumably, report back to Washington. It was perhaps the presence of this particular fly on the wall that persuaded Carlos Coelho and the committee's rapporteur, the German MEP Gerhard Schmid, that in the spring of 2001, having completed most of their investigation, they should go to Washington and give the Americans an opportunity to reply.

"They were evidently very interested in what we were doing," David Lowe told me. "We wanted to give them a chance to have their say." A tall, trim British man with a gray beard and longish, thinning hair, Lowe is not an MEP but a career parliament bureaucrat. He was in charge of managing the committee from a logistical standpoint, an appointment he found strange, because many of the parliamentarians were incensed that Britain would be included in a network that spied on Europeans, and "my nationality could be regarded as a disadvantage." Over curry and beer at a restaurant behind the parliament, he recounted for me the disastrous trip that ensued.

In April 2001, the committee announced that parliament members would be meeting with various American agencies and departments and making a visit to Fort Meade. It remains a matter of great controversy whether the committee had obtained confirmation of any appointments, however. "You can't just arrive in Washington on the basis of a few phone calls and e-mails and expect to get very far," Ilka said to me. But Lowe insisted that they did have agreements, if not exact appointments, to meet with the CIA, the NSA, the State Department, and the Commerce Department.

The Advocacy Center at the Commerce Department was the one place where the committee had a definite appointment. But then about ten days before they left, a strange event took place. "The representative in the Advocacy Office telephoned and said, 'I'm sorry, Mr. Lowe, I've been instructed to refer your calls to the State Department,' " Lowe told me. "I spoke to a woman in the State Department, a director, and she said, 'We're sorry, but we don't think these meetings are going to be possible.' With the State Department? I asked. 'And with the Advocacy Center,' she said."

Lowe was furious and tried to appeal the decision at the Commerce Department. On the Wednesday before the committee's Monday departure, as Lowe was waiting to hear back from Commerce, he received a fax from Mike Hayden, saying that no one from the NSA would be meeting with the delegation. Shortly thereafter, a fax from the CIA arrived, saying the same thing. Finally, on Friday afternoon Lowe received a call from an assistant counsel at the Advocacy Center, saying that the appeal had been denied, and the meeting was off.

Lowe reported the news to the other members of the committee. "What do we do? Do we go?" he said they wondered. "Of course we go, because by now it's political. We made it clear to the State Department that we did not want to discuss intelligence. The bottom line was to discuss the implications on EU-U.S. relations. That's their *job!* I'm afraid the whole thing did a great disservice to the U.S."

Eleanor Lewis, the chief counsel for international commerce at the Commerce Department, told me that she and two other representatives from the department *had* met with David Lowe in March but that they told him they would not meet with the entire committee in May, because "we are not an intelligence agency." She would not respond to my specific questions about Lowe's impression that precisely such a meeting had been scheduled and wrote flatly that "because this email contains all the information we still have on this subject," it seemed unnecessary to discuss the matter further. At the time, CIA spokesman Mark Mansfield said, "We never led them to believe that a meeting with CIA officials would take place," and added that anything they might discuss was in the public domain anyway, so no meeting was necessary.

Nevertheless, on May 6, a dozen members of the committee arrived in Washington. They met with Representative Porter Goss, Representative Nancy Pelosi, and a few other congresspeople in charge of intelligence oversight. Porter Goss was furious at the snub. "What he said probably doesn't bear repeating," Lowe told me. "But he thought this was a major political mistake. He saw immediately what the implications were." When they asked him about Echelon, Lowe says Goss told them, "If you're asking me does Echelon exist, I will not answer you. If you're asking me do we have the capacity for considerable interception of global communications, the answer is yes."

The committee members met with Jim Woolsey as well, who, Lowe said, "was characteristically frank." They met with James Bamford and Jeffrey Richelson of the National Security Archive, as well as Wayne Madsen and a few of his old NSA colleagues. They tried to secure a last-minute meeting with the Department of Justice but were met by only a low-level functionary. "The chairman and rapporteur considered it insulting" to be pawned off in this manner, Lowe said. "So they didn't go." Humiliated and stuck in their hotel with no one to meet, the committee members cut their visit short and were back in the European Parliament's offices by Friday.

On hearing about the snub, President of the Parliament Nicole Fontaine released a statement blasting the American authorities for canceling "pre-arranged" meetings. "By taking such a decision, the U.S. authorities prevented the members of our temporary committee on the Echelon interception system from carrying out their work properly," she wrote. "I find this refusal to countenance dialogue all the more worrying because the very aim of the visit was to enable the U.S. government authorities to respond openly to the various allegations made." Coelho echoed Fontaine's remarks, suggesting that the Americans would have been "much wiser" to give the committee their side of the story and saying that the refusal to meet "can only increase the suspicion that there is indeed something to hide."

THERE WAS A STRAIN IN the protests of the parliamentarians that seemed to suggest that the Americans would regret their refusal to meet when, in the coming weeks, the committee's final report was released. So it came as a surprise that the final report was in fact such a bland document. "Satellite interception does not leave a fingerprint," Lowe said to me. "There *is* no smoking gun." And, indeed, the "Draft Report on the Existence of a Global System for the Interception of Private and Commercial Communications (Echelon Interception System)" did not present much in the form of incriminating evidence. Released on May 18, 2001, the report's key finding was that the existence of the system "is no longer in doubt" and that "it seems likely, in view of the evidence, that its name is in fact ECHELON, although this is a relatively minor detail." The purpose of the system was "to intercept private and commercial communications, and not military communications," though the report suggested that "the system cannot be nearly as extensive as some sections of the media have assumed." The system that had in the 1997 report been purported to listen to all telecommunications traffic passing from Europe now was said to be able to access a limited amount and analyze even less.

Most disappointing for the committee members was the failure to confirm a single case of industrial espionage. One subheading in the final report captured the acuteness of the committee's frustration: "Why Is It Necessary to Work on the Basis of Clues?" Again, David Lowe said that the nature of the charge was such that it was virtually impossible to confirm. "When we contacted Airbus, no one was able to say, 'Yes, we've been intercepted by Echelon.' " Ilka agreed, "What we got from the committee's work is that the proper monitoring of secret services is just not possible, because by definition it is secret, and it covers its tracks." And while they may not have been able to prove the allegations, they did not disprove them either. Carlos Coelho makes clear where he stands on industrial espionage: "If you have a tool, and you can gain an advantage from using that tool, and no one is going to control your use of this tool, are you going to use it?" he asks.

Still, the report was not a complete failure. The committee managed to find an extensive amount of information about the alliance between the five countries. A 2000 report from the British Intelligence and Security Committee held that "the quality of intelligence gathered clearly reflects the value of the close cooperation under the UKUSA agreement." A similar document from New Zealand from the same year said that GCSB was a member of a "longstanding collaborative intelligence partnership for the exchange of foreign intelligence and the sharing of communications security technology." It named the other four agencies and added, "New Zealand gains considerable benefit from this arrangement, as it would be impossible for New Zealand to generate the effectiveness of the five nation partnership on its own." A 1996 report from the auditor general of Canada pointed out that, as part of the relationship between the agencies, "intelligence products, including analysis and assessment, are exchanged, and technical assistance is provided by each to the others. These, and other relationships provide Canada with information and technological resources that would otherwise be unobtainable with current resources." And in case there was any remaining doubt about the existence of the UKUSA relationship, James Bamford told the committee: "I have been given several tours of NSA, and one of the things I saw there was a plaque on the wall at one point, and it was a plaque which was actually given to one of the directors in 1996, and it was given by GCHQ, and it said, 50 years of friendship and cooperation, BRUSA-UKUSA."

When the committee shut down in the summer of 2001, a story in Wired News joked that "the defining accomplishment of the European Parliament's temporary committee on Echelon may be that it is due to close up shop on schedule, less than a year after it began its work." Ilka Schroeder was more sanguine. "I think it's very good that the report states clearly that Echelon exists, so the work we've done is not in vain," she said. She might be right that due in part to the work of the committee, the quotation marks have disappeared from around the word *Echelon*. "Even the BBC now refers to it as the Echelon system, and not the 'so-called Echelon system,' " David Lowe told me. "A small advance, but, you know, we're proud of it."

INTERESTINGLY, THE DISSENTING OPINIONS appended to the final report held not that there was an absence of hard facts, but on the contrary that more sweeping conclusions should have been drawn on the basis of the committee's findings. An Italian MEP named Maurizio Turco filed a dissenting opinion that objected that the United States and the United

Kingdom were hardly alone in this kind of interception activity and that there were similar capabilities in Germany and Holland and "probably" in France. This was, of course, nothing new, as *Interception Capabilities 2000* had numbered the non-UKUSA countries with major Comint organizations at thirty.

Ilka also filed a dissenting opinion, and she went a little further. She realized that one proposal on the table was for Europe to develop its own unified Sigint capability, to fight fire with fire. "It is hypocritical for the European Parliament to criticize the Echelon interception practice while taking part in plans to establish a European secret service," she wrote. And here Ilka showed her stripes: "No effective public control mechanism of secret services and their undemocratic practices exists globally. It is in the nature of secret services that they cannot be controlled." Thus far, on the basis of my own research and experiences, I was inclined to agree with her. But Ilka went on: "They must therefore be abolished."

In the honeymoon of the End of History, Ilka's position may have seemed tenable. Secret intelligence agencies are impossible to regulate and oversee, so why not just do away with them? Her dissenting opinion was submitted right along with the final report when it went before the parliament, on September 5, 2001. And a mere six days later, her posturing seemed decidedly naïve. Still, I felt for Ilka. The report was widely regarded as a backing down, and people would thereafter refer to it as evidence that Echelon was much more limited than had originally been suggested. My sense was that the whole process had been hijacked, in a way, by the fears over industrial espionage. The parliament is a political organization like any other, and it was much easier to mobilize political momentum behind the notion of lost business and suffering industry than it was behind something so abstract as privacy. But by making the central focus of the investigation an effort to establish with forensic certainty that industrial espionage had taken place, the committee doomed itself, in some sense, to failure.

Ilka told me that for many of the MEPs, Duncan Campbell's allegations about industrial espionage were the reason that they got involved in the first place. "In the original reports, there wasn't much on industrial espionage. But when that came out, many MEPs became very concerned. Many from the Christian Democrats groups had been appointed by industrialists." She added that it was in the area of industrial espionage that the idea of betrayal by the United Kingdom seemed most acute.

During his testimony, Nicky Hager had implored the committee not to lose focus. "This committee has got too caught up in the question of whether Echelon has been used in the one narrow area of monitoring of European companies to the advantage of United States companies," he said. He suggested that the privacy implications of Echelon were far more consequential.

"The real issue is the maturing of public perception," the privacy advocate Simon Davies said. "Now it's conventional wisdom, people know they're spied on. Two years ago it was stunning news. But because people haven't heard personal horror stories . . . to some extent the issue has passed into legend."

LURKING BEHIND THE ECHELON investigation was an impending geopolitical dilemma. In the spring of 2000, Charles Grant, a young former defense editor for *The Economist* who moved on to head the Center for European Reform, published an influential paper called "Intimate Relations." The paper discussed the emergence of a European Common Foreign and Security Policy (CFSP). Grant suggested that many British officials assume the United Kingdom "can continue to have its cake and eat it—enjoying privileged access to U.S. intelligence, while counting as much as any in the embryonic CFSP." These officials argue that firewalls within the intelligence community will "allow the British to keep a foot in both camps: the U.S. will hand over certain reports on the understanding that Britain's European allies will not get to see them, while at the same time Britain can exchange other material with its European partners." But Grant believed this assessment was misguided, and while he would not go so far as a French official he quoted who said, "Britain must choose Europe or betray us," he did feel that the United Kingdom was too "insouciant" in the face of an approaching conflict.

Grant's paper discussed the UKUSA intelligence system at some length. He argued that the special intelligence bond connecting these countries runs deeper than a series of historical agreements and procedures. The affinity is apparent in the very manner in which they conceptualize intelligence. "Anglo-Saxons use intelligence in an empirical way: it is about gathering facts, and if the facts are significant the policies may get changed," Grant suggested. The French and other continentals, on the other hand, "being essentially deductive in their thinking, develop sophisticated analyses and policies and then draw on intelligence to support them; but that they seldom allow intelligence to shift policy."

Organizations are naturally jealous when it comes to sharing their information; a certain possessive tendency to hoard is an enduring feature of bureaucracies the world over. Grant argued that this particular trait will limit Great Britain's willingness to distribute intelligence within the larger European ecosystem. He noted that because so much intelligence in the Kosovo campaign was shared throughout NATO, much of it went straight to the Serbs. He cited the case of Pierre-Henri Bunel, a French NATO officer who was found in 1998 to have passed NATO target plans for Kosovo directly to a Yugoslav diplomat in Brussels.

As Europe develops its own intelligence identity, it does seem likely that this conflict of loyalties will become more of an issue. The EU has already developed a "satellite center," at Torrejón, in Spain, that processes information from commercial satellites. And France has its own satellite-interception system, dubbed *Frenchelon* by the press, with more than a dozen listening stations, in places like French Guiana, Nouvelle-Calédonie, Réunion, and Djibouti. Ilka worries that the message Europe took from the Echelon investigation is that it needs to beef up its own Sigint identity. "This report constantly plays down these dangers of Echelon," she said in her dissent, "while it remains silent to the . . . interception planning in the EU." Even Charles Grant argues that "the precise capabilities of Echelon are less important than the fact that it remains a symbol of the continuing mistrust between, on the one hand, France and some other European countries, and on the other, the Anglo-Saxon nations."

When I asked Glyn Ford, the British MEP who ran STOA and commissioned the first report that touched on Echelon, where he thought Britain's future lies, he said, "Our future eventually is with Europe. Politically, economically—and in terms of intelligence. There is no question in my mind." When I raised the same question with David Lowe, he objected. "The relationship between the United States and the U.K. is virtually umbilical," he said. "There's no way the British will share anything with the Germans or the Italians. There's no way. And intelligence can only operate effectively, for better or for worse, with that level of cooperation the U.K. and the U.S. have. And I don't think the EU is in any position to supplement that level of cooperation." He shrugged his shoulders. "Either we do it with the United States, or we simply won't have that capacity."

THE JIHAD PHONE

Listening to Terrorists

ON THE FIFTH OF February 2003, Secretary of State Colin Powell took the dais at the United Nations Security Council in New York and prepared to make his case for an invasion of Iraq. What followed was a dynamic eighty-three-minute performance, featuring video, satellite images, and the broadcast of three tantalizing, scratchy communications intercepts.

"Just a few weeks ago we intercepted communications between two commanders in Iraq's Second Republican Guard Corps," Powell said. "One commander is going to be giving an instruction to the other." He had indicated that the Arabic recording would be accompanied by large slides on which the translation would appear against a blue background. "You will hear as this unfolds that what he wants to communicate to the other guy," Powell continued, "he wants to make sure the other guy hears clearly, to the point of repeating it so that it gets written down and completely understood. Listen."

The room was suddenly filled with two male voices, speaking Arabic. They spoke in a call-and-response recitation, their voices frayed by the static.

The slides read:

COL. Captain Ibrahim?
CAPT. I am with you, Sir.
COL. Remove.
CAPT. Remove [Repeats instructions].
COL. The expression.
CAPT. The expression.
COL. "Nerve agents."

CAPT. "Nerve agents."

COL. Wherever it comes up.

CAPT. Wherever it comes up.

COL. In the wireless instructions.

CAPT. In the instructions.

COL. Wireless.

CAPT. Wireless.

"Why does he repeat it that way?" Powell asked when the tape had run. "Why is he so forceful in making sure this is understood? And why did he focus on wireless instructions? Because the senior officer is concerned that somebody might be listening." Powell paused for effect. "Well," he said, "*somebody was.*"

In terse, prosecutorial tones, Powell said that the conversation confirmed the Bush administration's "conservative estimate" that Iraq had a stockpile of between one and five hundred tons of chemical-weapons agents. "That is enough agent to fill sixteen thousand battlefield rockets," Powell said. "Even the low end of one hundred tons of agent would enable Saddam Hussein to cause mass casualties across more than one hundred square miles of territory, an area nearly five times the size of Manhattan."

As Powell rolled out his case, with Director of Central Intelligence George Tenet sitting just behind him, those in attendance were awed by the apparent clairvoyance of the American espionage establishment. But another group of people listening was shocked. For anyone familiar with Sigint and secrecy, the public unveiling of intercepts so fresh that they had been gathered in the last few weeks was virtually unheard-of. One former high-ranking NSA employee who watched the presentation said, "I can only assume that everyone else had the same sense of shock when they actually heard it—a sense of that great sucking sound as all the business goes south."

This was not actually the first time intercepts had been revealed by the United States. On April 5, 1986, a bomb ripped through the La Belle discotheque in Berlin, killing two U.S. soldiers and a Turkish woman and injuring 230 others. The NSA had intercepted telex messages between Tripoli, Libya, and the Libyan diplomatic mission in East Berlin that proved that the action was performed on orders from the Libyan secret service. One of the messages read, "Kill as many people as possible." President Reagan revealed the Libyan connection, because he needed to justify for the public his decision to launch air strikes on Tripoli and Benghazi ten days after the attack. General William Odom was director of the NSA in those years, and in his own words he proceeded to "raise holy hell," because now the Libyans would know the NSA was listening. The transcripts were ultimately used in the 1997 trial of five conspirators in the bombing.

But never had so dramatic a series of intercepts been played in public. It emerged in the days after Powell's presentation that the decision to present the conversations had been widely debated within the intelligence community. Much of the intelligence used in the presentation did not in fact come directly from U.S. agencies but from various allies around the world. In the final analysis, ten different intelligence services, from both Europe and the Middle East, signed off on the presentation. In the months preceding Powell's presentation, Mike Hayden had personally ordered that $300 million to $400 million of the NSA's annual budget be redirected to "Iraq unique" operations and targets. The Bush administration and its allies were effectively betting the farm on persuading the international community that the time was ripe to depose Saddam Hussein. The overwhelming reason that the intercepts were used was that they were regarded as unassailably incriminating. In the days before the presentation, one intelligence official told *Newsweek,* "Hold on to your hat. We've got it." As Powell made his presentation, thousands of NSA employees gathered to watch in cafeterias at Fort Meade. While more seasoned hands grumbled, the rank and file were thrilled. Such was their confidence in the evidence they had gathered and their exhilaration at the unusual experience of having their work publicly commended that when Powell played the intercepts, the NSA employees cheered. Powell announced that the intercepts revealed Iraq's "policy of evasion and deception that goes back twelve years, a policy set at the highest levels of the Iraqi regime."

THE TROUBLE WAS, THEY didn't. Eight months after Powell's presentation, on October 2, 2003, David Kay, the weapons expert appointed by Tenet to run the CIA's Iraq Survey Group, told the congressional intelligence committees that he could produce no evidence of nerve agents. In fact, he went so far as to say that to the best of the group's knowledge, there had been no chemical-weapons program in Iraq since 1991. While the intercepted phone calls had appeared to offer conclusive proof of Powell's claims, they ended up doing no such thing. The resulting controversy and investigations called seriously into question the general state of American intelligence in the run-up to Iraq, but the intercepts in Powell's speech called particular attention to whether Sigint actually *works*. It is difficult to overstate the importance of this question. As I have suggested already, the terms *privacy* and *national security* have become ossified in our political discourse, assuming a certain inert and uncontested status in the minds of those who wield them. But if the various steps that are being taken at the expense of privacy and in the name of security are *not* in fact enhancing security, then the whole equation changes. And it is not merely our privacy that is at stake, after all—it is our safety as well. The 9/11 Commission learned that when it came to investigating "overseas threats," "officials believed that signals intelligence was more reliable than human intelligence." If that belief was demonstrably false or even merely controversial, it reflects a reckless misallocation of priorities.

IF THE TASK OF intelligence is, in essence, to see the future, then American intelligence has an abysmal track record. Pundits tend to suggest that the only antecedent to the events of September 11, 2001, was the Japanese attack on Pearl Harbor, but in fact the last half century is littered with significant events that the CIA, FBI, and NSA simply did not foresee. Less than a decade after Pearl Harbor, there was the North Korean invasion and the Chinese intervention in the Korean War in 1950; then the Tet Offensive against American forces in Vietnam in 1968; the fall of the Shah in Iran *and* the Soviet invasion of Afghanistan in 1979; the Hezbollah attacks on the U.S. embassy and marine barracks in Lebanon in 1983; the collapse of the Soviet Union in 1991; the intense resistance to U.S. forces seeking to capture Mohammed Farah Aideed in Somalia in 1993; the nuclear test by India *and* the truck bombs at American embassies in Kenya and Tanzania in 1998; the attack on the USS *Cole* in Yemen in 2000; and finally the attacks on the World Trade Center and the Pentagon in September 2001.

But the public hears only about the failures, a chorus of intelligence officers objects when confronted with this litany of blunders. When you think about the sheer omniscience involved in successful counterintelligence and the multitude of threats against the United States, what is more remarkable is that there have been so *few* dramatic intelligence failures. David Kahn says, "Before you complain too loud about intelligence failures, tell me what the stock market's going to do tomorrow. Go to the horse races, and you'll see a lot of people betting wrong—

and that's a far more restricted set of possibilities than intelligence analysts face." And he is quite right. But of course, the stakes are rather higher for intelligence agencies than they are for traders at the stock exchange or bettors at the track—and so, it is not insignificant to point out, is the budget.

In a spring 2002 article called "Time for a Rethink," *The Economist* posed a pithy hypothetical:

> Imagine a huge $30-billion conglomerate. It operates in one of the few businesses that might genuinely be described as cut-throat. Its competitors have changed dramatically, and so have its products and technologies. But its structure is the same as when it was founded, in 1947. Nobody leads this colossus (there is just an honorary chairman) and everyone exploits it. Demoralized and bureaucratic, it has just endured its biggest-ever loss. The response: the firm has been given even more money, and nobody has been sacked.

The scenario captures the peculiar paradox of the intelligence agency. The nature of the job is such that some measure of failure is more or less inevitable. But the human stakes involved are so high that failure cannot properly be penalized. On the contrary, given that it is the appearance of weakness that can really move money in Washington, it is often the case that failure is rewarded. The intelligence historian Rhodri Jeffreys-Jones regards this as a cycle, wherein appropriations-hungry intelligence agencies "con" Congress into throwing more funding their way in times of crisis. "A disaster happens," Jeffreys-Jones writes. "The government sets up a preemptive inquiry to deliberate until the fuss dies down; the confidence men now say the disaster happened because they had too little money to spend on intelligence; the President and Congress authorize more intelligence funds." He points out that the CIA and the NSA were born out of the intelligence failure at Pearl Harbor and that the NSA's technical shortcomings in the 1990s inspired not punitive cuts but larger appropriations.

Jeffreys-Jones may overstate the case somewhat. I tend to believe that the people who run our intelligence agencies are sincere in their beliefs that they are underresourced to do the job they must do. It may also be absurd to adopt the corporate model that underlies the views of *The Economist* and Jeffreys-Jones, which would hold that you could penalize an organization for failing. The intelligence community is not a corporation, after all. Any penalties levied against it could be felt by the entire country, if it meant that agencies were less vigilant for any period of time. Senator Gary Hart told me that "heads should have rolled," on September 12, 2001, because people had failed to do their jobs. But given the continued risk of attack, firing intelligence and defense officials at that time would have clearly been irresponsible.

NEVERTHELESS, IT SEEMS THAT after September 11 and Iraq, America should give some real thought to the utility and reliability of signals intelligence. Because the NSA is so secretive and the press colludes in this secretiveness, because as a result most Americans have little understanding of the technical apparatus that produces "chatter," because our understanding of the dimensions of our own privacy is similarly undeveloped, Sigint remains the one major element of our intelligence apparatus that has not been discussed or debated in the years since September 11.

The CIA's Directorate of Operations has roughly four thousand employees, and of those fewer than fifteen hundred are actual case officers deployed overseas. By contrast, the NSA has tens of thousands of eavesdroppers. Does this disparity make sense? Doesn't Powell's presentation indicate that intercepts are as or more faulty a source of intelligence than humans? Isn't one salutary lesson of the whole presentation that we cannot perform intelligence by remote control? When India carried out its nuclear tests in the desert southwest of New Delhi, officials involved in the tests knew when American imaging satellites were passing above and suspended the tests during that period. "What we didn't have was the humans who would have given us an insight into their intentions," Frank Wisner, the American ambassador to India at the time of the tests, told me. In this case, an active human source inside the Indian defense establishment would have been much more valuable than any overhead assets. Perhaps the problem is the fallibility of listening itself.

BETWEEN *THE GODFATHER* AND *The Godfather II,* Francis Ford Coppola made a smaller, lesser-known film, *The Conversation,* that is an object lesson in why Sigint sometimes does not work. Gene Hackman plays a man named Harry Caul, who is an eavesdropper for hire: a freelance surveillance expert who will tap phones, trace unsuspecting spouses, and bug conversations for a fee. When Caul is hired by the director of a corporation, played by Robert Duvall, to record a conversation between his wife, Ann, and her lover, Mark, as they stroll around Union Square in San Francisco, he collects a rough soundtrack of their talk, which he pares down, eliminating distortion and static, trying to isolate the two voices from the sound of a brass band playing "Red Red Robin" in the background. At one point in Caul's recording, Mark says to Ann, "He'd kill us if he had the chance." Listening to that phrase over and over, Caul becomes convinced that his employer, the cuckolded husband, plans to murder the adulterous pair. The movie does climax in a murder, and the murder is foretold in that snippet of Mark and Ann's private conversation—but it's not the murder that Harry Caul expects. Playing and replaying the conversation, Caul hears Mark say to Ann, "He'd *kill* us if he had the chance." Perhaps it's the other conversations in the square that day, or the static and whine of the microphone, or the jaunty strains of the brass band, but Harry Caul misreads the intonation. Too late, he realizes that Mark is actually proposing a murder, saying, "*He'd* kill *us* if he had the chance."

This is the Achilles' heel of Echelon and the whole leviathan of global electronic eavesdropping: conversation is such a mutable, ambiguous thing, so laden with deception and doublespeak, flattery and obfuscation, that one can see the world by listening in only as through a glass darkly. It is one thing to intercept a signal and quite another to understand what it *means*. Even assuming that everything else goes according to plan—that a conversation is intercepted, punctually translated, understood at the level of literal meaning, and disseminated to the appropriate parties—sifting through conversations for indications of future events seems as arbitrary and uncertain as sifting through tea leaves.

In the early hours of October 12, 2000, the USS *Cole* was bombed, ripping a forty-foot hole in the hull of the ship, killing seventeen sailors and wounding thirty-nine. The men were having a meal while it happened, and the blast hit the mess deck. Several hours *after* the attack, the NSA distributed a highly classified report warning that terrorists were involved in "operational planning" for an attack on U.S. or Israeli personnel or property in the Middle East. There are conflicting accounts of whether Yemen was specified or whether the warning related to the Persian Gulf region more generally. When the report was disseminated, it was not sent over Intelink, the intelligence community's global computer network, which is the most widely used intelligence-reporting channel. NSA reports are not distributed over Intelink because of their sensitivity. But here a problem really develops, as action is shackled by the need for secrecy. NSA reports are sent to the CIA, the Defense Intelligence Agency (DIA), the State Department, and the intelligence arms of the military services, then incorporated into the reports of those agencies. This process tacks additional time onto the NSA reporting schedule, which, from interception to translation to dissemination can often already take twenty-four to forty-eight hours. But even had the NSA's warning arrived earlier, what would it have told us? The warning was extremely broad and applied to a region where, even before September 11, threats on American interests were more or less perpetual. The knowledge that an attack was planned for the region would hardly narrow down the scope of possibilities. The staff of the *Cole* might have been more careful about the boat approaching, but would the word have gotten to the entire crew of the ship?

Much was made of the two intercepted phone calls from September 10, 2001, that were not translated until September 13. The fact that it took the NSA that long to get to them was used as a rationale for giving the agency greater resources. But in fact, what could we possibly have ascertained from "Tomorrow is the zero hour"? What kind of actionable intelligence could that have produced? When Mike Hayden testified before the congressional inquiry into the attacks, he said, "This information did not specifically indicate an attack would take place on that day. It did not contain any details on the time, place, or nature of what might happen. It also contained no suggestion of airplanes being used as weapons." In fact, Hayden later acknowledged that during the summer before September 11, the agency intercepted thirty similar messages obliquely promising imminent disaster. "We dutifully reported these, yet none of these subsequently correlated with terrorist attacks. The concept of 'imminent' to our adversaries is relative; it can mean soon or imply sometime in the future," he said. Even a fairly specific threat can produce little in the way of actionable intelligence. When New York City police were told that chatter between terrorist suspects had included the word *underground,* what were they to do? The New York subway system covers 722 miles of track and 466 stations and carries nearly five million people per day. If "underground" was as specific as the threat got, how were authorities to determine where to allocate their inevitably finite resources in preventing an attack?

"After any particular turning point or big event, yes, you can go back and say there were lots of pointers," Sir Peter Heap told me, in his elegant Victoria flat in London. "But there were lots of other things saying something different. So it's usually afterward rather than before that you know which are the ones that were telling you what was going to happen." Heap had a long and distinguished career as a British diplomat posted to nine different embassies overseas and was on the Foreign Office's Vietnam desk during the Tet Offensive. He believes that it is misleading to go back and endeavor to "connect the dots" after an attack, because while one string of dots may have forecast a calamity in retrospect, in real time there are many different dots leading in many different directions. "A lot of credence is given to the volume of the stuff," Heap told me,

> the fact that everyone is chattering, so something's going to happen. But they don't know *what*. That's what happened with the Tet Offensive. In the immediate day or two before, there was a lot of apprehension that something was going to happen, but there wasn't any material there that told us there was going to be a simultaneous uprising all over the country in the way it happened.

At the same time, he said, "there were massive indications that something like the Tet Offensive was going to happen on *other* occasions," when in fact nothing did. "Picking it out is easy afterward but not so easy beforehand."

ONE INSTANCE IN WHICH intercepts were used to connect the dots very carefully after the fact was the 2001 trial of the bombers of the American embassies in Kenya and Tanzania in 1998. The challenge for the prosecution was proving that the bombings in Africa were in fact the work of a shadowy terrorist network based in Afghanistan. The federal prosecutors made their case by pointing at Osama Bin Laden's satellite phone. Bin Laden had long since stopped using the phone, but Marilyn Morelli, who worked for a New York–based company called Ogara Satellite Networks, testified that she sold the $7,500 phone and hundreds of minutes to Ziyad Khalil, a Bin Laden associate and student at the University of Missouri at Columbia, on November 1, 1996. The phone number was (873)682505331, and over the next two years, according to trial records, a total of 2,200 minutes were used. Bin Laden called England, Yemen, Sudan, Iran, Saudi Arabia, Pakistan, and Azerbaijan. He also made fifty calls to Kenya. During the trial, the prosecutors spent hours laying out hundreds of intercepted calls for the Manhattan jury, using transcripts and call records. Assistant U.S. Attorney Kenneth Karas referred to one London cellphone that often called Bin Laden's phone in Afghanistan as the Jihad Phone. "That's the phone that Bin Laden and the other co-conspirators [used] to carry out their conspiracy to murder U.S. nationals," he told the court. "It is the phone that gives you a window into how it is that Al Qaeda operates." And it was. Prosecutors were able to reconstruct in elaborate detail Al Qaeda's maneuvers in advance of the embassy bombings. But of course, this vivid picture was visible only in retrospect. The intercepts had not predicted the bombings themselves. And in fact, the prosecutors had to go to great pains, in the spring of 2001, to remind the jurors who Osama Bin Laden was, to jog their memories about this strange organization they had never heard of, Al Qaeda.

Part of the reason the prosecutors were able to reconstruct Al Qaeda's activities was that they were fairly certain the terrorists were not deliberately misleading one another. But one reason to be skeptical about information obtained in intercepts and to question the notion of intercepts as a coherent chain of predictive dots is that you cannot take for granted that people are always so straightforward. Henry Stimson, who said that gentlemen don't read one another's mail, also pointed out that reading someone's mail is not the same as reading his mind. Milt Bearden, the veteran CIA officer, told me that part of the problem is just the nature of human conversation. He said that on one occasion he had been at an American-embassy function in a foreign city and had a conversation with someone, only to receive a transcript the next day of that person reporting back to their superiors and totally mischaracterizing the conversation. Was the functionary trying to please his masters, inflating his own behavior? Would he have known better than to do so had he understood that Bearden was listening in? When I questioned a senior American diplomat about this, he asked rhetorically, "Does what one foreign minister says to another in any way express what he really believes? Or is that just maneuver?"

In the spring of 1995, the NSA intercepted a communication from the Iranian Ministry of Intelligence and Security in Tehran to one of its foreign stations. The message indicated that the CIA, under cover of the National Security Council, was planning to assassinate Saddam Hussein. The message went on to explain that the plot was the work of a CIA officer in northern Iraq who was using the code name Robert Pope. The day after the message was intercepted, a report on it reached the desk of Anthony Lake, Bill Clinton's national-security adviser. Lake was furious, as assassinations of foreign leaders, if they were to happen at all, should most certainly not be happening without his authorization—and in any event were illegal. At Lake's request, the FBI began an investigation into the incident, and several weeks later Robert Baer, a veteran field officer and one of the few CIA case officers who could speak Arabic, was called back to Langley from northern Iraq, where he was managing a covert operation to back the Iraqi opposition to Saddam. Baer flatly denied that any assassination plan was afoot, and it emerged that he was right. The intercept was disinformation— whether deliberate or not it is unclear, but in any event erroneous.

Intercepts are anything but infallible divinations of what is happening in the world and what will happen in the future. *Chatter* is, as it turns out, a perfect word for the conversations culled from the airwaves: fickle, misleading, most often inconsequential. To be sure, Sigint has occasionally been extremely effective in averting disaster. In 2003, British Airways canceled flights to and from Kenya because electronic eavesdropping on Al Qaeda suspects indicated a specific attack. A satellite-phone call gave away the Karachi hideout of Ramzi Binalshibh, the senior Al Qaeda suspect caught in September 2002. Likewise, an intercepted e-mail allegedly led to the arrest in March 2003 of another suspected Bin Laden aide, Khalid Shaikh Mohammed. Intercepts and GPS reportedly played a role in locating and killing Qusay and Uday Hussein. And in March 2004, *The New York Times* revealed that a complex international operation code-named Mont Blanc had succeeded in capturing dozens of suspected Al Qaeda operatives by tracing the Swisscom SIM (subscriber identity module) cards built into their mobile phones. But when I asked Britt Snider, the former inspector general of the CIA who as a young man worked on the Church committee, whether the fact that there had not been another major attack on U.S. soil since September 11 could be attributed to the success of the American intelligence community or Al Qaeda biding its time, he echoed the answer I received from virtually every other person I interviewed for this book: "I'd have to say it's more Al Qaeda biding its time."

One of the odd ironies of the summer of 2001 and the intense speculation then about the all-powerful nature of Echelon was that a mere week after the European Parliament voted to adopt the final Echelon report, a massive and devastating attack occurred that had not registered meaningfully in the ears of the agencies involved. The system that

Mike Frost said "covers everything that's radiated worldwide at any given instant . . . [e]very square inch" somehow failed to pick up and process so much as a tremor of warning. It was difficult to deny after September 11, 2001, that Sigint had had its day and failed.

ON OCTOBER 1, 1993, a twelve-year-old girl named Polly Klaas was having a slumber party with two friends in the affluent San Francisco suburb of Petaluma when a strange man entered the room, threatened the girls with a knife, and took Polly away. The community was traumatized and launched into action to find Polly, posting flyers, soliciting calls with tips, and presenting the story to the media. Thousands of volunteers in the Bay Area were joined in the search by people all over the country. Despite the fact that hundreds of children are kidnapped every year, the case somehow caught people's attention, and when Polly's body was eventually found on December 4, the public was outraged. It emerged that Polly's murderer, a man named Richard Allen Davis, had prior convictions for robbery, burglary, assault, and kidnapping, as well as a long history of violence against females.

In response to the Klaas case, a movement got under way to pass a "three strikes" law for California, which would mandate sentences of twenty-five years to life, without possibility of parole, for anyone with two serious felony convictions who was convicted a third time. Some protested at the time that the law cut too broadly, that a heavy sentence for people convicted of a third *violent* felony—as opposed to any felony at all—would be a better solution. But the California legislature was reacting to a sense of public indignation and insecurity and proceeded to pass a law that, from a criminal-justice point of view, has been an ill-considered disaster. Since the law passed in 1994, the number of inmates in the California state prison system has grown by almost 25 percent. One in four prisoners, or some forty-two thousand inmates, is serving a life term under the three-strikes law. In the last decade, just housing these third strikers cost the state $8 billion, and nearly five billion of this was for convicts whose third strike was not a violent crime. By 2003, there were 344 California inmates serving twenty-five years to life for thefts worth less than four hundred dollars.

In times of panic, we overreact; we overlegislate; we get it wrong. What the Klaas case demonstrates is the degree to which we are willing to pass outlandish or draconian provisions in response to events we find threatening or alarming. But it also reveals something more specific: after a jarring event like the murder of Polly Klaas, we overreact in a particular way. We strive for more *control*. This tendency to want to simply jail anyone who might be a threat has more in common with signals intelligence than it might at first appear. The assumption that there are various antisocial, anarchic, or simply evil entities out there and that if we can just find them, trap them, confine them, or watch them everything will be all right, animates not only our attachment to penitentiaries but our fondness for surveillance as well.

The new orthodoxy expressed by lawmakers and commentators in the weeks after September 11 that the United States needed more spies on the ground was somehow absent in the massive piece of legislation that was promptly rushed through Congress: the USA Patriot Act. The Patriot Act was an omnibus bundle of laws, with scores of provisions dealing with a broad variety of issues, but it did seem oddly fixated on electronic intelligence. There were provisions broadening the ability to search various financial, library, travel, video-rental, phone, medical, church, synagogue, and mosque records (section 215); lowering the procedural bar to obtain a FISA warrant (section 218); lengthening the terms of FISA warrants (section 207); and extending this broader authority to wiretap to the Internet (section 206). The act allowed for the warrantless interception of any Internet information "relevant to an ongoing criminal investigation." Section 216 authorized roving wiretaps—rather than focusing on a particular phone or computer, authorities can now track one individual in whatever media the individual uses. Section 220 allowed judges to authorize national wiretaps rather than taps for a single jurisdiction.

Like the Polly Klaas law, the Patriot Act went from bill to law very quickly, in this case in under six weeks. The bill bypassed the committee stage and floor debate in the Senate, and while it did receive consideration and adjustment by the House Judiciary Committee, the chaos of the anthrax scares on Capitol Hill meant that the proposed law was not subjected to anything resembling rigorous or sustained scrutiny. Moreover, intense political pressures from a panicked electorate and executive branch conspired to rush the bill through the legislative process. (Sounding oddly unacquainted with this process, John Ashcroft announced at the time that he wanted broader authority to pursue terrorists in days, not weeks.)

Part of the reason Congress was able to get the Patriot Act passed with such alacrity was that numerous provisions in it were already on different lawmakers' and lobbyists' legislative agendas prior to September 11. The proponents of these issues were referred to by the press as "hitchhikers": individuals who cynically took advantage of the new momentum on the Hill, where Congress seemed eager to pass anything that could be plausibly alleged to stop terrorism. The bill shot through the House (357–66) and Senate (98–1) and became law. And despite the fact that in the ensuing years dozens of American communities would pass resolutions opposing the act, by the spring of 2004, with the four-year deadline for some of the provisions in the act to "sunset" approaching, several senators argued that they should not be allowed to do so.

One is tempted to ask, as Kevin Hogan, an editor at *MIT Technology Review* did several months after September 11, "Now that it is apparent that these supposedly all-seeing government systems are not all-knowing, how can we ascertain that they work at all?" In broadening wiretapping capabilities with the USA Patriot Act, Congress signaled that it is not willing to ask that particular question and would much rather take it on faith that signals intelligence does work. Noel C. Koch, a top Pentagon official in the Reagan years, has said that some electronic intelligence "has a damn short shelf life" but that the secrecy accorded to intercepts imparts "an illusion of competence." This illusion seems to weather even catastrophic intelligence failures, and because the world of signals intelligence is so closed no outside authority is ever able to actually weigh the merits and effectiveness of listening in. "Because of the nature of the intelligence, it is often surrounded by a great deal of secrecy," Sir Peter Heap told me.

> Then when it gets into the government sphere, because of that secrecy the people who are best able to evaluate that intelligence are not able to do so. Once people know that it came through electronic methods, it takes on a certain aura of respectability, whereas the same information obtained differently—and very often the same information is obtained differently—doesn't have that.

"THE ONLY PEOPLE WHO think that intelligence wins wars—hot *or* cold—are intelligence people," a Defense Department policy official told me between mouthfuls of smoked salmon, over breakfast one morning at a club in New York. "Whenever major decisions are made, intelligence is only one factor that goes into the making of that decision, and it's usually not the decisive factor. . . . A lot of what they're working with is anecdotes." He shook his head and chuckled.

> In Washington, *data* is the plural of *anecdotes*. The way they produce their product, we read it, but we read it with a grain of salt. There was a time when U.S. and allied capabilities to intercept and decrypt message traffic was underappreciated by pretty much everybody else. Then you could put more reliance on the intercepts. People were telling the truth, as they understood it.

But this official believes that now foreign adversaries are aware of America's ability to listen in and can be more cryptic or downright misleading in their communications. He added that an intercepted conversation, like any piece of intelligence, can be read different ways. "If you bring your signals people in . . . it's hard to get a straight answer. [It's] like what Truman said about economists: they can point at one time in all directions. That might be healthy, but it's not always for healthy reasons—they're protecting themselves. They'd rather cover themselves and be fuzzy than stick their necks out and be wrong."

I asked how you could get a firmer grounding in intelligence, and the official echoed the wisdom that had prevailed in Washington since September 11. "What we need most of is what we have least of—which is Humint," he said. When I objected that the Patriot Act is long on eavesdropping provisions and short on actual spies, he said that the Humint problem was not something that could be solved overnight by changing the laws. "It takes years to develop capabilities in that area, recruiting and training the right kind of people, getting them out there to put their skills to use," the official said. "It goes back to when Stansfield Turner was DCI [Director of Central Intelligence]. He really wasn't interested in anything that wasn't produced by machinery. He basically wanted to get the CIA out of the spying business. Strong human intelligence takes years to build up. But you can eliminate it at the stroke of a pen." When I asked him whether the community would reform in this new climate of criticism and self-examination, the Pentagon official shook his head and smiled. "Career bureaucrats—speaking as one myself—are very good at waiting out political appointees. They're going to be here for a few years and then go, and their agendas will go with them. I'll still be here. And you won't be."

He seemed to believe that further investment in electronic assets would produce diminishing returns, because the enemy had figured out how to adapt to American interception capabilities. "Remember the CIA strike in Yemen?" he asked, referring to an attack by an unmanned Predator aircraft on a senior Al Qaeda leader and five associates in November 2002. "That was because they'd gone on the air. When they went out and picked up the pieces, they found the bad guy carrying seven different cellphones. It's the old armor and the shell competition. One side produces better armor, the other side produces a better shell to penetrate the armor, and so forth."

I pointed out that in that particular case, we had actually caught our man. Mightn't that counsel further investment in Sigint? The official replied that increasingly those cases are the exception. "The bad guys have learned the hard way to stay off the air. Use the cellphone and you might have an unpleasant visit from the Navy Seals." But interestingly, he didn't seem to think this was all bad. Whereas most of the other people I had spoken with had bemoaned the idea that Al Qaeda would go off the air, because it meant we would no longer be able to listen in, the Pentagon official believed that we had hurt the terrorists by keeping them off the phone. "It exacts a price," he said. "They have to use couriers. This has really slowed them down. We've introduced some dysfunction—if they can't go on the air, use the cellphone, e-mail, things are going to slow down. It significantly impacts their operations as a result."

ONE INTRIGUING ASPECT OF the challenge of connecting the dots is that a lot of the time the most telling dots are not secret intercepts but eloquent arguments and evidence that lie under analysts' noses, in the public domain. The cold-war historian George Kennan remarked in 1997 that

> The need by our government for secret intelligence about affairs elsewhere in the world has been vastly overrated. I would say that something upward of 95 percent of what we need to know about foreign countries could be very well obtained by the careful and competent study of perfectly legitimate sources of information open and available to us in the rich library and archival holdings of [the United States]. Much of the remainder, if it could not be found here . . . could easily be non-secretively elicited from similar sources abroad.

Kennan may overstate the case here, and the remark betrays its pre–September 11 vintage, but the broader point is inescapable: useful intelligence can often be gleaned from open-source material, without resort to the vagaries of covert collection techniques.

In his remarks to the UN Security Council, Colin Powell praised the most recent report on Iraq from British intelligence, but it emerged in the next several days that much of that dossier was drawn from—or simply copied verbatim from—several articles from the *Middle East Review of International Affairs* and *Jane's Intelligence Review*. Sir Peter Heap told a similar story about a British ambassador he was working for throwing down a report describing raw intelligence that had been furnished by MI6 in London. The ambassador asked Heap if the contents looked familiar, and he replied that they did, but he could not think why. The ambassador handed him an article that had run in the local newspaper on the previous day, which was practically identical in wording and content to the supposedly top-secret report, and said, "That's why."

But if these are instances in which warmed-over information from the public sphere masquerades as intelligence, there are other instances in which intelligence agencies overlook warnings from the public sphere at their peril. In May 1997, an analyst at the DIA named Russ Travers published an astonishingly prescient article in the CIA journal *Studies in Intelligence*. The article was titled "The Coming Intelligence Failure" and opened with the words, "The year is 2001. . . . The [Intelligence] Community could still collect 'facts,' but analysts had long ago been overwhelmed by the volume of available information and were no longer able to distinguish consistently between significant facts and background noise. . . . From the vantage point of 2001, intelligence failure is inevitable." Auguring not only the calamity of September 11 but also the reaction by officials in its aftermath, Travers continued, "The Community will try to explain the failure(s) away, and it will legitimately point to extenuating circumstances. . . . When we do the postmortems and try to reconstruct the broader institutional causes for the failure, we will find them spread throughout the national security apparatus." During the same period that the NSA was bringing in the Technical Advisor Group and determining that it should reinvest in technological solutions, Travers declared, "Technology is our panacea. Technology can help sort and rapidly move information, but finding the right piece of data, assimilating the information, and putting it in context is never going to be the job of a machine."

How could the intelligence community have not heeded Travers' prognostications? After all, the article was published in 1997, when (we can say in retrospect) there was still plenty of time, even at the glacial rates of intelligence bureaucracies, to change priorities and procedures. Similarly, how could the community overlook the Hart-Rudman report, produced in February 2001, which predicted imminent "mass-casualty terrorism directed against the U.S. homeland." After the attacks, Warren Rudman reportedly joked, "We printed 100,000 copies of the report, and 99,800 were stored in a warehouse until September 11. On September 12, they were all gone." One unsettling explanation is the tendency that Heap identified to perceive an "aura of respectability" around any intelligence that is gathered through Sigint or other secret means and disregard as inconsequential anything that does not appear to be elicited from a privileged source. "Intelligence community leaders have little regard for unclassified information," Michael Scheuer, the CIA official who wrote the 2004 book *Imperial Hubris* declares. "It cannot be important if it is not secret, after all."

ONE NAGGING QUESTION THAT persistently underlies these discussions of intelligence failure is whether, technologically speaking, the cat is simply out of the bag: whether in the form of laptops, Internet technology, disposable cellphones, and encryption, the United States has not ultimately endowed the world with precisely those tools that will destroy it.

In January 2001, the thirty-six-year-old hacker Kevin Mitnick walked out of Lompoc Federal Correctional Institute in California, having served five years on fraud convictions for breaking into the computer networks of Fujitsu, Motorola, Sun Microsystems, and numerous other companies. Stocky and bespectacled, Mitnick had been the FBI's most-wanted hacker before going away. For a two-year probation period following his release, he was obliged to abide by a most unusual condition of supervised release: he could not touch a computer, go near a keyboard, or use a cellular or cordless phone. He believed that the judge in his case had bought into what he called "the myth of Kevin Mitnick—that I could launch nuclear missiles by whistling into a phone." And there *was* something slightly ridiculous about the conditions of his release. He was able to have his girlfriend connect his laptop to the Internet and hit "send" and "receive" for him, but he could not punch the buttons himself.

This image of Mitnick stuck with me as emblematic of the gulf between those who understand new communications technologies and those who do not. The notion of physically separating Mitnick from a keyboard betrays a frank admission of defeat on the part of the authorities and a superstitious sense that it was a kind of black magic he practiced—as lethal as it was incomprehensible.

It seems lamentably clear that the zealots of Al Qaeda today possess a similar shape-shifting advantage, a similar ability to feint and jab and disappear, and a similarly mythic quality in the minds of those who fear them. The name *Al Qaeda* is itself a misnomer. In Arabic the word means "the base," and yet Al Qaeda is in some respects precisely the opposite: diffuse and scattered, constituting and reconstituting itself around a series of ever-changing nuclei. "Their recruiting grounds, moreover, are confusingly amorphous, disguised as they are within communities of recently arrived immigrants," John Keegan observes, "many of them young men without family or documented identity, often illegal border-crossers who take on protective coloring within the large groups of 'paperless' drifters." But how do you net paperless drifters when what you're good at is following a paper trail? How does what some privacy advocates have referred to as "the dossier society" work against adversaries without dossiers?

In its final report, the 9/11 Commission pointed out that cold-war adversaries presented fairly straightforward targets, from a Sigint point of view, with their hierarchical, predictable military command-and-control methods. "With globalization and the telecommunications revolution, and with loosely affiliated but networked adversaries using commercial devices and encryption," however, "the technical impediments to signals collection grew at a geometric rate. . . . Modern adversaries are skilled users of communications technologies. The NSA's challenges, and its opportunities, increased exponentially in 'volume, variety, and velocity.' " Reading that assessment, you can almost miss the suggestion that it is not only the challenges that increase but the opportunities as well. While terrorist organizations are shrewd users of technology, they are at least in theory vulnerable, because they are using that technology all the time. In *Imperial Hubris*, Scheuer, who has spent much of his career in counterterrorism and published a previous study of Al Qaeda, claims that the most important growth of Al Qaeda since September 11 "has not been physical but has been, rather, its expansion into the Internet." Peter Bergen, the CNN analyst and author of *Holy War, Inc.*, has referred to this "virtual" aspect of Al Qaeda's operations as, "Al Qaeda 2.0."

It is an extraordinary coincidence, and one that has gone largely overlooked in the various postmortems of September 11, that in the months leading up to the attacks, at least six of the hijackers were living and working just miles from NSA headquarters, in the towns of Laurel, Bowie, and Greenbelt, in northern Prince George's County, Maryland. Nawaf al-Hazmi, Salem al-Hazmi, Hani Hanjour, Khalid al-Mihdhar, and Majed Moqed all lived in the area and would ultimately hijack American Airlines Flight 77. A sixth, Ziad Jarrah, also spent time in Maryland and was on United Airlines Flight 93. The suspects lived in the Valencia Motel and the Pin-Del Motel on U.S. Route 1, the main drag running through Laurel, and yet they went completely undetected by the thousands of eavesdroppers listening in just miles away.

It is precisely modern communications technologies that facilitate Al Qaeda's cell-like structure, so how could it possibly be that these men could go undetected? Part of the answer is that the terrorists of Al Qaeda are shrewd and opportunistic and, like Kevin Mitnick, simply know how to play the game. The September 11 hijackers communicated by hundreds of e-mails sent from copy shops and public libraries. From a Kinko's in Minnesota, Zacarias Moussaoui, the alleged twentieth hijacker, accessed his e-mail account, Xdesertman@hotmail.com, the name giving no clue about the user or his activities. From an Internet café in Hamburg, Germany, Mohammed Atta researched flight schools in the United States. In libraries and cafés from Morocco to Yemen, solitary individuals create new accounts and communicate. They buy phone cards and disposable cellphones, and these connective tendrils, while they should be precisely what the UKUSA Sigint apparatus zooms in on, often go unnoticed. These connections have been used to slowly regroup and reestablish Al Qaeda in the years since the fall of the Taliban, and today they sustain an organization that is thought to be present in as many as sixty countries.

Moreover, in the years since September 11, the Al Qaeda organization appears to have given way to something that better resembles a loosely connected global movement. The great advantage for the Unites States during the cold war was that it faced a threat that was monolithic, and as such readily identifiable. The challenge for intelligence agencies when confronted with Al Qaeda in the 1990s and the early years of the new century was that the organization was so widespread. But even this menacing new entity began with a banal organizational meeting of fifteen men at Osama Bin Laden's house in Afghanistan in August 1988 and had a discernible membership. The organizers kept minutes of meetings, and it was at this initial gathering that they settled on the name Al Qaeda. Sixteen years later, the perpetrators of the attacks of March 11, 2004, in Madrid, were a different breed. The pursuit of Al Qaeda leaders and their deputies has driven the "organization" underground, but the broader movement is Hydra-headed, and any decline in the ranks of Bin Laden's lieutenants has been more than answered by a profusion of new and eager foot soldiers. Driven by the infectious ideology of Islamic extremism and their own political agendas, rather than by orders from above, they are emblematic of a new species of copycat terrorists, who take up the violent techniques of Al Qaeda not because they have satisfied the rigorous screening that new recruits to the organization traditionally endured, but because they are inspired by broader calls to Jihad broadcast over the Internet. In the long run this more atomized adversary may prove to be an even greater and more resilient threat than the terrorist group that gave birth to it.

The evidence suggests that Al Qaeda and its affiliates know that the United States is listening. James Bamford claims that Bin Laden used to be aware of this and talked anyway. He reports that prior to September 11, officials at the NSA used to impress visitors by playing recordings of Bin Laden talking to his mother. At the same time, we know that Al Qaeda members have access to cutting-edge encryption. After officials in the Philippines found a computer in the apartment of Ramzi Yousef, the architect of the 1993 World Trade Center bombing, NSA code breakers went to work endeavoring to break the encryption on Yousef's files. It reportedly took them a year. When troops entered caves abandoned by Al Qaeda in Afghanistan, they found manuals explaining how to evade various Sigint systems, including detailed instructions regarding the orbits of overhead satellites. Bin Laden himself was so familiar with the techniques employed by Sigint agencies that he foiled the efforts of Task Force Dagger, the Delta Force team sent into Afghanistan in 2001 to capture him, by using a low-frequency radio that could transmit communications via a satellite phone in another location. Even if the Delta team could get the NSA to locate the satellite phone, they could not pinpoint the radio relay or the remote transmitter over which Bin Laden was talking.

If this is the case, the listeners have to wonder when they hear something that sounds valuable whether they are hearing it because Al Qaeda wants them to. In mid-June 2001, electronic intercepts indicated that Al Qaeda would shortly attack U.S. military forces in the

Persian Gulf. The Fifth Fleet moved to Threatcon Delta, which is its highest state of alert. The aircraft carrier *Constellation* and its battle group headed out to sea. The whole port of Bahrain was emptied. But the attack did not happen. When U.S. forces started looking for actual terrorists, moreover, there weren't any to be found. According to press reports, a significant number of military-intelligence insiders now believe that the whole episode was a spoof by Al Qaeda, designed to test the efficiency of American eavesdropping systems and also possibly to create a "never cry wolf" dynamic, whereby U.S. intelligence would be less inclined to believe the next warning. "It was one of those hair on the back of your neck things," said a source familiar with the alert and subsequent analysis. "You're watching him, and suddenly, you realize, he may be watching you."

"Do the terrorists use disinformation?" says Porter Goss. "Absolutely." When I told Milt Bearden that it seems to stand to reason that at least some of the chatter-induced panics the United States had experienced in the last several years were based on deliberate red herrings from Al Qaeda, he replied, "Of course they're fooling with us on the chatter game. I think they'll have us tied in knots with it. At the very least they can bankrupt any number of municipalities by keeping us up in the orange range."

WHAT SEEMS CERTAIN IS that the effectiveness of signals intelligence is an issue that is ripe for discussion in the United States. The self-interest of the agencies, the bureaucratic inertia of Washington, and the reflexive secrecy surrounding Sigint have all conspired to prevent the American people from addressing the misguided but by all appearances widely held assumption that just listening to everybody all the time is the best way to avert further terrorist attacks. There did seem to be some sense, in Mike Hayden's appearances before the congressional committees to discuss September 11, that the NSA was ready to talk—to open the door a crack and acknowledge that as a publicly funded institution entrusted with the safety of the American people, the agency had to concede some level of accountability to the public and could no longer retreat behind the veil of anonymity. But my repeated requests for interviews with Hayden and other officials at the NSA were ignored. I corresponded for a while with a public-affairs officer named Don Weber who was processing my requests, but at a certain point Weber stopped returning my e-mails. When I finally got a woman from the publicaffairs office at Fort Meade on the telephone, I tried to explain to her that in the spirit of the new openness of Hayden's tenure, and in light of the many charges I had come across from former members of Congress, diplomats, Pentagon officials, analysts, linguists, technologists, activists, and so forth, the NSA should provide at the very least some assurances to the American people. Her blithe, almost smug reply was a simple, "Uh, yeah, we're not going to honor your request." My request had been in detail and in writing. I had expected the agency to turn it down, but not in so offhand a manner. After all, the public-affairs office at the NSA numbered at least half a dozen people. What did these people do all day?

"No interviews? No official comment or response—nothing?" I stammered.

"Nothing," the woman said.

"Why not?" I asked. "Can you at least give me a reason why you're rejecting the request out of hand?"

"We just have no information to offer," said the woman from the NSA.

CODA

From the dew of the few flakes that melt on our faces, we cannot reconstruct the snowstorm.

—*John Updike*

THERE'S ONLY ONE decent restaurant in Assab, the southernmost town in Eritrea, a war-torn sliver of a country that separates Ethiopia from the Red Sea. A deepwater harbor once made Assab a major center of commerce for the region, but peacetime assets are often wartime liabilities, and the port was contested and eventually shut down. Now Assab is languorous and dusty; hulking pieces of machinery for unloading ships rust by the docks; a mild-mannered population still takes the ambling after-dinner *passeggiata* from the days when Eritrea was an Italian colony. It is said to be the hottest place on earth.

I was visiting my girlfriend Justyna, who was working as a lawyer in the protracted exchange of prisoners of war with Ethiopia. She was based in Asmara, the sleepy colonial capital that the war somehow froze in the late 1950s: cafés and faded art-deco facades, cobwebbed but elegant. A Miss Havisham of cities.

As the inky night descended, we strolled out of our hotel in search of the restaurant we were told was the only Italian place remaining, run by an old woman who came before the war with Ethiopia and never left. The restaurant was big, a large room with seventies-era posters for macaroni and cruises to the Mediterranean curling off the walls. Dilapidated fans turned lazily overhead. Apart from a solitary diner in the corner and the matron, who was, true to form, a brusque holdout from another era, amply proportioned, slow moving, and neither impressed nor surprised by my college Italian, the place was empty.

It was agreed that we would have the only item available, fresh-caught fish, haphazardly breaded and grilled. We smiled in the direction of the other diner, a dark-haired man in his late thirties, dressed in a uniform the starch of which had given way to the wrinkle and sag of tropical heat. He was aggressively devouring his platter of fish and making good progress on a bottle of Chianti, and as we looked over he smiled, raised the bottle in one hand, lifted his plate of food in the other, and made his way to our table.

"Would you like some wine?" he asked, by way of introduction. He sat and filled our glasses and explained that he was a Spaniard working for the UN, monitoring the fragile peace in the area. He said he had been here for ten weeks and hated Eritrean food and thus was forced to dine at this restaurant every night. He questioned Justyna about the work she was doing in Asmara, nodding along and interjecting in fractured English. Then he turned to me. I braced myself for the usual exchange. "I'm writing a book," I said, knowing that you can never leave it at that. I'd found, since I started researching Sigint years before, that when talking to people in the States about my work I invariably had to explain what signals intelligence was, how it worked, and why I was interested in it.

"About what?" the Spaniard asked.

I decided that I should explain as thoroughly as possible, as here we were in the middle of nowhere, the Horn of Africa heat still intense in the air around us, the neorealist restaurateur lounging by the bar, half listening. "Well," I began, "it's about how when you communicate, by phone or e-mail, you send out electronic signals." The Spaniard nodded. "And it's very easy to intercept those signals—"

"Oh," he interrupted, nodding vigorously and taking another mouthful of fish, "of course. Ekelon."

This encounter illustrated the strange dynamic of American signals-intelligence secrecy in general and the debate about Echelon in particular. Here we were very far from major newspapers or cable news or Washington or London, in a place that felt like the last restaurant on earth. And while the average American has never heard of Echelon, our dinner companion knew all about it.

Of course, it turns out that the remote locale was not so remote after all. There may be Eritreans who remember April 1943, when an American second lieutenant landed in Eritrea during his search for a good place to put a radio station in North Africa. Because Eritrea is just north of the equator and has a high altitude, it is, in the words of James Bamford, "practically an audio funnel," perfect for an American interception station and relay facility. Indeed, the Kagnew station became so important to the NSA that when Eritrea began organizing to rebel against Ethiopian rule in the 1970s, the agency contrived, with the help of GCHQ, to eavesdrop on both the Ethiopians and the rebels to monitor and attempt to control the situation.

But I wondered, as we sat with the Spaniard and finished his wine, whether the name *Echelon* would ever intrude in a serious way on the minds of most Americans, whether a full grasp of the gargantuan scope and perhaps insurmountable weaknesses of our eavesdropping alliance would ever be reflected in our national debates. When Bamford appeared before the European Parliament committee, he was asked about reaction in America to the recent revelations about Echelon. He was at a loss to explain it, he said, but there had been no reaction. "In terms of public debate, there *is* no real debate in the U.S.," he told the committee. "It's just not an issue that has caught the public's attention in the U.S. the way it has caught the attention over here."

I thought that perhaps the aftermath of September 11 would thrust the Sigint issue into the public realm and actually foster some debate about it, but oddly enough the terrorist attacks had the opposite effect. Debate over the Echelon system and global eavesdropping in general suddenly seemed trivial. The few voices in Congress that had pursued greater accountability for the NSA opted to leave the agency alone to do its job. Civil libertarians and privacy advocates moved on to other issues: the Patriot Act, Total Information Awareness, the detention of "enemy combatants." And the NSA seemed to recede even farther into the background. The attacks and the later invasion of Iraq inspired the greatest period of self-examination for the intelligence community since the Church committee hearings in the 1970s. Yet somehow the NSA did not feature in national discussions about the need for change. Despite the colossal size of the agency and its manifest difficulty at working with the rest of the intelligence community, the NSA appeared only fleetingly in the 9/11 Commission's 500-page final report. Journalists and analysts all gave lip service to the notion that America needs more human linguists and spies on the ground, but few commentators ventured beyond these platitudes to ask what the intelligence community was doing in that regard.

Curiously enough, one year after September 11, Mike Hayden took the unprecedented step of *asking* for some national debate on Sigint himself. "I am not really helped by being reminded that I need more Arabic linguists or by someone second-guessing an obscure intercept sitting in our files that *may* make more sense today than it did two years ago," he told the congressional intelligence committees. "What I really need you to do is to talk to your constituents and find out where the American people want the line between security and liberty to be."

But so far as I can ascertain, Hayden's entreaty fell on deaf ears. His request is an exceedingly difficult one to honor, certainly, but that is no reason for Americans to refuse to try to answer him, or at the very least to endeavor to gather the basic information that would allow them to do so. We must begin to articulate what privacy means to us and what it is worth, and we must recognize that "national security" is not an undifferentiated absolute but, on the contrary, an eclectic series of competing strategies and agendas, some of which will inevitably be more effective than others. And we must start insisting on less secrecy and more oversight, not just across the intelligence community but with particular reference to the single biggest intelligence agency on the planet, the NSA.

If we do not, it seems inevitable that the agency and its partners will get things wrong. They will remain isolated from view and will make strategic errors. How do we know this? Because in fact they already have. In the aftermath of September 11, as the CIA and the FBI were calling back employees from retirement, the NSA began firing people. Mike Hayden felt that too many of his employees had "the right skills for the wrong targets," so he politely asked many to leave, going so far as to pay people to retire. Soviet linguists and old analog-intercept officers unfamiliar with new technologies were shown the door, and the agency sought to recruit fresh blood for the new tasks of the war on terror. But what were those tasks? As it turns out, they were not what you might expect. Recruiting went up, and by 2004 the NSA was hiring 1,500 new employees per year. But of those, the single greatest number were security guards for Fort Meade. Puzzling though it is, this development might be excusable. It could be argued that one of the lessons of September 11 was that nothing is safe from direct terrorist attack. An assault on Fort Meade would be devastating, and perhaps new guards would go some way in preventing that scenario.

But after security guards, the agency's next hiring priority was not new linguists or analysts but new polygraph examiners. *Polygraph examiners?* Nowhere, in any of the various diagnoses of intelligence failures after September 11, had anyone concluded that a mole or infiltrator was responsible for the attacks. And even if it were true that Al Qaeda had somehow insinuated itself into the NSA, does it make sense that the agency would solve that problem by administering a test that had implicated the innocent Wen Ho Lee and cleared the guilty Aldrich Ames? A test that even in the best of circumstances is plagued by "doubts and uncertainties," according to the Supreme Court? Linguists ranked only third in the NSA's hiring scheme and analysts fourth. How could the agency recruit more polygraph examiners than linguists?

The answer lies in the obsession in the Sigint community with secrecy. Like the army, which a year after September 11 fired six Arab linguists at the Defense Language Institute in Monterey, California, because they were gay, the NSA has allowed its own prevailing institutional culture to prevent it from changing, even in the face of the greatest challenge in its history. But unlike the army, the NSA has managed to evade scrutiny or criticism for these nearsighted and dangerous decisions.

More than three years have gone by since the most dramatic intelligence failure of our time, and during that period the simplest lessons of that event have become a mantra, repeated to the point where they verge on cliché: we did not have enough linguists, and we did not have enough spies on the ground. Obviously, it takes time to develop the language capabilities to master the obscure dialects of a shadowy terrorist network, but it would appear that the NSA has been truly unwilling to make that task a priority. And as for the number of human spies, that lesson appears to have gone unheeded as well. As of May 2004, thirty-two months after September 11, the CIA had fewer than 1,100 case officers posted overseas—fewer than the number of FBI agents assigned to the New York City field office alone.

History will remark on one paradoxical outcome of September 11, 2001: a dangerous refusal to assign responsibility. As a country, we were unready to lay blame for the devastating attacks on the doorstep of any individuals. For a variety of reasons the American public refrained from assigning blame. George Tenet's resignation in June 2004 was largely perceived as a reaction to the intelligence community's blunder on Iraq and Tenet's own assertion that the evidence that Saddam Hussein possessed weapons of mass destruction was a "slam dunk." But the events of September 11 were too brutal and had left too indelible a mark to simply designate a fall guy. Instead, almost from the start, the general consensus in this country was that the problems were "structural" or "institutional." The structure of the intelligence community was invoked by the joint congressional investigation into the attacks and also by the independent 9/11 Commission. Some said we needed an office of homeland security, others a new cabinet-level intelligence czar. The debates continue. But underlying this discussion is a prevailing cynicism about any real possibility for change. Between the fall of the Berlin Wall and the time the 9/11 Commission issued its final report in the summer of 2004, the intelligence community had been subject to no fewer than sixteen federal studies, many of which called for major structural reforms. But the fundamental characteristics of the community had weathered the scrutiny and remained basically unaltered. Part of what makes institutions institutions, after all, is precisely their unwillingness—or inability—to change.

And all the while the largest and most powerful institutional element in that community pulled the veil of secrecy even tighter. In December 2003, the NSA won the authority to automatically turn down requests by citizens, pursuant to the Freedom of Information Act, for records on the agency. The agency argued that this was a "labor saver," because agency officials were wasting too much time processing requests about the NSA's operations, only to reject them all anyway.

The world of global eavesdropping remains, in Joseph Conrad's formulation, a blank space on the map. Having finished my investigation, I realized that I had not filled in that void so much as circled it, discerned where it begins and ends, spent time among the bizarre denizens of the periphery, and staked out the various vanishing points in our understanding of these issues. In terms of wrestling with the conflict between security and liberty, I became no more assured of one position or the other as I went along, pushing through an initial instinctive paranoia about the privacy of my own communications to a broader unease about a Sigint network that has grown so colossal and so hampered by its own devotion to secrecy that it has become clumsy and inept. But the one conviction I came away with is that if we ignore this issue, put off by the level of secrecy or the technical complexity involved, we do so at our own peril. Communications interception will be a major feature of twenty-first-century life, in terms of how we construe our privacy and safety and in terms of how accountable we as citizens want our government to be. If Mike Hayden does not get an answer about where the line should be drawn between security and liberty, it is not difficult to guess in which direction he will err. But he should get an answer, and there should be a debate. On the tricky issue of line drawing, this book is designed not to be the last word but the first. I'm still not certain I know where that line between security and liberty should be. Do you?

AFTERWORD TO THE PAPERBACK EDITION

LESS THAN A YEAR after the publication of *Chatter*, my speculation in the final pages that Mike Hayden would err on the side of security over liberty was proved correct. In an eerie parallel to the 1974 Seymour Hersh scoop that eventually led to the Church committee hearings, the reporters James Risen and Eric Lichtblau published a story in *The New York Times* on December 16, 2005, that revealed that under a new program initiated after September 11, 2001, the NSA had been conducting warrantless electronic surveillance inside the United States. The Bush administration confirmed the existence of the program, described it as a targeted "terrorist surveillance program," and made frequent use of the clever sound bite, "If Al Qaeda is calling you, we want to know why."

But as details about the program emerged, it began to appear that it was not as precisely targeted as administration officials suggested. The surveillance was conducted with high-level cooperation from American telecommunications and Internet providers—including AT&T, MCI, and Sprint—that furnished the agency with backdoor access to the hubs and switches of America's communications infrastructure. Russ Tice, a former NSA employee who had worked on secret Special Access Programs, went public, alleging abuses by the agency, volunteering to testify before Congress, and explaining that NSA analysts can start with a single phone call that is of interest and "spiderweb" outward, looking at everyone else the two parties to the call have contact with, and everyone *those* people have contact with, until the list of vicariously implicated individuals contains thousands of names.

Increasingly, it began to appear that the program was not geared so much to figuring out why Al Qaeda had been calling any particular individual, as to performing a broader kind of social network analysis in order to ascertain who might be a member of a terror cell. The ambition was not to listen in on innocent Americans, but, rather, to scan the communications of everyone in the country in order to extrapolate the answer to an all-important threshold question: whom precisely should we be listening to? If that sounds rather akin to the kind of crystal ball intelligence device envisioned by Admiral Poindexter and the bright minds at DARPA, it's worth noting that after being briefed on the program in 2003—in a secret session at which he was not allowed to consult his staff or take any notes—Senator Jay Rockefeller, D-WV, wrote a handwritten letter to Dick Cheney, saying, "John Poindexter's TIA Project sprung to mind, exacerbating my concern regarding the direction the Administration is moving with regard to security, technology, and surveillance."

Suddenly Sigint was in the news in a way that it hadn't been since the Church committee hearings. The same press outlets that had spent years ignoring government eavesdropping were all over the story: in the first days after the *Times*'s initial revelations, cable news anchors, finding themselves on unfamiliar turf, could often be heard describing the scandal involving wiretapping by the National Security *Council*. President Bush blasted the *Times* for running the story, as if to suggest that terrorist groups might change their behavior on the basis not of whether they were being listened to, but of whether the listening was done pursuant to a warrant; and almost immediately the Justice Department launched an investigation to determine the sources of the leak to Risen. The administration made no allowances for the fact, mentioned in passing in the original story and further elaborated elsewhere, that Risen had actually learned of the warrantless eavesdropping a year earlier but that the *Times*'s Washington bureau had acquiesced to a White House request not to run with the story. It was only as Risen prepared to publish the revelations in his own book, *State of War,* that the newspaper suddenly mustered the courage to inform Americans about the wiretapping program, lest it get scooped by its own reporter.

Justice Department investigation to the contrary, it was clear that the reason the administration did not want the program revealed had less to do with the exposure of sources and methods than with the brashness of the decision to jettison altogether the procedures and protections established by the FISA. Days after the revelations, James Robertson, a U.S. district judge who served on the FISA court, resigned his post in protest, expressing to associates an understandable worry that the extrajudicial spying undermined the legitimacy of the work of the court. The program was being carried out with an unmistakable *sneakiness* that was enormously unsettling. Suddenly, all of the national debate surrounding the passage of the Patriot Act in 2001 seemed like a charade: all the while there were a series of procedures taking shape that were not even reflected in the text of the new law. According to Risen's account, intelligence obtained through the program is "laundered" by the NSA before being distributed through broader intelligence community channels to hide the fact that it is obtained illegally. He suggests that in some instances authorities applied for legitimate FISA warrants of individuals they were already monitoring, and redundant warrants of this sort would certainly be a form of masking the existence of the program. Though the administration claimed that there had never been any doubts about the legality of the wiretapping, it emerged that, on the contrary, the decision to circumvent the FISA court had occasioned serious debate among Justice Department lawyers, some of whom had preemptively hired private attorneys to defend themselves, on the off chance that the program should ever be exposed.

When the program was exposed, members of Congress announced that they would investigate, but any hopes that this might result in another Church committee–style assessment of the uses and abuses of intelligence were soon dashed by the meek proceedings that followed. With much fanfare, the Senate Judiciary Committee announced hearings on the legality of the program, but the major portion of those hearings was a one-day session in early February in which the only witness was Attorney General Alberto Gonzales. With an implacable smile and the slightest hint of smugness, Gonzales resisted the senators' questions by repeating, ad nauseum, that while he would assert the general legality of the program, he would not comment on any specifics. At one point Senator Patrick Leahy, D-VT, shot back, "Oh, I'm sorry. I forgot: you can't answer *any* questions that might be relevant." The essential nature of the proceedings, in which members of Congress endeavored to assess the legality of a program that they didn't understand, and that Gonzales refused to tell them anything about, was absurd, and Gonzales was quick to adopt the eavesdroppers' mantra: Just Trust Us. The program targets terrorists and protects civil liberties, he suggested. How does it select those targets, the senators wondered. Gonzales didn't want to get into specifics. How does it protect civil liberties? "There are guidelines, minimization procedures," he said vaguely. Could he make available those guidelines and procedures? Nope. "They're classified."

Had they been serious about determining what precisely the program had involved, the senators might have subpoenaed the telecom CEOs who cooperated with the program. This was a tactic adopted with great success by congressional investigators of the 1970s, and despite the unprecedentedly broad interpretation of executive power that the administration used to justify the NSA program, it is unlikely that "executive privilege" not to testify could be extended to private citizens like the CEOs. But the committee took no such initiative, and the abortive investigation served instead to underline how hopelessly compromised a body Congress had become.

In fact, Congress had demonstrated its lack of ability or interest to pursue NSA infractions months earlier, when another scandal—as shocking, in some ways, as the warrantless wiretapping program, but completely overlooked—came and went. During the confirmation hearings for John Bolton's candidacy for the position of U.S. ambassador to the United Nations in April 2005, it emerged that on a number of occasions while he was an undersecretary at the State Department, he had received reports of intercepted phone calls between a party the NSA was targeting and a "U.S. Person." Part of the fallacy of the Bush administration's line "If Al Qaeda is calling you, we want to know why" was of course that even prior to 9/11, the NSA was always allowed to continue listening if a target telephoned someone in the United States. It *never* required a FISA warrant to listen in on Al Qaeda's calls to America. The one requirement was always that, as reports of these conversations were distributed to different offices and agencies in Washington, the name of the American be redacted and replaced by a generic "U.S. Person." But when Bolton received these reports, he would occasionally contact the NSA and ask to know the identity of the U.S. person in question. And without any showing of cause on his part, or process of review, the agency turned over the names.

Following this revelation, *Newsweek* discovered that from January 2004 to May 2005, the NSA had supplied the names of some 10,000 American citizens in this informal fashion to policy makers at many departments, other American intelligence services, and law enforcement agencies. The trouble here was that the loophole had clearly grown bigger than the law itself. If the agency provides officials with the identities of Americans, what is the use of redacting those names in the first place? The exposure of this informal practice was the first indication that the assurances of Mike Hayden and others that rigorous safeguards governed the agency's activities, and that Americans should trust that the agency was not listening to them, were less than credible. After all, the reports Bolton was reading involved not people Al Qaeda was calling but, on the contrary, his own colleagues and rivals in Washington who happened to correspond with foreign dignitaries. At one point, Bolton sought out and congratulated a colleague whose performance in an intercepted telephone call he particularly admired.

Senate Democrats took advantage of Bolton's transgression in the nomination battle, playing up his reputation as a sharp-elbowed bureaucratic brute and implying that he might have used the intercepts to intimidate Washington adversaries, assembling information gleaned from intercepted conversations and playing a kind of Beltway Richelieu. Bolton, for his part, told Congress that he had asked the spy agency for the names in order "to better understand" summaries of intercepted conversations. "It's important to find out who is saying what to whom," he said. Stewart Baker, the former NSA general counsel, essentially conceded that the requests were vetted with a rubber stamp. "We typically would ask why" disclosure of an identity was necessary, he said, "but we wouldn't try to second-guess" the rationale. But when President Bush curtailed the confirmation process by using a "recess appointment" to install Bolton at the United Nations, the Senate Democrats, interested more in the partisan utility of the revelations than their intrinsic significance, let the matter drop altogether.

IN THIS MANNER, the reassuring narrative offered by officials, in which the history of intelligence cleaves neatly into two acts—the bad old days that preceded the Church committee hearings and the decades of responsibility that followed—has suddenly eroded. The contest between security and liberty described in *Chatter* seems, for the moment, to have gone to security—or some semblance thereof—and the move to write human analysts and legal constraints out of the intelligence equation, and replace them with pervasive, Orwellian systems that can deliver results at the touch of a button, is on the ascendant.

The single largest item in the intelligence budget for 2005 was a $9.5 billion "stealth" photoreconnaissance satellite code-named Misty. Satellites are better adapted to tracking tank divisions than locating terrorists, and as India's nuclear tests made clear, they are of dubious utility even in monitoring the atomic ambitions of other countries. This particular satellite was described by Senator Ron Wyden, D-OR, a member of the intelligence committee, which vetoed it twice, as "unnecessary, ineffective, over-budget, and too expensive." Several independent reviews found that other programs already in existence or development could produce the same intelligence at far less cost and technological risk. Even the supposed "stealthiness" of the satellite was dubious: when the NRO launched the first generation of Misty in 1990, it was spotted almost immediately—not by Russian satellite trackers, but by a team of amateur space observers. Nevertheless, Misty was saved by the appropriations committee, and is currently being developed by Lockheed Martin. Intelligence by remote control has never been more in vogue; one official familiar with Misty said of its colossal price tag, "With the amount of money we're talking about here, you could build a whole new CIA."

In February 2006, the *National Journal* revealed that the Total Information Awareness program had never in fact gone out of business after Congress "killed it." Instead it had been given a new name ("Basketball" was the code name used by one contractor), new and secret sources of funding, and a new home. After Congress pulled its funding in late 2003, several of the components of TIA were shifted—to the NSA. The NSA appears to be augmenting its ranks at an impressive rate: in the summer of 2005, Maryland's largest employer announced plans for as many as 10,000 new jobs at Fort Meade within seven years. The agency took out a patent on a new geo-location technology that could pinpoint the physical location of an Internet user by comparing it to a "map" of IP addresses with known locations. After Hayden assumed the position of principal deputy director for national intelligence, Lieutenant General Keith Alexander, who had most recently served as the army's intelligence chief, was appointed the new head of the NSA. Demonstrating some of Hayden's PR instincts, Alexander granted a long inaugural interview to the Baltimore *Sun,* and was amiable, even chipper, but scrupulously unrevealing. He was happy to disclose his fondness for golf, and spoke in the most generic terms possible about the agency's need to transition from the "industrial age" to the "information age."

But there are also signs that new investments in surveillance technologies are encountering problems. The long-term effort to modernize the NSA's eavesdropping infrastructure, Trailblazer, which Hayden had launched in 2000, fell years behind and hundreds of millions of dollars over budget. The FBI acknowledged that in its own wiretapping operations, it was not unusual that agents mistakenly targeted the wrong phone numbers, intercepting the communications not of terror suspects, but of innocent civilians. And the backlog of conversations intercepted as part of terror investigations, but still untranslated due to a shortage of linguists, grew to 8,300 hours.

As details began to emerge about the NSA program, it became clear that it was not old-fashioned targeted wiretapping that had taken place, but a broader intercept-first-and-sort-through-it-later approach more akin to Echelon and other systems. Officials familiar with the program said that computers scanned the "metadata" of large flows of communications—the origin, destination, duration, and time of phone calls and the header information of e-mails—looking for particular identities or patterns, before actually listening in on anyone. In some respects this might have proved reassuring. After all, it's far less intrusive to have a computer analyzing the metadata of your communications than it would be to have a human analyst actually listening to your spoken words. If you're not calling Al Qaeda, you might be inclined to think, then you're in the clear.

But the problem with having government computers effectively play six degrees of Osama Bin Laden is that most of us are connected by two degrees of separation to thousands of people, and by three degrees to hundreds of thousands. The system will inevitably ensnare innocent individuals who are connected, however tenuously or accidentally, to the original target. Thus it turns out that the FBI grew frustrated each time the NSA delivered a new batch of leads generated by the wiretapping program, because most of the leads were dead ends, which is to say, innocent civilians. They reportedly joked about how new tips could only mean "more calls to Pizza Hut." In fact, it emerged that the vast majority of names generated by the program were false positives—innocent people implicated in an ever-expanding associational web. The National Counterterrorism Center's database of suspected terrorists contains 325,000 names—a number that, logic would suggest, must include at least tens of thousands of innocent false positives. Thus, even as it grows, the NSA continues to struggle with the challenge of triage— what good do red flags do when there are 325,000 of them? A report on new data-mining initiatives by the Congressional Research Service recently found that the agency is at risk of being "drowned" in information.

IN DECEMBER 2004, Admiral Bobby Ray Inman, who had been director of the NSA from 1977–1981, granted an interview to the online magazine

Slate. The interviewer, the journalist A. L. Bardach, inquired about a variety of contemporary intelligence-related issues, and then asked Inman about the Echelon system. "I have difficulty in talking to you, Annie, in a recorded, print interview about Echelon," Inman said, "because it was a classified project and it's never been declassified to me." Nevertheless, with a little prodding from Bardach, Inman became the first NSA official to confirm the existence of the system. He described Echelon in the past tense. When asked whether it had focused exclusively on Europe, he corrected, "It wasn't just Europe; it was worldwide." In an admission that must have given the European parliamentarians some belated vindication, he added, "Its real impact was economic, on financial issues."

Inman was adamant, however, that the system could not be used inside the United States. Reading his reassurances today, one is struck by how antique they sound, how quaint. The interview took place a year before the Bush administration's program was revealed, and Inman, of course, was the first director of the NSA in the FISA era. But even as he spoke, the new warrantless program was under way. At the time of this writing, it is difficult not to believe that the FISA era effectively ended on September 11, 2001. While some wrangling persists in Washington, proposals for an extensive investigation into the NSA program have met with no success, and without any concrete grasp of how it is that targets are selected, what constitutes a link between a terror suspect and his immediate and distant associates, and how long data on innocent civilians are maintained, any ruling on the part of Congress about the legality or constitutionality of the program will be tentative and hypothetical at best.

The debate about security and privacy does seem to have come and gone already. The greatest revelations in three decades about abuses by the NSA had their brief moment of significance and public outcry, but stories like this are driven by the momentum of the Congress and the revelations of muckraking journalists, and as Congress resigns itself to defeat, and the press moves on to other things, the wiretapping story already seems to have lost traction. On March 7, 2006, the Senate intelligence committee voted along party lines not to investigate the wiretapping, effectively abdicating its role as an oversight body. Senator Jay Rockefeller, D-WV, pointed out that the move could only mean the committee would sink "further into irrelevancy." *The New York Times* declared it dead. The committee—one of the two institutional safeguards that grew out of the tumult of the Church committee era—sacrificed itself for the Bush administration and the NSA, and it took the other of those institutions, the FISA, along with it. This is lamentable, most especially because what we have learned about the NSA's program points to a bitter truth: in its illegality, its pervasiveness and its invasiveness, and in its false-positive afflicted manifest inefficiency, the NSA program seems to indicate that contrary to the assumptions that undergirded much of *Chatter*, Americans do not even have the luxury of a zero-sum choice between security and liberty. It may be that in our very passivity, in our refusal to confront these issues head on, we will end up not more free and less safe, or more safe and less free—but less safe and less free.

March 28, 2006
New York

ACKNOWLEDGMENTS

THE FIRST AND only time I was aware of being bugged, I was with the South African writer Rose Moss, tagging along while she interviewed Popo Molefe, one of the leaders of the United Democratic Front, in Johannesburg. It was 1990, and I was fourteen. We turned the radio up and whispered. It was Rose's notion that a boy who was curious about South Africa should go there. I want to thank her for taking me along on that early adventure and instilling in me that same sense of intellectual exploration.

While *Chatter* contains a great deal of original reporting, it owes its existence to the pioneering work of a number of writers and researchers who have written on intelligence, technology, surveillance, and secrecy. In particular, I owe debts to the work of Steven Aftergood, Desmond Ball, James Bamford, Sissela Bok, Duncan Campbell, Skipper Elkjaer, David Ensor of CNN, Anna Funder, Timothy Garton Ash, Bill Gertz of *The Washington Times,* Nicky Hager, Seymour Hersh, Declan McCullagh, Richard Norton-Taylor of *The Guardian,* John Pike, Jeffrey Richelson, Jon Ronson, Jeffrey Rosen, Kenan Seeberg, Scott Shane and Laura Sullivan of the Baltimore *Sun,* and Nigel West.

Simon Davies supervised a graduate thesis on Sigint and cryptography at the London School of Economics and pointed me in the right direction when I first embarked on the book. Milt Bearden promised he would show me "the mines in the minefield" and from the beginning was extremely generous with his advice and his time. David Kahn was an early inspiration for and champion of this book. He is a shrewd and prolific scholar and has become a great friend.

Eli Abir, Steven Aftergood, Bob Baer, Rep. Bob Barr, Mark Bearce, Doron Ben-Atar, Lincoln Caplan, Mike Castelaz at PARI, Helen De

Witt, Skipper Elkjaer, Michael Erskine, Glyn Ford, Johannes Geiger, Milosz Gudzowski, Katharine Gun, Alistair Harley, Anthony Hawley, Sen. Gary Hart, Sir Peter Heap, Maureen Howard, Dan Kearney, Charles Keith, Sen. Bob Kerrey, Steve Klein, Herb Lebowitz, David Lowe, Wyatt Mason, Bob McNally at GCHQ, Karl Nastrom, Marty Nee, Charles Osborne at PARI, Lindis Percy, the pseudonymous Ralph J. Perro, Ilka Schroeder, Kenan Seeberg, Mike Sims, Aiste Skarzinskaite, Britt Snider, Sai Sriskandarajah, Ned Sublette, John Jeremiah Sullivan, Steve Warby, David Weld, Sean Westmoreland, and Robert Windrem at NBC all helped in ways large and small. Thanks also to the small handful of individuals who talked to me and helped me out but requested that I withold their names.

In London, I repeatedly abused the generosity of Paul Morrison and Penny Dixon, and much of the early thinking on this book occurred in conversation with Paul.

Mike Becker was kind enough to put me up in Brussels and take the edge off days at the parliament with evenings at Le Blue Note.

Over the last several years, I have benefited immeasurably from friendships and conversations with former professors, in particular James Mayall at Cambridge, Richard Bulliet, Simon Schama and Fritz Stern at Columbia, and Jay Winter at Yale.

At Yale Law School, I am grateful in various ways to Jack Balkin, Jim Silk, Kate Stith, and Kenji Yoshino, and in the graduate school I am especially thankful to Paul Kennedy, John Gaddis, and Charles Hill for their excellent seminar in grand strategy.

John Swansburg, my editor at *Legal Affairs,* read the manuscript and made extremely useful suggestions on sharpening it. Barbara Epstein at *The New York Review of Books* saw promise in the Katharine Gun story and ran an early draft of it. Thanks also there to Evan Hughes and Amanda Gill.

My interest in Sigint began while I was studying in Britain on a Marshall scholarship. Deep thanks to the Foreign & Commonwealth Office and the Marshall Aid Commemoration Commission for that extraordinary opportunity.

Much of this book was written during a one-year fellowship at the Cullman Center for Scholars and Writers, a remarkable and wonderful institution created by Dorothy and Lewis B. Cullman. My deepest gratitude goes to the Cullmans, who gave me an excuse to devote myself full-time to the book and meet a group of brilliant individuals. Everyone at the center had the opportunity to comment on various sections of this book in two workshops during the course of the year, and I thank each and every fellow, as well as Amy Azzarito, Rebecca Federman, Peter Gay, and Pamela Leo for their insights and support.

But in particular I owe a great debt to Jean Strouse and Melanie Rehak, who talked me through the peculiar neuroses of birthing a book and, when they tired of book talk, steered the conversation in the more agreeable direction of movies or food. They have both become dear friends, and Melanie has read and remarked on more sections of the book in more different forms than I care to think about.

This book would never have been were it not for Tina Bennett, agent extraordinaire. Tina in action is a wonder to behold: advocating, editing, and when necessary effusing. There's something awe inspiring about watching someone so exceedingly good at what she does; the awe is tinged with gratitude when she's doing it on your behalf. Many thanks also to Cecile Barendsma, Svetlana Katz, and everyone else at Janklow and Nesbit.

Joy de Menil saw potential in the book and from the start spotted weaknesses and opportunities with surgical precision. After Joy, the book fell in the lap of Ileene Smith. Having known me only a short few months and having read half the manuscript, Ileene displayed the extraordinary empathetic instincts that set her in such good stead as an editor, intuited that I had approached a crossroads in terms of which direction the book would go, and gently nudged me down the road I'd wanted to pursue all along. I'm deeply indebted to her and also to Robin Rolewicz, Luke Epplin, and everyone else at Random House. A particular thanks to Timothy Mennel, for the gentle but scrupulous copyedit the manuscript so desperately needed, and to Evan Camfield for steering me through production.

Martin Eisner has been my first reader for a decade. He's a great editor and a great friend, and—to his chagrin, I suspect—I rarely send a sentence out into the world without running it by him first.

My family has also been extraordinarily supportive throughout the writing of the book. With her customary tact, Beatrice contributed such marginalia as "Dear God cut that joke out, or I'll about die." And Tristram reminded me that technical details are fine, but it's the stories that stay with you. My mother and father, Jennifer and Frank, are the two sharpest, funniest people I know. The years it took to write this book have felt at times like one protracted and fascinating conversation with my mum and dad. *Chatter* is dedicated to them.

But most important has been the quiet and unstinting support of

Justyna Paulina Gudzowska. In eight apartments, in four cities, in two countries, she has suffered through the early mornings and the late nights and known when to rein in my rhetorical excesses and when to tell me to kick off for the day. She is dazzlingly smart and a joy to be around. I am lucky to know her.

NOTES

All of the material in *Chatter* was drawn from public sources; no classified documents were used, and with a few possible exceptions none of what the various people I interviewed told me was classified. In addition to pointing the reader to the sources for various assertions in the book, the notes that follow occasionally clarify or elaborate on points made in the text and make suggestions for further reading.

INTRODUCTION

xi   IN FEBRUARY 2003 William Rashbaum, "Police Are Focusing More on Protecting the Subways," *The New York Times*, February 14, 2003; Larry Celona and Brad Hunter, "Target: Subway," *New York Post*, February 9, 2003.

xii   IN THE WEEKS BEFORE James Risen, "U.S. Increased Alert on Evidence Qaeda Was Planning 2 Attacks," *The New York Times*, February 14, 2003; "Slowdown in 'Chatter' Worries Officials," CNN, August 6, 2004.

xiii OUR SMALL VOCABULARY Sir William Blackstone, *Commentaries on the Laws of England*, vol. 4 (Chicago: University of Chicago Press, 1979), p. 169.

xiv   WHEREAS THE CIA The exact figures are notoriously difficult to ascertain, as they are highly classified and have fluctuated considerably over the last two decades, declining steadily after the cold war, then growing suddenly again after September 11, 2001. The website of the Federation of American Scientists has good material on the staff and budget numbers of intelligence agencies, though all the federation can do is speculate on the basis of public source information. James Bamford, the civilian authority on the NSA, claims in *Body of Secrets* that each working day, 38,000 employees come to work at Fort Meade, and press accounts tend to refer back to this number and hold that the NSA has some 40,000 employees. But Bamford adds that the agency has an additional 25,000 employees stationed at listening posts overseas. That could bring the total number of people employed in some capacity by the agency to more than 60,000. See James Bamford, *Body of Secrets* (New York: Doubleday, 2001), p. 482. Conservative estimates of the NSA's budget put it at around $3 to $4 billion before September 11, but that number has likely been significantly augmented in the intervening years. In *Plan of Attack,* Bob Woodward estimates that the agency's budget might be as high as $6 billion (Bob Woodward, *Plan of Attack* [New York: Simon and Schuster, 2004], p. 213). It's also worth remembering that budget figures just for the NSA are misleading, because the National Reconnaissance Office (NRO), the secret agency that builds and maintains America's satellites, also has an annual budget of roughly $7 billion (Douglas Pasternak, "Lack of Intelligence," *U.S. News and World Report,* August 11, 2003). On the budget issue, the Federation of American Scientists is again a good place to start. See "Intelligence Agency Budgets," at http://www.fas.org (hereinafter "the FAS site"). As for the CIA figures, the 20,000 figure comes from the FAS site, but of that number, fewer than 5,000 are actually in the Directorate of Operations, which overseas active human spying ("Time for a Rethink," *The Economist,* April 18, 2002). And of *that* number, fewer than 1,100 are case officers posted overseas. Douglas Jehl, "Abundance of Caution and Years of Budget Cuts Are Seen to Limit CIA," *The New York Times,* May 11, 2004.

xv   MARLOW, JOSEPH CONRAD'S Joseph Conrad, *Heart of Darkness* (New York: Alfred A. Knopf, 1967 [1902]), p. 9.

xv   "THE MOST PROFOUND TECHNOLOGIES" Mark Weiser, "The Computer for the Twenty-first Century," *Scientific American,* September 1991.

CHAPTER 1: RADOMES IN THE DESERT, RADOMES ON THE MOOR: THE INVISIBLE ARCHITECTURE OF ECHELON

5   THEY MOVE THEIR BELONGINGS An article by Barbara E. Scott in the April 1991 issue of the internal *NSA Newsletter* announces Field Recruitment Week at Fort Meade and suggests that the question "for those who are looking for diversity of experience, the chance to live in a different culture, marvelous opportunities to travel to exotic countries, and even to save money, should be, 'Why *not* take a field tour?' "

5   THERE ARE LINGUISTS Duncan Campbell, *Interception Capabilities 2000,* report to the Director General for Research of the European Parliament, 1999. Available at http://www.iptvreports.mcmail.com/interception_capabilities_2000.htm.

5   HE SAID THAT AS FAR A rare, if not especially revealing, glimpse inside Menwith Hill is presented by Senator Bob Graham (D-Fla.), who toured the base with other members of the congressional intelligence committees in the summer of 2001.

> Inside the facility were a series of wide-open spaces occupied by several hundred people grouped into mission-based clusters of roughly twenty-five people. Within each cluster, the workers were divided into two areas. The technicians tended the sophisticated monitors and computer systems that were collecting the information, and the analysts were prioritizing and analyzing the data. As we toured the complex, we saw analysts poring over data that was streaming in from thousands of miles away, including real-time observations of events that merited the observation of the Menwith Hill staff. Of course, it wasn't that obvious to us. A worker would punch a

button and say, "Look at this!" We'd see a series of squiggly lines, which for the Menwith staff contained a world of information. Such information may well be more important than armaments in this new century.

Bob Graham with Jeff Nussbaum, *Intelligence Matters* (New York: Random House, 2004), p. 86.

6   "IT IS FAIR TO SAY" Walter Pincus, "CIA's Espionage Capability Found Lacking," *The Washington Post,* May 10, 1998.

7   "THE THEORY WAS" Robert Baer, *See No Evil* (New York: Crown, 2002), p. xvii.

7   STANSFIELD TURNER Christopher Andrew, *For the President's Eyes Only* (New York: HarperCollins, 1995), p. 429.

7   IN THE JULY/AUGUST 2001 ISSUE Reuel Marc Gerecht, "The Counterterrorist Myth," *Atlantic Monthly,* July/August 2001.

7   THIS DESPITE THE FACT David Kahn, *The Codebreakers* (New York: Scribner, 1996), pp. 677, 689.

8   THE FORMER INVOLVES In fact, *Sigint* is a broad umbrella term that encompasses a variety of subsidiary "ints." Communications interception is often referred to, as I do in this book, as Sigint, but it is more specifically known as Comint, or communications intelligence. Other types of Sigint include Imint (imagery), Radint (radar), Elint (electrical), and so forth.

8   IT JUST SITS AND LISTENS This particular organizational characteristic would in fact come under fire from the 9/11 Commission in their final report: "The NSA did not think its job was to research [suspected terrorist] identities. It saw itself as an agency to support intelligence consumers, such as CIA. The NSA tried to respond energetically to any request made. But it waited to be asked." National Commission on Terrorist Attacks upon the United States, *The 9/11 Report: Final Report of the National Commission on Terrorist Attacks upon the United States* (New York: W. W. Norton, 2004) (hereinafter "9/11 Commission Report"), p. 353.

8   WHEN THE PRESS Walter Pincus, "The Reasons Behind a White House Rebuke," *The Washington Post,* June 24, 2002. For a fascinating account of the point at which Bin Laden jettisoned the phone, see Steve Coll, "A Secret Hunt Unravels in Afghanistan," *The Washington Post,* February 24, 2002; also see *Ghost Wars,* Coll's terrific history of CIA operations in Afghanistan and the emergence of Al Qaeda (New York: The Penguin Press, 2004). The original article containing the leaked information was Ernest Blazar, "Inside the Ring," *The Washington Times,* August 24, 1998. Michael Scheuer, the author of *Imperial Hubris,* blasts Blazar and other journalists who print leaks, as well as the officials who supply them, arguing that this activity is tantamount to treason. Anonymous, *Imperial Hubris* (Dulles, Va.: Brassey's, 2004), pp. 192–200.

9   THUS IT WAS NOT Nicky Hager, *Secret Power* (Nelson, N.Z.: Craig Potton, 1996), p. 40.

10   IN A TRIAL Geoffrey Robertson, *The Justice Game* (London: Chatto and Windus, 1998), p. 125.

11   THE BEST WAY As with the word *Sigint,* when I use *cryptography* I am for the sake of convenience huddling a series of different technical terms under one semantic umbrella. By *cryptography* I mean the art of making and breaking

codes and ciphers, in the broadest possible terms. For a more nuanced exploration of the differences between cryptography, cryptology, steganography, and so forth, delve into Kahn, *Codebreakers.*

11 "IT MUST BE THAT" Kahn, *Codebreakers,* p. 84.

11 IN *THE HISTORY,* HERODOTUS Herodotus, *The History,* trans. David Greene (Chicago: University of Chicago Press, 1987), 5:35.

11 IN ANCIENT CHINA Kahn, *Codebreakers,* p. 73.

11 ACTUALLY, NEITHER OF THESE Simon Singh, *The Code Book* (New York: Doubleday, 1999), p. 15.

12 IN THE 1500S Kahn, *Codebreakers,* p. 109.

12 HIS NAME WAS GIOVANNI SORO Ibid.

12 ANTOINE ROSSIGNOL Ibid., p. 159.

13 IT WAS ROSSIGNOL See Mark Urban, *The Man Who Broke Napoleon's Codes* (London: Faber and Faber, 2001).

13 AND THE ROYAL NAVY Nigel West, *GCHQ* (London: Hodder and Stoughton, 1987), pp. 24–26.

13 ON JANUARY 16, 1917 Barbara Tuchman, *The Zimmermann Telegram* (New York: Macmillan, 1996), illustration after p. 180, details of maneuverings, chap. 10.

14 THE BRITISH INTERCEPTED Singh, *Code Book,* pp. 112–15.

14 THE CHARTER FOR ROOM 40 David Stafford, *Roosevelt and Churchill: Men of Secrets* (New York: Overlook Press, 1999), p. 34.

15 WHEREAS THE U.S. ARMY Kahn, *Codebreakers,* p. 611.

15 "THIS WAS THE SECRET WAR" Winston Churchill, *Their Finest Hour* (Boston: Houghton Mifflin, 1949), p. 381.

15 DURING THE WAR Stafford, *Roosevelt and Churchill,* p. 223.

15 HE RELISHED THIS Ibid., pp. 36–37.

16 IN FACT, IT WASN'T West, *GCHQ,* p. 20.

16 IN THE SPRING OF 1941 James Bamford, *The Puzzle Palace* (New York: Penguin, 1983), p. 312.

16 FIRST, THE PURPLE MACHINE Stafford, *Roosevelt and Churchill,* p. 56.

17 THE BRITISH DID NOT William Stevenson, *A Man Called Intrepid* (New York: Harcourt Brace Jovanovich, 1976), p. 48.

17 ONCE THE AMERICANS Bradley F. Smith, *The Ultra-Magic Deals and the Most Secret Special Relationship, 1940–1946* (Novato, Calif.: Presidio Press, 1992), pp. 150–52.

18 IT HELD THAT The BRUSA Agreement of May 17, 1943, as published in *Cryptologia* 21. 1 (January 1997).

18 AFTER BRUSA WAS SIGNED Smith, *Ultra-Magic Deals,* pp. 160–63.

18 SIX MONTHS LATER West, *GCHQ,* p. 287.

18 ON SEPTEMBER 12, 1945 Smith, *Ultra-Magic Deals,* p. 212.

19 THE AMERICANS WORRIED Ibid., pp. 217–25.

19 AND SO IN FEBRUARY 1946 Andrew, *For the President's Eyes,* pp. 162–63.

19 AT THE MEETINGS Jeffrey Richelson and Desmond Ball, *The Ties That Bind,* 2d ed. (Boston: Unwin and Hyman, 1990), p. 3.

20 BEFORE HE DIED Andrew, *For the President's Eyes,* pp. 162–63.

20 THE INITIAL PHASE Bamford, *Body of Secrets,* p. 40.

20 THE ARRANGEMENT PROVIDED Richelson and Ball, *Ties That Bind*, pp. 5–6.

20 EVEN BRITAIN Ibid., p. 8.

20 INDEED, MOST OF THE AMERICAN BASES Nicholas Rufford, "Spy Station F83," *Sunday Times*, June 1, 1998.

20 THE TERMS OF THE AGREEMENT West, *GCHQ*, p. 287.

21 YET SINCE 1981 Hager, *Secret Power*, p. 94.

21 IN OCTOBER 2002 Audrey Young, "PM Backs CIA Over Warnings," *New Zealand Herald*, October 17, 2002. Also, Murray Horton, "Government Still Coy About UKUSA Agreement," *Peace Researcher*, at http://www.converge.org.nz/abc/pr27-79.htm.

21 ONE DAY IN 1970 Desmond Ball, *Pine Gap* (Sydney: Allen and Unwin, 1988), chaps. 2, 4. Robert Lindsey, *The Falcon and the Snowman* (New York: Simon and Schuster, 1979), chap. 9. William Burrows points out that this first model was an "experimental operational version," which was eventually succeeded by the first "fully operational" Rhyolite bird in 1973. William Burrows, *Deep Black: Space Espionage and National Security* (New York: Random House, 1986), p. 191.

22 AS SUCH, IN THE WORDS Lindsey, *Falcon and the Snowman*, p. 57.

22 JAMES BAMFORD Bamford, *Body of Secrets*, pp. 367–68.

22 PACKED INTO A LARGE CONTAINER Ibid., p. 368.

22 BIRD 1 WAS A SQUAT Burrows, *Deep Black*, p. 193.

22 DEEP IN THE SWELTERING Details drawn from Ball, *Pine Gap*.

23 OF COURSE, THE LOCATION Ibid., p. 90.

24 WHILE THIS KIND Bamford, *Body of Secrets*, p. 368.

24 THE SEVEN SQUARE MILES Ball, *Pine Gap*, pp. 90–91.

24 YET THE AGREEMENT Ibid., appendix 1, 2.

24 THE AUSTRALIAN MINISTER Ibid., p. 92.

25 BUT EVEN AT THE HEIGHT Ibid.

25 MOREOVER, AS BALL MAKES CLEAR Ibid., p. 53.

25 TODAY, THE BASE EMPLOYS "Aussie War Spies Go on Strike," *Northern Territory News* (Australia), March 18, 2003.

25 THEY NEVER DISCUSS THEIR JOBS "A Yankee Spy Base in the Outback," *U.S. News and World Report*, June 20, 1983.

25 INITIALLY, PINE GAP Bamford, *Body of Secrets*, p. 368.

25 BUT RON HUISKEN "Ex-Official Speaks on Role of Australian-U.S. Pine Gap Monitoring Station," BBC Monitoring International Reports, March 13, 2003.

26 TODAY, PINE GAP See Desmond Ball, *A Suitable Piece of Real Estate: American Installations in Australia* (Sydney: Hale and Iremonger, 1980).

26 THE LABOUR PARTY INITIATED INQUIRIES Lindsey, *Falcon and the Snowman*, pp. 140–41.

26 "CIA IS PERPLEXED" Ibid., p. 141.

27 WHITLAM PERSERVERED, HOWEVER Ibid., p. 142.

27 THOUGH INITIALLY AUSTRALIAN EMPLOYEES Remarks of Desmond Ball, Commonwealth of Australia, Proof Committee Hansard, Joint Standing Committee on Treaties, Reference: Pine Gap, August 9, 1999.

27 THE DIRECTORS OF THE FIVE Hager, *Secret Power*, p. 22.

27 Numerous other Richelson and Ball, *Ties That Bind,* p. 135.
27 In 1999, Bill Blick Andrew Bomford, "Echelon Spy Network Revealed," *BBC News,* November 3, 1999.

CHAPTER 2: THE LEAK WAS ME: LISTENING TO DIPLOMATS

29 On the afternoon of Unless otherwise specified, details in this chapter are drawn from an extensive interview with Katharine Gun conducted in Cheltenham on April 1, 2004.
31 "As you've likely heard" Martin Bright, Ed Vulliamy, and Peter Beaumont, "Revealed: U.S. Dirty Tricks to Win Vote on Iraq War," *The Observer,* March 2, 2003. For the full text of the memo, see "U.S. Plan to Bug Security Council: The Text," *The Observer,* March 2, 2003.
31 On the morning of March 2 Ibid.
32 American coverage was limited Column Lynch, "Spying Report No Shock to UN," *The Washington Post,* March 4, 2003; Bob Drogin and Greg Miller, "Purported Spy Memo May Add to U.S. Troubles at UN," *Los Angeles Times,* March 4, 2003.
32 "Well, it's not that" Norman Solomon, "Stop Dodging the Awkward Truth," *The Observer,* March 9, 2003.
32 By the evening of the day See the Drudge Report (www.drudgereport.com) for March 2, 2003; see also Stephen Pritchard, "Our Spy Story Spelt Conspiracy to Some," *The Observer,* March 9, 2003.
32 The president of Chile Martin Bright, Ed Vulliamy, and Peter Beaumont, "UN Launches Inquiry into American Spying," *The Observer,* March 9, 2003.
32 And the British police Martin Bright, "GCHQ Arrest over Observer Spying Report," *The Observer,* March 9, 2003; Jeevan Vasagar and Richard Norton-Taylor, "GCHQ Worker Held After Leak," *The Guardian,* March 10, 2003.
36 Meanwhile, outside the courtroom Jefferson Morley, "British Press Hails Wiretap Whistleblower," *The Washington Post,* February 26, 2004.
36 ("GCHQ Mother: My Girl") Martin Bright, "GCHQ Mother: My Girl Is Not a Traitor," *The Guardian,* February 22, 2004.
36 Ellsberg called the leak Solomon, "Stop Dodging the Awkward Truth."
39 Since the invasion of Iraq Martin Bright, Antony Barnett, and Gaby Hinsliff, "Army Chiefs Feared Iraq War Illegal Just Days Before Start," *The Guardian,* February 29, 2004.
39 On Wednesday, February 25 "Charges Against ex-GCHQ Employee Dropped," Liberty press release, February 25, 2004; Mark Oliver, "GCHQ Whistleblower Cleared," *The Guardian,* February 25, 2004. See also Richard Norton-Taylor and Ewen MacAskill, "Spy Case Casts Fresh Doubt on War Legality," *The Guardian,* February 26, 2004. Interestingly, Attorney General Lord Goldsmith announced several days later that the decision to drop the charges was not related to his advice on the legality of the war, but he refused to disclose that advice just the same. "GCHQ Decision: War 'Not Political,' " *BBC News,* February 26, 2004.
39 The moment the case Patrick E. Tyler, "Britain Drops Charges in Leak of U.S. Memo," *The New York Times,* February 26, 2004; Glenn Frankel,

"Britain Accused of Spying on Annan Before Iraq War," *The Washington Post,* February 27, 2004.

39 AND LATE WEDNESDAY Clare Short, interviewed by John Humphreys, "The World Today," BBC Radio Four, February 25, 2004.

40 A FIERCE ANIMOSITY BETWEEN Jeremy Paxman, Interview with Clare Short, *Newsnight,* BBC, February 26, 2004. The *Daily Telegraph* was quick to take up Paxman's suggestion that Short was in violation of the act. "Disclosure Appears to Breach Official Secrets Act," *Daily Telegraph,* February 27, 2003.

40 ON FRIDAY, FEBRUARY 27 "Blix, Butler 'Bugged,'" Australian Broadcasting Corporation (ABC) Online, February 27, 2004. Also see Andrew Fowler, "Blix Wants Transcripts of Bugged Talks," ABC Online, April 7, 2004.

41 DURING THE GREAT DEPRESSION Fritz J. Roethlisberger and William J. Dickson, *Management and the Worker: An Account of a Research Program Conducted by the Western Electric Company, Hawthorne Works, Chicago* (Cambridge, Mass.: Harvard University Press, 1939); George Elton Mayo, *The Human Problems of an Industrial Civilization* (New York: Macmillan, 1933).

42 STILL, WHEN QUESTIONED ABOUT Daily Press Briefing by the Office of the Spokesman for the Secretary-General of the United Nations, February 27, 2004. Available online, through www.un.org/news/briefings/docs/2004.

43 THROUGHOUT THE PLANNING The Signal Security Agency had access to the cables because, under wartime censorship laws, Western Union and other commercial telegraph companies were turning over copies of all foreign cables to the government. Some of the smaller countries represented at the meetings did not use the commercial cable companies. In these cases, the U.S. Army Communications Service was only too happy to make available its own radio and wire facilities. Stephen Schlesinger, *Act of Creation: The Founding of the United Nations* (Boulder, Colo.: Westview, 2003), pp. 93–94.

43 WHEN *THE WASHINGTON POST* Lynch, "Spying Report No Shock to UN."

43 IN FACT, THE PAPER Ibid.; Morley, "British Press Hails Wiretap Whistle-blower."

43 FORMER SECRETARY GENERAL Katherine Baldwin, "Blair Battles to Calm Iraq Bugging Claim," Reuters, February 27, 2004.

43 *THE OBSERVER* REPORTED Bright et al., "Army Chiefs Feared Iraq War Illegal."

44 QUERIED ABOUT EAVESDROPPING "Spy on the Wall Treatment a Given," http://www.cbsnews.com/stories/2004/02/26/iraq/main602328.shtml, March 4, 2003.

44 THE ARTICLE SAID THE AGENCY For a more straightforward introduction to the Doughnut, see Richard Norton-Taylor, "The Doughnut, the Less Secretive Weapon in the Fight Against International Terrorism," *The Guardian,* June 10, 2003.

45 THE BBC, MEANWHILE, SAID Vasagar and Norton-Taylor, "GCHQ Worker Held After Leak"; Paul Reynolds, "The World's Second Oldest Profession," *BBC News,* February 26, 2004.

46 SHE TOLD ME THAT THE RECRUITMENT In 2003, GCHQ released one such newspaper, *The Daily Observer,* under the tagline, "GCHQ—Where Careers Make Headlines." The inaugural article was headlined "GCHQ Intercepted Me—Claims Electronic Signal" and reported that "Signals Analysts at GCHQ—starting on a salary of £17,490–£21,600—play a leading behind-

the-scenes role in many front page stories, it was revealed today." This recruitment bulletin used to be available at www.gchqinterceptedme.co.uk and linked to GCHQ's main recruitment page, www.gchq.gov.uk. It may still be available at http://www.gchq.gov.uk/recruitment/brochure.zip

CHAPTER 3: FOOTPRINTS OF FREEDOM: A CONSTELLATION OF BASES

48   IN THE WONDERFUL OPENING Krzysztof Kieslowski, *Rouge* ("Red") (Miramax, 1995).

49   OVER THE NEXT SEVERAL HOURS Interview with Alistair Harley, in and around Ely, U.K., July 15, 2002.

50   A SINGLE GEOSTATIONARY SATELLITE Figures taken from Intelsat's website, http://www.intelsat.com.

51   WHAT WAS NOT REPORTED Jean Strouse, "Triumph at Heart's Content," *The New York Review of Books,* June 12, 2003.

51   THE LAUNCH OF A SECOND SATELLITE Intelsat website: http://www.intelsat.com.

51   THE ORGANIZATION HAD ALSO Chalmers Johnson, *The Sorrows of Empire* (New York: Metropolitan Books, 2004), p. 161.

52   THE INTELSAT SATELLITES ARE ACCOMPANIED Pasternak, "Lack of Intelligence."

53   MORWENSTOW WAS THE FIRST Hager, *Secret Power,* p. 33.

53   IN THE 1970s Ibid., p. 30.

53   "IF IT HAS TO LEAVE" Harley interview, July 15, 2002.

54   IN THE 1980s Hugh Lanning and Richard Norton-Taylor, *A Conflict of Loyalties: GCHQ 1984-1991* (Cheltenham, U.K.: New Clarion Press, 1991), p. 69.

54   "WE'RE INTERESTED IN" GCHQ Recruitment, "Morwenstow—Technical Vacancies" announcement, February 27, 2003. Available at http://cndyorks.gn.apc.org/caab/articles/morwenstowvacancies.htm.

54   THE SECOND OF THE THREE Bamford, *Puzzle Palace,* pp. 224–25.

54   THOUGH THE BASE HAD Hager, *Secret Power,* p. 31.

55   IN A LEAGUE OF One of the few times the mainstream American media has ever made reference to Yakima was on *NBC Nightly News,* May 11, 1995, when Mike Jensen reported that transmissions intercepted at Yakima had produced evidence of bribes by foreign companies.

55   THE CENTER IS AN ARMY For information on the training center see John Pike's excellent website, http://www.GlobalSecurity.org.

55   WHILE THE AREA Yakima Training Center website: http://www.lewis.army.mil/yakima.

55   THE FRONTIER-STYLE ISOLATION Hager, *Secret Power,* p. 166.

55   (THE BUILDING IS NAMED) See the dedication of the building, at http://uss liberty.org/linnops.jpg.

55   THE STATION BEGAN Bamford, *Puzzle Palace,* pp. 219–23.

56   SUGAR GROVE IS RUN History of NSGA. This history was available at http://www.nsgafm.navy.mil/history.asp in 2003, but is no longer as of summer 2004.

56   THE CASE WENT *Reinbold v. Evers,* 187 F.3d 348 (4th Cir. 1999).

56 IN 2000, THE INTELLIGENCE Jeffrey Richelson, "The National Security Agency Declassified," January 13, 2000 (http://www.gwu.edu/~nsarchiv/NSAEBB/NSAEBB23/index2.html).

56 BEFORE IT WAS HANDED BACK Desmond Ball, "Nasty Time for Our Men in Hong Kong," Sydney Morning Herald, June 30, 1997.

57 BEFORE THE BASE Hager, Secret Power, pp. 32–33.

57 THE CHINESE INSISTED Jon Swain, "Britain to Close 'Spy' Station," The Times, August 11, 1991.

57 ULTIMATELY, THE OPERATIONS Michael Evans, "The Truce That Changed Everything," The Times, January 27, 1997.

57 THE BRITISH THEN PROCEEDED Glenn Schloss, "UK Spy Site Razed to Keep Its Secrets," South China Morning Post, November 30, 1997.

58 THE BASE HAD James Clark, "Americans Expand Top Spy Base in UK," Sunday Times, June 10, 2001.

58 WHILE THIS SHIFT Heiner Effern, "BND übernimmt die Abhör-Station der USA," Süddeutsche Zeitung, December 20, 2003.

59 THE ISLAND IS SO SMALL Simon Winchester, The Sun Never Sets: Travels to the Remaining Outposts of the British Empire (New York: Prentice Hall, 1985), p. 115.

59 JOHANSON MANAGED A SMOOTH LANDING, Melissa King, "Arrest Scare for Solo Pilot After Emergency Landing," The Advertiser (Australia), July 19, 1996.

59 TO HIS RELIEF Jon Johanson, Trip West Journal, available at http://www.vansaircraft.com/public/jj-tripw.htm.

59 AND YET, AS SIMON WINCHESTER Winchester, Sun Never Sets, p. 118.

60 IN 1922, ASCENSION WAS Ibid., p. 119.

60 DURING THE COLD WAR Andrew Marshall, "Flying the Flag," The Independent, May 31, 1997.

60 IN 1815, THE BRITISH Michael Brooke, "No Place Like Home: Imported Cats Led to the Decline of the Booby," The Independent, November 18, 2002.

61 ASCENSION WAS A VITAL James Feron, "Gateway to the Falklands," The New York Times, July 28, 1982.

61 AS THE COLD WAR WANED, Anthony Browne, "Ascension Islanders Ready to Revolt for Democracy," The Times, June 15, 2002.

61 THE LARGER ISLANDS Winchester, Sun Never Sets, pp. 33–35.

62 BUT THE BRITISH GOVERNMENT Tom Pelton, "Displaced Tribe a Shadow over U.S. Base," Chicago Tribune, October 3, 2001.

62 THIS WAS PROBABLY Winchester, Sun Never Sets, pp. 35–39.

63 THE MAN WHOM Ibid., p. 39.

63 IN 1966 Pelton, "Displaced Tribe a Shadow."

63 BUT DIEGO GARCIA'S ACTUAL Richelson and Ball, Ties That Bind, p. 205.

64 DAYS AFTER SEPTEMBER 11 Eric Ellis, "Sites Go Silent as Base Gets Supplies," The Australian, September 19, 2001.

64 THE REASON EMERGED Ewan MacAskill, "Attack on Afghanistan: Diego Garcia: Foreign Office Faces Moral Dilemma," The Guardian, October 9, 2001; Paul Harris and Martin Bright, "Exiled from Paradise to Crawley New Town," The Observer, July 27, 2003.

64 WHAT IS INSIDE Unless otherwise noted, details in this section are drawn from a visit to PARI, on May 13–14, 2004, and Laura Sullivan, "When NSA Moves Out, Its Mysteries Remain," Baltimore *Sun*, January 5, 2001.

66 IN 1986, ROBERT Robert Windrem, e-mail to Cypherpunks, January 12, 2001. Available at http://www.mail-archive.com/cypherpunks@cyberpass. net/msg03165.html. Also, telephone interview with Windrem, September 24, 2003.

68 "SUGAR GROVE?" I GUESSED Windrem speculates that much of the material was actually transferred to another eavesdropping facility, at Sebana Seca, Puerto Rico. Ibid.

70 GLOBALLY, THERE ARE Hager, *Secret Power*, p. 36.

70 THE MOST ADVANCED Campbell, *Interception Capabilities 2000*.

70 THE NSA HAS RADIO-COLLECTION Hager, *Secret Power*, p. 36.

71 "I AM NOW" E-mail from Mike Frost, October 20, 2003.

71 NEVERTHELESS, THERE IS ONE Mike Frost and Michael Gratton, *Spyworld* (Toronto: McClelland Bantam, 1995), p. 19–20.

71 LEAKS IN THE 1980S Hager, *Secret Power*, p. 38.

71 FOR MORE DARING OPERATIONS Stephen Cass, "Listening In," *Institute of Electrical and Electronics Engineers Spectrum*, April 2003; See also Wayne Madsen and Jason Vest, "A Most Unusual Collection Agency," *The Village Voice*, February 24, 1999.

71 DATING BACK AS FAR For information on these successive code names and programs, see William Burrows, *Deep Black: Space Espionage and National Security* (New York: Random House, 1986); Christophe Anson Pike, "CANYON, RHYOLITE, and AQUACADE: U.S. Signals Intelligence Satellites in the 1970s," *Spaceflight* magazine, November 1995; Jeffrey Richelson, *America's Space Sentinels* (Lawrence: University Press of Kansas, 1999).

72 IN THE LAST FOUR DECADES Pasternak, "Lack of Intelligence."

72 THE NRO HAS COME Ibid.

72 IN 1998, THE OFFICE See description of IOSA at www.globalsecurity.org/intell/systems.iosa.htm.

73 IN ITS FINAL REPORT *9/11 Commission Report*, p. 93.

73 DURING THE COLD WAR For an edge-of-your-seat account of the cold-war submarine maneuvers of the Americans and the Soviets, see Sherry Sontag, Christopher Drew, and Annette Lawrence Drew, *Blind Man's Bluff* (New York: PublicAffairs, 1998).

73 BUT FIBER OPTICS ARE ANOTHER Cass, "Listening In."

73 IN THE EARLY 1990S Seymour Hersh, "The Intelligence Gap," *The New Yorker*, December 6, 1999.

73 IN 1990, SADDAM HUSSEIN Dan Verton, "Intelligence Ops in Baghdad Show Need for Physical Security Back Home," *Computerworld*, April 8, 2003.

74 BUT AS EARLY AS 1999 Michael Smith, *The Spying Game* (London: Politico's, 2003), p. 318. See also M. E. Kabay, "Tapping Fiber Optics Gets Easier," *Network World Security Newsletter*, March 4, 2003.

74 SOME AGREEMENT SEEMS TO "Fiber Optic Intrusion Detection Systems," a White Paper from the Marketing Group of Norscan Instruments, Limited, 2003. Available at http://www.norscan.com/web/news/norscan-whitepaper. pdf.

74 BY APRIL 2003, COMPUTERWORLD Verton, "Intelligence Ops in Baghdad."

74 JOHN PESCATORE Ibid.

74 IN 1999, CONGRESS Michael Moran, "America's Global Embrace," MSNBC News, April 6, 2001, http://www.msnbc.com/news/546845.asp?0sp=n5b4&cp1=1.

74 AND WHILE FIBER OPTICS See Richard Sale, "Three CIA Assets Killed in Baghdad," United Press International, April 4, 2003; Charles Madigan, "Fast, Furious, Relentless; Lighting-Quick Campaign Ousts Hussein in 4 Weeks," *Chicago Tribune,* April 20, 2000.

75 IN 1965, THREE Gordon E. Moore, "Cramming More Components Onto Integrated Circuits," *Electronics,* April 19, 1965.

75 "THE HIGHEST CAPACITY SYSTEMS" Campbell, *Interception Capabilities 2000.*

76 "IT FOLLOWS THAT" Ibid.

76 AND INDEED, ACCORDING TO Wayne Madsen, "Puzzle Palace Conducting Internet Surveillance," *Computer Fraud and Security Bulletin,* June 1995.

76 TERRY THOMPSON James Bamford, "NSA Confidential," *Newsweek,* May 19, 2001.

76 "ALL INTERNET TRAFFIC" Interview with Alistair Harley, July 15, 2002.

77 "THE PROBLEM THEY'RE" Telephone interview with Bob Baer, November 3, 2003.

77 HE AND HIS ASSOCIATES Declan McCullagh, "Bin Laden: Steganography Master?" *Wired News,* February 7, 2001.

77 MUSLIM EXTREMISTS WHO ATTENDED Jack Kelley, "Terror Groups Hide Behind Web Encryption," *USA Today,* February 5, 2001.

78 HOWEVER, AFTER IT WAS REPORTED Walter Pincus, "The Reasons Behind a White House Rebuke," *The Washington Post,* June 24, 2002; Blazar, "Inside the Ring."

78 AND HE ABSTAINS FROM "Where electronic communications were regarded as insecure, Al Qaeda relied even more heavily on couriers." *9/11 Commission Report,* p. 169.

CHAPTER 4: BLACK PHONE/GRAY PHONE: THE HAZARDS OF SECRECY

79 LATE ONE APRIL AFTERNOON Details of the Prime story are drawn from D. J. Cole, *The Imperfect Spy* (London: Robert Hale, 1998), and Rhona Prime, *Time of Trial* (London: Hodder and Stoughton, 1984).

82 "TO PROVIDE SIGNALS INTELLIGENCE" Lanning and Norton-Taylor, *Conflict of Loyalties,* p. 49.

82 THE GOVERNMENT WAS ALSO Cole, *Imperfect Spy,* p. 181.

82 "VAST AMOUNTS OF INFORMATION" NSA Security Guidelines Handbook. The handbook has been available in numerous places online, including http://www.tscm.com/NSAsecmanual1.html and http://www.politrix.org/foia/nsa/nsasecman.html.

83 EVEN THE TRASH David Martin, "National Security Meltdown," http://www.CBSNews.com/stories/2001/01/24/60ll/main266857.shtml (June 19, 2002); also see Rona Kobell and Ariel Sabar, "NSA Says Its Toxic Waste is Classified," *Baltimore Sun,* December 30, 2003.

83 ON APRIL 1, 2000, A NAVY For an interesting examination of the EP-3E and

the future of Sigint collection by plane, see Robert Wall, "Navy May Join Army on New Sigint Aircraft," *Aviation Week and Space Technology,* July 13, 2003.

84 A NAVY REPORT LATER Robert Burns, "China 'Likely' Saw U.S. Secrets," Associated Press, September 12, 2003; Bill Gertz, "China Blamed in '01 Air Collision," *The Washington Times,* September 13, 2003; Bill Gertz, "Beijing Gets Voice Data from Plane," *The Washington Times,* May 15, 2001.

84 THIS UNFLINCHING DEVOTION Hager, *Secret Power,* p. 106. It should be noted that in an August 1992 edition of the *NSA Newsletter* an article on such emergencies advises employees to "Stop work immediately—do not pause to secure materials." Sandie Ginn, "This is Only a Drill . . ." *NSA Newsletter,* August 1992.

85 "FOR THE LAST FOUR YEARS" Alice Kimball Smith and Charles Weiner, eds., *Robert Oppenheimer: Letters and Reflections* (Cambridge, Mass.: Harvard University Press, 1980), p. 289.

85 "IT SOUNDS STRANGE TO SAY" "I Couldn't Even Talk to My Husband," *Gloucestershire Echo,* October 25, 2002.

85 "I DO NOT KNOW" Cole, *Imperfect Spy,* p. 25.

87 ON JUNE 24, 1960 Wayne Barker and Rodney Coffman, *The Anatomy of Two Traitors* (Laguna Hills, Calif.: Aegean Park Press, 1981), p. 4.

87 MITCHELL AND MARTIN WERE Ibid., p. 25.

87 "WE WERE EMPLOYEES" Ibid., p. 51.

87 "THEIR APPEARANCE IN MOSCOW" Ibid., p. 55.

87 THE HOUSE UN-AMERICAN ACTIVITIES Bamford, *Puzzle Palace,* p. 191.

88 "THIS MANIA FOR SECRECY" James Rusbridger, *The Intelligence Game* (New York: New Amsterdam, 1989), p. 208.

88 NEVERTHELESS, THERE WERE THOSE James Adams, "Sidelined by History, The Fantasy Is Over for the Spy Who Never Was," *The Times,* February 20, 1994.

89 IT WAS WITH A SHUDDER Nick Pryor, "Riddle of ex-MI6 Spy Hanged in Gas Mask," *The Evening Standard,* February 17, 1994; Richard Norton-Taylor, " 'Scourge of Whitehall' Found Hanged in Loft," *The Guardian,* February 17, 1994.

89 HAVING PEERED INTO Unless otherwise noted, all Steven Aftergood–related material is drawn from an interview with Aftergood at the FAS offices in Washington, D.C., January 5, 2004.

90 EACH DAY, HE CHECKS For an argument against unauthorized disclosure of intelligence and defense-related information, see James B. Bruce, "The Consequences of Permissive Neglect," *Studies in Intelligence* 147. 1 (www.cia.gov/csi/studies/vol47no1/article04.html).

92 THE COMMISSION ALLOWED THAT *9/11 Commission Report,* p. 416.

92 MOYNIHAN FAMOUSLY ESTIMATED D. P. Moynihan, *Secrecy* (New Haven: Yale University Press, 1999), introduction, p. 2.

92 MOYNIHAN ESTABLISHED Ibid., p. 11.

92 MOYNIHAN PUBLISHED Ibid., p. 59.

93 IN THE SUMMER OF 2002 "Rumsfeld Wants Leaks Plugged," *CBS News,* July 17, 2002.

93 AND SURE ENOUGH Interview with a Department of Defense policy official who did not want to be named, New York City, January 16, 2004.

93 **"IN MATTERS SO FUNDAMENTAL"** Sissela Bok, *Secrets: On the Ethics of Concealment and Revelation* (New York: Pantheon, 1982), p. 202.

94 **THE TIDE OF CLASSIFICATION** There is a burgeoning literature on how the administration of George W. Bush has been the most secretive in American history. See for example, Dana Milbank, "Under Bush, Expanding Secrecy," *The Washington Post*, December 23, 2003; Christopher Schmitt and Edward Pound, "Keeping Secrets," *U.S. News and World Report*, December 22, 2003; David E. Rosenbaum, "When Government Doesn't Tell," *The New York Times*, February 3, 2003.

94 **PERRO WAS A MIDCAREER** Ralph J. Perro, "Interviewing with an Intelligence Agency (or, A Funny Thing Happened on the Way to Fort Meade)," November 2003. Available through the FAS site and elsewhere online (www.fas.org/irp/eprint/nsa-interview.pdf).

96 **"IN ORDER FOR SECRETS"** Edward Shils, *The Torment of Secrecy* (Chicago: Ivan R. Dee, 1996), p. 201.

96 **WHEN THE LOS ALAMOS SCIENTIST** Steven Aftergood, "Polygraph Testing and the DOE National Laboratories," *Science*, November 3, 2000.

96 **IN 1998, THE SUPREME COURT** *U.S. v. Scheffer*, 523 U.S. 303 (1998).

97 **IN THE LETTER** Aldrich Ames to Steven Aftergood, November 28, 2000, posted on the FAS website (http://www.fas.org/sgp/othergov/polygraph/ames.html).

97 **"THERE CAN BE NO PRESUMPTION"** Bok, *Secrets*, p. 27.

98 **"ONE IS TOTALLY SEEN"** Michel Foucault, *Discipline and Punish: The Birth of the Prison*, trans. Alan Sheridan (New York: Vintage, 1995), p. 202.

98 **"THERE WAS NO WAY"** George Orwell, *Nineteen Eighty-four* (New York: Alfred A. Knopf, 1992), p. 5.

98 **BUT AS THE WAR** Unique Signatures Program, which seeks to identify genetically determined odor types, DARPA website, February 4, 2004.

98 **"THE SECRET WORLD"** John Keegan, *Intelligence in War* (New York: Alfred A. Knopf, 2003), p. 318.

99 **(AN EARLY OVERVIEW)** John Poindexter, Information Awareness Office Overview, available at http://www.darpa.mil/DARPATech2002/presentations/iao_pdf/speeches/POINDEXT.pdf.

99 **"NO ONE SPENDS MONEY"** Lawrence Lessig, *Code and Other Laws of Cyberspace* (New York: Basic Books, 1999), p. 152.

100 **ACCORDING TO THE PROGRAM-OBJECTIVE** Total Information Awareness System, System Diagram, available on DARPA's website in fall 2002 (http://www.darpa.mil/iao/TIASystems.htm) but no longer available.

100 **"FOCUSED WARNING"** Ibid.

100 **"THE PERFECT STORM"** John Markoff, "Threats and Responses: Intelligence—Pentagon Plans a Computer System That Would Peek at Personal Data of Americans," *The New York Times*, November 9, 2002.

101 **"ANYONE WHO DELIBERATELY SET OUT"** "Total Information Awareness," *The Washington Post*, November 16, 2002, editorial page.

102 **(IT WAS POINDEXTER)** Robert O'Harrow, Jr., "U.S. Hopes to Check Computers Globally," *The Washington Post*, November 12, 2002.

102 **ON NOVEMBER 27, 2002** Matt Smith, "Calling All Yahoos," *SF Weekly*, December 3, 2002.

102 **DARPA's CLUMSINESS** William Safire, "You Are a Suspect," *The New York Times,* November 14, 2002.

103 **HE TOLD ME RECENTLY** Telephone interview with Matt Smith, March 17, 2004.

104 **GILMORE'S SUGGESTION WAS** Gilmore's letter is also posted at http://www. politechbot.com/p-04206.html. His home page is http://www.toad.com/gnu.

105 **DURING THE SUMMER OF 2003** Eric Schmitt, "Poindexter to Resign Following Terrorist Futures Debacle," *The New York Times,* August 3, 2003.

105 **IN EARLY 2003** William Safire, "Privacy Invasion Curtailed," *The New York Times,* February 13, 2003.

105 **STILL, AFTERGOOD IS QUICK** Alarmingly enough, there is in fact some sugges-tion that TIA may never actually have ceased existing. A June 7, 2004, article quotes an unnamed DARPA technician saying, "When Congress cut the fund-ing, the Pentagon—with administration approval—simply moved the program into a 'black bag' account. Black bag programs don't require Congressional approval and are exempt from traditional oversight." Teresa Hampton and Doug Thompson, "Where Big Brother Snoops on Americans 24/7," *Capitol Hill Blue,* June 7, 2004.

106 **HE WAS VISITED BY THE FBI** John Young, "Gestapo Harasses John Young, Ap-peals to Patriotism, Told to Fuck Off," e-mail to Cypherpunks, November 15, 2003 (http://www.mail-archive.com/cypherpunks-moderated@minder.net/msg 07413.html).

CHAPTER 5: GOLIATH PROTESTS: MAKING SENSE OF SIGNALS

109 **ON JANUARY 24, 2000** Laura Sullivan, "Computer Failure at NSA Irks Intel-ligence Panels," *Baltimore Sun,* February 2, 2000.

110 **IN JULY 1999** Sen. Bob Kerrey, speaking during hearings on Intelligence Au-thorization Act for Fiscal Year 2000, Motion to Proceed, July 19, 1999 (available at http://www.fas.org/sgp/news/1999/07/kerrey.html).

110 **"THE WHOLE WORLD IS"** Interview with Department of Defense policy official, New York City, January 16, 2004.

110 **HAYDEN HAS AN OPEN** For more on Hayden, see Bamford, *Body of Secrets,* particularly Chapter 11; Scott Shane, "Director of NSA Shifts to New Path," *Baltimore Sun,* August 8, 2004.

111 **"HE MIGHT BE"** Telephone interview with Wayne Madsen, October 13, 2003.

111 **"FORTY YEARS AGO"** Lt. Gen. Michael V. Hayden, Director, National Security Agency, address to Kennedy Political Union of American University, Wash-ington, D.C., February 17, 2000.

112 *THE GUARDIAN* RAN "Big Brother Echelon," *The Guardian,* June 6, 2001; "Grandes Oreilles Américaines," *Le Monde diplomatique,* March 1999.

113 **THE ARTICLE WAS CALLED** Hersh, "The Intelligence Gap."

114 **AT A LUNCH** John Millis, address at CIRA luncheon, October 5, 1998, reprinted in *CIRA Newsletter* 23. 4, (winter 1998/1999).

115 **"DECLINING BUDGETS AND OBSOLETE EQUIPMENT"** Special Report of the Select Committee on Intelligence, U.S. Senate, 106th Congress, 1st Session, Wash-ington: U.S. Government Printing Office, February 3, 1999 (available at http://www.loyola.edu/dept/politics/intelsrpt106-3.pdf).

115 ONE OFFICIAL INVOLVED Hersh, "Intelligence Gap."

116 THE WATCH LIST IS *The National Security Agency and Fourth Amendment Rights,* Hearings Before the Select Committee to Study Government Operations with Respect to Intelligence Activities, U.S. Senate, 94th Congress, First Session, Volume 5, Washington: U.S. Government Printing Office, 1976.

116 ACCORDING TO FORMER NSA EMPLOYEES Campbell, *Interception Capabilities 2000.*

116 EACH AGENCY IS Hager, *Secret Power,* p. 206.

116 THIS SWIFT AND INTRICATE PROCESS Ibid., p. 47.

116 WHEN A MESSAGE Campbell, *Interception Capabilities 2000.*

116 THE LISTS OF KEYWORDS Hager, *Secret Power,* p. 115.

116 BUT THE WHOLE PROCESS Ibid., p. 157.

117 WHEN AN INTERCEPTED MESSAGE Ibid., p. 48.

117 THUS, FOR EXAMPLE Campbell, *Interception Capabilities 2000.*

117 EVERETTE JORDAN David Ensor, "Linguist Up to His Ears Tracking Security Threats," CNN.com, March 22, 2001. There's also a funny article in *NSA Newsletter,* January 1991, about the fact that there is an Everett E. Jordan in the Installations and Logistics Organization Section of the NSA and an Everette E. Jordan (the listener) in the Operations Organization. Two African-American men with almost identical names, both working for the same gargantuan and highly compartmentalized organization. Hilarity ensues.

118 A FORMER ANALYST Hager, *Secret Power,* p. 107.

118 ERSKINE WORKED IN A VARIETY E-mail from Michael Erskine, November 5, 2003.

118 A TRAFFIC ANALYST IS For an interesting explanation of traffic analysis, see Hazel Muir, "Email Traffic Patterns Can Reveal Ringleaders," *New Scientist,* March 27, 2003.

119 "GO TO GOOGLE" Ibid., October 31, 2003.

119 ACCORDING TO MIKE FROST Frost and Gratton, *Spyworld,* p. 152.

119 TO ILLUSTRATE THE MANNER Mike Frost, interviewed by Steve Kroft on *60 Minutes II,* CBS, February 27, 2000.

119 "THE PROCESSING OF TELEPHONE CALLS" Campbell, *Interception Capabilities 2000.*

120 MOREOVER, WHEN IN 1993 Jeffrey Richelson, "Desperately Seeking Signals," *Bulletin of the Atomic Scientists,* March/April 2000.

120 "DOCUMENTS SHOW THAT" Campbell, *Interception Capabilities 2000.*

120 ON IJET'S WEBSITE The profile of McIndoe was posted through at least October 2003. By December, McIndoe's profile had been removed from the site, but was subsequently restored with the name Echelon II removed.

120 IN THEIR ARTICLE Bo Elkjaer and Kenan Seeberg, "Echelon's Architect," *Ekstra Bladet,* May 18, 2002. (Trans. from the Danish by Bo Elkjaer.)

121 "OSAMA BIN LADEN HAS" Michael Hayden, quoted on *60 Minutes II,* CBS, February 12, 2001.

121 BUT IT TAKES VERY LITTLE U.S. Patent 6,169,969 (http://www.uspto.gov).

122 WE KNOW, FOR INSTANCE Campbell, *Interception Capabilities 2000.*

122 TO THIS END U.S. Patent 5,991,714.

122 AS FOR SPEECH U.S. Patent 5,937,422.

123 IN NOVEMBER 2000 U.S. Patent 6,144,934.

123 BUT ON FEBRUARY 11 U.S. Patent 6,519,362.

123 IN 2002, MAUREEN MAGINSKI Cited in Lt. Gen. Michael V. Hayden, USAF, Director, National Security Agency, Chief, Central Security Service, Statement for the Record Before the Joint Inquiry of the Senate Select Committee on Intelligence and the House Permanent Select Committee on Intelligence, 107th Congress, 2nd Session, October 17, 2002. Available at http://intelligence.senate.gov/0210hrg/021017/hayden.pdf.

123 CURRENTLY, WHEN DICTIONARY Hager, *Secret Power,* pp. 44–45.

124 ON SEPTEMBER 10, 2001 "Al Qaeda Tied to Intercepted Phone Calls," CNN.com, June 20, 2002.

124 ONE OF THE MESSAGES Scott Shane and Ariel Sabar, "Coded Warnings Become Clear Only in Light of Sept. 11 Attacks," *Baltimore Sun,* June 21, 2002.

124 DURING THE 1990s Figures taken from Hayden, Statement for the Record, October 17, 2002.

124 "THOUSANDS OF TIMES A DAY" Ibid.

125 IN A MARCH 2002 SPEECH Harvey A. Davis, Associate Director, Human Resource Services, NSA, Statement for the Record Before the Governmental Affairs Subcommittee on International Security, Proliferation and Federal Services, Hearing on Critical Skills for National Security and the Homeland Security Federal Workforce Act, March 12, 2002 (available at http://www.senate.gov/~gov_affairs/031202davis.pdf).

126 "AS AN NSA LINGUIST" Job posting, National Security Agency, February 7, 2002.

126 IN FACT, ACCORDING TO Joint Inquiry into Intelligence Community Activities Before and After the Terrorist Attacks of September 11, 2001, *Report of the U.S. Senate Select Committee on Intelligence and U.S. House Permanent Select Committee on Intelligence,* 107th Cong., 2d sess., December 2002.

127 "WE TAKE AS MANY COURSES" Ensor, "Linguist Up to His Ears."

127 IN THE FALL OF 2003 John Mintz, "U.S. Agencies Surf for Translators," *The Washington Post,* November 6, 2003. Also see Michael Errard, "Translation in an Age of Terror," *MIT Technology Review,* March 2004, for a fuller explanation of the National Virtual Translation Center and another interview with Jordan.

127 "TO THEM, IT'S HAVING" Mintz, "U.S. Agencies Surf for Translators."

127 EVEN THE BEST LINGUISTS Interview with Milt Bearden in Washington, March 10, 2003.

128 BOB BAER TOLD ME Telephone interview with Bob Baer, April 9, 2003.

128 "YOU CAN'T GET" Gary Hart, interviewed by Joe Trento of the Public Education Center (http://www.publicedcenter.org/stories/cia-interviews/hart.shtml), 2003.

129 THE NAME MOHAMMED Steve Mollman, "Wanted: What's His Name Again?" Wired.com, January 13, 2003 (http://www.wired.com/news/conflict/0,2100,57167,00.html).

129 "THIS WAS LARGELY DUE" Davis, Statement for the Record, March 12, 2002.

130 THERE IS A HUGE AMOUNT Chip Walter, "The Translation Challenge," *MIT Technology Review,* June 2003.

130 CURRENTLY, ACCURACY RATES Ibid.

131 STEVE WAS RELUCTANT Leslie Walker, "Making Computers Understand," *The Washington Post*, May 15, 2003.

132 (THAT'S ABOUT 5 PERCENT) It has been estimated that the text in all of the printed collections in the Library of Congress amounts to roughly twenty terabytes.

132 THE NSA IS DEVELOPING Biometrics exhibit, http://www.nsa.gov/museum/museu00011.cfm.

133 THE HUMAN VOICE VARIES Brendan I. Koerner, "Speak of the Devil," *Harper's*, April 2003.

134 EVEN IF MACHINES Wade Roush, "Computers That Speak Your Language," *MIT Technology Review*, June 2003.

134 WHAT THEY MEAN Ensor, "Linguist Up to His Ears."

134 "AN ANALYST COSTS" Millis, address at CIRA luncheon, October 5, 1998.

134 IN THE YEAR AFTER Hayden, Statement for the Record, October 17, 2002.

134 BUT CARBONELL Errard, "Translation in an Age of Terror."

134 AFTER A THREE-DECADE CAREER Ensor, "Linguist Up to His Ears."

CHAPTER 6: ROGUE ELEPHANT ON A RAMPAGE: PRIVACY ON THE LINE

135 "IF I WANT TO KISS" Unless otherwise noted, details from the Bill Brown episode are drawn from a surveillance-camera walking tour of Soho, in New York City, June 8, 2002.

136 IN ENGLAND, THIS APPEALING "CCTV: Does It Work?" *BBC News*, August 13, 2002. For a broad and critical take on the closed circuit television phenomenon in the United Kingdom, also see Jeffrey Rosen, "Being Watched: A Cautionary Tale of the New Surveillance," *The New York Times Magazine*, October 7, 2001.

136 AFTER THE CITY Timothy Egan, "Surveillance: From 'Big Brother' to Safety Tool," *The New York Times*, December 6, 2001.

137 IN NEW YORK Samuel Bruchey, "Surveillance Camera Activist Charged in Harassment," *Newsday*, January 24, 2004. Bill Brown pled guilty to the charges and was convicted and sentenced to nine months in prison, which he began serving in October 2004.

138 "FEW VALUES SO FUNDAMENTAL" Alan Westin, *Privacy and Freedom* (New York: Athenaeum, 1967), p. 7.

138 ONE REASON PRIVACY Isaiah Berlin, "Two Concepts of Liberty," in *The Proper Study of Mankind* (New York: Farrar, Straus, and Giroux, 1998), p. 194.

138 IN *LEGISLATING PRIVACY* Priscilla Regan, *Legislating Privacy* (Chapel Hill: University of North Carolina Press, 1995), p. 4.

138 EVEN JUSTICE LOUIS BRANDEIS Samuel Warren and Louis Brandeis, "The Right to Privacy," *Harvard Law Review* (1890): 4 193, 213.

138 BUT THE SUPREME COURT *Olmstead v. United States*, 277 U.S. 438 (1928).

139 *KATZ* INVOLVED AN FBI WIRETAP *Katz v. United States*, 389 U.S. 347, 353 (1967).

139 THUS, WHILE *KATZ California v. Greenwood*, 486 U.S. 35, 39 (1987).

139 BECAUSE WE PAY *Smith v. Maryland*, 442 U.S. 735, 741 (1979).

139 "No doubt it is" Telford Taylor, *Two Studies in Constitutional Interpretation* (Columbus: Ohio State University Press, 1969), p. 114.

140 In a 1994 essay Stewart Baker, "Should Spies Be Cops?" *Foreign Policy* 97 (winter 1994–1995).

140 In 1978, Timothy Garton Ash Details and figures drawn from Timothy Garton Ash, *The File* (New York: Random House, 1997).

140 Under the Third Reich Details and figures from Anna Funder, *Stasiland* (London: Granta, 2003), p. 57.

141 They developed Ibid., pp. 191–92.

141 As the 1980s Ibid., pp. 67, 268.

142 "I was not a victim" Garton Ash, *File*, p. 131.

142 "The East European dissident's" Ibid., p. 253.

142 The public/private distinction Milan Kundera, *Testaments Betrayed* (New York: HarperCollins, 1995), pp. 260–61.

142 "A liberal state" Jeffrey Rosen, *The Unwanted Gaze* (New York: Random House, 2000), p. 11.

142 "It is in order" Bok, *Secrets*, p. 21.

143 In 1975, a young Unless otherwise noted, details in the Church committee section are drawn from an interview with L. Britt Snider, in Washington, D.C., March 23, 2004; as well as "Unlucky Shamrock: Recollections of the Church Committee's Investigation of NSA," *Studies in Intelligence* 43. 1 (1999).

143 One damage-control plan William Colby, *Honorable Men* (New York: Simon and Schuster, 1978), p. 398.

143 The case for Katherine S. Olmsted, *Challenging the Secret Government* (Chapel Hill: University of North Carolina Press, 1996), p. 49.

144 "Perhaps I revealed" Colby, *Honorable Men*, p. 340.

146 (The outright hostility) Gerald Haines, "Looking for a Rogue Elephant: The Pike Committee Investigations and the CIA," *CIA Studies*, winter 1998–1999.

146 As it turned out Kahn, *Codebreakers*, p. 515.

146 The Radio Intelligence Division Ibid., pp. 526–30.

147 It later emerged Hearings before the Select Committee to Study Governmental Operations with Respect to Intelligence Activities of the United States Senate, *The National Security Agency and Fourth Amendment Rights*, 94th Cong., 1st Sess., vol. 5, November 6, 1975 (Washington, D.C.: U.S. Government Printing Office, 1976).

148 The findings John Crewdston, "Church Doubts Plot Link to Presidents," *The New York Times*, July 19, 1975.

148 The public learned Seymour Hersh, *The Price of Power: Kissinger in the Nixon White House* (New York: Simon and Schuster, 1983), p. 83.

148 Kissinger's penchant for wiretaps Ibid., pp. 88–89.

148 In a bizarre permutation Ibid., pp. 92–93.

148 In fact, Kissinger Ibid., p. 207.

148 "Too many people" United States Senate, Final Report of the Select Committee to Study Governmental Operations with Respect to Intelligence Activities, *Intelligence Activities and the Rights of Americans*, book 2: 94th Cong. (Washington: U.S. Government Printing Office, 1976), p. 5.

149 IN 1997, DURING A TRIAL Duncan Campbell, "BT Condemned for Listing Cables to U.S. Sigint Stations," September 4, 1997. (This story appears to be self-published on the Web at www.gn.apc.org/duncan/menwith.htm. The link no longer works, but the article is available in Google's cached file of the page.)

150 FIRST ANNOUNCED Dan Eggen, "Ashcroft: TIPS Plan Won't Have Central Database," The Washington Post, July 26, 2002.

150 AFTER SEPTEMBER 11 Michael Moss, "False Terrorism Tips to FBI Uproot the Lives of Suspects," The New York Times, June 19, 2003.

151 WHEN IN 2002 Christopher Lee, "Agencies Fail Cyber Test," The Washington Post, November 20, 2002.

151 NO LESS AN AUTHORITY William H. Rehnquist, All the Laws but One: Civil Liberties in Wartime (New York: Alfred A. Knopf, 1998), p. 221.

151 THE WHOLE PASSAGE The passage is from a letter from Lord Acton to Bishop Mandell Creighton, April 5, 1887. Lord Acton, Selected Writings of Lord Acton, vol. 2, ed. J. Rufus Fears, (Indianapolis: Liberty Fund, 1985), p. 385.

152 THE SOCIOLOGIST ANTHONY GIDDENS Anthony Giddens, The Consequences of Modernity (Palo Alto, Calif.: Stanford University Press, 1990), chap. 3.

152 "OVERSIGHT," ONE FRIEND The friend was Jean Strouse.

152 "THERE'S AN AWFUL LOT" Interview with Bob Kerrey, New School for Social Research, New York, February 3, 2004. Kerrey's views were, if anything, moderate next to the conclusions of the 9/11 Commission. The commission's final report, published in July 2004, held that

> traditional review of the administration of programs and the implementation of laws has been replaced by "a focus on personal investigations, possible scandals, and issues designed to generate media attention." The unglamorous but essential work of oversight has been neglected, and few members past or present believe it is performed well. . . . Staff tended as well to focus on parochial considerations, seeking to add or cut funding for individual (often small) programs, instead of emphasizing comprehensive oversight projects.

In fairness to the intelligence committees, the commission indicates that these problems are typical of congressional committees in general.

> Committees with oversight responsibility for aviation focused overwhelmingly on airport congestion and the economic health of the airlines, not aviation security. Committees with responsibility for the INS focused on the Southwest border, not on terrorists. Justice Department officials told us that committees with responsibility for the FBI tightly restricted appropriations for improvements in information technology, in part because of concerns about the FBI's ability to manage such projects. Committees responsible for South Asia spent the decade of the 1990's imposing sanctions on Pakistan, leaving presidents with little leverage to alter Pakistan's policies before 9/11. Committees with responsibility for the Defense Department paid little heed to developing military responses to terrorism and stymied intelligence reform. All committees found themselves swamped in the minutiae of the budget process, with little time for consideration of

longer-term questions, or what many members past and present told us was the proper conduct of oversight.

9/11 Commission Report, pp. 106–7.

154 "RARE IS THE" William Odom, *Fixing Intelligence* (New Haven: Yale University Press, 2003) , p. x.

154 "WE DO BELIEVE THIS" Gary Hart, interviewed by Joe Trento of the Public Education Center (http://www.publicedcenter.org/stories/cia-interviews/hart.shtml), 2003.

154 IN THE MEMORABLE PHRASE Loch K. Johnson, *A Season of Inquiry: Congress and Intelligence* (Chicago: Dorsey Press, 1998), p. 263.

154 IN ITS POSTMORTEM *9/11 Commission Report*, p. 103.

155 TODAY, THE INTELLIGENCE COMMITTEES James Bamford, testimony before the European Parliament Temporary Committee on the Echelon Interception System, Brussels, April 23 and 24, 2001 (hereafter "Bamford, Testimony).

155 "THE BASIC STRUCTURE" Telephone interview with Bob Barr, April 9, 2003.

156 THE COMMITTEE CHAIRMAN, PORTER GOSS Additional views of Chairman Porter Goss, Intelligence Authorization Act for Fiscal Year 2000, 106th Congress, 1st Sess., Part 1, rept. 106–30, May 7, 1999.

156 IN LATE 1999 Bob Barr, "Is the U.S. Spy Shop Listening to Your Call?" *Insight*, December 13, 1999.

157 "AS IS THE LONG-STANDING POLICY" NSA, letter to Congressional Offices, February 24, 2000 (available at the FAS website: http://www.fas.org/sgp/news/2000/02/nsalet.html).

157 ON APRIL 12, 2000 George Tenet, Statement Before the House Permanent Select Committee on Intelligence, April 12, 2000 (available at the FAS website: http://www.fas.org/irp/congress/2000_hr/tenet.html).

157 THERE IS AN EXECUTIVE ORDER Executive Order 12333 (available at http://www.cia.gov/cia/information/eo12333.html).

158 THERE IS A CONCEPT Toby Lester, "The Reinvention of Privacy," *Atlantic Monthly*, March 2001.

158 THIS NEW LAW Foreign Intelligence Surveillance Act, 50 U.S.C. Section 1803 (available at http://www4.law.cornell.edu/uscode/50/1803.html).

158 THE COURT IS COMPOSED Patrick S. Poole, "Inside America's Secret Court: The Foreign Intelligence Surveillance Court." (available at http://fly.hiwaay.net/~pspoole/fiscshort.html). For the names of the judges on the court, see http://www.fas.org/irp/agency/doj/fisa/court2003.html.

158 THE COURT MEETS Scott Shane, "Secret U.S. Court Handed New Power to Fight Terror." *Baltimore Sun*, October 29, 2001.

158 THE PANEL'S 7–0 RULING U.S. Foreign Intelligence Surveillance Court, "In Re All Matters Submitted to the Foreign Intelligence Surveillance Court," memorandum opinion, May 17, 2002. (Available at the FAS website: http://www.fas.org/irp/agency/doj/fisa/fisc051702.html.)

159 THE WASHINGTON POST DESCRIBED "Chipping Away at Liberty," *The Washington Post*, November 19, 2002, editorial page.

159 IT WAS ESTABLISHED Foreign Intelligence Surveillance Act, Section 1803(b).

159 IN NOVEMBER 2002, THE PANEL Civil libertarians predicted in 2001 and 2002 that lowering the wall would be an invitation to overzealous cops and prose-

cutors, and it appears they were correct. In June 2003, federal prosecutors used the Patriot Act to bring a charge of "terrorism using a weapon of mass destruction" against a California man after a pipe bomb he had made exploded in his lap while he was sitting in his car. A county prosecutor in North Carolina charged a man accused of running a methamphetamine lab with violating a state law banning the manufacture of chemical weapons. ("Terror Law Nabs Common Criminals," Associated Press, September 14, 2003.) In New York, prosecutors used new state antiterror legislation to indict nineteen gang members in May 2004 for such crimes as conspiracy, murder and gang assault, claiming that these were acts of terror. ("Anti-Terrorism Law Used to Indict Gang Members," Associated Press, May 14, 2004.)

159 ONE PERSON WHO Stewart Baker, "Wall Nuts," Slate.com, December 31, 2003.

160 BY AUGUST 2001 Joint Inquiry into Intelligence Community Activities report, p. 153.

160 "WE HAD IMPOSED" Stewart Baker, "Wall Nuts."

161 THE BIPARTISAN 9/11 9/11 Commission Report, p. 80; also see nn. 37, 38.

161 IN FACT, THERE IS EVIDENCE Ibid., pp. 87–88.

161 IN THE FALL OF 2002 David Johnston and Don Van Natta, Jr., "Agencies Monitor Iraqis in the U.S. for Terror Threat," The New York Times, November 17, 2002.

161 SINCE SEPTEMBER 11 Dan Eggen and Robert O'Harrow, Jr., "U.S. Steps Up Secret Surveillance," The Washington Post, March 24, 2003.

161 IN A 2002 STATEMENT Hayden, Statement for the Record, October 17, 2002.

CHAPTER 7: VOICES IN THE DARK: MUCKRAKERS, WHISTLEBLOWERS

163 AT FIFTY-TWO, DUDAYEV For photographs and biographical sketches of Dudayev, see http://www.aeronautics.ru/chechnya/dudayev/htm.

163 "WE HAVE PROPOSED NEGOTIATIONS" Steve McNally, "Yeltsin Announces Mediators for Chechen Peace Talks," CNN.com, April 6, 1996.

164 DUDAYEV HEADED INTO A FIELD For some of the details of that evening, so far as we understand them, see "Chechen Leader Confirmed Dead," CNN.com, April 26, 1996 (http://www.cnn.com/WORLD/9604/24/dudayev/); Wayne Madsen, "Did NSA Help Target Dudayev?" Covert Action Quarterly, 61, (1997); Art Villasanta, "Satellites That Kill," Philippine Daily Inquirer, December 30, 2001.

164 HAD THE KILLING OCCURRED TODAY Brendan Koerner, "Your Cellphone Is a Homing Device," Legal Affairs, May/June 2003.

165 "FROM WHAT I HEARD" Telephone interview with Wayne Madsen, October 13, 2003.

165 MADSEN SPECULATES THAT Madsen, "Did NSA Help Target Dudayev?"

165 A SIMILAR POINT Patricia Reaney, "Defense Experts Question How Dudayev Was Killed," Reuters, April 24, 1996.

165 THUS, HE NORMALLY KEPT "Russia's New Air Force Chief Took Part in Elimination of Former Chechen Leader," AVN Military News Agency, Moscow, December 23, 2002.

165 IN FACT, DURING Madsen, "Did NSA Help Target Dudayev?"

166 THE CLINTON ADMINISTRATION Seymour Hersh, "The Wild East," *Atlantic Monthly,* June 1994.

166 YELTSIN HAD ADMITTED Bruce Nelan, "Cutting off the Head," *Time* Europe, May 6, 1996.

166 IN FACT, IN A TWIST Ibid.

166 WHEN THE COUP Hersh, "The Wild East."

166 WHEN I ASKED MILT Interview with Milt Bearden in Washington, March 10, 2003.

166 IN ANY EVENT Tom de Waal, " 'Dual' Attack Killed President," BBC News, April 21, 1999.

167 STILL, MADSEN INSISTS Telephone interview with Wayne Madsen, October 13, 2003.

168 "ECHELON COVERS EVERYTHING" Mike Frost, *60 Minutes II* interview, February 27, 2000.

168 "AROUND THE WORLD" Rusbridger, *Intelligence Game,* p. 21.

168 AS A RESULT Regan, *Legislating Privacy,* p. 14.

168 "WE HAVE ALL GLIMPSED" Susan Harding and Kathleen Stewart, "Anxieties of Influence: Conspiracy Theory and Therapeutic Culture in Millennial America," in Harry G. West and Todd Sanders, eds., *Transparency and Conspiracy, Ethnographies of Suspicion in the New World Order* (Durham, N.C.: Duke University Press, 2003).

169 IN COPENHAGEN, NOBODY Unless otherwise noted, all material related to Kenan Seeberg and Bo Elkjaer is drawn from an extensive interview in Copenhagen on July 18, 2002.

170 THE RESULT WAS Bo Elkjaer and Kenan Seeberg, "Echelon Was My Baby," *Ekstra Bladet,* November 17, 1999. (Trans. from the Danish by Bo Elkjaer.)

171 SHE BROUGHT A LAWSUIT *United States of America, ex rel. Margaret A. Newsham and Margaret Overbeek Bloem v. Lockheed Missiles and Space Company, Inc.,* 907 F. Supp. 1349 (1995).

172 IN 1991, THE BRITISH TELEVISION PROGRAM Nick Davies, *World in Action* (Granada Television, 1991), as quoted in Hager, *Secret Power,* p. 51.

172 A YEAR LATER, IN THE SUMMER John Merritt, "GCHQ Spies on Charities and Companies," *The Observer,* June 28, 1992.

174 BUT THE CODEBREAKERS Telephone interview with David Kahn, May 19, 2004.

174 AS THE BOOK NEARED COMPLETION Bamford, *Puzzle Palace,* pp. 168–69. There is some disparity between Bamford's account of this, which was put together in the early 1980s, and Kahn's recollections in 2004. Kahn says he cannot remember anything about the agency endeavoring to buy the copyright, nor can he recall that one of the passages the agency wanted deleted involved GCHQ. He concedes, however, that this may simply be the vagaries of memory, and he did cooperate with Bamford when Bamford was researching the episode.

174 KAHN WAS FOLLOWED All of this material is from Paul Constance, "How Jim Bamford Probed the NSA," *Cryptologia* 26. 1 (January 1997).

176 WHEN BAMFORD WAS DOING Bamford, Testimony.

176 TWO DECADES AFTER THE BOOK APPEARED Odom, *Fixing Intelligence,* p. 129.

176 THE BOOK BECAME George Lardner, Jr., "An Angry Reaction to Disclosure of History," *The Washington Post,* March 18, 1990.

176 THUS, ON THE FIFTIETH ANNIVERSARY David Kahn, Remarks Commemorating the 50th Anniversary of the National Security Agency, November 1, 2002, Fort Meade (available at the FAS website: http://www.fas.org/irp/eprint/kahn.html).

177 WHEN HE WAS PURSUING Duncan Campbell, "Shhh . . . They're Listening," *UNESCO Courier,* March 1, 2001.

177 SIX MONTHS EARLIER Duncan Campbell and Mark Hosenball, "The Eavesdroppers," *Time Out,* June 1976. It is worth mentioning that particularly in the case of the George W. Bush presidency, a critical point of view will often lose a journalist access to sources. See Harry Jaffe, "Pentagon to Washington Post Reporter Ricks: Get Lost," *The Washingtonian,* December 29, 2003.

178 JOHN BERRY HAD BEEN Roberston, *Justice Game,* pp. 108–10.

179 "WHAT THE SECURITY SERVICES WANTED" Ibid., p. 111.

179 "SOMEBODY'S LISTENING, AND THEY" Duncan Campbell, "Somebody's Listening," *New Statesman and Society,* August 12, 1988.

180 READING AN ACCOUNT Robertson, *Justice Game,* p. 121.

181 THEY HAVE EXPOSED Bo Elkjaer and Kenan Seeberg, "Where the Spies Are Listening," *Ekstra Bladet,* February 11, 2000. (Trans. from the Danish by Bo Elkjaer.)

181 IN 1999, THE DANISH MINISTER Bo Elkjaer and Kenan Seeberg, "The Danish Minister for Defense Admits," *Ekstra Bladet,* September 27, 1999. (Trans. from the Danish by Bo Elkjaer.)

185 "IF THIS BOOK" Hager, *Secret Power,* pp. 13–14.

185 "LISTS OF NAMES" Nicky Hager, Testimony before the European Parliament Temporary Committee on the Echelon Interception System, April 23 and 24, 2001 (hereafter "Hager, Testimony.")

185 "THE PERSON WORKING" Ibid.

186 LIKE LINDIS, NICKY HAGER Nicky Hager, "Researching Echelon," posted on www.heise.de, April 11, 2000.

186 EARLY ON IN HIS INVESTIGATION Hager, Testimony.

186 "AN ASTONISHING NUMBER OF PEOPLE" David Lange, foreword to Hager, *Secret Power.*

CHAPTER 8: TOOTHLESS TALKING SHOP: THE EUROPEAN PARLIAMENT INVESTIGATES

189 THE PLAUSIBILITY THE PARANOID STYLE Richard Hofstadter, *The Paranoid Style in American Politics and Other Essays* (Cambridge, Mass.: Harvard University Press, 1996), p. 37.

189 "WITHIN EUROPE, ALL EMAIL" Steve Wright, Omega Foundation, "An Appraisal of the Technologies of Political Control," European Parliament, 1998.

189 "FRANKLY, THE ONLY PEOPLE" Niall McKay, "Eavesdropping on Europe," *Wired News,* September 30, 1998.

189 THE IDEA BORROWS FROM See Francis Fukuyama, *The End of History and the Last Man* (New York: Free Press, 1992).

190 "THERE IS NOT ENOUGH" Niall McKay, "Did EU Scuttle Echelon Debate?" Wired News, October 5, 1998.

190 "THIS REPORT DESCRIBES" Campbell, Interception Capabilities 2000.

192 IN 1994, AIRBUS INDUSTRIE Ibid.; also Scott Shane and Tom Bowman, "America's Fortress of Spies," Baltimore Sun, December 3, 1995.

192 THE "HIGHLY PLACED" John Merritt, "GCHQ Spies on Charities and Companies," The Observer, June 28, 1992.

192 IN FACT, KATHARINE GUN Interview with Katharine Gun, April 1, 2004, Cheltenham. See also Richard Norton-Taylor, "Former GCHQ Official Confirms Monitoring," The Guardian, June 17, 1992; Michael Evans, "Spy Centre 'Monitored Maxwell Money Deals,' " The Times, June 16, 1992.

192 "WE LISTENED TO MANY" Ball, Pine Gap, p. 53.

192 "IN THE POST–COLD WAR WORLD" Warren Christopher, "The Strategic Priorities of American Foreign Policy," U.S. Department of State Dispatch, November 4, 1993.

192 "NO IS THE SHORT ANSWER" Suzanne Daley, "An Electronic Spy Scare Is Alarming Europe," The New York Times, February 24, 2000.

193 JAMES RUBIN, THE STATE David Ensor, "Spy Agency Tells Congress It Is Breaking No Law," CNN, February 29, 2000.

193 (WHEN THE NSA ACKNOWLEDGED) Vernon Loeb, "NSA Admits to Holding Secret Information on Princess Diana," The Washington Post, December 12, 1998.

193 "I RECOGNIZE THAT" George Tenet, Statement before the House Permanent Select Committee on Intelligence, April 12, 2000 (available at the FAS website).

193 "SIGINT DOES PROVIDE" Ibid.

194 "SOME THINGS WERE PUBLISHED" Steve Kettmann, "U.S. Eyes Europe's Echelon Probe," Wired News, July 6, 2000.

194 "I HAVE NEVER FOUND" Bamford, Testimony.

195 HE CAUTIONED THE COMMITTEE Ibid.

196 "I WISH YOU" Shane and Bowman, "America's Fortress of Spies."

196 "MY EUROPEAN FRIENDS" R. James Woolsey, "Why We Spy on Our Allies," The Wall Street Journal, March 17, 2000, editorial page.

196 "THAT'S RIGHT, MY CONTINENTAL FRIENDS," Ibid.

196 "I DON'T BELIEVE" Quoted in Kettmann, "U.S. Eyes Europe's Echelon Probe."

196 A GREEN PARTY MEMBER Cited in Steve Kettmann, "Echelon Panel Calls It a Day," Wired News, June 21, 2001.

199 HE TOLD THE COMMITTEE Hager, Testimony.

199 "IN THE TORRENT OF PRESS" Duncan Campbell, Testimony before the European Parliament Temporary Committee on the Echelon Interception System, January 22 and 23, 2001 (hereafter "Campbell, Testimony").

199 "NOT EVERY SATELLITE" Ibid.

199 WHILE HE CONFIRMED Ibid.

199 JAMES BAMFORD AGREED Bamford, Testimony.

199 IF A SINGLE STATION GATHERS Ibid. Senator Bob Graham renders these numbers differently:

> To clarify the concept of "raw data," if the NSA collects a million phone calls, a computer will narrow the million down to one hundred, and a

human being will listen to the hundred to determine if there's anything significant about them. If there is, that person will distill that information into a report. The report is the intelligence; the hundred calls are the raw data.

Bob Graham with Jeff Nussbaum, *Intelligence Matters,* p. 176.

200 HE TOLD THE STORY Bamford, Testimony; the Dècle story is recounted in greater detail in Bamford, *Body of Secrets,* chap. 11.

201 "DISEMBODIED SNIPPETS OF CONVERSATIONS" James Bamford, "What Big Ears You Have," *The Guardian,* September 14, 2002.

201 "THEY WERE EVIDENTLY" Interview with David Lowe, Brussels, July 9, 2002.

202 IN APRIL 2001 Declan McCullagh, "Euros Continue Echelon Probe," *Wired News,* April 24, 2001.

202 THE ADVOCACY CENTER Interview with David Lowe.

202 ELEANOR LEWIS E-mail from Eleanor Lewis, U.S. Department of Commerce, March 18, 2004.

203 "WE NEVER LED THEM" Carter Dougherty, "U.S. Snubs EU Trade-Spying Team," *The Washington Times,* May 11, 2001.

203 ON HEARING ABOUT THE Steve Kettmann, "U.S. Echelon Snub Angers Europe," *Wired News,* May 18, 2001.

203 COELHO ECHOED FONTAINE'S REMARKS Juliana Gruenwald, "U.S. Officials Snub EU Echelon Fact Finders," *ZDNet,* May 11, 2001.

204 AND, INDEED, THE Draft Report on the Existence of a Global System for the Interception of Private and Commercial Communications (Echelon Interception System), May 18, 2001 (available as a pdf at http://www.europarl.eu.int/tempcom/echelon/pdf/prechelon_en.pdf).

204 "IF YOU HAVE A TOOL" Kettmann, "Echelon Panel Calls It a Day."

205 A 2000 REPORT Annual report for 1999–2000 of the Intelligence and Security Committee, Chairman Tom King, Ch MP, Intelligence Services Act 1994, chap. 13 (Crown Copyright, 2000).

205 A SIMILAR DOCUMENT FROM *Securing Our Nation's Safety, How New Zealand Manages Its Security and Intelligence Agencies* (Wellington, N.Z.: Domestic and External Secretariat Department of the Prime Minister and Cabinet, December 2000).

205 A 1996 REPORT Report of the Auditor General of Canada—November 1996—to the House of Commons, chap. 27, "The Canadian Intelligence Community—Control and Accountability" (Canada, Minister of Public Works and Government Services, 1996).

205 "I HAVE BEEN GIVEN" Bamford, Testimony.

205 WHEN THE COMMITTEE SHUT Kettmann, "Echelon Panel Calls It a Day,"

205 "EVEN THE BBC" Interview with David Lowe, Brussels, July 9, 2002.

206 "IT IS HYPOCRITICAL" Ilka Schroeder, "Second Minority Opinion on Echelon," European Parliament, July 2, 2001.

207 "THIS COMMITTEE HAS" Hager, Testimony.

207 "THE REAL ISSUE" Matthew Broersma, "Europe Stumbles on Echelon Spy Network," *ZDNet,* March 28, 2002.

207 LURKING BEHIND THE ECHELON Charles Grant, "Intimate Relations," Center for European Reform, 2000 (available at http://www.cer.org.uk/pdf/cerwp4.pdf).

208 "THIS REPORT CONSTANTLY" Ilka Schroeder, "Secret Services: The European

Parliament's Echelon Committee Minority Vote,"July 4, 2001 (available at the FAS website: http://www.fas.org/irp/program/process/eu_dissent.html).
208 EVEN CHARLES GRANT Charles Grant, "Intimate Relations."
208 WHEN I ASKED Interview with Glyn Ford, Brussels, July 8, 2002.
208 WHEN I RAISED Interview with David Lowe.

CHAPTER 9: THE JIHAD PHONE: LISTENING TO TERRORISTS

209 ON THE FIFTH OF FEBRUARY Secretary of State Colin Powell, "Remarks to the United Nations Security Council," February 5, 2003. (Transcript available at http://www.state.gov/secretary/rm/2003/17300.htm).
210 "I CAN ONLY ASSUME" Laura Sullivan, "Powell's Iraq Revelations Come at Intelligence Cost," Baltimore Sun, February 7, 2003.
211 THE TRANSCRIPTS WERE Bill Gertz, "U.S. Intercepts from Libya Play Role in Berlin Bomb Trial," The Washington Times, November 19, 1997; Sullivan, "Powell's Iraq Revelations."
211 IT EMERGED IN THE DAYS Dana Priest, "Telling Secrets: Not Just What, but How," The Washington Post, February 6, 2003.
211 IN THE MONTHS PRECEDING Woodward, Plan of Attack, p. 217.
211 IN THE DAYS BEFORE Michael Hirsh and Michael Isikoff, "Iraq: No More Hide and Seek," Newsweek, February 5, 2003.
211 SUCH WAS THEIR CONFIDENCE Woodward, Plan of Attack, p. 309.
211 POWELL ANNOUNCED THAT Secretary of State Colin Powell, "Remarks to the United Nations Security Council," February 5, 2003.
211 EIGHT MONTHS AFTER See Thomas Powers, "The Vanishing Case for War," The New York Review of Books 50.19 (December 4, 2003).
212 THE 9/11 COMMISSION LEARNED 9/11 Commission Report, n. 43.
212 "BEFORE YOU COMPLAIN" Scott Shane, "How Intelligence Fails More Often Than Not," Baltimore Sun, February 8, 2004.
213 "IMAGINE A HUGE $30-BILLION CONGLOMERATE" "Time for a Rethink," The Economist, April 18, 2002.
213 THE INTELLIGENCE HISTORIAN Rhodri Jeffreys-Jones, Cloak and Dollar (New Haven: Yale University Press, 2002), p. 9.
214 SENATOR GARY HART Telephone interview with Senator Gary Hart, February 2, 2004.
214 THE CIA'S DIRECTORATE OF OPERATIONS The Economist puts the ratio at 30,000 eavesdroppers/4,000 spies ("Time for a Rethink"). But The New York Times reports that of the 4,000 employees in the D.O., only 1,100 are case officers deployed overseas. Douglas Jehl, "Abundance of Caution and Years of Budget Cuts Are Seen to Limit CIA," The New York Times, May 11, 2003.
214 WHEN INDIA CARRIED OUT Bill Gertz, "American Intelligence Is Taken by Surprise," The Washington Times, May 12, 1998.
214 "WHAT WE DIDN'T HAVE" Telephone interview with Ambassador Frank Wisner, March 17, 2004.
214 GENE HACKMAN PLAYS Francis Ford Coppola, The Conversation (Paramount/American Zoetrope, 1974).
215 SEVERAL HOURS AFTER THE ATTACK Bill Gertz, "NSA's Warning Arrived Too Late to Save the Cole," The Washington Times, October 25, 2000.

216 "THIS INFORMATION DID NOT" Hayden, Statement for the Record, October 17, 2002.

216 "WE DUTIFULLY REPORTED THESE" Ibid.

216 WHEN NEW YORK CITY POLICE Rashbaum, "Police Are Focusing More on Protecting the Subways."

216 "AFTER ANY PARTICULAR TURNING POINT" Interview with Sir Peter Heap, London, April 2, 2004. Also see Peter Heap, "The Truth Behind the MI6 Façade," *The Guardian,* October 2, 2003.

217 THE FEDERAL PROSECUTORS *United States v. Usama Bin Laden et al.,* United States District Court, Southern District of New York, trial transcript, Day 37, May 1, 2001; Scott Shane, "Bin Laden, Associate Elude Spy Agency's Eavesdropping," Baltimore *Sun,* September 16, 2001.

218 HENRY STIMSON, WHO SAID Keegan, *Intelligence in War,* p. 5.

218 MILT BEARDEN, THE VETERAN Interview with Milt Bearden, Washington, D.C., March 10, 2003.

218 "DOES WHAT ONE FOREIGN MINISTER" Interview with a U.S. diplomat who wished not to be named, New York City, May 24, 2004.

218 IN THE SPRING OF 1995 Bill Gertz, *Breakdown: How America's Intelligence Failures Led to September 11* (Washington, D.C.: Regnery, 2002), pp. 53–54.

219 IN 2003, BRITISH AIRWAYS Megan Lane, "How Terror Talk Is Tracked," BBC News Online, May 21, 2003 (http://news.bbc.co.uk/2/hi/uk_news/3041151.stm).

219 AND IN MARCH 2004 Don Van Natta, Jr. and Desmond Butler, "How Tiny Swiss Cellphone Chips Helped Track Global Terror," *The New York Times,* March 4, 2004.

219 BUT WHEN I ASKED Interview with Britt Snider, Washington, March 23, 2004.

219 THE SYSTEM THAT MIKE FROST Mike Frost, *60 Minutes II* interview, February 27, 2000.

220 ON OCTOBER 1, 1993 For an account of the Klaas case, see Court TV's Crime Library, at http://www.crimelibrary.com/serial_killers/predators/klaas/1.html.

220 SINCE THE LAW PASSED "Cost of 'Three Strikes' Law," *San Francisco Chronicle,* March 5, 2004, editorial page. See also Joe Domanick, *Cruel Justice: Three Strikes and the Politics of Crime in America's Golden State* (Berkeley: University of California Press, 2004).

220 BY 2003, THERE WERE Harper's Index, *Harper's,* February 2003.

221 THE NEW ORTHODOXY Part of the reason for the continued emphasis on Sigint may be that in the absence of effective Humint assets, electronic assets, however fallible, were the only available source of useful intelligence. As cochair of the joint inquiry into the terrorist attacks of September 11, Sen. Bob Graham "found, as had [Richard] Clarke, that the NSA was the agency within the intelligence community that provided the most credible intelligence." Bob Graham with Jeff Nussbaum, *Intelligence Matters,* p. 202.

221 THE PATRIOT ACT WAS For a useful clause-by-clause discussion of the Patriot Act, see "A Guide to the Patriot Act," a four-part series by Dahlia Lithwick and Julia Turner, on Slate.com, September 8–11, 2003 (first part begins at http://Slate.msn.com/id/2087984/).

221 (SOUNDING ODDLY) John Lancaster, "Hill Puts Breaks on Expanding Police Powers," *The Washington Post,* September 30, 2001.

222   AND DESPITE THE FACT Evelyn Nieves, "Local Officials Rise Up to Defy the Patriot Act," *The Washington Post,* April 21, 2003.

222   "NOW THAT IT IS APPARENT" Kevin Hogan, "Will Spyware Work?" *MIT Technology Review,* December 2001.

222   NOEL C. KOCH Shane and Bowman, "America's Fortress of Spies."

222   "BECAUSE OF THE NATURE" Heap interview, April 2, 2004.

222   "THE ONLY PEOPLE WHO" Interview with a Department of Defense policy official, who did not want to be named, January 16, 2004.

224   THE COLD-WAR HISTORIAN Letter from George Kennan to Senator Daniel Patrick Moynihan, March 25, 1997 (available at FAS website). Kennan published a version of these reflections as "Spy and Counterspy," *The New York Times,* May 18, 1997.

225   IN HIS REMARKS Sarah Lyall, "Britain Admits That Much of Its Report on Iraq Came from Magazines," *The New York Times,* February 8, 2003.

225   SIR PETER HEAP TOLD Heap, "Truth Behind the MI6 Façade."

225   IN MAY 1997, AN ANALYST Russ Travers, "The Coming Intelligence Failure," *Studies in Intelligence* (declassified) 1.1 (1997).

226   SIMILARLY, HOW COULD "Road Map for National Security: Imperative for Change," report by the United States Commission on National Security in the 21st Century, February 15, 2001 (available at http://www.aaas.org/spp/yearbook/2002/ch34.pdf).

226   AFTER THE ATTACKS, WARREN RUDMAN Morton Kondracke, "Congress Should Heed Hart-Rudman Report," *The Daily Ardmoreite,* June 26, 2002.

226   "INTELLIGENCE COMMUNITY LEADERS" Anonymous, *Imperial Hubris,* p. xiii.

226   IN JANUARY 2001 Clive Thompson, "Connected Again," *The New York Times Magazine,* January 12, 2003.

227   THE NAME AL QAEDA For a fascinating discussion of the image and reality of Al Qaeda, see John Gray, *Al Qaeda and What It Means to Be Modern* (London: Faber and Faber, 2003).

227   "THEIR RECRUITING GROUNDS" Keegan, *Intelligence in War,* p. 318.

227   IN ITS FINAL REPORT *9/11 Commission Report,* p. 87.

227   IN *IMPERIAL HUBRIS* Anonymous, *Imperial Hubris,* p. 78. See pp. 78–86 for a full account of this development. The study of Al Qaeda was Anonymous, *Through Our Enemies' Eyes* (Dulles, Va.: Brassey's, 2003).

227   PETER BERGEN Peter Bergen, "Al Qaeda's New Tactics," *The New York Times,* November 15, 2002; See also Lawrence Wright, "The Terror Web," *The New Yorker,* August 2, 2004.

228   IT IS AN EXTRAORDINARY COINCIDENCE Gertz, *Breakdown,* p. 130.

228   THESE CONNECTIONS HAVE BEEN James Risen and David Johnston, "Intercepted Al Qaeda E-Mail Is Said to Hint at Regrouping," *The New York Times,* March 6, 2002.

228   BUT EVEN THIS Douglas Farah, *Blood from Stones* (New York: Broadway Books, 2004), p. 135. Also see Alan Cullison, "Inside Al-Qaida's Hard Drive," *The Atlantic,* September 2004, for a glimpse of the organization's internal bureaucracy.

229   SIXTEEN YEARS LATER For an alarming investigation of the new Al Qaeda, see Lawrence Wright, "The Terror Web," *The New Yorker,* August 2, 2004.

229   JAMES BAMFORD CLAIMS Bamford, *Body of Secrets,* p. 410.

229 IT REPORTEDLY TOOK THEM Lou Dolinar, "America's Ordeal: Bin Laden's Electronic Arsenal," *Newsday,* September 23, 2001.

229 WHEN TROOPS ENTERED CAVES Eli J. Lake, "Noise Pollution," *The New Republic,* November 4, 2002.

229 BIN LADEN HIMSELF Robin Moore, *The Hunt for Bin Laden: Task Force Dagger* (New York: Random House, 2003), p. 154.

229 IN MID-JUNE, 2001, ELECTRONIC INTERCEPTS Lou Dolinar, "Bin Laden Embraces Technology to Thwart U.S. Intelligence Efforts," *Chicago Tribune,* October 1, 2001.

230 "DO THE TERRORISTS USE" Lake, "Noise Pollution."

CODA

233 FROM THE DEW John Updike, "The Blessed Man of Boston," *Early Stories* (New York: Knopf, 2003), p. 92.

235 BECAUSE ERITREA IS Bamford, *Body of Secrets,* p. 160.

235 HE WAS AT A LOSS Bamford, Testimony.

236 "I AM NOT REALLY" Hayden, Statement for the Record, October 17, 2002.

236 IN THE AFTERMATH James Bamford, *Pretext for War* (New York: Doubleday, 2004), pp. 356–57.

237 LIKE THE ARMY "U.S. Army Sacks Gay Arabic Experts," *BBC News,* November 15, 2002.

237 AS OF MAY 2004 Jehl, "Abundance of Caution and Years of Budget Cuts."

238 BETWEEN THE FALL David E. Kaplan, "Mission Impossible," *U.S. News and World Report,* August 2, 2004.

238 IN DECEMBER 2003 Ariel Sabar, "NSA Can Summarily Reject Requests for Information," Baltimore *Sun,* December 11, 2003.

AFTERWORD TO THE PAPERBACK EDITION

239 LESS THAN A YEAR James Risen and Eric Lichtblau, "Bush Lets U.S. Spy on Callers Without Courts," *The New York Times,* December 16, 2005.

239 THE SURVEILLANCE WAS CONDUCTED The program is described in great detail in James Risen's book *State of War: The Secret History of the CIA and the Bush Administration* (New York: Free Press, 2006), pp. 42–60. See, also, Leslie Caulie and John Diamond, "Telecoms Let NSA Spy on Calls," *USA Today,* February 6, 2006; Scott Shane with Ken Belson, "Attention in NSA Debate Turns to Telecom Industry," *The New York Times,* February 11, 2006.

239 RUSS TICE Brian Ross, "NSA Whistleblower Alleges Illegal Spying," ABC News, January 10, 2006; on Tice, see, also, Patrick Radden Keefe, "The Professional Paranoid," *Slate,* January 17, 2006.

240 IF THAT SOUNDS Letter from Sen. Jay Rockefeller, D-WV, to V.P. Dick Cheney, July 17, 2003. Rockefeller kept a sealed copy of the letter in a safe, and released it to the public after the program was revealed in December 2005.

240 PRESIDENT BUSH BLASTED Dan Eggen, "Justice Dept. Investigating Leak of NSA Wiretapping," *The Washington Post,* December 31, 2005.

240 THE ADMINISTRATION MADE NO ALLOWANCES See Gabriel Sherman, "Why

Times Ran Wiretap Story, Defying Bush," *The New York Observer,* December 26, 2005.

240 DAYS AFTER THE REVELATIONS Carol D. Leonnig and Dafna Linzer, "Spy Court Judge Quits in Protest," *The Washington Post,* December 21, 2005.

241 ACCORDING TO RISEN'S ACCOUNT Risen, *State of War,* pp. 42-60.

241 THOUGH THE ADMINISTRATION CLAIMED Daniel Klaidman, Stuart Taylor, Jr., and Evan Thomas, "Palace Revolt," *Newsweek,* February 6, 2006.

241 WITH MUCH FANFARE Patrick Radden Keefe, "Trust the Professionals," *Slate,* February 7, 2006. For Gonzales's legal argument, see the Justice Department's White Paper on the program, "Legal Authorities Supporting the Activities of the National Security Agency Described by the President," January 19, 2006, U.S. Dept. of Justice. (Available at http://www.epic.org/privacy /terrorism/fisa/doj11906wp.pdf.)

242 AND WITHOUT ANY SHOWING Greg Miller, "Experts Call Spy Agency Practice an Eye-Opener," *Los Angeles Times,* April 25, 2005.

242 FOLLOWING THIS REVELATION Mark Hosenball, "Spying: Giving Out U.S. Names," *Newsweek,* May 2, 2005.

243 AT ONE POINT Sen. Joseph Biden, Floor Statement: Nomination of John Bolton to Be the U.S. Representative to the United Nations, May 26, 2005. (Available at: http://biden.senate.gov/newsroom/details.cfm?id=239193.)

244 EVEN THE SUPPOSED "STEALTHINESS" Patrick Radden Keefe, "I Spy," *Wired,* February 2006.

244 INTELLIGENCE BY REMOTE CONTROL Dana Priest, "New Spy Satellite Debated on Hill," *The Washington Post,* December 11, 2004.

244 IN FEBRUARY 2006 Shane Harris, "TIA Lives On," *National Journal,* February 23, 2006.

244 THE NSA APPEARS Tom Pelton and Phillip McGowan, "Fort Meade May Gain Up to 10,000 New Jobs," Baltimore *Sun,* June 3, 2005.

244 THE AGENCY TOOK OUT U.S. Patent 06947978, "Method for Geolocating Logical Network Addresses," September 20, 2005. (Available at www.uspto .gov.)

244 AFTER HAYDEN ASSUMED Siobhan Gorman, "NSA Director Poised to Update Spy Agency," Baltimore *Sun,* August 22, 2005.

244 THE LONG-TERM EFFORT Alice Lipowicz, "NSA Modernization Effort Suffers Cost Overruns, Delays," *Washington Technology,* September 12, 2005.

244 THE FBI ACKNOWLEDGED "Sorry, Wrong Wiretap," Associated Press, September 30, 2005.

245 AND THE BACKLOG Eric Lichtblau, "FBI's Translation Backlog Grows," *The New York Times,* July 28, 2005.

245 OFFICIALS FAMILIAR WITH THE PROGRAM Barton Gellman, Dafna Linzer, and Carol D. Leonnig, "Surveillance Net Yields Few Suspects," *The Washington Post,* February 5, 2005.

245 THUS IT TURNS OUT Lowell Bergman, Eric Lichtblau, Scott Shane, and Don Van Natta, Jr., "Spy Agency Data After Sept. 11 Led F.B.I. to Dead Ends," *The New York Times,* January 17, 2006. See, also, Patrick Radden Keefe, "Can Network Theory Thwart Terrorists?" *The New York Times Magazine,* March 12, 2006.

245 THE NATIONAL COUNTERTERRORISM CENTER'S DATABASE Walter Pincus and

Dan Eggen, "325,000 Names on Terrorism List," *The Washington Post*, February 15, 2006.

245 A REPORT ON NEW DATA-MINING "Data Mining and Homeland Security: An Overview," Congressional Research Service Report, January 27, 2006.

245 IN DECEMBER 2004 A. L. Bardach, "Listen to the Admiral," *Slate,* December 16, 2004.

246 SENATOR JAY ROCKEFELLER Patrick Radden Keefe, "Orwell Would Be Proud," *Slate,* March 9, 2006.

246 *THE NEW YORK TIMES* "The Death of the Intelligence Panel," *The New York Times* (Editorial), March 9, 2006.

BIBLIOGRAPHY

The bibliography below details the websites and books that *Chatter* draws from, as well as some of the more significant government reports. Some of the books may be hard to get hold of; many are out of print, were never published in the United States, or both. If your library fails you, try http://www.bookfinder.com. Articles from the press and other government documents are too numerous to list here but are fully cited in the notes.

Websites

www.fas.org: The website of the Federation of American Scientists contains an invaluable trove of information and documents, and is the home of Steven Aftergood's Project on Government Secrecy. You can register at the site to receive Aftergood's "Secrecy News," which was also extremely useful in preparing this book.

www.globalsecurity.org This site is run by John Pike, formerly of FAS, who is an expert on an extremely broad array of defense and intelligence issues. Pike has highly informative and accessible entries on more or less every acronym in the glossary of this book.

www.epic.org The site of the Electronic Privacy Information Center is an excellent resource for documents and commentary on various emerging issues on the tech side of the privacy issue.

www.cryptome.org This site run by John Young is a huge searchable repository of information on military and intelligence operations and organizations, government secrecy, and cryptography. The site is also a good litmus test for your attachment to freedom of speech. When the press mentions new locations that might serve as potential targets for terrorist attacks, Young helpfully uploads satellite photographs and road maps of the places in question.

www.politechbot.com Politech is an excellent site, run by technology journalist Declan McCullagh, that deals with a wide array of issues at the intersection of technology and politics and is one of the few sites mentioned here that encourages and exhibits a broad range of opinion on current debates.

www.gwu.edu/~nsarchiv/ The National Security Archive at George Washington University is an excellent source for documents on Sigint and other matters. Jeffrey Richelson, one of the foremost civilian experts on intelligence technology in the United States, is based at the archive and has compiled a rich collection of material.

www.echelonwatch.org A useful resource for Echelon information, maintained by the ACLU, though since September 11 it has been updated only sporadically.

fly.hiwaay.net/~pspoole/echres.html Patrick Poole's Echelon Research Resources has a great series of links to hundreds of articles on Echelon, the European Parliament investigation, and UKUSA Sigint.

Finally, the agencies themselves all have websites these days and will occasionally (*very* occasionally) post revealing or useful information. See www.nsa.gov; www.gchq.gov.uk; www.cse-cst.gc.ca; www.dsd.gov.au; www.gcsb.govt.nz; and naturally, www.darpa.mil. And remember, should you stumble across anything interesting on one of these sites: *print it out!*

Books

Acton, Lord John. *Selected Writings of Lord Acton,* vol. 2. Ed. J. Rufus Fears. Indianapolis: Liberty Fund, 1985.

Agre, Philip, and Marc Rotenberg, eds. *Technology and Privacy: The New Landscape.* Cambridge, Mass.: MIT Press, 1998.

Aide, Matthew, and Cees Wiebes, eds. *Secrets of Signals Intelligence During the Cold War and Beyond.* London: Frank Cass, 2001.

Andrew, Christopher. *For the President's Eyes Only.* New York: HarperCollins, 1995.

Anonymous [Michael Scheuer]. *Imperial Hubris.* Dulles, Va.: Brassey's, 2004.

———. *Through Our Enemies' Eyes.* Dulles, Va.: Brassey's, 2003.

Baer, Robert. *See No Evil.* New York: Crown, 2002.

Ball, Desmond. *Pine Gap.* Sydney: Allen and Unwin, 1988.

———. *A Suitable Piece of Real Estate: American Installations in Australia.* Sydney: Hale and Iremonger, 1980.

Bamford, James. *Body of Secrets.* New York: Doubleday, 2001.

———. *Pretext for War.* New York: Doubleday, 2004.

———. *The Puzzle Palace.* New York: Penguin, 1983.

Barker, Wayne, and Rodney Coffman. *The Anatomy of Two Traitors.* Laguna Hills, Calif.: Aegean Park Press, 1981.

Barkun, Michael. *Culture of Conspiracy.* Berkeley: University of California Press, 2003.

Bergen, Peter. *Holy War, Inc.* New York, Free Press, 2001.

Berlin, Isaiah. *The Proper Study of Mankind.* Farrar, Straus & Giroux, 1998.

Blackstone, William. *Commentaries on the Laws of England,* vol. 4. Chicago: University of Chicago Press, 1979.

Bok, Sissela. *Secrets: On the Ethics of Concealment and Revelation.* New York: Pantheon, 1982.

Brin, David. *The Transparent Society.* Reading, Mass.: Perseus, 1998.

Burrows, William. *Deep Black: Space Espionage and National Security.* New York: Random House, 1986.

Campbell, Duncan. *Interception Capabilities 2000.* Report to the Director General for Research of the European Parliament, 1999.

———. *The Unsinkable Aircraft Carrier.* London: Picador, 1986.

Churchill, Winston. *Their Finest Hour.* Boston: Houghton Mifflin, 1949.

Clarke, Richard. *Against All Enemies.* New York: Simon and Schuster, 2004.

Colby, William. *Honorable Men.* New York: Simon and Schuster, 1978.

Cole, D. J., *The Imperfect Spy.* London: Robert Hale, 1998.

Coll, Steve. *Ghost Wars: The Secret History of the CIA, Afghanistan, and Bin Laden, from the Soviet Invasion to September 10, 2001.* New York: The Penguin Press, 2004.

Conrad, Joseph. *Heart of Darkness.* New York: Alfred A. Knopf, 1967 [1902].

Davies, Simon. *Big Brother.* East Roseville, N.S.W.: Simon and Schuster, 1992.

Dodd, Annabel Z. *The Essential Guide to Telecommunications,* 3rd ed. Upper Saddle River, N.J.: Prentice Hall, 2002.

Domanick, Joe. *Cruel Justice: Three Strikes and the Politics of Crime in America's Golden State.* Berkeley: University of California Press, 2004.

Elton Mayo, George. *The Human Problems of an Industrial Civilization.* New York: Macmillan, 1933.

European Parliament, Temporary Committee on the ECHELON Interception System, Report on the Existence of a Global System for the Interception of Private and Commerical Communications (ECHELON Interception System), July 11, 2001 (available at www.europarl.eu.int/tempcom/echelon/pdf/rapport_echelon_en.pdf).

Farah, Douglas. *Blood from Stones.* New York: Broadway Books, 2004.

Foucault, Michel. *Discipline and Punish: The Birth of the Prison.* Trans. Alan Sheridan. New York: Vintage, 1995.

Frost, Mike, and Michael Gratton. *Spyworld.* Toronto: McClelland Bantam, 1995.

Fukuyama, Francis. *The End of History and the Last Man.* New York: Free Press, 1992.

Funder, Anna. *Stasiland.* London: Granta, 2003.

Garton Ash, Timothy. *The File.* New York: Random House, 1997.

Gaylin, Ann. *Eavesdropping in the Novel from Proust to Augustine.* Cambridge, U.K.: Cambridge University Press, 2002.

Gerson, Joseph, and Bruce Berchard, eds. *The Sun Never Sets: Confronting the Network of Foreign U.S. Military Bases.* Boston: South End Press, 1991.

Gertz, Bill. *Breakdown: How America's Intelligence Failures Led to September 11.* Washington, D.C.: Regnery, 2002.

———. *Treachery: How America's Friends and Foes Are Secretly Arming Our Enemies,* New York: Crown Forum, 2004.

Gibson, William. *Pattern Recognition.* New York: Putnam, 2003.

Giddens, Anthony. *The Consequences of Modernity.* Palo Alto, Calif.: Stanford University Press, 1990.

Graham, Senator Bob, with Jeff Nussbaum. *Intelligence Matters.* New York: Random House, 2004.

Gray, John. *Al Qaeda and What It Means to Be Modern.* London: Faber and Faber, 2003.

Hager, Nicky. *Secret Power.* Nelson, N.Z.: Craig Potton, 1996.

Herodotus. *The History.* Trans. David Greene. Chicago: University of Chicago Press, 1987.

Hersh, Seymour. *The Price of Power: Kissinger in the Nixon White House.* New York: Simon and Schuster, 1983.

———. *"The Target Is Destroyed."* New York: Random House, 1986.

Hofstadter, Richard. *The Paranoid Style in American Politics and Other Essays.* Cambridge, Mass.: Harvard University Press, 1996.

Jeffreys-Jones, Rhodri. *Cloak and Dollar.* New Haven: Yale University Press, 2002.

Johnson, Chalmers. *The Sorrows of Empire.* New York: Metropolitan Books, 2004.

Johnson, Loch K. *A Season of Inquiry: Congress and Intelligence.* Chicago: Dorsey Press, 1998.

Joint Inquiry into Intelligence Community Activities Before and After the Terrorist Attacks of September 11, 2001. *Report of the U.S. Senate Select Committee on Intelligence and U.S. House Permanent Select Committee on Intelligence,* 107th Cong., 2d sess., December 2002.

Kahn, David. *The Codebreakers.* New York: Scribner, 1996.

——. *The Reader of Gentlemen's Mail*. New Haven: Yale University Press, 2004.

Keegan, John. *Intelligence in War*. New York: Alfred A. Knopf, 2004.

Kessler, Ronald. *The CIA at War*. New York: St. Martin's, 2003.

Kundera, Milan. *Testaments Betrayed*. New York: HarperCollins, 1995.

Lanning, Hugh, and Richard Norton-Taylor. *A Conflict of Loyalties: GCHQ 1984–1991*. Cheltenham, U.K.: New Clarion Press, 1991.

Laudon, Kenneth. *The Dossier Society: Value Choices in the Design of National Information Systems*. New York: Columbia University Press, 1986.

Lerner, Mitchell. *The Pueblo Incident: A Spy Ship and the Failure of American Foreign Policy*. Lawrence: University Press of Kansas, 2002.

Lessig, Lawrence. *Code and Other Laws of Cyberspace*. New York: Basic Books, 1999.

Levy, Steven. *Crypto: Secrecy and Privacy in the New Code War*. London: Penguin, 2000.

Lindsey, Robert. *The Falcon and the Snowman*. New York: Simon and Schuster, 1979.

Littman, Jonathan. *The Fugitive Game*. New York: Little, Brown, 1997.

Marrs, Jim. *Rule by Secrecy*. New York: HarperCollins, 2000.

Miller, John, and Michael Stone. *The Cell: Inside the 9/11 Plot, and Why the FBI and CIA Failed to Stop It*. New York: Hyperion, 2002.

Moore, Robin. *The Hunt for Bin Laden: Task Force Dagger*. New York: Random House, 2003.

Moynihan, Daniel Patrick. *Secrecy: The American Experience*. New Haven: Yale University Press, 1999.

Nabokov, Vladimir. *Nikolai Gogol*. New York: New Directions, 1961.

National Commission on Terrorist Attacks upon the United States. *The 9/11 Report: Final Report of the National Commission on Terrorist Attacks upon the United States*. New York: W. W. Norton, 2004.

Odom, William. *Fixing Intelligence*. New Haven: Yale University Press, 2003.

Olmsted, Katherine S. *Challenging the Secret Government*. Chapel Hill: University of North Carolina Press, 1996.

Orwell, George. *Nineteen Eighty-four*. New York: Alfred A. Knopf, 1992.

Poe, Edgar Allan. *Complete Stories and Poems of Edgar Allan Poe*. New York: Doubleday, 1966.

Powers, Thomas. *Intelligence Wars*. New York: New York Review Books, 2002.

——. *The Man Who Kept the Secrets*. New York: Alfred A. Knopf, 1979.

Prime, Rhona. *Time of Trial*. London: Hodder and Stoughton, 1984.

Regan, Priscilla. *Legislating Privacy*. Chapel Hill: University of North Carolina Press, 1995.

Rehnquist, William. *All the Laws but One: Civil Liberties in Wartime*. New York: Alfred A. Knopf, 1998.

Richelson, Jeffrey. *America's Space Sentinels*. Lawrence: University Press of Kansas, 1999.

———. *The U.S. Intelligence Community*, 4th ed. Boulder, Colo.: Westview, 1999.

Richelson, Jeffrey, and Desmond Ball. *The Ties That Bind*, 2nd ed. Boston: Unwin Hyman, 1990.

Robertson, Geoffrey. *The Justice Game*. London: Chatto and Windus, 1998.

Roethlisberger, Fritz J., and William J. Dickson. *Management and the Worker: An Account of a Research Program Conducted by the Western Electric Company, Hawthorne Works, Chicago*. Cambridge, Mass.: Harvard University Press, 1939.

Rosen, Jeffrey. *The Naked Crowd*. New York: Random House, 2004.

———. *The Unwanted Gaze*. New York: Random House, 2000.

Rusbridger, James. *The Intelligence Game*. New York: New Amsterdam, 1989.

Schlesinger, Stephen. *Act of Creation: The Founding of the United Nations*. Boulder, Colo.: Westview, 2003.

Shils, Edward. *The Torment of Secrecy*. Chicago: Ivan R. Dee, 1996.

Singh, Simon. *The Code Book*. New York: Doubleday, 1999.

Smith, Alice Kimball, and Charles Weiner, eds. *Robert Oppenheimer: Letters and Reflections*. Cambridge, Mass.: Harvard University Press, 1980.

Smith, Bradley F. *The Ultra-Magic Deals and the Most Secret Special Relationship, 1940–1946*. Novato, Calif.: Presidio Press, 1992.

Smith, Michael. *The Spying Game*. London: Politico's, 2003.

Sontag, Sherry, Christopher Drew, and Annette Lawrence Drew. *Blind Man's Bluff*. New York: PublicAffairs, 1998.

Stafford, David. *Roosevelt and Churchill: Men of Secrets*. New York: Overlook Press, 1999.

Stafford, David, and Rhodri Jeffreys-Jones, eds. *American-British-Canadian Intelligence Relations, 1939–2000*. Portland, Oreg.: Frank Cass, 2000.

Stevenson, William. *A Man Called Intrepid*. New York: Harcourt Brace Jovanovich, 1976.

Taylor, Telford. *Two Studies in Constitutional Interpretation*. Columbus: Ohio State University Press, 1969.

Tuchman, Barbara. *The Zimmermann Telegram*. New York: Macmillan, 1996.

Turnbull, Malcolm. *The Spycatcher Trial.* Topsfield, Mass.: Salem House, 1998.

Updike, John. *The Early Stories.* New York: Alfred A. Knopf, 2003.

Urban, Mark. *The Man Who Broke Napoleon's Codes.* London: Faber, 2001.

———. *UK Eyes Alpha.* London: Faber and Faber, 1996.

U.S. Commission on National Security/21st Century (the Hart-Rudman Commission). *Road Map for National Security: Imperative for Change, the Phase III Report,* February 15, 2001.

U.S. Senate, *Intelligence Activities and the Rights of Americans,* Book 2: *Final Report of the Select Committee to Study Governmental Operations with Respect to Intelligence Activities,* 94th Cong. Washington: U.S. Government Printing Office, 1976.

West, Harry G., and Todd Sanders, eds. *Transparency and Conspiracy, Ethnographies of Suspicion in the New World Order.* Durham, N.C.: Duke University Press, 2003.

West, Nigel. *GCHQ: The Secret Wireless War 1900–96.* London: Hodder and Stoughton, 1986.

———. *The Sigint Secrets: The Signals Intelligence War, 1900 to Today.* New York: William Morrow, 1998.

West, Rebecca. *The Vassall Affair.* London: Sunday Telegraph Books, 1963.

Westin, Alan. *Privacy and Freedom.* New York: Athenaeum, 1967.

White, Leslie. *The Science of Culture: A Study of Man and Civilization.* New York: Farrar, Straus, and Cudahy, 1949.

Winchester, Simon. *The Sun Never Sets: Travels to the Remaining Outposts of the British Empire.* New York: Prentice Hall, 1985.

Woodward, Bob. *Bush at War.* New York: Simon and Schuster, 2002.

———. *Plan of Attack.* New York: Simon and Schuster, 2004.

———. *Veil: The Secret Wars of the CIA, 1981–1987.* New York: Simon and Schuster, 1987.

Wright, Peter. *Spycatcher.* New York: Dell, 1988.

GLOSSARY OF ACRONYMS, AGENCIES, AND TERMS

ACLU American Civil Liberties Union

BIOT British Indian Ocean Territory. The British colony that contains Diego Garcia.

BRUSA The precursor to the UKUSA agreement, binding Britain and the United States on communications-interception matters during the Second World War.

BT British Telecom

CAAB The Campaign for Accountability for American Bases

CIA Central Intelligence Agency

COMINT Communications Intelligence. The interception and analysis of communications by intelligence agencies. Comint is used synonymously with Sigint in this book, though technically speaking Comint is a subcategory of Sigint.

Cryptography The art of rendering "plain text" communications as code or cipher.

CRS Congressional Research Service

CSE Communications Security Establishment. Canada's Sigint agency, and one of the five principal partners in the UKUSA agreement.

CSO Composite Signals Organization. The overseas arm of GCHQ.

DARPA The Defense Advanced Research Projects Agency. DARPA is the research and development wing of the Department of Defense.

DCI Director of Central Intelligence

DIA Defense Intelligence Agency

Dictionary The name of a program used by the UKUSA agencies to sort very rapidly through intercepted communications in search of items containing certain preselected keywords or numbers.

DSD Defense Signals Directorate. Australia's Sigint agency and one of the five principal partners in the UKUSA agreement.

Echelon Strictly speaking, Echelon refers to a program used by some of the satellite interception stations run by UKUSA countries to gather, analyze, and distribute civilian communications conveyed over satellite networks. More broadly, Echelon is used, in this book and elsewhere, to refer to the whole system whereby the five UKUSA countries cooperate on intercepting and processing various forms of civilian communications around the planet.

EPIC Electronic Privacy Information Center

E-Systems One of the principal contractors for the NSA, E-Systems is now part of Raytheon.

FAS Federation of American Scientists

FBI Federal Bureau of Investigation

FOIA Freedom of Information Act

GAO General Accounting Office

GCHQ Government Communications Headquarters. The United Kingdom's Sigint agency, one of the five principal UKUSA partners, and by far the closest partner to America's NSA.

GCSB Government Communications Security Bureau. New Zealand's Sigint agency, and one of the five principal partners in the UKUSA agreement.

GDR German Democratic Republic

GPS Global Positioning Systems

HUMINT Human Intelligence. Old fashioned, cloak and dagger, man-on-the-ground spying.

Intelsat The company that runs a network of commercial communications satellites which transmit communications around the planet.

IOSA Integrated Overhead Sigint Architecture. An initiative by the NRO to consolidate various functions traditionally performed by numerous Sigint systems into one system.

ICJ International Court of Justice

IXPs Internet Exchange Points

Lockheed Lockheed Martin. A massive aerospace and defense contractor that is one of the principal contractors for the NSA.

MEP Member of the European Parliament

MP Member of Parliament

MI5 Britain's domestic intelligence agency

MI6 Britain's international intelligence agency

NATO The North Atlantic Treaty Organization

NRO The National Reconnaissance Office. The NRO is the agency in charge of designing, building and managing America's intelligence satellites. In this capacity it works very closely with the NSA.

NSA The largest and most secretive intelligence agency in the United States. The NSA is America's communications interception, code making, and code breaking organization. It is the dominant party to the UKUSA agreement, with nearly 40,000 employees in the United States, and another 25,000 scattered at listening stations around the world.

NYPD New York Police Department

OSS Office of Strategic Services

PARI Pisgah Astronomical Research Institute

RAF Royal Air Force

Rhyolite The name of the first generation of American spy satellites devoted to gathering Sigint and other forms of intelligence.

Room 40 The British admiralty's code breaking operation during the First World War.

Shamrock A secret program initiated by the precursor to the NSA during the Second World War, and exposed three decades later, whereby commercial cable companies turned over copies of all cables leaving the U.S. to American intelligence.

Sigint Signals Intelligence. This broad term refers to any intelligence gathered by intercepting electronic signals. This includes communications, and in this book Sigint refers primarily to communications interception. But Sigint also includes things like photoreconnaissance intelligence and telemetry, which involves monitoring nuclear testing by intercepting electronic signals.

SCS Special Collection Service. A partnership between the NSA and the CIA whereby agents deposit bugs and interception equipment, or physically tap into lines, in situations where remote interception would be impossible.

STASI The secret police of the German Democratic Republic.

Steganography Similar to cryptography, but rather than converting the writing itself, you are hiding it. In ancient times, this simply involved concealing the writing. These days, steganography is so sophisticated that whole text messages can be implanted by special computer programs in a single image on the web, or in another letter of text.

TAG Technical Advisory Group. A group of experts brought into the NSA in the mid 1990s to assess the agency's problems with new technology.

Telemetry One function performed by intelligence satellites. Monitoring nuclear testing by foreign countries by reading various electromagnetic emissions associated with that testing.

TIA Total Information Awareness

TIPS Terrorism Information and Prevention System A program introduced and then abandoned by the Justice Department in the wake of September 11 that would have solicited a million "volunteers" around the United States who would serve as the eyes and ears of the government and report any suspicious happenings.

TRW The company that manufactured the Rhyolite satellites.

UKUSA The UKUSA agreement is an actual physical document that is sitting in vaults in the countries associated with it, though it is so secret that the specifics of its text remain a mystery. The agreement was negotiated during the years following the Second World War, and a final draft was signed in 1948. The agreement is a pact to cooperate fully on the interception and analysis of communications, between the United States, the United Kingdom, Canada, Australia, and New Zealand.

UNSC United Nations Security Council

INDEX

Kahn, David, 11, 174, 175, 176–77, 212–13
Kalb, Marvin, 148
Karamursel listening station (Turkey), 70
Karas, Kenneth, 218
Katz v. United States, 139
Kay, David, 211
Keegan, John, 98, 227
Kennan, George, 224–25
Kenya, 212, 217–18, 219
Kerrey, Bob, 110, 115, 152–54, 156
Kerr, John, 27
KH-11 "Keyhole" satellites, 52
Khalil, Ziyad, 217
Kieslowski, Krzysztof, 48
King, Martin Luther, Jr., 148
Kirby, Colonel, 20
Kissinger, Henry, 143, 148, 149
Kittiwake Project, 57
Klaas, Polly, 220–21
Klein, Steve, 129–30, 131–32
Koch, Noel C., 222
Korean War, 212
Kosovo campaign, 208
Koza, Frank, memo of, 30–32, 33, 36, 42, 43, 45, 46, 47
Kraus, Karl, 104–5
Kucinich, Dennis, 36
Kundera, Milan, 142

Lagos, Ricardo, 32
Lake, Anthony, 219
Lakenheath, England, American air force base at, 49–50
Lamumba, Patrice, 144
Lange, David, 186
law enforcement, wall between intelligence and, 159–60, 161
Lawrence Livermore National Laboratory, 115
Lebanon, Hezbollah attacks on U.S. in, 212
Le Carré, John, 6
Lessig, Lawrence, 99
Lewis, Eleanor, 202–3
libertarians, 160
Liberty (human rights organization), 34, 35, 36, 38, 39
Liberty, USS, 55

Libya, 210–11
Lindsey, Robert, 22
linguists, 125–29, 235, 237
listening, and types of interception, 53–54
listening stations
    abandoned, 64–69
    characteristics of, 52–53
    choosing sites for, 23–24, 58
    during Cold War, 57–58
    description of, 64–68
    importance of, 52
    radio, 69
    secrecy about, 54
    and types of interception, 54
    See also specific station
Lockheed Martin, 51–52, 170–71, 195
London, England, visual surveillance in, 136
Los Angeles Times, and Gun case, 32
Louis XIV (king of France), 12–13
Lourdes, Cuba, 66–67
Lowe, David, 201–3, 204, 205, 208
Luhrmann, Anna, 197

Maclean, Donald, 82
Madrid, Spain, bombing in 2004 in, 229
Madsen, Wayne, 111, 165–66, 167, 169, 203
Mail on Sunday (London), 34
Mansfield, Mark, 203
Marconi, Guglielmo, 13
Martin, William, 82, 86, 87
Marzocchi, Ottavio, 198
Mauritius, 61–64
Maxwell, Tom, 103
McCormack, Alfred, 17, 18
McDonnell Douglas, 192
McIndoe, Bruce, 120–21
McNally, Bob, 21
Meaningful Machines, 129–32
media
    and distrust of NSA and GCHQ, 112
    and effectiveness of signals intelligence, 214

PHOTO: © NANCY CRAMPTON

PATRICK RADDEN KEEFE is a fellow at The Century Foundation and the recipient of a 2006 Guggenheim Fellowship. He was educated at Columbia College, Cambridge University, the London School of Economics, and Yale Law School, and was a Marshall Scholar and a 2003 fellow at the Cullman Center for Scholars and Writers at the New York Public Library. He has written for *The New Yorker, The New York Times Magazine, The New York Review of Books, The Boston Globe, Wired, Slate,* and other publications, and is a frequent commentator on intelligence and security issues on national television and radio. Visit his website www.patrick raddenkeefe.com.